UNIVERSITY TREATISE SERIES

FEDERAL TAX RESEARCH

GUIDE TO MATERIALS AND TECHNIQUES

Eleventh Edition

Gail Levin Richmond
Professor of Law Emerita
Nova Southeastern University, Shepard Broad College of Law

Kevin M. Yamamoto
Professor of Law
South Texas College of Law Houston

FOUNDATION PRESS

444 Cedar Street, Suite 700
St. Paul, MN 55101
1-877-888-1330

Printed in the United States of America

ISBN: 978-1-64708-283-3

GLR
To my grandchildren

KMY
To my wife and son

Preface

This book had its genesis in a 1975 Tax Practice Seminar involving current issues in taxation. Students selected issues and presented their findings as ruling requests, audit protest memoranda, and statements before congressional committees. Unfortunately, they could not use their first-year legal research texts as guides; the standard legal research texts devoted little, if any, space to materials commonly used for tax research. The first edition of this book was designed as a brief introduction to tax research.

Research techniques are highly personalized. While the format of this text reflects our preferences, it can be adapted to almost any variation the user may devise. Although most frequently used as an instructional guide for students, many practitioners have also used it as an aid to finding materials.

The problems at the end of most chapters cover both historical materials and fairly recent items. Both types have value as teaching tools. Most problems involving recent law can be solved using electronic sources—both government and commercial; those problems enhance or introduce electronic research skills. Historical materials appear for a different reason. Although electronic databases continue to add retrospective coverage, some materials are not yet available electronically or are available only on commercial sites. In those cases, users must consult print or microform materials. In addition, electronic searches may involve usage fees. Researchers who are familiar with print materials should be able to use them in a cost-effective manner.

Each new edition benefits from suggestions made by tax professors, practitioners, and librarians. Library staff members at our institutions have been particularly generous with their time and their budget allocations. We could not describe and explain so many sources without their support. A special thank you to librarian Monica Ortale of South Texas College of Law Houston, and to Varvara Marmarinou, Elizabeth Nevle, Mia Romano, Jacqueline Thomason, and Lindsay Thomason for their help as research assistants.

We would also like to acknowledge the late Professor Roy M. Mersky, then-Director of the University of Texas Tarlton Law Library, for suggesting the first edition of this book; Tessa Boury, former Executive Editor at Foundation Press, for suggesting we collaborate on recent editions; and Staci Herr, our current editor at Foundation Press.

GAIL LEVIN RICHMOND
KEVIN M. YAMAMOTO

August 2020

Summary of Contents

Table of Contents

FEDERAL TAX RESEARCH

GUIDE TO MATERIALS AND TECHNIQUES

Eleventh Edition

Chapter 1

OVERVIEW

A. Introduction

This book is about federal tax research. If you covered tax in a general legal research course, you already know that tax research has much in common with other types of legal research. If this is your first experience with tax research, this book will introduce you to those common features.

Common features are a good starting point, but there are complicating factors. First, a single tax problem often involves authority generated by all three branches of government. You may need to find legislation, administrative rulings, and judicial opinions. Second, you may be planning a transaction rather than litigating a completed event. Planning involves researching alternative ways to structure the transaction—and you may still encounter after-the-fact litigation. Third, tax law changes rapidly, and some changes are retroactive; keeping current is a time-consuming task. Fourth, certain specialties within tax are—to say the least—extraordinarily complex or involve interactions with other areas of law. Given these facts, it is not surprising that many attorneys believe tax research has nothing in common with traditional legal research.

B. Format of This Book

This book has five functions. First, it lists and describes primary and secondary sources of federal tax law. Second, it provides information about finding those materials. Third, it discusses evaluating what you have found. Fourth, it covers methods for updating your research results. Fifth, and perhaps most important, it includes problems designed to exercise your tax research skills. In carrying out these functions, this book builds on techniques covered in a general legal research class.

This chapter describes how the book is organized and lists certain conventions used throughout the book. Chapter 2 introduces various types of authority, and Chapter 3 describes factors affecting the research process.

The next seven chapters cover documents produced by the government. Chapter 4 begins with the Constitution. That document's first three articles describe powers (and limits on those powers) of the three branches of government we encounter in Chapters 5 through 10. Although those chapters focus on primary authority—legislation, treaties, administrative pronouncements, and judicial opinions—they also cover some secondary authority produced by government entities. Those chapters discuss what is available and how to find it, why it is important, how to interpret it, and what deference it may receive in court.

The next five chapters cover secondary sources. Chapter 11 discusses citators, including two that cover only tax materials. Chapters 12 through 15 cover looseleaf services and treatises, periodical articles, form books, and newsletters. Some of these materials (e.g., looseleaf services) also include primary source material.

The last two chapters cover microforms and materials available online. We refer to and illustrate materials available online throughout the book, but the earlier discussions focus only on particular items. Chapter 17 provides more information about databases and search terms. Because online websites and their content undergo continuous change, both as to format and coverage, you should focus on the type of material available online.

The book concludes with four Appendixes:

- Appendix A Commonly Used Abbreviations
- Appendix B Alternate Citation Forms
- Appendix C Potential Research Errors
- Appendix D Commonly Owned Publishers

C. User Notes

1. Describing Sources

As noted in Section B, we may describe a service in several chapters because it is relevant to the topics covered in those chapters. We also cover online services in more detail in a separate chapter. In making decisions about where to describe services, we have tried to avoid unnecessary repetition. Where possible, we have also included several cross-references to other chapters.

A caveat is in order. Our descriptions and illustrations cannot substitute for a service's user's guide or for your experience in using the service. This is particularly important for online services, which vary in their search command structures and continually change both coverage dates and sources included. Research guides and other library-prepared reference materials are also useful guides for accessing materials.

2. Problem Assignments

Many chapters include short problems. Locating the primary source materials you need for solving problems in Chapters 4 through 10 often requires using materials described in later chapters. You should consult those descriptions on an as-needed basis. Although you can easily solve many of the problems using online sources, you may need to use print or microform materials when you search for older items.

3. Illustrations and Tables

This book includes illustrations and tables. Illustrations show primary and secondary source material as it appears in the source from which extracted.[1] Tables present useful information about particular topics.

Because we refer to some illustrations and tables in more than one chapter they are numbered by chapter to make them easier to locate. All references to illustrations and tables appear in brackets rather than in parentheses [e.g., Illustration 3-1; Table 5-C].

4. Bold Typeface and Arrows

To emphasize terms discussed in this book, we put them in **bold typeface**. Arrows (→) indicate discussion relating to an illustration or table.

---

[1] Because several of the illustrations are obtained by scanning or using a screen capture function, the font or text size may differ slightly from a publisher's original version. The final product is close to the original and should not inconvenience or confuse you.

5. Citation Format

Legal citation format is prescribed in a variety of sources, including The Bluebook, the ALWD Guide, and the Internal Revenue Manual.[2] These sources differ in their treatment of various items, and their citation format often differs from that used by the material's original publisher. Citation differences are particularly notable for IRS material. Depending on which source you use, you might encounter the following citations for a private letter ruling issued in 2020.

- PLR 202020010
- P.L.R. 2020–20–010
- I.R.S. P.L.R. 202020010 (Feb. 4, 2020)
- I.R.S. Priv. Ltr. Rul. 2020–20–010 (Feb. 4, 2020)

Note that the IRS itself does not use hyphens and is likely to use PLR rather than the other identifiers. If you search for "PLR 202020010," you can easily find it online; if you search for "PLR 2020–20–010," you may be less successful. Thus, it is critical to determine which format(s) the service you use recognizes. Print services are likely to use a single format; an electronic service might recognize more than one format.

Because citation manuals, law reviews, and courts use different citation formats, Appendix B includes several variations for selected primary sources. Before submitting your research, remember to format each citation in the style your recipient mandates.

Note that we try to limit signals (such as "see" and "compare") in text or footnotes. We generally limit our use of italics and small capitals. We made these formatting decisions to enhance readability. They do not reflect a preference for a particular citation system.

6. Abbreviations and Acronyms

During your research sessions, you will probably encounter abbreviations, initials, and acronyms. A true abbreviation is simply a truncated word (e.g., Cong. instead of Congress). As the example in Subsection 5 illustrates, different services use different abbreviations for the same item. Even if every service uses the same abbreviation, you may not know what the letters mean.

Initials are simply a short-hand means of referring to an item (e.g., IRS for Internal Revenue Service); instead of abbreviating the words, we use the relevant initial letters. If we pronounce the initials as if they were an actual word, we have made them into an acronym. In addition to names of services or types of authority, tax lawyers frequently encounter acronyms (e.g., FATCA, FOIA, and REIT).

Appendix A provides an extensive list of abbreviations. Note that some of the items listed involve initials or acronyms instead of actual abbreviations.

---

[2] THE BLUEBOOK: A UNIFORM SYSTEM OF CITATION (21st ed. 2020) (compiled by the editors of the Columbia Law Review, Harvard Law Review, University of Pennsylvania Law Review, and The Yale Law Journal); ALWD GUIDE TO LEGAL CITATION (6th ed. 2017) (compiled by the Association of Legal Writing Directors and Coleen M. Barger); the INTERNAL REVENUE MANUAL 4.10.7.2 (Jan. 1, 2006). Websites for The Bluebook and ALWD include additional material. Another citation manual, TAXCITE: A FEDERAL TAX CITATION AND REFERENCE MANUAL (1995) (compiled by The Virginia Tax Review, Tax Law Review, and the ABA Section of Taxation; the ABA group received assistance from student editors of The Tax Lawyer), has not been revised to cover government sources released since 1995, but it is possible that it is still in use.

7. Cut-Off Dates

This edition went into production on September 9, 2020. Most illustrations and descriptions were completed by mid-July 2020. It is likely that some services, particularly those delivered electronically, will change their layout or coverage before a new edition appears.

8. A Note on Free Sources

As this book illustrates, there are numerous subscription and free services available, and many items are available in multiple formats and from multiple publishers. If you are a student, you may never use some of the materials described here. For example, you may not need to read public comments on proposed regulations or determine if a proposed regulation has an impact on small business. Likewise, because you probably have free access to several subscription services, you may not need to access free government websites or print materials. If you are a practitioner, or a student clerking for one, you may find that free sources provide the information you need in a cost-effective way. We have tried to accommodate both groups in discussing research materials.

Chapter 2

TYPES OF AUTHORITY

A. Introduction

Because many factors influence the process, there is no "right" way to begin and end a tax research project. Your method of attack depends on the nature of the problem and your familiarity with the subject matter. While many research efforts begin with the relevant statutory provisions, others start with explanatory materials. The appropriate ending place depends on the type of problem and the number of sources you need to consult before resolving the issues raised. At various points between the start and finish, most research efforts involve both primary and secondary authority.

B. Primary and Secondary Authority

Primary authority emanates from a branch of government: legislative; executive (including administrative agencies); or judicial. In addition to the Constitution, it includes statutes, treaties, Treasury regulations, Internal Revenue Service (IRS) documents, and judicial decisions. If a problem has international aspects, you may encounter primary authority from other countries or from international organizations.

Secondary authorities include treatises, looseleaf services, and articles. These authorities explain (and sometimes criticize) primary authorities.

Some publications (e.g., Code of Federal Regulations) contain one type of primary authority; others (e.g., Internal Revenue Bulletin) contain several types. Many services (e.g., Bloomberg Law, Checkpoint, Cheetah,[1] Lexis+, and Westlaw Edge) contain both primary and secondary authorities.

In considering primary authority, remember two facts. First, some government-produced documents do not qualify as primary authority. These include the legislative histories discussed in Chapter 6, which have characteristics of both primary and secondary authority.[2] Second, an authority doesn't lose its status as primary when it is reproduced by a nongovernment publisher. Nevertheless, if you can obtain the original version, you avoid the risk of errors introduced by the second publisher.

C. Hierarchy of Authority

Not all authorities are equal in value. Primary authorities carry more weight than do secondary authorities, and some primary authorities carry more weight than others. An authority's value varies depending upon the body reviewing it and the purpose for

[1] Wolters Kluwer has two platforms for their tax materials, Cheetah, and their older user interface, IntelliConnect. Because many schools will no longer have IntelliConnect when this book is published, we use the term Cheetah to refer to both. There is no difference in content between the two platforms.

[2] This book describes legislative histories in the chapters on primary sources because (1) they emanate from a branch of government; (2) the IRS considers them authority for avoiding the substantial understatement penalty described later in this chapter; and (3) you would consult them immediately after reading statutory text in many research efforts. Nevertheless, many legislative history documents are considered secondary sources.

which it is being submitted. The subsections below, covering precedential, persuasive, and substantial authority, illustrate these distinctions.

1. Precedential and Persuasive Authority

The Treasury Department and IRS recognize a hierarchy of sources. Courts also value some authorities more than others. Certain holdings constitute **binding precedent**; these must be followed. Others are considered merely **persuasive** and receive little, if any, deference. Secondary sources fall into the latter category, but so do many primary sources. For example, the IRS will follow a Supreme Court decision in its dealings with other taxpayers. It may, however, choose to ignore an adverse lower court opinion and continue litigating a particular issue.[3]

An authority is not precedential merely because a court or administrative agency issued it. The type of document is also important. In some instances, for example, the IRS is not bound by its own pronouncements. For example, the IRS issues both officially published revenue rulings and publicly available private letter rulings. Third parties with comparable facts may rely on the revenue rulings but not on the letter rulings.

The relationship of one deciding body to another is also relevant. One trial court (e.g., the Tax Court) may refuse to treat as precedential an opinion issued by another trial court (e.g., the Court of Federal Claims). These limitations are discussed further in Chapters 8 through 10, which cover administrative and judicial sources.

2. Substantial Authority

An authority may have value even if the IRS rejects it. First, the IRS might be incorrect. A court (perhaps even the Supreme Court) may rely on the particular authority in rendering its decision. Second, litigation involves more than the underlying substantive issue; penalties are also relevant. If the IRS asserts the Code section 6662(b)(2) penalty for substantial understatement of income tax liability, the authority you find may shield the taxpayer from liability.

Section 6662(d)(2)(B)(i) waives this 20% penalty if the taxpayer has **substantial authority** for a position. This determination requires that the taxpayer's position be backed by recognized authority and that the authority be substantial.

A Treasury regulation lists the items below as authority for this purpose.[4] Note that this list includes both items that are binding precedent and items that are at best persuasive authority.

- applicable provisions of the Internal Revenue Code and other statutory provisions;
- proposed, temporary and final regulations construing such statutes;
- revenue rulings and revenue procedures;
- tax treaties and regulations thereunder, and Treasury Department and other official explanations of such treaties;

---

3 IRS announcements concerning its litigation plans are discussed in Chapters 9 and 10.

4 Treas. Reg. § 1.6662–4(d)(3)(iii). Taxpayers can also avoid this penalty by adequately disclosing the relevant facts if there is a reasonable basis for the tax treatment claimed. I.R.C. § 6662(d)(2)(B)(ii). The section 6662 regulations also constitute authority for avoiding the understatement penalty imposed on tax return preparers for taking an unreasonable position. See I.R.C. § 6694(a)(2)(A); Treas. Reg. § 1.6694–2(b).

- court cases;
- congressional intent as reflected in committee reports, joint explanatory statements of managers included in conference committee reports, and floor statements made prior to enactment by one of a bill's managers;
- General Explanations of tax legislation prepared by the Joint Committee on Taxation (the Blue Book);
- private letter rulings and technical advice memoranda issued after October 31, 1976;
- actions on decisions and general counsel memoranda issued after March 12, 1981 (as well as general counsel memoranda published in pre-1955 volumes of the Cumulative Bulletin);
- Internal Revenue Service information or press releases; and
- notices, announcements and other administrative pronouncements published by the Service in the Internal Revenue Bulletin.

Conclusions reached in treatises or other legal periodicals and opinions rendered by tax professionals do not constitute authority for avoiding this penalty. In addition, the regulation provides rules by which overruled and reversed items lose their status as authority and older items receive less regard.[5]

3. Compiling a Table of Authorities

As part of your research effort, you could categorize authorities you locate in a table format. Table 2-A illustrates one possible format. If you use this method, remember that an item's status as precedential is affected by the entity to which you are submitting it. Thus, a Fourth Circuit decision is precedential in a District Court located in Virginia but is only persuasive if you are litigating in Tennessee, which is located in the Sixth Circuit. A recent private letter ruling is more valuable as authority than one issued many years earlier.

Table 2-A. Categorizing Authority

Item	*Precedential Authority*	*Substantial Authority*
Supreme Court decision	Yes	Yes
Fourth Circuit decision	Maybe	Yes
Private Letter Ruling	No	Maybe
Field Service Advice	No	No
Law Review Article	No	No

[5] "An older private letter ruling, technical advice memorandum, general counsel memorandum or action on decision generally must be accorded less weight than a more recent one. Any document described in the preceding sentence that is more than 10 years old generally is accorded very little weight." Treas. Reg. § 1.6662–4(d)(3)(ii). This limitation does not apply to other IRS documents, such as revenue rulings. See Field Service Advisory (Nov. 17, 1994), 1994 WL 1725562, 1994 FSA LEXIS 464.

D. Examples

Examples of statements concerning precedent appear in Chapters 8 through 10, which cover regulations, IRS rulings, and judicial decisions.

The judicial decisions and IRS ruling[6] below involved taxpayers who claimed they had substantial authority. You can find these items on Bloomberg Law, Checkpoint, Cheetah, Federal Research Library, Lexis+, Westlaw Edge, and other free and commercial sources.[7]

- *Bhatia v. Commissioner*, T.C. Memo. 1996–429 (unsuccessful)
- *Estate of Kluener v. Commissioner*, 154 F.3d 630 (6th Cir. 1998) (successful)
- Technical Advice Memorandum 200326034 (June 27, 2003) (unsuccessful)
- *Ackerman v. Commissioner*, T.C. Memo. 2009–80 (unsuccessful)
- *TIFD III-E, Inc. v. United States*, 666 F.3d 836 (2d Cir. 2012) (unsuccessful)
- *Cohen v. United States*, 999 F. Supp. 2d 650 (S.D.N.Y. 2014) (unsuccessful)
- *Chemtech Royalty Associates, L.P. v. United States*, 823 F.3d 282 (5th Cir. 2016) (unsuccessful)

---

6 Litigation remains an option for a taxpayer whose claim is denied by the IRS.

7 The 2003 TAM is also available on the IRS website, which is discussed in Chapter 9.

Chapter 3

RESEARCH PROCESS

A. Introduction

This chapter continues the overview discussion begun in Chapters 1 and 2. As noted there, your research will involve primary and secondary authorities and will consider the relative weight of each authority you find. This chapter focuses on process. What are your research goals? What methods will you use to find the materials you need? What factors favor using print or online sources? These questions reappear in later chapters as part of the discussion of various sources.

B. Research Tasks

As is true in other areas of the law, tax research begins with an assignment. To complete that assignment, you must (1) determine the relevant facts and issues; (2) find authorities that are on point (either directly or by analogy); (3) try to reconcile conflicting findings; (4) update your findings; and (5) communicate your conclusions. These are techniques you learned in a basic legal research course.

The type of assignment will influence the course your research takes and the product you produce. Are you structuring a new transaction? Are you litigating the tax consequences of a completed transaction? Are you testifying before Congress or the Treasury Department to advocate a statutory or administrative change?

In the first situation, future legislation and regulations may be as important as existing law. Because retroactive effective dates are a fact of life, you must be able to locate pending legislation and proposed regulations. You may even have to locate IRS revenue procedures and notices describing regulations that may be proposed in the future. Because your client does not want unexpected tax consequences after the transaction closes, you may consider requesting a letter ruling to provide comfort that the IRS agrees with your tax analysis. Your ruling request will include authority that supports your position.

When the IRS challenges a completed transaction, the statutes and regulations in effect when the transaction closed are more important than future legislation or administrative guidance.[1] You may also search for judicial opinions and for information about cases currently being litigated, as they may provide authority for (or against) your client's position. If your client is unsuccessful with respect to his substantive position, you may need to find authority for avoiding the substantial understatement penalty described in Chapter 2.[2]

In testifying at congressional or Treasury Department hearings, you may want to include detailed history supporting your position. You can find previous legislative and

---

1 But technical corrections bills may affect transactions that took place several years earlier.

2 I.R.C. § 6662(b). In addition, you may need to avoid I.R.C. § 6694(a) preparer penalties. See also Treas. Dept. Circular 230, § 10.34 (31 C.F.R. § 10.34, Standards with respect to tax returns and documents, affidavits and other papers). On the other hand, if the client prevails, you may look for authority to justify charging part of your legal fees to the government. I.R.C. § 7430 provides for recovery of attorneys' fees if the government's position was not substantially justified and the taxpayer meets certain other requirements.

regulatory changes and their effects by tracing rules back to their inception and reading cases and commentary about prior versions.

The above list is not exclusive. You may be researching sources for a law review article or note, bibliography, CLE presentation, or class assignment. Your assignment may be narrow in scope (e.g., go to the Tax Court website and find all opinions authored by Judge Greaves in 2020 or find the most recent revenue procedure on changes in accounting method), or it may require consulting several primary and secondary sources (e.g., research and write an article arguing that Congress should reinstate the deduction for state gasoline taxes). No matter what your goal is, successful research requires an ability to locate relevant sources.

C. Research Methodology

1. In General

As noted above, tax research has much in common with the research techniques you learned in a basic research course. Using a set of facts presented, you determine the relevant issues and ascertain any additional facts that might be important. Because a project may be completed over a period of weeks or months, you must regularly update your research by looking for newer materials and using a citator. For the same reason, you must compile a list of sources you consulted and dates you used them.

2. Primary Sources

To resolve the issues you isolate, you must locate the governing statutes. Legislative history or administrative pronouncements would be the next step if you desire guidance in interpreting those statutes. You may then search for judicial decisions interpreting the statutes or administrative provisions. In addition to interpreting statutes or regulations, judges may rule on their validity. Judicial decisions may cover constitutional challenges to statutes and regulations. Judges may also determine whether a regulation or ruling appropriately interprets a statute or was issued in compliance with the Administrative Procedure Act.[3] If your problem involves non-U.S. source income or citizens of other countries, your research expands to include applicable treaties and related materials.

3. Secondary Sources

If you are familiar with the subject matter involved, you probably can locate relevant primary sources without using any secondary materials other than a citator. When you lack familiarity, you might start with secondary materials. Those materials have two advantages. First, they explain the topic you are researching. Second, they provide citations to the relevant Code sections and other primary sources. Looseleaf services, treatises, and periodical articles are particularly useful for this purpose. You may also resort to legal dictionaries or even annotated form books.

The "knowledgeable researchers start with primary sources, others start with secondary sources" rule does not always apply. Even an experienced researcher may begin the project by consulting a treatise or looseleaf service. The discussion of potential

---

[3] Chapters 8 and 9 discuss the degree of deference courts give administrative determinations. They also discuss issues regarding the Administrative Procedure Act.

issues is particularly important if the experienced researcher knows the tax rules but is less comfortable with the problem's nontax issues.[4]

How much time should you spend using secondary sources? Your level of knowledge may be the most important factor. Even if you have taken a basic tax course, you may know very little about a particular specialty within tax law. You may not have encountered—or only brushed the surface of—employment taxes, exempt organizations, natural resources, health care, and pensions. These areas involve complex Code sections and overlap with nontax rules (e.g., ERISA). Because tax law changes rapidly and there are so many sources to consult, even less-complex topics may initially seem overwhelming.

How much secondary material is likely to be available? A clearly written statute should require less explanation than a complex one, and settled questions are written about less often than litigated issues.

Timing is also important. For example, older statutes probably have been explained more thoroughly than newer ones.[5] You may need to be creative when researching recent changes. For example, if materials discussing a recent statutory amendment are limited, secondary materials criticizing the original provision may be useful guides to the change. If the change involves a completely new Code section, look for Joint Committee reports and newsletter articles for explanations.

D. Locating Materials

1. In General

As discussed above, tax research involves techniques used in other types of research. Likewise, you can often use traditional legal research sources in solving tax research problems.[6] Even if you can use traditional materials, you will find that materials focusing on taxation make research easier.

Before starting your research in print materials, make sure you know what tax materials are available and where they are located.[7] Most library collections contain tax-oriented print materials but differ in how they shelve them. Some libraries shelve them together in a "tax alcove." Other libraries group some tax-oriented materials (e.g., treatises, looseleaf services, and legislative histories) together and shelve others (e.g., tax-oriented periodicals) in the general collection. Even if dispersed throughout the collection, tax research sources are no more difficult to locate or use than are traditional research tools.

Online research follows a similar pattern. You can select from general services (e.g., Bloomberg Law, Lexis+, and Westlaw Edge) that include tax libraries, or you can use services (e.g., Checkpoint, Cheetah, and Federal Research Library) that focus on tax. In

---

4 If the research project involves a relatively recent statute or administrative pronouncement, articles in practitioner-oriented journals or newsletters are likely to be better starting points.

5 These factors also influence the availability of explanatory sources for administrative materials and judicial opinions.

6 Because we assume you are familiar with traditional legal research tools, we devote relatively little space to such items. In some instances, particularly if a library lacks a tax-oriented tool, you may need to consult traditional materials.

7 As library costs escalate, many libraries are canceling print subscriptions to materials that are also available online. If the library has a research guide focusing on taxation, it may include the location for each print and microform service. It may also indicate materials available only electronically.

addition to subscription services, you can use general or tax-only government websites. Each service operates somewhat differently and varies in the material covered.

If your university has a business or public policy school, its library (or the general university library) may carry print or electronic services that aren't available in the law school library. You may have access to those sources by virtue of your status as a law student.[8]

2. Subscription Services

Because there are so many available materials, a library or database may lack some materials discussed in this book or may contain materials omitted here. Fortunately, many alternative services cover primary and secondary sources. Because it focuses on the types of materials available, this book should help you conduct successful tax research in virtually any law library or electronic resource.

If you are still in school, you have free access to subscription services that may not be available to you in practice. Your firm may limit itself to Bloomberg Law, Lexis+, or Westlaw Edge. It may carry only one of the tax-oriented electronic services; it may not carry any of them. Even if it carries a particular service, it may not subscribe to all of its available databases. It may carry some services in print and others electronically.

You don't know today what subscription services you can access in practice, and clients don't want to pay for you to learn how to use them. Using all available services now can pay dividends in the future.

3. Government Websites

Don't overlook government websites. They include significant amounts of primary source material, and often provide original text in PDF. They are not as easy to use as the commercial services, their coverage generally begins much later, and you may have to access multiple sites to obtain your information, but access is free.

E. Print Versus Other Formats

Given the large number of materials available in both print (bound and looseleaf), microform, and electronic formats, how do you decide which format to select? Although that question has no single correct answer, factors discussed in the following paragraphs and in the materials covering online research are relevant.

1. Availability of Materials

What is available in your library? Although online services continue to add retrospective coverage, older materials are often available only in print or in microform. For example, if you don't have access to a source such as HeinOnline or ProQuest Congressional, you may be limited to print or microform versions of early legislative history materials. In other situations, the library may not carry print subscriptions to materials available online. Decisions not to carry might reflect shelf space and filing costs,[9] availability of similar services from another publisher, or relative lack of use by library patrons.

---

[8] If you are a business or public policy school student, you may have similar privileges with respect to the law school's collection.

[9] For example, IRS letter ruling services and the Daily Tax Report require extensive shelf space.

If you subscribe to an online service, to which of its files do you have access? Many subscription services have pricing options that allow access to different databases. The service may carry a particular item, but you can't access it unless your library subscription covers it.

Another aspect of availability relates to mobility. If you have Internet access, you can access online services from remote locations. The biggest inconvenience may involve remembering your passwords. Your access to print materials depends on your being close to a library during the hours it is open.

2. Updating Frequency

How often is each source updated? Some print materials are updated weekly; others receive less-frequent supplementation. Online databases should be updated at least as often as print sources and often are updated more frequently. Primary source materials posted by the government body that produces them may be available immediately after being issued. This is particularly true for judicial opinions available at a court's website and for IRS items.[10]

3. Type of Search

a. Indexes and Tables

Is the research best conducted based on indexes or tables of contents? Or would you be better off searching for words or concepts? Indexes are useful if you don't know all the relevant words or concepts. Tables of contents provide a structure for topics you are researching. Although both print and electronic services have indexes and tables of contents, the print versions are easier to browse than their online counterparts. In addition, it is harder to overlook them. A print volume (or set of volumes) has a table of contents at the beginning and an index at the end. It may also have tables indicating where the service covers specific cases, rulings, and other material. In an online environment, you may be tempted to go directly to the word search feature and skip the table of contents or index. That may not be the most effective way to research.

b. Words and Concepts

Judicially declared concepts such as "step-transaction doctrine" are not specifically covered in citators because they are neither case names nor Code sections. Although you can find materials relevant to concepts using a print source's index, you can find them more quickly by searching in the relevant online database. The same is true for concepts that do appear in the Code (e.g., "effectively connected").

There are two risks associated with online word searches. These involve spelling and specificity. First, if you (or the service itself) make a spelling error, you may not retrieve a document even though it exists. Words with variant spellings are particularly likely to cause problems. For example, "includible" and "excludible" might also be spelled "includable" and "excludable." If you know a word has variant spellings, you can use wildcards (discussed in Chapter 17) in your search.

---

10 You can subscribe to GuideWire, a free email service the IRS provides for I.R.B. items. The emails often arrive several weeks before these items appear in the I.R.B. The IRS website also has a page on which it lists advance releases; that page does not indicate the Code section or subject matter involved. It is located at https://www.irs.gov/downloads/irs-drop. I.R.B. items are discussed further in Chapter 9.

The second problem occurs if your search terms are too specific. For example, if you search for "car," you may miss sources that discuss automobile or motor vehicle. If an online service has a thesaurus option, using it reduces the risk of this type of error. Although specificity may also be a problem when you use indexes, "see also" references in a service's index may point you in the right direction.

c. Code Cross-References

Online searches are more effective than print searches if you want to know which Code sections cite other sections. Online databases may be updated more frequently than Code cross-reference tables. In addition, because you can search by Code section, you do not have to worry about editorial errors in compiling the tables. Finally, because online databases have hyperlinks, you can jump directly from one Code section to another.

d. Names of Judges or Attorneys

Searches involving particular judges or attorneys are difficult to accomplish using print materials. Finding every case in which Senior Judge L. Paige Marvel authored an opinion after joining the Tax Court would require reading many volumes of opinions. The search would be impossible to conduct using print sources if you needed to include Summary Opinions. These decisions are not compiled in bound volumes.

As illustrated below, that search can be easily accomplished online. Online searches can be restricted by judge name, attorney name, or date. If we wanted to know whether any of these cases involved a particular topic, such as "compensation," we could add that as a search term.

Illustrations 3-1 through 3-6 illustrate searches performed in May 2020 using both Westlaw Edge and the Tax Court's website. The results were very similar. The Westlaw Edge search found 318 opinions, while the Tax Court's website returned 313 opinions. Using either platform, you can select a specific day, month, year, or range of years. The Tax Court site has only two sorting options: alphabetical by taxpayer name or release date. Westlaw Edge offered more sorting options (at least on some of its screens).

Illustration 3-1. Westlaw Edge Search

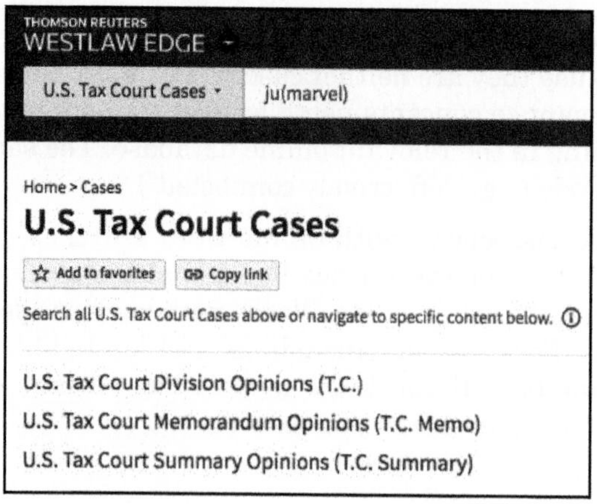

→ Westlaw Edge allows searches by type of decision as well as searching all decisions.

Illustration 3-2. Westlaw Edge Search: Results Screen

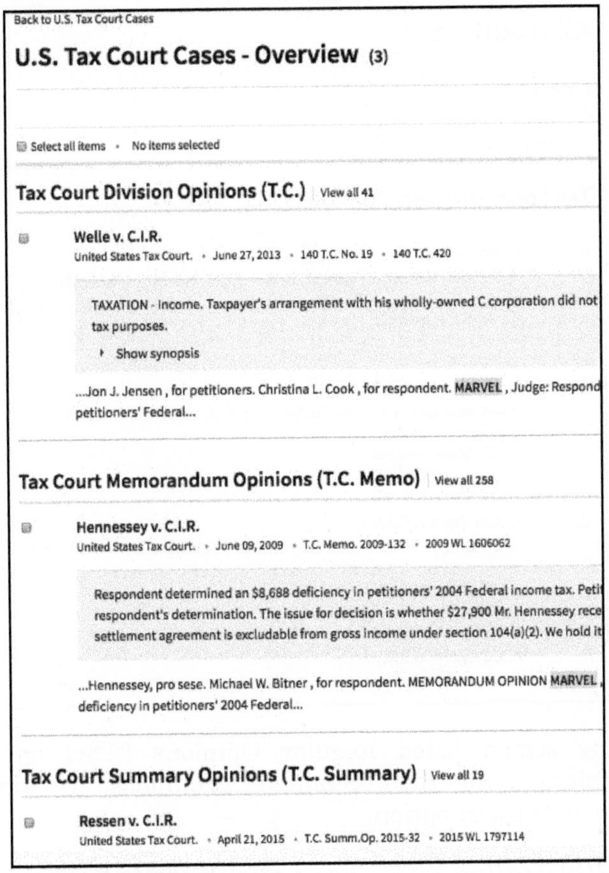
Back to U.S. Tax Court Cases

U.S. Tax Court Cases - Overview (3)

Select all items • No items selected

Tax Court Division Opinions (T.C.) View all 41

Welle v. C.I.R.
United States Tax Court. • June 27, 2013 • 140 T.C. No. 19 • 140 T.C. 420

TAXATION - Income. Taxpayer's arrangement with his wholly-owned C corporation did not
tax purposes.
Show synopsis

...Jon J. Jensen, for petitioners. Christina L. Cook, for respondent. MARVEL, Judge: Respond
petitioners' Federal...

Tax Court Memorandum Opinions (T.C. Memo) View all 258

Hennessey v. C.I.R.
United States Tax Court. • June 09, 2009 • T.C. Memo. 2009-132 • 2009 WL 1606062

Respondent determined an $8,688 deficiency in petitioners' 2004 Federal income tax. Peti
respondent's determination. The issue for decision is whether $27,900 Mr. Hennessey rece
settlement agreement is excludable from gross income under section 104(a)(2). We hold it

...Hennessey, pro sese. Michael W. Bitner, for respondent. MEMORANDUM OPINION MARVEL,
deficiency in petitioners' 2004 Federal...

Tax Court Summary Opinions (T.C. Summary) View all 19

Ressen v. C.I.R.
United States Tax Court. • April 21, 2015 • T.C. Summ.Op. 2015-32 • 2015 WL 1797114

→ The initial results screen showed one case of each type. It also indicated the number of each type found. The total was 318 "hits."

Illustration 3-3. Westlaw Edge Search: Summary Opinions Only

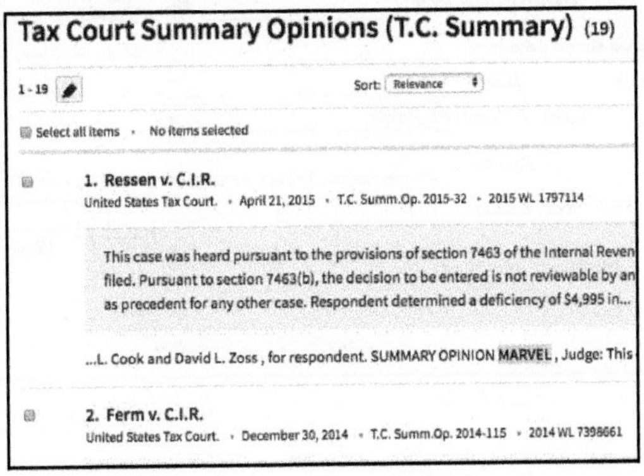
Tax Court Summary Opinions (T.C. Summary) (19)

1 - 19 Sort: Relevance

Select all items • No items selected

1. Ressen v. C.I.R.
United States Tax Court. • April 21, 2015 • T.C. Summ.Op. 2015-32 • 2015 WL 1797114

This case was heard pursuant to the provisions of section 7463 of the Internal Reven
filed. Pursuant to section 7463(b), the decision to be entered is not reviewable by an
as precedent for any other case. Respondent determined a deficiency of $4,995 in...

...L. Cook and David L. Zoss, for respondent. SUMMARY OPINION MARVEL, Judge: This

2. Ferm v. C.I.R.
United States Tax Court. • December 30, 2014 • T.C. Summ.Op. 2014-115 • 2014 WL 7398661

→ Searches confined to a particular type of opinion can be sorted by Relevance, Date, Most Cited, Most Used, Court Level, and Term Frequency.

Illustration 3-4. Westlaw Edge Search: All Decisions

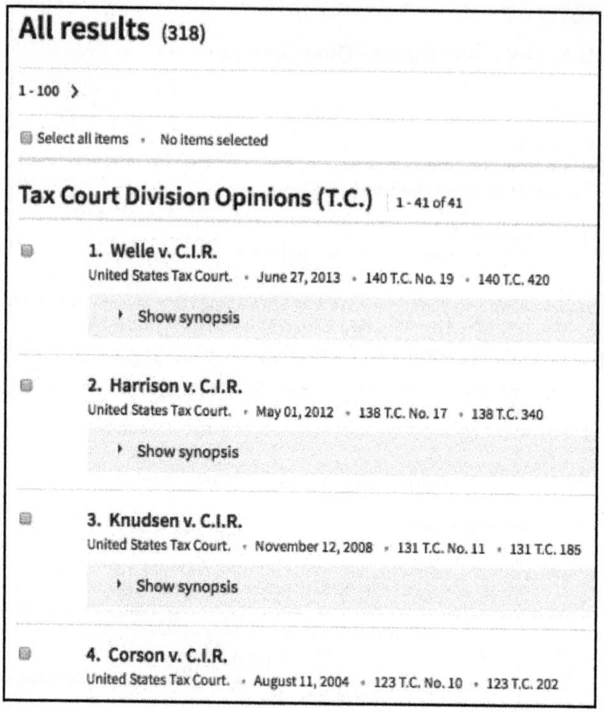

All results (318)

1 - 100 ›

Select all items • No items selected

Tax Court Division Opinions (T.C.) | 1 - 41 of 41

1. Welle v. C.I.R.
United States Tax Court. • June 27, 2013 • 140 T.C. No. 19 • 140 T.C. 420
› Show synopsis

2. Harrison v. C.I.R.
United States Tax Court. • May 01, 2012 • 138 T.C. No. 17 • 138 T.C. 340
› Show synopsis

3. Knudsen v. C.I.R.
United States Tax Court. • November 12, 2008 • 131 T.C. No. 11 • 131 T.C. 185
› Show synopsis

4. Corson v. C.I.R.
United States Tax Court. • August 11, 2004 • 123 T.C. No. 10 • 123 T.C. 202

→ The All results screen listed Regular Opinions ("Division" Opinions), then Memorandum Opinions, and then Summary Opinions. It did not list them chronologically or include a sort option.

Illustration 3-5. Tax Court Website Search

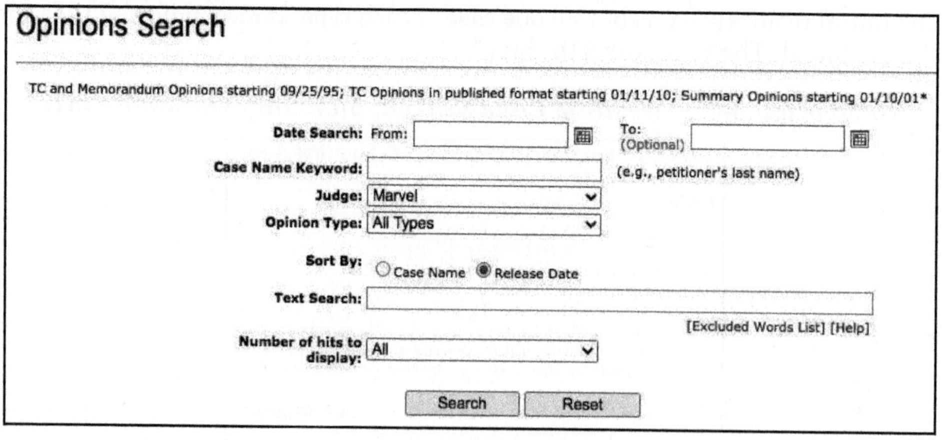

Opinions Search

TC and Memorandum Opinions starting 09/25/95; TC Opinions in published format starting 01/11/10; Summary Opinions starting 01/10/01*

Date Search: From: [ ] To: (Optional) [ ]
Case Name Keyword: [ ] (e.g., petitioner's last name)
Judge: Marvel
Opinion Type: All Types
Sort By: Case Name / Release Date
Text Search: [ ]
[Excluded Words List] [Help]
Number of hits to display: All

Search | Reset

Illustration 3-6. Tax Court Website Search: Results Screen

Max. Results per Page: 25 Page 1 of 13 << < > >>

Case Name	Type	Released
Anargyros George Mylonas	Memorandum	12/14/1998
Thomas M. and Dolores F. Gomez	Memorandum	03/25/1999
Ruby Jean Stevens	Memorandum	08/04/1999
Cheryl J. Miller	Memorandum	08/12/1999
Agapito Fajardo and Clara S. Fajardo	Memorandum	09/16/1999
Gregg Chernik	Memorandum	09/23/1999
Hugh D. and Nancy L. Sims	Memorandum	12/22/1999
William J. Fleischaker and Donni L. Fleischaker	Memorandum	12/30/1999
Michael C. Hollen and Joan L. Hollen	Memorandum	03/24/2000
Cheryl J. Miller	TC Opinion	03/24/2000

→ You can sort opinions alphabetically by Case Name or chronologically by Release Date. Sorting by release date shows the oldest opinions first.

e. Articles

Online searching will be more efficient than print if you are searching for articles by author or topic. Print articles indexes are not cumulative. Each volume covers one or more years, necessitating a lengthy search. The process is further complicated because each index covers slightly different publications; the Index to Legal Periodicals has imposed minimum page requirements for articles; these have varied over time.

Although their online versions also have coverage limitations, you can search these databases more quickly. In addition, the online service may compile a list of "hits" that you can print out and return to as needed.

Two important limitations apply in selecting between print and online articles indexes. The first relates to availability; the second, to coverage dates. The Index to Federal Tax Articles (which has extensive retrospective coverage) is not available online. Both Index to Legal Periodicals and Current Law Index are available in electronic formats. Coverage for Index to Legal Periodicals begins in 1908 if you have access to both ILP and ILP Retrospective; otherwise, online coverage begins in 1982. Online coverage for Current Law Index (Legal Resource Index online) begins in the late 1970s or early 1980s.[11] Articles indexes are discussed further in Chapter 13.

f. Citators

There are at least three advantages to using a citator online. First, the online version is more current than the print version. Second, you can accomplish the search more quickly because you won't have to consult several volumes of print materials. Third, online citators provide easy access to the citing material. You can print out a list of citations or jump to them directly using hyperlinks. Citators are discussed further in Chapter 11.

Electronic services can also quickly perform citator-like searches. Even if, for example, an electronic service lacks a citator, you can use the initial case name or citation as a search term and find all later cases or other material citing it. You can also do this for words and phrases, which would not be covered by a print or online citator.

11 Lexis+ indicates that its coverage of Legal Resource Index (the electronic version of Current Law Index) begins in 1977. Westlaw Edge coverage for Legal Resource Index begins in 1980.

4. Cost

Research tools are not free. You should consider both your time and the cost of materials when you decide between competing sources. As noted in Section E.1, your library may have limited your choice by deciding which materials it carries. Cost may determine which materials you select from those available to you.

You do not pay separately to use print or microform materials; the subscription price is a fixed cost. You pay nothing to use free online materials, such as those available at government websites. Although law students have unlimited, free access to services such as Bloomberg Law, Lexis+, and Westlaw Edge, that may not be true for law firms.[12] Pricing for subscription services may be based on a fixed fee or may include time or search charges. You should consider both the time savings in speed (your "hourly rate" as a practitioner) and any incremental cost (fee for use) associated with subscription services.

If you need to familiarize yourself with a topic, print services may be preferable to online sources. The less you know about the topic, the more time you should spend reading explanatory material. Although you can reduce online time by downloading text, your lack of familiarity with the topic may result in your downloading too much or too little. If you have difficulty reading large amounts of text from a computer screen, you must factor in physical "costs" when deciding between print and online sources. The print version also forces you to keep reading. There are no hyperlinks to primary sources to distract you from the analytical material. This can be an important distinction if you are relatively unfamiliar with the topic.

5. Need for Original Page Citations

If you must cite to the original volume and page numbers, the original print source obviously provides that information. Many online services also include original pagination. If you need to cite more than one publication (e.g., official and unofficial citations), online services are more likely to include parallel citations (and page numbers within each service) than are print materials.

When using electronic sources, you take a slight risk that citations or pagination will be incorrect. Many websites, particularly those of government entities, avoid this problem by providing documents in PDF format. Westlaw Edge also does this for West reporter services. Federal Research Library offers Original Source PDFs for many judicial and administrative items. HeinOnline also provides original pages. This format doesn't merely add pagination at appropriate breaks; it actually reproduces the original document. In most cases, you can perform word searches in these PDF documents.[13] If you need the original source's format (e.g., italics or bold), you are more likely to obtain correct formatting from a PDF version than from an HTML or XML version; this is true even on government websites.

---

[12] See, e.g., Simon Canick, *Infusing Technology Skills into the Law School Curriculum*, 42 CAP. U. L. REV. 663, 700 (2014); Laura K. Justiss, *A Survey of Electronic Research Alternatives to LexisNexis and Westlaw in Law Firms*, 103 LAW LIBR. J. 71, 73 (2011); Heidi W. Heller, *The Twenty-First Century Law Library: A Law Firm Librarian's Thoughts*, 101 LAW LIBR. J. 517, 518–19 (2009); Patrick Meyer, *Law Firm Legal Research Requirements for New Attorneys*, 101 LAW LIBR. J. 297, 311–13, 329–30 (2009).

[13] If the service offers both text (with hyperlink) and PDF options, you can use the text version's hyperlinks to follow sources cited within the document while relying on the easy-to-read pagination of the PDF version.

F. External Factors Affecting Research

Three phenomena affect the research process: proliferation of sources, technological change, and publishing industry consolidation.

The number of primary and secondary authorities continually expands. Since this book's first edition, for example, the Internal Revenue Service has stopped issuing some types of guidance but has added different items. The Tax Court began public release of Summary Opinions in 2001, and additional law reviews focusing on tax have appeared.[14]

Technology, particularly online research sites and even blogs, enhances the research process by covering many sources and allowing for easy database searching.[15] Although some online sites require subscriptions, many others offer free access to materials. The federal government has been quite active in providing free online access to primary source materials and in making its sites more user-friendly.[16] Many libraries have reduced their print collections of materials that are available online. Recognizing the increasing importance of these sources, we have increased this book's focus on online materials (both government and private).

Finally, the publishing industry continues to consolidate. As indicated in Appendix D, several once-independent companies are now commonly owned. Many services have been renamed, eliminated, or limited to online format. Others now appear only on platforms (e.g., Bloomberg Law, Lexis+, or Westlaw Edge) owned by their common parent. No one knows when this process will end. Because this book focuses on general tax research principles, you should be able to adapt your research strategy to the appearance of new materials and the disappearance of old ones.

G. Summary

Research generally involves using both primary and secondary sources. Various factors influence the order in which you consult them and the format in which you conduct your research. These factors include:

- how complicated the problem is in relation to your knowledge of the subject matter;
- the specific tools available in your library;
- the frequency with which services are updated;
- where you are located when conducting your research;
- the usefulness of tables of contents, indexes, and other finding aids;
- the cost-effectiveness of each service for the particular task;
- your need for correct page citations; and
- personal preferences you develop as you gain research expertise.

Remember that your research is not complete until you use appropriate updating tools to check your authorities.

---

14 For a partial list of tax-specific law reviews and publications, see Table 13-A, *infra* page 262.

15 Your clients can access a wide array of free, but not necessarily authoritative, electronic sources. Don't be surprised if they ask you about tax results based on misleading information they've read online.

16 In recent years, it replaced FDsys with govinfo.gov and THOMAS with Congress.gov.

Chapter 4

CONSTITUTION

A. Introduction

The United States Constitution serves several functions. First, in articles I, II, and III, it establishes the three branches of government: legislative, executive, and judicial. Second, it lists powers exercised by each branch and indicates situations in which a second branch is involved. For example, Congress (the legislative branch) has the power to impose taxes but legislative proposals generally do not become law without the President's signature. The President (executive branch) has the power to make treaties but only with the concurrence of the Senate. The judicial branch has the power to hear cases arising under the Constitution, statutes, and treaties, but the Constitution establishes only the Supreme Court; it gives Congress the power to establish any lower courts.

The Constitution also imposes limitations on the exercise of each branch's powers. One limitation is alluded to above—certain powers require the participation or acquiescence of a second branch of government. In addition, the Constitution imposes limitations that do not involve a second branch of government. Many of those limitations, covered in the next section, relate to the imposition of taxes.

B. Taxing Power and Limitations

The Constitution gives Congress the power to impose taxes but provides several limitations on its ability to do so. Some limitations are substantive: direct taxes must be apportioned, and other taxes must be uniform throughout the United States. Other limitations are procedural: bills for raising revenue must originate in the House of Representatives. Table 4-A includes provisions that specifically mention taxation.

Because the income tax is specifically authorized by the Constitution's sixteenth amendment, it avoids an earlier holding that it was a direct tax subject to apportionment based on population.[1] The estate and gift taxes, on the other hand, are indirect taxes; they are subject only to the requirement that they be uniform throughout the United States.

Table 4-A. Constitutional Provisions Regarding Federal Taxes

Art. I, § 2, cl. 3: Representatives and direct Taxes shall be apportioned among the several States which may be included within this Union, according to their respective Numbers . . . . (Before amendment)
Art. I, § 7, cl. 1: All Bills for raising Revenue shall originate in the House of Representatives; but the Senate may propose or concur with Amendments as on other Bills.
Art. I, § 8, cl. 1: The Congress shall have Power To lay and collect Taxes, Duties, Imposts and Excises, to pay the Debts and provide for the common Defence and

1 *Pollock v. Farmers' Loan & Trust Co.*, 158 U.S. 601 (1895); cf. *Springer v. United States*, 102 U.S. 586 (1881), involving an income tax for the year 1865.

general Welfare of the United States; but all Duties, Imposts and Excises shall be uniform throughout the United States;

Art. I, § 9, cl. 4: No Capitation, or other direct, Tax shall be laid, unless in Proportion to the Census or Enumeration herein before directed to be taken.

Art. I, § 9, cl. 5: No Tax or Duty shall be laid on Articles exported from any State.

Art. I, § 9, cl. 6: No Preference shall be given by any Regulation of Commerce or Revenue to the Ports of one State over those of another; nor shall Vessels bound to, or from, one State, be obliged to enter, clear, or pay Duties in another.

Amend. XVI: The Congress shall have power to lay and collect taxes on incomes, from whatever source derived, without apportionment among the several States, and without regard to any census or enumeration.

→ Article I, § 10, includes limitations on the power of states to impose taxes and duties.

C. Constitutional Litigation

1. Items Challenged

Because several constitutional provisions explicitly mention taxation, courts may be asked to decide if a Code section violates the limitations shown in Table 4-A. Examples of such litigation appear in Table 4-B. Most cases discussing constitutional claims involve provisions that do not mention taxation, such as those listed in Table 4-C. Tax claims involving the Constitution rarely generate a substantial body of important litigation in any year.

Table 4-B. Litigation Involving Tax Provisions

Mobley v. United States, 8 Cl. Ct. 767 (1985) (the apportionment clause—art. I, § 2, cl. 3)

Hotze v. Burwell, 784 F.3d 984 (5th Cir. 2015) (the origination clause—art. I, § 7, cl. 1)

National Federation of Independent Business v. Sebelius, 567 U.S. 519 (2012) (the power to lay and collect taxes—art. I, § 8, cl. 1)

United States v. Clintwood Elkhorn Mining Co., 553 U.S. 1 (2008) (the export clause—art. I, § 9, cl. 5)

Murphy v. Internal Revenue Service, 460 F.3d 79 (D.C. Cir. 2006) (definition of income—amend. XVI)[2]

Nathel v. Commissioner, 615 F.3d 83 (2d Cir. 2010) (definition of income—amend. XVI)

[2] The decision above was later vacated. In its later decision, the court upheld the tax as an excise tax that met the uniformity requirement. 493 F.3d 170 (D.C. Cir. 2007).

Table 4-C. Litigation Involving Nontax Provisions[3]

Clinton v. City of New York, 524 U.S. 417 (1998) (the presentment clause—art. I, § 7, cl. 2)

Freytag v. Commissioner, 501 U.S. 868 (1991) (the appointments clause—art. II, § 2, cl. 2)

United States v. Hatter, 532 U.S. 557 (2001) (the compensation clause—art. III, § 1)

Battat v. Commissioner, 148 T.C. 32 (2017) (whether the President's ability to remove Tax Court judges under § 7443(f) interferes with art. III judicial power)

Hernandez v. Commissioner, 490 U.S. 680 (1989) (establishment of religion and free exercise of religion—amend. I)

United States v. Windsor, 570 U.S. 744 (2013) (due process and equal protection—amend. V)

Northern California Small Business Assistants Inc. v. Commissioner, 153 T.C. 65 (2019) (excessive fines—amend. VIII)

South Carolina v. Baker, 485 U.S. 505 (1988) (infringement on powers reserved to states—amend. X)

2. Supreme Court Litigation Versus Constitutional Litigation

Keep two facts in mind. First, lower courts dismiss many constitutional claims; most of these claims never reach the United States Supreme Court. Second, most substantive tax litigation involves interpreting statutes or other rules rather than resolving constitutional claims. If Congress disagrees with a Supreme Court decision regarding interpretation, it can "overrule" the Court by amending the statute.

D. Consideration of Constitutional Challenges

Only a court can declare a statute or administrative interpretation unconstitutional. But the IRS can consider constitutional challenges in its dealings with taxpayers. If it decides a challenge is valid, it can concede the disputed tax before the matter reaches a court. Many of these challenges are so-called "frivolous" challenges—e.g., that the sixteenth amendment was not properly ratified. An IRS document, "The Truth About Frivolous Tax Arguments," includes citations to cases and rulings covering constitutional and other challenges to federal taxes. It is available on the IRS website.

E. Research Process

You can use citators to determine if a court or the IRS has considered a challenge based on constitutional grounds. KeyCite, the online version of Shepard's, and the Bloomberg Law citators (BCite/Smart Code) are all good citators for this purpose.[4]

---

[3] Other provisions that have been litigated are: nondelegation doctrine—judicially derived from art. I, § 1; separation of powers doctrine—art. I, § 7, cl. 2; ex post facto laws—art. I, § 9, cl. 3; freedom of speech and association—amend. I; equal protection—amend. V; retroactivity as a denial of due process—amend. V; and cruel and unusual punishments—amend. VIII.

[4] Many of the print Shepard's series did not cover IRS material or Tax Court Memorandum decisions; the CCH and RIA citators do not provide citations to statutes or regulations.

Instead of using a citator, you can search online services for specific constitutional provisions or common terms (e.g., "due process").

The sources listed below discuss constitutional challenges. Each includes citations to authority.

- Bittker & Lokken, Federal Taxation of Income, Estates and Gifts chapter 1, available in print and on Westlaw Edge
- Cummings, The Supreme Court, Federal Taxation, and the Constitution (available in print from the American Bar Association Section of Taxation)
- Mertens, Law of Federal Income Taxation chapter 4, available in print and on Westlaw Edge
- Standard Federal Tax Reporter volume 1, available in print and on Cheetah
- The Truth About Frivolous Tax Arguments, available on the IRS website

Because substantive tax research rarely involves the Constitution, you may decide to perform your research using nontax materials.[5]

F. Problems

1. Indicate which of the Constitution's tax provisions was involved in
   a. *United States v. Ptasynski*, 462 U.S. 74 (1983)
   b. *Moore v. United States House of Representatives*, 733 F.2d 946 (D.C. Cir. 1984)
   c. *Miller v. United States*, 868 F.2d 236 (7th Cir. 1989)
   d. *United States v. International Business Machines Corp.*, 517 U.S. 843 (1996)
   e. *Retfalvi v. United States*, 930 F.3d 600 (4th Cir. 2019)
2. Indicate which of the Constitution's nontax provisions was involved in
   a. *Melton v. Kurtz*, 575 F.2d 547 (5th Cir. 1978)
   b. *United States v. Darusmont*, 449 U.S. 292 (1981)
   c. *Ianniello v. Commissioner*, 98 T.C. 165 (1992)
   d. *United States v. Vallone*, 698 F.3d 416 (7th Cir. 2012)
   e. *Fonticiella v. Commissioner*, T.C. Memo. 2019–74

3. Cite to the 2007 Second Circuit opinion involving challenges based on the Ninth Amendment and the Free Exercise Clause of the First Amendment.

4. Cite to and indicate the constitutional challenge addressed in the 1991 Second Circuit opinion involving challenges by a company to the Tax Court's assigning of a case with complex issues to a special trial judge.

---

[5] The most useful materials are annotated Constitutions, such as those included in United States Code Annotated and United States Code Service, and digests.

5. Indicate what conclusion about the Takings Clause the authors reached in this Congressional Research Service 2012 report: *Constitutionality of Retroactive Tax Legislation*.

6. Indicate any constitutional challenge the authors discussed in this Congressional Research Service 1993 report: *Constitutionality of Limiting the Deductibility of Tobacco Advertising*.

Chapter 5

STATUTES

A. Introduction

This chapter discusses statutes authorized by the United States Constitution and enacted by Congress. It covers terminology used to describe statutes, lists sources in which you can locate current, repealed, and pending statutes, and introduces rules of interpretation. The primary focus of this chapter is the Internal Revenue Code.

In interpreting statutes, judges and administrative agencies may look to legislative history, a topic covered in Chapter 6. If a taxpayer has ties to another country, treaties may also be relevant. Treaties and their relationship to statutes are discussed in Chapter 7.

Your goals for Chapters 5 and 6 include finding relevant documents, determining their relative importance, and updating your research to encompass pending items. In accomplishing these goals, you should become familiar with the process by which statutes are enacted and the terminology used to describe statutory and legislative history documents.

B. Functions of Statutes

The Constitution gives Congress the power to "lay and collect" taxes. As noted in Chapter 4, the Constitution provides limitations on congressional power, but it does not provide rules for measuring income or value, allowing deductions or credits, or determining rates. Congress accomplishes those tasks by enacting statutes covering taxation.

Statutes define the tax base and penalties for noncompliance, provide effective dates, authorize administrative agencies to interpret the laws, and direct those same agencies to make reports to Congress. Your research may require you to locate statutes serving these purposes.

C. Terminology

This chapter's discussion of statutes uses terms related both to the statutes themselves and to the process by which they are enacted. The latter topic is discussed in more detail in Chapter 6.

1. Internal Revenue Code and United States Code

The **United States Code** is a subject-based codification of federal statutes. It is currently divided into more than 50 titles, and each title is further subdivided into smaller units. A tax research project may involve several U.S.C. titles, but your primary focus is usually title 26, **Internal Revenue Code**. Most titles of U.S.C. are referred to by title number rather than by name. For example, you would generally say title 29 rather than the Labor title. Title 26, on the other hand, is generally referred to as the Internal Revenue Code.[1] Because other titles of U.S.C. include tax-related material,

1 Title 26 is currently the only U.S.C. title that has the word Code in its name.

make sure you know whether you are looking for an answer in the I.R.C. or in another title of U.S.C.

The Internal Revenue Code contains most of the statutes covering income, estate and gift, excise, and employment taxes. The 1986 Code replaced the 1954 Code, which had replaced the 1939 Code. Throughout this book, references to either the Code or the I.R.C. refer to the 1986 statutory materials. Any references to the two previous Codes (1939 and 1954) include the relevant Code year.[2]

Although the current Code was enacted in 1986, it has been amended many times. You will frequently see references to the Internal Revenue Code of 1986, as amended. That usage is appropriate. A reference to the Internal Revenue Code of 2021 would be incorrect.

2. Bills and Acts

No provision can be added to the Internal Revenue Code (or to any other part of U.S.C.) until it is enacted.[3] The starting point is the introduction of a **bill** in Congress. A bill contains the initial draft of proposed legislation. That language may be changed at various points before the bill is finally enacted.

Each bill is assigned a bill number. Each chamber numbers its bills separately. Bills are usually numbered in the order in which they are introduced. A House bill is referred to as H.R. (e.g., H.R. 3838); a Senate bill is identified as S. Senators introduce bills involving taxation despite the constitutional requirement that bills for raising revenue originate in the House.[4]

Even though a bill may die because it failed to pass both the House and Senate, don't be surprised to hear it referred to as an act.[5] The term "act" is not reserved for actual statutes, and the bill's original name often includes the word "Act."

3. Public Laws, Slip Laws, and Statutes at Large

Each enacted bill that affects society as a whole is called a **Public Law** and receives a Public Law number (Pub. L. No.).[6] These numbers are chronological by Congress. They bear no relation to the original bill number and provide no information about the session of that Congress. Congress began using Public Law numbers in 1957; bills enacted before then have chapter numbers instead of Public Law numbers.

---

[2] Before 1939, tax statutes were reenacted in their entirety, or with necessary changes, on a regular basis. Because many current provisions can be traced back to the 1939 Code or even earlier—I.R.C. § 263, for example, contains language taken almost verbatim from § 117 of the 1864 Act—cross-references to these earlier materials are extremely useful. See Act of June 30, 1864, ch. 173, 13 Stat. 223, 281–82. Chapter 6 covers materials used to trace statutory language.

[3] Amendments to, or repeal of, statutory provisions, go through the same process.

[4] If the House objects, it "blue-slips" the bill and returns it to the Senate.

[5] Unless a bill is enacted by the time a particular Congress ends, it dies. Its supporters must reintroduce it in a subsequent Congress and start the legislative process over. This rule does not apply to treaties (Chapter 7), which remain alive for action by a subsequent Congress.

[6] This book does not discuss Private Laws, which affect an individual, family, or small group. The govinfo.gov site provides more information about Public Laws and Private Laws.

Table 5-A. Examples of Public Law Numbering System

Public Law	*Number*	*Location in Statutes at Large*
Revenue Act of 1943	ch. 63	58 Stat. 21
Revenue Act of 1962	Pub. L. No. 87–834	76 Stat. 960

Public Laws are first published in pamphlet form as **slip laws**. Slip laws published since 1995 (104th Congress) are available in PDF on the govinfo.gov website (Public and Private Laws collections). They are later printed in **Statutes at Large** in Public Law number order [Illustration 5-1]. Even though it is a separate pamphlet, each slip law includes the volume and page numbers it will have in Statutes at Large.

Illustration 5-1. First Page of Pub. L. No. 116–127

134 STAT. 178 PUBLIC LAW 116–127—MAR. 18, 2020

Public Law 116–127
116th Congress

An Act

Mar. 18, 2020
[H.R. 6201]

Making emergency supplemental appropriations for the fiscal year ending September 30, 2020, and for other purposes.

Be it enacted by the Senate and House of Representatives of the United States of America in Congress assembled,

Families First Coronavirus Response Act. 29 USC 2601 note.

SECTION 1. SHORT TITLE.

This Act may be cited as the "Families First Coronavirus Response Act".

→ In addition to the Public Law number, the first page includes the enactment date (March 18, 2020) and original bill number (H.R. 6201).

→ The first page also includes the official title (Making emergency supplemental appropriations for the fiscal year ending September 30, 2020, and for other purposes) and the overall short title (Families First Coronavirus Response Act).

→ If an act has additional short titles, those will appear in the relevant parts of the act. This particular act has several additional short titles.

Statutes at Large prints Public Laws in chronological order by session of Congress. United States Code rearranges statutes, as amended by Public Laws. As noted in Section C.1, U.S.C. is arranged by subject matter.

Public Laws can affect multiple I.R.C. sections. A Public Law can also affect multiple titles of U.S.C. Although Congress regularly enacts laws focused on tax, it also includes I.R.C. provisions in Public Laws enacted for other purposes. Language that appears together in Statutes at Large, because it is part of a single act section, may be dispersed into several titles of U.S.C.

If statutory language will be added to U.S.C., the Public Law generally refers to the relevant U.S.C. title. In addition to language that will be added to U.S.C., the Public Law includes enactment dates, effective dates, instructions to administrative agencies, and substantive provisions that will not be codified in U.S.C.

Illustration 5-2. First Page of Pub. L. No. 114–239

Public Law 114–239
114th Congress

An Act

To amend the Internal Revenue Code of 1986 to exclude from gross income any prizes or awards won in competition in the Olympic Games or the Paralympic Games.

Oct. 7, 2016
[H.R. 5946]

Be it enacted by the Senate and House of Representatives of the United States of America in Congress assembled,

SECTION 1. SHORT TITLE.

This Act may be cited as the "United States Appreciation for Olympians and Paralympians Act of 2016". United States Appreciation for Olympians and Paralympians Act of 2016. 26 USC 1 note.

SEC. 2. OLYMPIC AND PARALYMPIC MEDALS AND USOC PRIZE MONEY EXCLUDED FROM GROSS INCOME.

(a) IN GENERAL.—Section 74 of the Internal Revenue Code of 1986 is amended by adding at the end the following new subsection: 26 USC 74.

"(d) EXCEPTION FOR OLYMPIC AND PARALYMPIC MEDALS AND PRIZES.—

"(1) IN GENERAL.—Gross income shall not include the value of any medal awarded in, or any prize money received from the United States Olympic Committee on account of, competition in the Olympic Games or Paralympic Games.

"(2) LIMITATION BASED ON ADJUSTED GROSS INCOME.—

"(A) IN GENERAL.—Paragraph (1) shall not apply to any taxpayer for any taxable year if the adjusted gross income (determined without regard to this subsection) of such taxpayer for such taxable year exceeds $1,000,000 (half of such amount in the case of a married individual filing a separate return).

"(B) COORDINATION WITH OTHER LIMITATIONS.—For purposes of sections 86, 135, 137, 199, 219, 221, 222, and 469, adjusted gross income shall be determined after the application of paragraph (1) and before the application of subparagraph (A).". Determination.

(b) EFFECTIVE DATE.—The amendment made by this section shall apply to prizes and awards received after December 31, 2015. 26 USC 74 note.

→ The marginal notes indicate the Code sections being amended. The enrolled bill sent to the President does not include marginal notes. The Office of the Federal Register assigns an act number and adds the notes before the slip law is published.

→ The "note" language indicates provisions that are not codified but are related notes following a particular Code section.

There are three important differences between Statutes at Large and United States Code. The first, discussed above, is arrangement: Statutes at Large is chronological; U.S.C. is subject-based. The second relates to uncodified items. U.S.C. deletes Statutes at Large language that won't be added to any of its titles or includes this language only in notes.

The third difference relates to how each Code section appears. Statutes at Large prints only the language in the Public Law. If a Public Law amends an existing Code section, it includes only the amending language. As a result, Statutes at Large does not show how the pre- or post-amendment Code section reads. [See Illustration 5-3.] If you need to see current Code language, the I.R.C. is more useful than Statutes at Large.[7]

Illustration 5-3. Original, Amending, and Amended Language of I.R.C. § 24(a)

I.R.C. § 24(a) Before 2008 Amendment	*Pub. L. No. 110–351, § 501(c)(1), Amending I.R.C. § 24(a)*	*I.R.C. § 24(a)(1) After 2008 Amendment*
(a) Allowance of credit.—There shall be allowed as a credit against the tax imposed by this chapter for the taxable year with respect to each qualifying child of the taxpayer an amount equal to $1,000.	(c) Restrict Qualifying Child Tax Benefits to Child's Parent. (1) Child tax credit.—Section 24(a) of such Code is amended by inserting "for which the taxpayer is allowed a deduction under section 151" after "of the taxpayer".	(a) Allowance of credit.—There shall be allowed as a credit against the tax imposed by this chapter for the taxable year with respect to each qualifying child of the taxpayer for which the taxpayer is allowed a deduction under section 151 an amount equal to $1,000.

→ The Public Law section number (501(c)(1)) has nothing to do with the Code section number (24(a)). Because there is a Code section 501(c)(1), you will not find what you need if you search for Code section 501(c)(1).

4. Codified and Uncodified Provisions

Most act provisions are **codified** in the I.R.C. or in another title of U.S.C. Three types of provisions are not likely to be codified: effective and enactment dates (discussed below); directions to another branch of government (usually an administrative agency); and statutory provisions that Congress did not codify.

5. Enactment Date, Effective Date, and Expiration Date

These terms are critical aspects of tax research. Because pending legislation may add new Code sections or amend or repeal existing law, it can totally change the outcome of a planned transaction.

a. Enactment Date and Effective Date

Most acts have two relevant dates. The **enactment date** is the date the President signs the act (or allows it to become law without a signature) or Congress overrides a presidential veto. The **effective date**, on which the act's provisions apply to particular transactions, may coincide with, follow, or even precede the enactment date.[8]

---

[7] Congress has enacted about half of the U.S.C. titles into positive (statutory law), making their text legal evidence of the law. The I.R.C. and other titles that have not been enacted into positive law are only prima facie evidence of the law. If I.R.C. language varies from Statutes at Large language (including amendments), the latter document governs.

[8] If the effective date precedes the enactment date, aggrieved taxpayers may challenge the retroactivity. Constitutional challenges are discussed in Chapter 4.

Tax legislation often involves separate effective dates for individual sections of an act. It is risky to assume that the enactment date is the effective date or that the effective date of one section applies to every section of a new act. Remember that effective dates rarely become part of the Code, but they do appear in the act itself.[9] Sources that include statutory text are listed in Section G.

When working with effective dates, be careful to look for **transition rules**. In appropriate circumstances, Congress provides exemptions from a particular effective date. This is particularly likely to occur for transactions that occur after the new effective date but that were subject to a binding contract on a specified earlier date.[10] An example appears in Table 5-B.

Table 5-B. Timeline in Polone v. Commissioner

Action	*Date*
Employer fires Polone	April 21, 1996
Polone sues for defamation	April 24, 1996
Settlement of $4 million; Polone receives first $1 million installment	May 3, 1996
Bill (H.R. 3448) introduced in Congress	May 14,1996
I.R.C. § 104(a)(2) amended to include "physical" requirement	August 20, 1996 (effective date unless binding agreement, decree, or award in effect or issued before September 13, 1995)
Polone receives second installment	November 11, 1996
Polone receives third and fourth installments	May 5, 1997 & November 11, 1998

Illustration 5-2 (*supra* page 30) illustrates separate enactment and effective dates in Public Law Number 114–239. The act is effective for amounts received after December 31, 2015, which is earlier than the enactment date of October 7, 2016. Illustration 5-4 and Table 5-B show the importance of effective dates.

[9] Effective dates do appear in the Code for provisions that phase in over time or that apply in a different manner in different years. For example, the applicable percentage for bonus depreciation allowed under § 168(k) is 100 percent for property placed in service after September 27, 2017, and before 2023; 80 percent for property placed in service in 2023; 60 percent for property placed in service in 2024; 40 percent for property placed in service in 2025; and 20 percent for property placed in service in 2026. I.R.C. § 168(k)(6), as amended by Pub. L. No. 115–97, § 13201(a)(2) (2017).

[10] Some acts include transition rules that benefit specific taxpayers. See, e.g., Pub. L. No. 99–514, § 204, 100 Stat. 2085, 2146 (1986).

Illustration 5-4. Excerpt from Polone v. Commissioner[11]

> 1998 payments were taxable. The amended statute applies to any damages *received* after its effective date of August 20, 1996, unless the parties had contracted prior to September 13, 1995. P.L. 104–188, Title I, Subtitle F, Part 1, § 1605(d). Although Polone settled his claims with UTA in May 1996, he did not actually *receive* the three payments in question until well after the effective date of the amendments to § 104. Because the settlement was not in effect before September 13, 1995, it was not subject to the exception to amended § 104 for preexisting settlement agreements.

The statute's language is critical for determining an effective date. Table 5-C indicates effective date formats with quite different meanings.

Table 5-C. Effective Date Formats

Effective for transactions occurring in taxable years beginning after December 31, 2021
Effective for transactions occurring after December 31, 2021
Effective for transactions occurring in taxable years ending after December 31, 2021

→ If a taxpayer uses the calendar year to compute his or her taxes, the three effective dates above might yield the same results. If a taxpayer instead has a fiscal year that ends January 31, a transaction that occurs January 15, 2022, is covered by the second and third effective dates but not by the first.

A statute might refer to a taxable year, or it might refer to a calendar year. If the effective date is based on a calendar year, a taxpayer who normally reports on a fiscal year uses a calendar year effective date for activities covered by that provision.

b. Expiration Date

As a general rule, Code provisions remain in effect until amended, repealed, or declared unconstitutional. Congress may provide a specific **expiration date** for an individual Code provision. Unlike effective dates, expiration dates usually appear in the Code.[12] [See Illustration 5-5.]

Illustration 5-5. Expiration Date for I.R.C. § 4376

> **(e) Termination**. This section shall not apply to plan years ending after September 30, 2029.

Although expiration dates are generally calendar dates, specific events may also cause a provision to expire. [See Illustration 5-6.]

---

[11] 505 F.3d 966, 970 (9th Cir. 2007), cert. denied, 552 U.S. 1280 (2008) (footnotes omitted).

[12] Code sections generally refer to these provisions as termination dates. The Joint Committee on Taxation refers to them as expiring provisions.

Illustration 5-6. Expiration Date in I.R.C. § 4121(e)(2)

> (2) Temporary increase termination date. For purposes of paragraph (1), the temporary increase termination date is the earlier of—
>
> (A) December 31, 2020, or
>
> (B) the first December 31 after 2007 as of which there is—
>
> (i) no balance of repayable advances made to the Black Lung Disability Trust Fund, and
>
> (ii) no unpaid interest on such advances.

Unless extended by Congress in subsequent legislation, the Code section dies (expires). The term **extenders** is commonly used for tax bill provisions postponing expiration dates.

Another term sometimes used for expiration date is **sunset date**. While at times used interchangeably with expiration date, a "sunsetting" provision is one that does not apply at the end of a certain time period, but this fact is not within the Code itself.[13]

6. Act Names

a. Official Titles, Short Titles, and Popular Names[14]

A bill receives an official title when it is introduced into Congress. That title appears at the top of the bill. [See Illustration 5-1, *supra* page 29.] Although that is the official title, we are more likely to refer to the bill (and the act, if it becomes law) by its short title or by its popular name.

Congress often "names" legislation by including one or more **short titles** in the act's text. A short title appears in an act section, usually the first one, and reads: "This Act may be cited as . . . ." [Illustration 5-1, *supra* page 29.] Congress may also provide separate short titles for some (or all) of an act's major subdivisions. In that case, the beginning of the subdivision would read: "This [division, title, subtitle] may be cited as . . . ."

Short titles can be confusing. If an act has multiple short titles, you may not realize that you've been given the name of a subdivision.

Acts are often referred to by a so-called **popular title or popular name**. The name may be an acronym (e.g., the Economic Recovery Tax Act of 1981 is generally referred to

---

[13] An example of a sunsetting provision is section 2210, nullifying the estate and generation-skipping transfer taxes. Enacted in 2001 as part of the Economic Growth and Tax Relief Reconciliation Act of 2001 (EGTRRA), that section had a stated effective date applicable to estates of decedents dying after December 31, 2009. However, under Pub. L. No. 107–16, § 901 (entitled "Sunset of Provisions of Act"), none of the provisions enacted in 2001 would apply to taxable years beginning after December 31, 2010 or to estates of decedents dying after December 31, 2010. This provision, which did not appear in the Code, is often referred to as the EGTRRA sunset provision. It effectively eliminated the estate tax for exactly one year, 2010. Later legislation reinstated the tax, albeit with higher exemptions than existed prior to the enactment of EGTRRA. The temporary nature of the increased estate and generation-skipping transfer tax exemptions enacted in 2017, on the other hand, is included in the Code. I.R.C. § 2010(c)(3)(C), as added by Pub. L. No. 115–97, § 11061(a).

[14] Some examples of short titles appear in Table 5-I, *infra* page 56.

as ERTA). It may be a descriptive phrase (e.g., Cash for Clunkers[15]). It may be something as simple as Revenue Act of 1924. Keep in mind that many short titles are similar; in the case of Revenue Acts, the year may be the only differentiating part of their names.

A popular title is not necessarily part of the bill text, but one can be assigned by a chamber of Congress or by the Congressional Research Service to improve access. Practitioners aren't bound by the official title, short title, or popular title. For example, the Glossary listing for "popular title" in Congress.gov indicates that the Patient Protection and Affordable Care Act is commonly known as the health care reform bill. The USCA Popular Name Table and the Office of Law Revision Counsel Tool refer to the act as the Affordable Care Act, as the Patient Protection and Affordable Care Act, and as Obamacare. The USCS Popular Names Table refers to it as the Patient Protection and Affordable Care Act and as Obamacare.

Although short titles, popular titles, and popular names may differ, if an act has only one short title, the popular title and popular name will often be the same as the short title. This book generally uses the terms interchangeably.

b. Revenue Acts and Other Act Names

Acts with "Revenue" or "Tax" in their short titles clearly announce their relevance to taxation. Other acts that are likely to include substantive tax law include those with "Deficit Reduction," "Income," "Trade," "Reconciliation," or "Investment" in their short titles.

An act's short title may contain no hint that it includes tax provisions; the act may not even have a name. For example, the Ricky Ray Hemophilia Relief Fund Act of 1998 treated certain payments as damages for purposes of Code section 104(a)(2).[16] Public Law Number 107–22, which changed the name of Education IRAs to Coverdell Education Savings Accounts, has no short title or popular name.[17]

D. Internal Revenue Code

This section covers how the Code is organized. It introduces topics that are covered in greater detail in Section E.

1. Code Subdivisions

Because the Internal Revenue Code is a title of U.S.C., its first subdivisions are subtitles. The Code currently has 11 subtitles.

---

[15] The "Cash for Clunkers" program was enacted by the Consumer Assistance to Recycle and Save Act of 2009 (C.A.R.S. Act), which was title XIII of the Supplemental Appropriations Act of 2009, Pub. L. No. 111–32 (2009). It provided a voucher to individual taxpayers for trading-in a vehicle for a more fuel-efficient model. The program began in July 2009 and ended on August 24, 2009, when all the allocated funds were distributed. The voucher value was excluded from the taxpayer's gross income. Pub. L. No. 111–32, § 1302(h)(2).

[16] Pub. L. No. 105–369, § 103(h), 112 Stat. 3368, 3371 (1998).

[17] 115 Stat. 196 (2001). Pub. L. No. 107–22 began as a Senate bill. S. 1190, 107th Cong., 1st. Sess. (2001). It had no revenue implications and thus did not violate the origination clause. U.S. CONST. art. I, § 7, cl. 1. Because Paul Coverdell had been a Senator, it is not surprising that the bill originated in the Senate.

Table 5-D. Internal Revenue Code Subtitles

Subtitle	*Subject*
A	Income Taxes
B	Estate and Gift Taxes
C	Employment Taxes
D	Miscellaneous Excise Taxes
E	Alcohol, Tobacco, and Certain Other Excise Taxes
F	Procedure and Administration
G	The Joint Committee on Taxation
H	Financing of Presidential Election Campaigns
I	Trust Fund Code
J	Coal Industry Health Benefits
K	Group Health Plan Requirements

Each subtitle is subdivided into smaller units. Many Code sections also include references to sentences within a larger subdivision.

The section is the basic unit used in finding the law. The Code contains only one section 1, not one for each part, chapter, or other unit. Although sections are numbered sequentially, breaks in the sequence provide room for Congress to insert new sections as needed.

2. Code Subdivision Numbering System

As Table 5-E illustrates, titles, chapters, parts, and sections are identified by number. Subtitles, subchapters, and subparts are identified by letter. Most subsections are identified by letter (e.g., 163(d)), but a few are designated by number (e.g., 212(1)). Successive subdivisions bear letters or numbers, as appropriate. The Code uses both upper and lower case letters and both Roman and Arabic numerals.

Table 5-E. Code Subdivisions: I.R.C. § 45F(c)(1)(A)(i)(I)

Subdivision	*Heading or Text*
Title 26	Internal Revenue
Subtitle A	Income Taxes
Chapter 1	Normal Taxes and Surtaxes
Subchapter A	Determination of Tax Liability
Part IV	Credits Against Tax
Subpart D	Business Related Credits
Section 45F	Employer-provided child care credit
Subsection (c)	Definitions. For purposes of this section—

Subdivision	*Heading or Text*
Paragraph (1)	Qualified child care expenditure
Subparagraph (A)	In general. The term "qualified child care expenditure" means any amount paid or incurred—
Clause (i)	to acquire, construct, rehabilitate, or expand property—
Subclause (I)	which is to be used as part of a qualified child care facility of the taxpayer,

→ Subdivisions may include headings, text, or both headings and text.

Code section 45F is not unique. Many Code sections have so many subdivisions that it is easy to lose track of where you are. Checkpoint includes a tool that lets you know exactly what Code section subdivision you are reading. Bloomberg Law is similar; hovering your pointer over any subdivision gives the entire citation. Cheetah labels each subdivision.

Illustration 5-7. Checkpoint Compass Feature

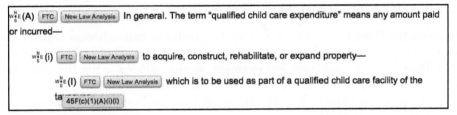

(A) FTC New Law Analysis In general. The term "qualified child care expenditure" means any amount paid or incurred—

(i) FTC New Law Analysis to acquire, construct, rehabilitate, or expand property—

(I) FTC New Law Analysis which is to be used as part of a qualified child care facility of the ta 45F(c)(1)(A)(i)(I)

→ Let your mouse hover over a compass sign to get the full citation.

Illustration 5-8. Bloomberg Law: Tax

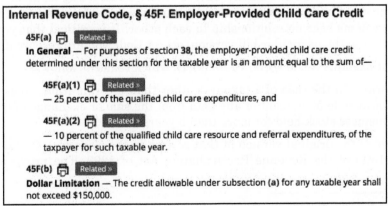

Internal Revenue Code, § 45F. Employer-Provided Child Care Credit

45F(a) Related »

In General — For purposes of section **38**, the employer-provided child care credit determined under this section for the taxable year is an amount equal to the sum of—

45F(a)(1) Related »

— 25 percent of the qualified child care expenditures, and

45F(a)(2) Related »

— 10 percent of the qualified child care resource and referral expenditures, of the taxpayer for such taxable year.

45F(b) Related »

Dollar Limitation — The credit allowable under subsection **(a)** for any taxable year shall not exceed $150,000.

→ Bloomberg Law: Tax shows the full Code section and relevant subdivisions.[18]

---

[18] Both Bloomberg Law and Tax Notes make free versions of the Code available online. Both include full citation information for each Code subdivision. Tax Notes does so with a scrolling "You are here" feature.

Illustration 5-9. Cheetah Code Labels

45F(c)(1)(A) In general.—The term "qualified child care expenditure" means any amount paid or incurred—
45F(c)(1)(A)(i) to acquire, construct, rehabilitate, or expand property—
45F(c)(1)(A)(i)(I) which is to be used as part of a qualified child care facility of the taxpayer,

→ Cheetah shows the full Code section and relevant subdivisions.

3. Unique and Repeated Code Subdivisions

Title, subtitle, chapter, and section numbers and letters are used only once. Other subdivision categories are used multiple times. For example, there is more than one Subchapter A, but there is only one Chapter 1 (which appears in Subtitle A). Subtitle B begins with Chapter 11.

Although subchapter, part, and subpart classifications are used multiple times, subchapters are the most likely to cause a problem if you aren't careful. Practitioners frequently refer to four groups of sections in Subtitle A by their subchapter designation—Subchapter C, Subchapter J, Subchapter K, and Subchapter S.[19] If you receive an assignment to research a particular subchapter, be sure to ascertain the correct chapter before you begin.

4. Similar Section Numbers

In using the Code's numbering system, be careful to note whether a letter is part of the section number or the subsection number. Code sections that include capital letters are most likely to cause problems. For example, section 2056(a) is not the same as section 2056A. Also, be careful when working with sections that share a common number followed by different capital letters. These include sections 45A[20] through 45T and sections 280A through 280H.

5. I.R.C. and Other Section Numbers

The Code, the Public Laws amending it or otherwise affecting taxation, and the bills that may become Public Laws all divide their provisions into sections. These section numbering systems bear no relationship to each other. It is critical that you match the section number to the particular bill version, act, or Code you are researching.[21]

Take for example, Code section 1202(a)(1), which reads as follows:

> In general.—In the case of a taxpayer other than a corporation, gross income shall not include 50 percent of any gain from the sale or exchange of qualified small business stock held for more than 5 years.

Congress added the original version of that section to the Code in 1993, including it as section 13113(a) of the Revenue Reconciliation Act of 1993. The provision began as

---

[19] These subchapters cover, respectively, corporations, trusts and estates, partnerships, and "small business" corporations. Although Subtitle A has several Subpart Fs, international practitioners often say "Subpart F" to refer to the controlled foreign corporation sections in Chapter 1, Subchapter N, Part III, Subpart F.

[20] There is also a section 45, with subsections (a) through (e).

[21] As noted in Section G.1 (*infra* page 51), the 1939 Code section numbers bear no relationship to the 1954 and 1986 Code section numbers.

section 14113(a) of H.R. 2264, the Omnibus Budget Reconciliation Act of 1993, a subtitle of which was the Revenue Reconciliation Act of 1993.

E. Working with the Internal Revenue Code

As noted earlier in this chapter, taxes are imposed by statutes, and most statutes relevant to tax research are in the Internal Revenue Code. These facts lead us to three tasks: finding the relevant Code provisions; reading them; and interpreting them.

Your research may involve two additional tasks. The first is using a citator to determine if a court has ruled on the statute's validity; Section H introduces citators, which are discussed in more detail in Chapter 11. The second is checking for pending legislation that could change the result. This is particularly important if you are researching a proposed transaction.

1. Finding Code Sections

Your research project will probably involve more than one Code section. If the person who assigned the project did not indicate which Code sections were involved, you will have to locate the relevant sections. You might do so using secondary sources, which discuss the issues raised in your project. Alternatively, you might use a Code section index to locate relevant Code sections. Think about the Code's structure and look for cross-references as you look for relevant Code sections.

a. Working with the Code's Structure

The Code has a structure that you should keep in mind in conducting your research. First, the subtitles [Table 5-D, *supra* page 36] give a starting point for research. For example, income tax provisions begin in Subtitle A; estate tax provisions begin in Subtitle B. Subtitle F includes various procedural rules.

Second, chapters and subchapters [Table 5-F] within each subtitle guide you to sections that may be relevant. This is particularly true for the income tax. In addition to issues related to credits, exclusions, deductions, timing, and character, your project may involve allocating income and deductions between individuals and entities or between United States and foreign sources. For example, if your client sold his home for a $1 million gain, and was receiving installment payments of the price, you would eventually read several sections located in Subtitle A, Chapter 1: section 1 (Subchapter A, Determination of Tax Liability); section 121 (Subchapter B, Computation of Taxable Income); and section 453 (Subchapter E, Accounting Periods and Methods of Accounting). You would have computed his gain using the rules in sections 1001 through 1016 (Subchapter O, Gain or Loss on Disposition of Property). You would also have consulted several sections in Subchapter P to determine if his gain was long-term capital gain.

Table 5-F. Subchapters in Subtitle A, Chapter 1

Subch.	*Heading*	*I.R.C. §§*
A	Determination of Tax Liability	1–59A
B	Computation of Taxable Income	61–291
C	Corporate Distributions and Adjustments	301–385

Subch.	*Heading*	*I.R.C. §§*
D	Deferred Compensation	401–436
E	Accounting Periods and Methods of Accounting	441–483
F	Exempt Organizations	501–530
G	Corporations Used to Avoid Income Tax on Shareholders	531–565
H	Banking Institutions	581–597
I	Natural Resources	611–638
J	Estates, Trusts, Beneficiaries, and Decedents	641–692
K	Partners and Partnerships	701–761
L	Insurance Companies	801–848
M	Regulated Investment Companies and Real Estate Investment Trusts	851–860G
N	Tax Based on Income From Sources Within or Without the United States	861–999
O	Gain or Loss on Disposition of Property	1001–1092
P	Capital Gains and Losses	1202–1298
Q	Readjustment of Tax Between Years and Special Limitations	1301–1351
R	Election to Determine Corporate Tax on Certain International Shipping Activities Using Per Ton Rate	1352–1359
S	Tax Treatment of S Corporations and Their Shareholders	1361–1379
T	Cooperatives and Their Patrons	1381–1388
U	Designation and Treatment of Empowerment Zones, Enterprise Communities, and Rural Development Investment Areas	1391–1397F
V	Title 11 Cases	1398–1399
Z	Opportunity Zones	1400Z-1–1400Z-2

Table 5-F illustrates some important facts. First, Code sections for several entity or business types have their own subchapters; these include corporations (Subchapters C and S), exempt organizations (Subchapter F), partnerships (Subchapter K), and insurance companies (Subchapter L). If your problem involves one of those taxpayers, start with the relevant subchapter. Second, an income tax project may include subchapters that are scattered throughout Subtitle A, Chapter 1. For example, gains and losses are relevant to the computation of taxable income, but the relevant Code sections are in Subchapters O and P rather than in Subchapter B.

Table 5-F suggests a third fact to remember. Although some subchapters involve only a few Code sections, others—such as Subchapter B—include many sections. If you want to use subdivision headings as a research guide, you should look to parts [Table 5-G] and subparts.

Table 5-G. Parts in Subtitle A, Chapter 1, Subchapter B

Part	*Heading*	*I.R.C. §§*
I	Definition of Gross Income, Adjusted Gross Income, Taxable Income, etc.	61–68
II	Items Specifically Included in Gross Income	72–91
III	Items Specifically Excluded from Gross Income	101–140
IV	Tax Exemption Requirements for State and Local Bonds	141–150
V	Deductions for Personal Exemptions	151–153
VI	Itemized Deductions for Individuals and Corporations	161–199A
VII	Additional Itemized Deductions for Individuals	211–224
VIII	Special Deductions for Corporations	241–250
IX	Items Not Deductible	261–280H
X	Terminal Railroad Corporations and Their Shareholders	281
XI	Special Rules Relating to Corporate Preference Items	291

→ Don't assume that the Code uses terms the same way that taxpayers do. The term "Itemized" (Parts VI and VII) above does not relate to where an item goes on the tax return.

Do not rely on the chapter or part headings for a list of included Code sections. Headings published by both the Office of the Law Revision Counsel of the U.S. House of Representatives and by the Government Publishing Office may include section numbers that have been repealed and omit section numbers that are included. The websites do not indicate why the headings do not reflect the actual language. The text in each website includes the current law.

b. Cross-References[22]

Subchapter B in Table 5-G includes several parts that list deductions, but it also includes Part IX, Items Not Deductible. The sections in Part IX modify those earlier sections. In other words, the Code provides for deductions in some Code sections but

[22] This chapter covers using statutory language, including cross-references within the Code. Chapter 6 covers using cross-reference tables to trace how a Code section has evolved over time.

might take them away in other sections. Ideally, there would be cross-references between sections in each group.

If two sections interact, each section may refer to the other. For example, section 267(e)(6) states: "For additional rules relating to partnerships, see section 707(b)." Section 707(b)(1) includes several references to section 267. This is the ideal situation because you find the relationship no matter which section you read first.

Alternatively, one section may refer to another section, but the second section may not mention the first. Section 104(a) refers to section 213, but section 213 does not mention section 104. Assume, for example, you are researching whether a particular outlay your client made qualified for the section 213 medical expense deduction. If you did not know about section 104, you might ask whether her outlays were covered by health insurance but not ask about damages from a prior lawsuit.[23]

In the worst-case scenario, neither section refers to the other. For example, section 280B contains no cross-references. It could be relevant to several sections, including 162, 165, 212, and 1016. None of those sections mentions section 280B.[24]

(1) Locating Cross-References

There are two methods you can use to determine if a particular Code section is mentioned by another section: cross-reference tools and electronic searches. Cross-reference tools, which are illustrated below, collect the information for you but are subject to editorial errors. Electronic searches for all Code sections that mention the section in which you are interested are less likely to include editorial errors. But, unless you search widely enough, you still may miss a relevant statute. For example, if you search only in the I.R.C., you may miss relevant provisions in other U.S.C. titles or in uncodified provisions.

As Illustrations 5-10 and 5-11 (*infra* page 43) indicate, different sources may yield different results. There is no substitute for reading the Code sections to be sure the cross-reference is valid and relevant to your project.

(2) Limitations of Relying on Cross-Reference Tools

As noted above, cross-reference tools are worthless if Code sections interact but don't explicitly refer to each other. Even if sections do refer to each other, an infrequently updated cross-reference tool may not reflect the most recent statutory changes. Using a term search in an online service presents much less risk that your source will not be current.

Cross-reference tools and online searches may induce a dangerous sense of security. After all, neither method can produce a cross-reference that doesn't exist. If you understand the Code's structure, you know which types of provisions affect others. In approaching a deductibility problem, for example, you would consider sections allowing the deduction as well as potential disallowance sections and timing provisions. You can locate these in the Code's table of contents, in a subject matter Code section index, or in a subject-oriented looseleaf service or treatise (Chapter 12). Less-experienced researchers should probably start with a looseleaf service or treatise.

---

[23] Careful reading of section 213(a) would avoid this result; the language covers expenses "not compensated for by insurance *or otherwise*." (emphasis added)

[24] Section 280B is mentioned in sections 179B and 198.

(3) Limitations on Using Cross-References as Interpretive Aids

While cross-references are useful in locating relevant statutory material, they lack independent interpretive significance. Code section 7806(a) provides that "[t]he cross references in this title to other portions of the title, or other provisions of law, where the word 'see' is used, are made only for convenience, and shall be given no legal effect." If you are using cross-references only to help you find relevant material, that limitation is not a problem.

Illustration 5-10. Cross-References for I.R.C. § 280B in U.S.C.A.

1. 26 USCA § 179B; § 179B. Deduction for capital costs incurred in complying with Environmental Protection Agency sulfur regulations

26 USCA § 179B

2. 26 USCA § 198; § 198. Expensing of environmental remediation costs

26 USCA § 198

3. CA REV & TAX § 24369.4; § 24369.4. Expensing environmental remediation costs; [ ]application of Internal Revenue Code provisions

CA REV & TAX § 24369.4

Illustration 5-11. Cross-References for I.R.C. § 280B in U.S.C.S.

Cross References:

Deductibility of trade or business expenses, generally, 26 USCS § 162.

Deductibility of losses, generally, 26 USCS § 165.

Expenses for production of income as deductible, generally, 26 USCS § 212.

This section is referred to in 26 USCS §§ 179B, 198.

→ Westlaw Edge includes U.S.C.A.; Lexis+ includes U.S.C.S.

2. Reading Code Sections

Illustrations 5-10 and 5-11 demonstrate that you can't rely on an editor's decision about cross-references. The same is true for explanations. If you rely on someone else's description of what the Code says, you risk missing an exception or election that applies to your client but was omitted in a general discussion.

Read each Code section carefully. First, determine what general rules it provides. Then look for exceptions, both within that section and in other sections that might apply. Finally, make sure that the applicable rules apply in the relevant time period. Focus on the effective date and the expiration date, if any. Remember that an effective date may include transition rules. These concepts are discussed in Section C.5 (*supra* page 31).

Subscription-based versions of the Code are generally more helpful than the official U.S.C. version. First, the print U.S.C. is revised only every six years, with annual supplements. Second, subscription-based services are more likely to alert you to incorrectly numbered sections, expiration or sunset dates that do not appear in the Code section, and pending legislation that might amend the section.

3. Interpreting Code Language

a. Definitions

As you read each Code section, you are likely to encounter terms that need to be defined. When searching for definitions, be cognizant of where they are likely to appear, but don't expect that every term will be defined.

The first place to look for a definition is in the Code section that uses the term. Unfortunately, the Code does not consistently use a "Definitions" label in each section. Definitions may appear in subsections (or smaller subdivisions) entitled Definitions, Special Rules, or [Term] Defined; often the heading for the definition is simply the term being defined. Examples appear in Table 5-H.

Table 5-H. Examples of Definition Placement

I.R.C. §	*Heading*
108(d)	Meaning of terms; special rules relating to certain provisions
108(i)(5)	Other definitions and rules
179(e)	Qualified real property
213(d)	Definitions
217(b)	Definition of moving expenses
453(b)	Installment sale defined

Another place to look is in a group of provisions that apply to more than one Code section. The sections in Subtitle F, Chapter 79, include numerous definition provisions, most of which apply to the entire Code. If you cannot locate a definition in an individual section, be sure to check the definitions in sections 7701–7705, especially section 7701.

Illustration 5-12. Excerpt from Definitions in I.R.C. § 7701(a)

> (24) Fiscal year. The term "fiscal year" means an accounting period of 12 months ending on the last day of any month other than December.
>
> (25) Paid or incurred, paid or accrued. The terms "paid or incurred" and "paid or accrued" shall be construed according to the method of accounting upon the basis of which the taxable income is computed under subtitle A.
>
> (26) Trade or business. The term "trade or business" includes the performance of the functions of a public office.

→ Section 7701(a)(24) defines "fiscal year," while section 7701(a)(26) simply indicates an item that is to be included in a definition.

Many terms are not defined in the Code. "Income" in section 61 is one example.[25] Other terms are defined in a section solely for purposes of that section. For example, section 1202(c) defines "qualified small business stock" for purposes of section 1202. Still other definitions apply only to a portion of a Code section. If you can't locate a Code definition that applies to your project, you should look in regulations, rulings, and judicial decisions. Researching in those sources is covered in Chapters 8 through 10.

If you find a definition, be careful to use it correctly. A Code section definition may apply to only a portion of that Code section, or it may contain a term that also needs defining. Many Code sections refer to definitions in other statutes [Illustration 5-13].

Illustration 5-13. Definitions in I.R.C. § 142(k)(2)–(4)

(2) Public-private partnership agreement described. A public-private partnership agreement is described in this paragraph if it is an agreement—

(A) under which the corporation agrees—

(i) to do 1 or more of the following: construct, rehabilitate, refurbish, or equip a school facility, and

(ii) at the end of the term of the agreement, to transfer the school facility to such agency for no additional consideration, and

(B) the term of which does not exceed the term of the issue to be used to provide the school facility.

(3) School facility. For purposes of this subsection, the term "school facility" means—

(A) any school building,

(B) any functionally related and subordinate facility and land with respect to such building, including any stadium or other facility primarily used for school events, and

(C) any property, to which section 168 applies (or would apply but for section 179), for use in a facility described in subparagraph (A) or (B).

(4) Public schools. For purposes of this subsection, the terms "elementary school" and "secondary school" have the meanings given such terms by section 14101 of the Elementary and Secondary Education Act of 1965 (20 U.S.C. 8801), as in effect on the date of the enactment of this subsection.

→ Note the references to I.R.C. §§ 168 and 179.

→ To determine the relevant language in the Elementary and Secondary Education Act of 1965, you must determine when I.R.C. § 142(k) was enacted because amendments to the Elementary and Secondary Education Act after that date would be ignored.

→ I.R.C. § 142(k) indicates where the Elementary and Secondary Education Act appears in U.S.C. If it omitted that information, you could use a popular name table to find that information.

[25] It is effectively defined under case law. *Commissioner v. Glenshaw Glass Co.*, 348 U.S. 426 (1955).

b. Scope Limitations

Definitions and scope limitations share a common trait: both indicate whether their rule applies to the entire Code (e.g., "this title") or to a smaller subdivision (e.g., "this subtitle" or "this paragraph"). Definitions define words or phrases. Scope limitations indicate when a particular rule applies. As is true for definitions, if you misread a scope limitation, you risk drawing erroneous conclusions.[26]

Illustration 5-14. Scope Limitation in I.R.C. § 1041(b)

> **(b) Transfer treated as gift; transferee has transferor's basis.** In the case of any transfer of property described in subsection (a)—
>
> (1) for purposes of this subtitle, the property shall be treated as acquired by the transferee by gift, and
>
> (2) the basis of the transferee in the property shall be the adjusted basis of the transferor.

→ The transfer is treated as a gift only for purposes of the income tax ("*this subtitle*"). It is not treated as a gift for purposes of other subtitles, including Subtitle B, which includes the gift tax.

c. Provisions Affecting Multiple Subtitles

When a Code section includes "for purposes of this title," it affects the entire Code. If it includes "for purposes of this subtitle," it affects only that subtitle (e.g., income tax or estate tax). Four sections affecting more than one subtitle appear in Subtitle F, Chapter 80, Subchapter C (Provisions Affecting More Than One Subtitle) (sections 7871–7874). Two of them, section 7872 (treatment of loans with below-market interest rates) and section 7874 (rules relating to expatriated entities and their foreign parents) have potentially broad application; the other two are relevant to tax professionals representing Indian tribal governments or taxpayers dealing with them.

Those four sections are not the only provisions that apply to multiple subtitles. Section 7520, for example, applies to multiple subtitles, and regulations interpreting it appear in several places in C.F.R.: Treas. Reg. § 1.7520–1 (income tax), Treas. Reg. § 20.7520–1 (estate tax), and Treas. Reg. § 25.7520–1 (gift tax).

d. Rules of Construction

When litigation involves what a statute means or whether it applies to a particular set of facts, someone must interpret it. The Code includes a negative rule of construction: "No inference, implication, or presumption of legislative construction shall be drawn or made by reason of the location or grouping of any particular section or provision or portion of this title, nor shall any table of contents, table of cross references, or similar outline, analysis, or descriptive matter relating to the contents of this title be given any legal effect." I.R.C. § 7806(b).

---

[26] One of us teaches students in the basic federal income tax class to focus on three things when reading a new Code provision: (1) to what does it apply (scope limitations); (2) when does it apply (the elements of the provision); and (3) what happens if the provision applies (outcome).

Because Congress has delegated the authority to issue interpretive rules to the Treasury Department (discussed in Chapter 8),[27] you should always look for regulations interpreting the relevant Code sections. In addition to administrative interpretations, or in their absence when none are available, courts may turn to legislative history documents (discussed in Chapter 6) as expressions of congressional intent. Legislative history materials take on particular significance if administrative rules are alleged to be unreasonable and the statute's "plain meaning" is in doubt.[28]

Judges cite various rules of statutory construction in the course of interpreting statutes. The decisions listed below state or repeat several of these rules. To appreciate their effect, you should read the opinions cited for each proposition. The weight given legislative history is discussed in Chapter 6; that given administrative interpretations is discussed in Chapters 8 and 9.

- "The fundamental principle of statutory construction, *expressio unius est exclusio alterius*, applies. There is a firm presumption that everything in the I.R.C. was intentionally included for a reason and everything not in the code was likewise excluded for a reason—the expression of one thing is the exclusion of another." *Speers v. United States*, 38 Fed. Cl. 197, 202 (1997).
- " 'Under the principle of *ejusdem generis*, when a general term follows a specific one, the general term should be understood as a reference to subjects akin to the one with specific enumeration.' In the usual instance, the doctrine of *ejusdem generis* applies where a 'catch-all' term precedes, or more often follows, an enumeration of specific terms in order to expand the list without identifying every situation covered by the statute." *Host Marriott Corp. v. United States*, 113 F. Supp. 2d 790, 793 (D. Md. 2000) (citations omitted).
- "[T]he presumption is against interpreting a statute in a way which renders it ineffective or futile." *Matut v. Commissioner*, 86 T.C. 686, 690 (1986).
- "[T]he courts have some leeway in interpreting a statute if the adoption of a literal or usual meaning of its words 'would lead to absurd results * * * or would thwart the obvious purpose of the statute.' Or, to put it another way, we should not adopt a construction which would reflect a conclusion that Congress had 'legislate[d] eccentrically.' " *Edna Louise Dunn Trust v. Commissioner*, 86 T.C. 745, 755 (1986) (citation omitted).
- "We should avoid an interpretation of a statute that renders any part of it superfluous and does not give effect to all of the words used by Congress." *Beisler v. Commissioner*, 814 F.2d 1304, 1307 (9th Cir. 1987).
- "[T]he whole of [the section's] various subparts should be harmonized if possible." *Water Quality Association Employees' Benefit Corp. v. United States*, 795 F.2d 1303, 1307 (7th Cir. 1986).

---

27 I.R.C. § 7805(a).

28 Supreme Court rulings on deference paid administrative interpretations are discussed in Chapters 8 and 9.

- "In terms of statutory construction, the *context* from which the meaning of a word is drawn must of necessity be the words of the statute itself." *Strogoff v. United States*, 10 Cl. Ct. 584, 588 (1986).
- "[H]eadings and titles are not meant to take the place of the detailed provisions of the text. Nor are they necessarily designed to be a reference guide or a synopsis. Where the text is complicated and prolific, headings and titles can do no more than indicate the provisions in a most general manner . . . . Factors of this type have led to the wise rule that the title of a statute and the heading of a section cannot limit the plain meaning of the text." *Stanley Works v. Commissioner*, 87 T.C. 389, 419 (1986) (citation omitted).
- "When a statute does not define a term, we generally interpret that term by employing the ordinary, contemporary, and common meaning of the words that Congress used." *United States v. Iverson*, 162 F.3d 1015, 1022 (9th Cir.1998).
- "As a matter of statutory construction, identical words used in different parts of the Internal Revenue Code are normally given the same meaning." *Disabled American Veterans v. Commissioner*, 94 T.C. 60, 71 (1990).
- "Stated another way, Congress must make a clear statement that a double benefit is intended before we will construe a provision to allow this result." *Transco Exploration Co. v. Commissioner*, 949 F.2d 837, 841 (5th Cir. 1992).

F. Working with Other Statutes

Several tax-related provisions appear outside the Internal Revenue Code. These include provisions codified in other titles of U.S.C. and provisions that are not codified. And, although it may ultimately be codified, pending legislation is at best a pre-statute.

1. Other United States Code Titles

Although most substantive tax provisions are included in the Internal Revenue Code, other titles of United States Code may include provisions relevant to your research. For example, some functions of the Treasury Department (and its subsidiary agencies) are codified in title 31 (Money and Finance) rather than in title 26. Section 330 of Title 31 authorizes the Treasury Department to regulate the practice of representatives before it. That provision is the basis for Circular 230, Regulations Governing Practice before the Internal Revenue Service.[29] Title 31 also includes provisions relating to the Office of Management and Budget and the Government Accountability Office; both entities are discussed in Chapter 6.

A provision may appear in another title of U.S.C. because an agency other than the Treasury Department or IRS has primary responsibility for the area of law involved. For example, many rules affecting retirement benefits appear in 29 U.S.C., the title that covers Labor; section 558 of Title 37 provides tax deferments for military personnel who are missing in action. In addition, as demonstrated in Illustration 5-13 (*supra* page 45),

[29] 31 C.F.R. §§ 10.0–10.93.

a Code section may refer to a nontax statute that appears in another title of U.S.C. or is uncodified.

You can locate provisions in other titles using a subject matter index to U.S.C. The Related Statutes materials in the Standard Federal Tax Reporter Code include many of these statutes. You can also perform an electronic search through U.S.C. to locate relevant material in other titles. Finally, you can use popular name tables if the Code includes the name of an act but doesn't give a cross-reference to U.S.C. Online versions generally provide links to either Statutes at Large or to the official or a subscription version of U.S.C.

2. Uncodified Provisions

As noted in Section C, many tax-related provisions are never added to U.S.C. Most uncodified provisions involve effective dates for particular Code sections. Others may direct an agency (usually the Treasury Department or IRS) to make a study or submit some other type of information. [See Illustration 5-15.] Congress may even use an uncodified provision to place a moratorium on regulations. A third group involves substantive law provisions. [See Illustration 5-16, *infra* page 50.]

Because we expect statutes to have effective dates, it is second nature to look for them in the act itself or in a Code publication that includes effective date notes. The other types of information are less common, however, and may well escape notice by someone who has not followed the progress of the particular legislation.

Uncodified substantive provisions are traps for the unwary. A very troublesome example involves so-called section 530 relief. Code section 530 governs Coverdell Education Savings Accounts. Section 530 relief has nothing to do with tax benefits for education. Instead, it is an act section involving guidance in the employee-independent contractor area.[30] It is not codified anywhere.

Illustration 5-15. Material Omitted from the Code

Strengthening EITC Compliance.--The Committee supports the Department and IRS' to increase compliance with and the accuracy of the Earned Income Tax Credit (EITC) program. The complexity of the EITC law makes it inherently difficult for families and individuals to avoid errors and inherently easy for criminals to make false claims. The Committee directs the Office of Tax Policy (OTP) and the IRS Office Research, Analysis and Statistics to conduct data-driven analysis to improve EITC compliance in collaboration with the tax preparation community. Successful analysis will identify solutions effective for both paid preparers and self-preparers, ensure ease of taxpayer understanding. The Committee directs OTP and IRS to submit a report to the Committees on Appropriations in the House and Senate not later than six months after enactment of this Act on meeting this goal.

→ This is an excerpt from H.R. Rep. No. 114–194, 114th Cong., 2d Sess. 21–22 (2015). Although the bill this report accompanied did not pass (but a larger bill did), the

[30] Revenue Act of 1978, Pub. L. No. 95–600, § 530, 92 Stat. 2763, 2885, extended indefinitely by the Tax Equity and Fiscal Responsibility Act of 1982, Pub. L. No. 97–248, § 269(c), 96 Stat. 324, 552, and amended by various subsequent acts. U.S.C. provides references to section 530 and its amendments in notes following Code section 3401.

Treasury issued the report requested by the Appropriations Committee. The 2016 report involves EITC compliance and is on the Tax Policy section of the Treasury website.

Illustration 5-16. Material Omitted from the Code

```
SEC. 2205. MODIFICATION OF LIMITATIONS ON CHARITABLE CONTRIBUTIONS
DURING 2020.
    (a) Temporary Suspension of Limitations on Certain Cash
Contributions.--
        (1) In general.--Except as otherwise provided in paragraph (2),
    qualified contributions shall be disregarded in applying
    subsections (b) and (d) of section 170 of the Internal Revenue Code
    of 1986.
```

→ This excerpt is from the Coronavirus Aid, Relief, and Economic Security Act (CARES Act), Pub. L. No. 116–136, § 2205 (2020). Although this provision affects tax consequences, it is not codified.

3. Pending Legislation

As illustrated earlier in this chapter, legislation occasionally has retroactive effect. Pending legislation is also relevant if you are doing research for a transaction that has not yet closed; the law could change before you finalize the transaction.

When you look for pending legislation, don't limit yourself to the first bill that you find. Several members of Congress may introduce bills covering the same Code section. Fortunately, because each Congress lasts only two years, searches for pending legislation generally involve current material and can be conducted electronically in Congress.gov or in a bill-tracking service. These searches are discussed in Section G.

4. Potential Legislation

Long before a bill is introduced, taxpayers may receive hints that legislation is likely. In presidential election years, for example, party platforms include potential legislative agendas. Presidential budget messages may also serve this function. Items of this nature appear in newsletters and in general interest newspapers. You can also find presidential documents at the President's website, www.whitehouse.gov. Political parties have their own sites.

Prior congressional action is another source of potential legislation. Treasury Department or IRS studies mandated in one act may lead to provisions enacted in a later year. The same is true for reports issued by the Government Accountability Office or other government entities.[31] In addition, bills that die in one Congress are often reintroduced in a later Congress. Legislators frequently issue press releases announcing they are working on bills.

Although Treasury regulations and IRS rulings usually follow (and interpret) statutes, there are occasional role reversals. Legislation may be enacted to codify positions taken in regulations.[32] Unpopular administrative positions or court decisions may also trigger legislative activity.[33]

---

[31] These and other government studies are discussed in Chapter 6.

[32] This occurred in 1996 for life insurance benefits paid before death during a terminal illness (I.R.C. § 101(g)) and in 1971 for asset depreciation range (ADR) depreciation (1954 I.R.C. § 167(m)).

[33] See, e.g., I.R.C. § 6501(e)(1)(B)(ii), a 2015 response to *United States v. Home Concrete & Supply, LLC*, 566 U.S. 478 (2012); I.R.C. § 108(d)(7)(A), a 2002 response to *Gitlitz v. Commissioner*, 531 U.S. 206 (2001). See

G. Finding Statutes

The methods you use to find statutes, and the service you read them in, depend on several interrelated factors. First, do you need Code section text or Public Law text? Second, are you looking for current law, repealed law, or pending law? Third, do you want to read one version of a Code or do you want to compare versions over time? Fourth, do you have a full citation to the material you want, only a short title or popular name, or neither? The paragraphs below discuss these interrelated concepts.

1. Using Citations

a. Code Section Citations

Once you have a citation, the source you use depends on whether you seek current law, post-1938 prior law, or pre-1939 law.

(1) Current Law

If you have a citation to the most recent Code, you can read the relevant section(s) in any commercial Code service. Unless the section was enacted before the most recent official version of the U.S.C., and not amended since then, the print U.S.C. is not the best choice. The official U.S.C. is completely revised every six years; it is supplemented annually in the interim.[34] Unofficial services are better choices. The four versions below are regularly updated during the year. Each is available in print and online.

- Standard Federal Tax Reporter Code (print and Cheetah)
- United States Code Annotated (print and Westlaw Edge)
- United States Code Service (print and Lexis+)
- United States Tax Reporter Code (semiannual print and Checkpoint)

You can use any of these for I.R.C. sections. Use U.S.C.A. and U.S.C.S. for provisions that are codified in other titles of U.S.C.

Bloomberg Law includes the Code in its Bloomberg Law: Tax area. Tax Notes provides it online in its Federal Research Library. Both publishers offer free online access to the Code outside their subscription databases.

(2) Prior Law: Since 1939

(a) In General

If you have a citation to the Code as it read in a previous year, use a source that covers the Code by year. Pay attention to dates when you use these sources. If you need to know how your section read on March 15, a Code that is current as of January 1 won't be accurate if the law changed on February 1. And, because it is possible that your section was revised again in November, a Code that is current as of January 1 of the following year could also cause problems. You need the version that includes the February change but not the November change.

---

also Pub. L. No. 111–5, § 1261, 123 Stat. 115, 342 (2009), prospectively repealing Notice 2008–83, 2008–42 I.R.B. 905.

[34] HeinOnline carries each version of U.S.C. since it began (1926). The government's govinfo.gov website begins with the 1994 edition of U.S.C.

Services that provide earlier versions of the Code include:

- Bloomberg Law (I.R.C. of 1939, 1954, 1986; yearly editions from 1986 to present)
- Checkpoint (annual since 1986; 1939 year-end version of 1939 Code; 1954 year-end version of 1954 Code)
- Cheetah (annual since December 1978; pre-1954 version of 1939 Code and pre-1986 version of 1954 Code)
- Federal Research Library (archived versions of the Code for 2001–2019)
- Internal Revenue Code of 1939 (Statutes at Large; doesn't reflect amendments)
- Internal Revenue Code of 1954 (Statutes at Large; doesn't reflect amendments)
- Lexis+ (archived versions of USCS Archive from end of each legislative session since 1992)
- Westlaw Edge USCA Historical Codes (annual USCA since 1990; original versions of 1939 and 1954 Codes)

If you don't have access to a source that provides statutory text on the date you want, you can recreate the prior text by starting with a Code version as close in time to your date as you can get. Then use the historical notes accompanying that Code to find amending language. You can use that language to recreate the Code as it read on the date you need.

Illustrations 5-17 and 5-18 illustrate reconstructing language using Checkpoint's Archives section. Checkpoint includes December 31 language beginning in 1986 and has a separate database for Code section history.

Illustration 5-17. Excerpt from I.R.C. § 104 as of December 31, 1990

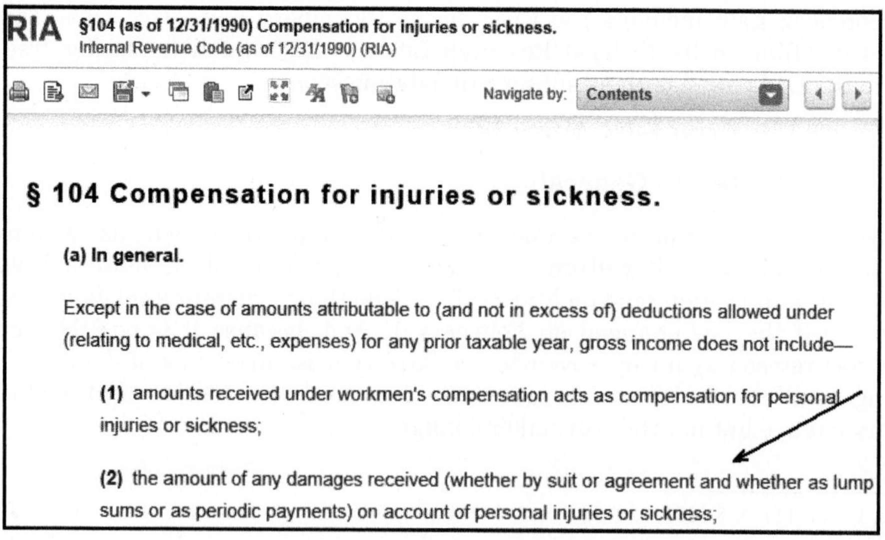
RIA §104 (as of 12/31/1990) Compensation for injuries or sickness.
Internal Revenue Code (as of 12/31/1990) (RIA)

Navigate by: Contents

§ 104 Compensation for injuries or sickness.

(a) In general.

Except in the case of amounts attributable to (and not in excess of) deductions allowed under (relating to medical, etc., expenses) for any prior taxable year, gross income does not include—

(1) amounts received under workmen's compensation acts as compensation for personal injuries or sickness;

(2) the amount of any damages received (whether by suit or agreement and whether as lump sums or as periodic payments) on account of personal injuries or sickness;

→ The current version of § 104(a)(2) differs from that shown above in two ways. It no longer allows punitive damages to be excluded, and it requires that the personal injury or sickness be physical.

Illustration 5-18. Excerpt from I.R.C. § 104 History as of December 31, 1990

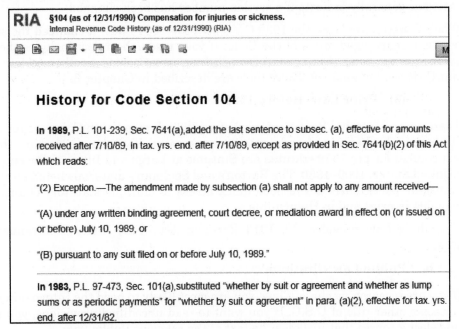

RIA **§104 (as of 12/31/1990) Compensation for injuries or sickness.**
Internal Revenue Code History (as of 12/31/1990) (RIA)

History for Code Section 104

In 1989, P.L. 101-239, Sec. 7641(a),added the last sentence to subsec. (a), effective for amounts received after 7/10/89, in tax. yrs. end. after 7/10/89, except as provided in Sec. 7641(b)(2) of this Act which reads:

"(2) Exception.—The amendment made by subsection (a) shall not apply to any amount received—

"(A) under any written binding agreement, court decree, or mediation award in effect on (or issued on or before) July 10, 1989, or

"(B) pursuant to any suit filed on or before July 10, 1989."

In 1983, P.L. 97-473, Sec. 101(a),substituted "whether by suit or agreement and whether as lump sums or as periodic payments" for "whether by suit or agreement" in para. (a)(2), effective for tax. yrs. end. after 12/31/82.

You can use the services below for tracing statutory language. All but Mertens are discussed in Chapter 6. Mertens is discussed in Chapter 12.

- Barton's Federal Tax Laws Correlated (1913–1952)[35]
- Internal Revenue Acts of the United States: 1909–1950; 1950–
- Legislative History of the Internal Revenue Code (1954–1965)
- Mertens, Law of Federal Income Taxation—Code (1954–1985)
- RIA Cumulative Changes (separate services for 1939, 1954, and 1986 Codes)
- Seidman's Legislative History of Federal Income and Excess Profits Tax Laws (1861–1953)[36]
- Tax Management Primary Sources (1969–2003)

Each of these services is available in print; all but Mertens, Cumulative Changes, and Primary Sources are also available in HeinOnline. Keep in mind that if a provision predates the 1954 Code, it has a different section number. You can locate the section numbers from earlier Codes by using the cross-reference tables discussed in Chapter 6.

---

[35] Barton's covers through 1969 but prints statutory text only through 1952.

[36] If Seidman's is unavailable, you can use Eldridge, The United States Internal Revenue Tax System. It provides annotated text for revenue acts prior to 1894 but does not give as much information as does Seidman's.

(b) Revised Code Section Numbers

Congress occasionally changed Code section numbers in the 1954 or 1986 Codes, but this was not a regular occurrence. And, when Congress replaced the 1954 Code with the 1986 Code, it generally retained the 1954 Code section numbers. Notes following Code sections generally indicate if a section number has been changed.

When Congress replaced the 1939 Code with the 1954 Code, it changed the section numbers and rearranged much of the Code. If your research project includes the 1939 Code, you can use tools that cross-reference from one Code to another to locate the relevant Code section number. These tools are described in Chapter 6.

(3) Prior Law: Before 1939

There was no Internal Revenue Code before 1939. Instead each Congress reenacted revenue laws with whatever amendments were necessary. If you have a citation, the best full-text sources for pre-1939 statutes are Statutes at Large and Internal Revenue Acts of the United States: 1909–1950. The Barton's and Seidman's materials listed above may also be useful, particularly if you need quick access to multiple statutory changes. All are available in print and in HeinOnline.

Bloomberg Law provides the 1913 Revenue Act in its Internal Revenue Code Archives.

b. Public Law Citations

If you are researching current law, you are most likely to need the Internal Revenue Code or some other title of U.S.C. If you want to read uncodified provisions, you might instead select a source that includes the text of the relevant Public Law.

When researching in an individual act, remember that the act section is not the same as the Code section. Act sections generally add, amend, or repeal Code sections. Illustration 5-18 (*supra* page 53) shows how section 101(a) of a Public Law enacted in 1983 amended Code section 104(a)(2).

If the act you are researching is particularly long, as is the case for appropriations acts, it is likely to repeat section numbers in multiple subdivisions. For example, the tax short title that appears in Table 5-I (*infra* page 56), is part of Division Q of the Consolidated Appropriations Act, 2016. Its first substantive provision is section 101; the first substantive provision in other divisions of that act is also section 101.

As was the case with the Code itself, your choice of service will be affected by how long ago the law was enacted. If you are using the print Statutes at Large (or the online version available in HeinOnline), you are not constrained by date. On the other hand, several of the services described below have limited retrospective coverage.

(1) Free Services

If you have the Public Law citation, you can find the act in the print version of Statutes at Large. Government websites include either Statutes at Large or individual Public Laws. The government's govinfo.gov website currently covers 1951 to 2013 for Statutes at Large; its Public and Private Laws collection begins in 1995. The Public and Private Laws collection includes Statutes at Large pagination but does not include its tables. It also includes legislative history information in its "Details" option. The site provides the statute in text and PDF formats.

The Congress.gov website also has a Public Law search function. Full-text coverage currently begins in 1989, with the 101st Congress; it provides information, but not text, for laws enacted between 1973 and 1988. Depending on the year and document, it provides text, PDF, and HTML/XML reading options. Congress.gov groups legislative history information for each bill, so you may prefer it to govinfo.gov.

Illustration 5-19. Advanced Search Option in govinfo.gov

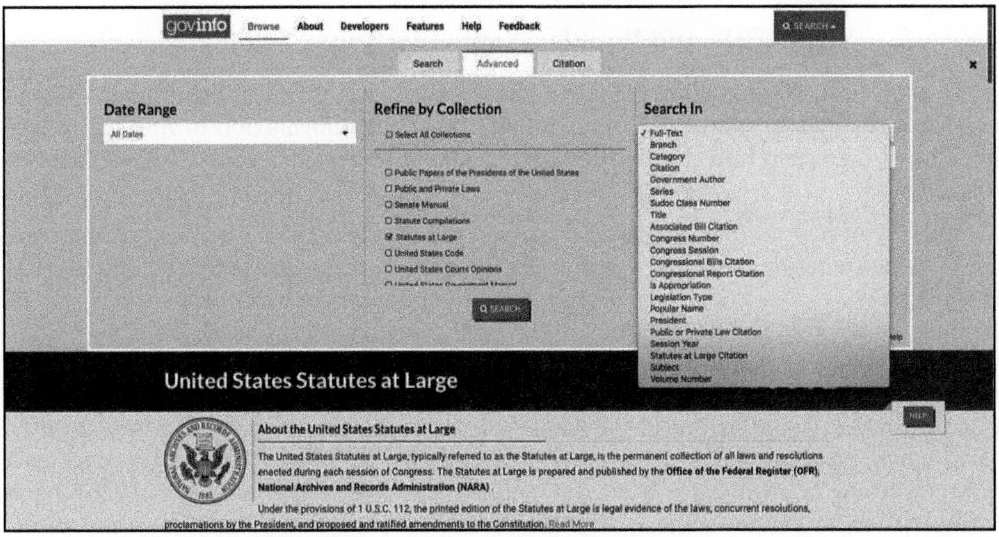

→ You can search the Statutes at Large collection by all of the categories listed above.

→ Each govinfo.gov collection has its own list of publications and metadata. For example, you can search the Statutes at Large collection by Popular Name. That option is not available in the Public and Private Laws collection, but a word search using the Title option will often yield the desired results.

(2) Subscription Services

You can also find Public Laws by citation on subscription services; however, there are large differences in coverage. HeinOnline has the most complete coverage, covering 1789–2012 in its U.S. Statutes at Large library.[37] Westlaw Edge's Statutes at Large database covers 1789–1972 and provides PDF versions of the Statutes at Large pages. Its U.S. Public Laws—Historical database lets you find legislation enacted beginning in 1973. ProQuest Congressional allows you to look at Public Laws in PDF format back to 1901.

The Cheetah citation feature lets you find a Public Law by its citation.[38] Cheetah divides older materials by year (2019–1978, 1953, and 1939) under Archives. The Lexis+

[37] Treaties with Indian tribes (1778–1842) and with foreign governments (1778–1845) appear in volumes 7 and 8. HeinOnline includes more recent statutes in its Public and Private Laws of the United States library.

[38] You can find this list in Cheetah under Tax-Federal>Laws & Regulations>Internal Revenue Code. Once you are in the I.R.C., look at the Table of Contents on the "Contents" side panel: "Public Laws Amending the Internal Revenue Code" is located under "Finding Lists" at the bottom of the list. You can search for any Public Law by using the Advanced Search function while in the Current Internal Revenue Code database.

USCS—Public Laws database begins in 1988. The Federal Research Library's Public Laws Amending the Internal Revenue Code database begins in 1979.

Checkpoint has the most limited coverage of Public Laws. It provides hyperlinks to enacted legislation in Public Law number order in its Pending and Enacted Legislation file. Coverage begins in 1995 with the 104th Congress. For older legislation, it links to the version printed in the Cumulative Bulletin, which may be limited to the act's tax provisions.

c. Short Title and Popular Name Citations

If you lack the Code section number and the Statutes at Large citation, but you have the act's short title or popular name, you can use that information to find the relevant Public Law. Once you find the Public Law, you can determine which Code sections have been affected.

When you search for popular names, keep four facts in mind. First, practitioners may refer to an act by its popular name. That name is not necessarily the official title or the short title that Congress assigned the act. The popular name may be descriptive (e.g., Obamacare or Tax Cuts and Jobs Act) or simply the act's initials. For example, practitioners often refer to the Tax Increase Prevention and Reconciliation Act of 2005 as TIPRA.[39] Second, Congress may assign one short title to an act and separate short titles to different subdivisions of the same act. An act might have only a main short title, only subdivision short titles, or no short titles at all. [See Table 5-I.] Third, some names are very similar to each other (e.g., Revenue Act of 1924, Revenue Act of 1926); be very careful with those names. Finally, Congress does not assign a short title to every act.

If the act's short title includes a year, it is usually easy to locate the act's text in Statutes at Large. Occasionally, the year in the act's name is the year before the year of enactment. That is the case for the Tax Increase Prevention and Reconciliation Act of 2005, which is mentioned in the preceding paragraph, and for the American Taxpayer Relief Act of 2012, which was enacted in 2013. The act's name might also be the year after the year of enactment. That is the case for the Consolidated Appropriations Act, 2016 [Table 5-I]. If the year is not part of the name, use Shepard's Acts and Cases by Popular Names to obtain a Statutes at Large citation. You can also obtain citations from popular names tables in the print or online versions of U.S.C.,[40] U.S.C.A., or U.S.C.S. These tables list short titles and popular names; they may also list acronyms by which an act is known.

Table 5-I. Short Title Information: Selected Legislation in the 114th Congress

Pub. L. No.	*Short Title: Act*	*Short Title: Tax Provisions*
114–14	Don't Tax Our Fallen Public Safety Heroes Act	No separate short title

[39] Pub. L. No. 109–222, 120 Stat. 345 (2006).

[40] The Office of the Law Revision Counsel U.S.C. Popular Name Tool has a scroll function and a searchable PDF listing. Both are available at https://uscode.house.gov/popularnames/popularnames.htm.

Pub. L. No.	*Short Title: Act*	*Short Title: Tax Provisions*
114–113	Consolidated Appropriations Act, 2016	Protecting Americans from Tax Hikes Act of 2015

You can also search in government websites using the act's short title. Congress.gov and govinfo.gov allow this type of search. Each gives you multiple versions of the act (e.g., bill as introduced, bill as passed in each chamber, bill sent to President, actual Public Law). Be sure to select the correct version.

Free services such as Statutes at Large are also available in online subscription services. You can also search subscription services by Public Law name and retrieve the full text of the act. Those services are covered in the discussion of finding statutes using Public Law citations in Section G.1.b (*supra* page 54).

d. Pending Legislation

(1) Citations

Pending legislation does not appear in either Statutes at Large or U.S.C. If you have a citation to the bill number, you can find the bill's text in Congress.gov or in the govinfo.gov Congressional Bills collection. Bloomberg Law, Lexis+, ProQuest, Westlaw Edge, and other commercial services have databases that provide the text of pending bills. Because the House and Senate both begin numbering at 1, include H.R. or S.[41] in your database search.

Illustration 5-20. Results of Bill Number Search in Congress.gov

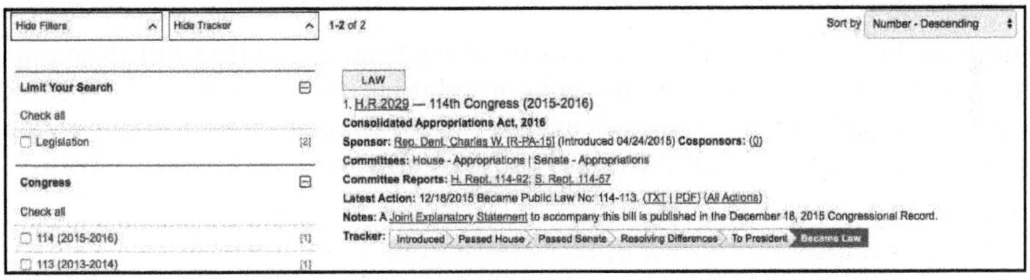

→ If you click on the bill number (H.R. 2029), you will learn what actions occurred, whether there was a committee report, whether there were related bills introduced, and whether the bill was amended after introduction.

→ There are hyperlinks for bill text, committee reports, and related bills.

[41] The database may accept HR or S in addition to (or instead of) H.R. or S.

Illustration 5-21. Actions Overview for H.R. 2029 in Congress.gov

Date	Actions Overview
04/24/2015	Introduced in House
04/24/2015	The House Committee on Appropriations reported an original measure, H. Rept. 114-92, by Mr. Dent.
04/30/2015	Passed/agreed to in House: On passage Passed by the Yeas and Nays: 255 - 163 (Roll no. 193).

→ The Congress.gov site provides a full list of actions taken on the bill. Above are the first three of eleven actions.

(2) Code Section Number

Many commercial services alert you that pending legislation may affect an existing Code section. Bloomberg Law, Lexis+, and Westlaw Edge use symbols to indicate pending legislation and provide links to the pending material.[42]

You can also search by Code section number in Congress.gov to see if a pending bill would modify an existing Code section. When conducting this type of search, you might want to include both the section number and a word or phrase that is likely to appear (or include the term Internal Revenue Code). Your search may initially provide only a list of bills rather than take you directly to the relevant language.

Searching by section number always involves risk: a pending bill may not amend an existing section directly. It may instead amend it indirectly with a second section that affects, but doesn't include a cross-reference to, the original section. Commercial services that track legislation may point out these indirect effects.

e. Unenacted Legislation

Because a bill that was not enacted during an earlier Congress may be introduced again, you may want to read the earlier bill. If you know the H.R. or S. number for the earlier bill, and the Congress in which it was introduced, you can find it in Congress.gov. Full-text coverage in Congress.gov currently begins in 1989. Govinfo.gov lets you search for legislation introduced since 1993 in its Congressional Bills collection. You can search by bill number or by words and phrases. The Federal Research Library includes the text of bills in its Proposed Legislation file; it begins with the 113th Congress.

2. No Citations

What if you need information about actual or proposed legislation, but you have no citations to the Code, Public Law, bill number, or other identifier? For example, you have been asked to find current Code sections covering employee achievement awards. Alternatively, you are preparing a survey article and need to know which Code sections were amended in a particular year. Or perhaps you need to find a statute indicating

[42] Checkpoint shows pending legislation; click on Bill Tracker above the statute.

whether "Cash for Clunkers" rebates were taxable. Finally, what if you need to know which Code sections are going to expire and when that will occur?

The particular assignment determines how you proceed. The first problem is relatively simple. You should be able to find sections 74 and 274 by using the Code's table of contents or index. You could also use a subject-based looseleaf service to find the relevant materials.

The second type of problem initially looks more time-consuming. You know that I.R.C. sections are amended by Public Laws that focus on taxation as well as by Public Laws that primarily deal with other areas of the law. Certainly, you don't want to read every Public Law enacted in a given year. Even searching Congress.gov or another site for the terms Internal Revenue Code or 26 U.S.C. will be a time-consuming effort. This research assignment is probably best accomplished using a table of Code sections affected during that year. The ideal format for such a table would be a list of changes in Code section order by year (or at least by Congress). Less useful, but still better than no listing, is a table of changes by Public Law. Illustrations 5-22 through 5-24 demonstrate Office of Law Revision Counsel[43] and Checkpoint tables. USCCAN tables provide information comparable to that provided by the Office of Law Revision Counsel.

If you cannot locate a table, you may have to find each act. The Joint Committee on Taxation Bluebook (discussed in Chapter 6) lists tax legislation passed in a particular Congress or a particular year.[44] However, it won't appear until after the relevant period ends.

Illustration 5-22. Office of Law Revision Counsel Listing: 115th Congress, 1st Sess.

26	1		115-97	11001(a)	2054
26	6695		115-97	11001(b)	2058
26	1	nt new	115-97	11001(c)	2059
26	1		115-97	11002(a)-(c)	2059
26	23		115-97	11002(d)(1)(A)	2060
26	25A		115-97	11002(d)(1)(B)	2060

→ The Office of Law Revision Counsel Classification Tables begin in 1995. Beginning in 1997, there is a separate table for each session of Congress.

→ The tables show the U.S.C. title, section number, Public Law number, and act section. They also include (not shown above) the Statutes at Large page.

→ The table above is in Public Law order. There are also U.S.C. section order tables.

---

43 http://uscode.house.gov/browse.xhtml.

44 The JCT staff issued separate Bluebooks for Pub. Law. No. 115–97 (JCS–1–18) and for other tax legislation enacted in the 115th Congress (JCS–2–19).

Illustration 5-23. Checkpoint Listing: 116th Congress

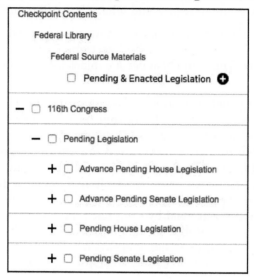

Checkpoint Contents

Federal Library

Federal Source Materials

☐ Pending & Enacted Legislation

– ☐ 116th Congress

– ☐ Pending Legislation

+ ☐ Advance Pending House Legislation

+ ☐ Advance Pending Senate Legislation

+ ☐ Pending House Legislation

+ ☐ Pending Senate Legislation

→ Checkpoint has a table for each Public Law, grouped by Congress. This list covers the second session of the 116th Congress as of May 2020.

→ Checkpoint also has tables covering Code sections that were affected by enacted legislation.

→ To reach these tables, use the Table of Contents function and select Federal Library>Federal Source Materials>Pending & Enacted Legislation.

Illustration 5-24. Checkpoint Table: Pub. L. No. 116–136

RIA **P.L. 116-136: Table of Code Sections Amended.**
116th Congress - Tables of Code Sections Amended (RIA)

Code Sec. 6428	**Bill Sec. 2201(a)DivA**
Code Sec. 6211(b)(4)(A)	**Bill Sec. 2201(b)(1)DivA**
Code Sec. 6213(g)(2)(L)	**Bill Sec. 2201(b)(2)DivA**
Code Sec. 402(c)(4)	**Bill Sec. 2203(b)DivA**
Code Sec. 127(c)(1)(A)	**Bill Sec. 2206(a)DivA**
Code Sec. 127(c)(1)(B)	**Bill Sec. 2206(a)DivA**
Code Sec. 127(c)(1)(C)	**Bill Sec. 2206(a)DivA**
Code Sec. 221(e)(1)	**Bill Sec. 2206(b)DivA**
Code Sec. 172(a)	**Bill Sec. 2303(a)(1)DivA**

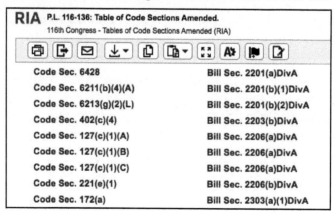

→ The Checkpoint table is in act section order, and you have to search each act individually.

→ Checkpoint does not include Statutes at Large page numbers but does provide hyperlinks.

With respect to the third search, you should check a popular names table to see if the term "Cash for Clunkers" appears. A search using Google or another search engine is also likely to succeed. Once you obtain the citation, you can read the act in Statutes at Large.

Illustration 5-25. USCA Popular Name Table on Westlaw Edge

Cars Act (Consumer Assistance to Recycle and Save Act of 2009)
Carter Act (Alaska Civil Code)
Carter G. Woodson Home National Historic Site Act
Carter G. Woodson Home National Historic Site Study Act of 2000
Case-Zablocki Act
Cases Act (Creating Advanced Streamlined Electronic Services for Constituents Act of 2019)
Cash Discount Act
Cash for Clunkers (Consumer Assistance to Recycle and Save Act of 2009)

→ Click on the popular name to get a citation and other information.

→ This table also lists the name formed by the act's acronym (Cars Act).

→ The Office of Law Revision Counsel lists the act by its short title but not by either of the popular names. The same is true for Lexis+, which includes the USCS Popular Names Table.

The final search, involving tax provisions that will expire, depends on what sources you have available. Cheetah has three Federal Tax Expiring Provisions Charts: Code section [Illustration 5-26], expiration year, and topic.[45]

Illustration 5-26. Cheetah Chart of Expiring Code Sections

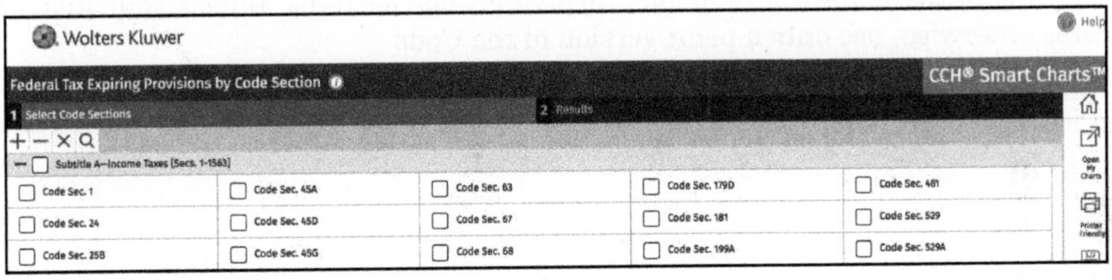

→ Click on the Code section to obtain the expiration date and additional information about the provision.

Bloomberg Law also has a list of expiring tax provisions in its "Expiring Tax Provisions" file. The file is located in Bloomberg Law: Tax under "Tables, Charts & Lists."

If you don't have access to Bloomberg Law or Cheetah, you can use the Joint Committee on Taxation pamphlet "Expiring Provisions," available on the JCT website.[46] The version available as of July 2020 (JCX–1–20) covers provisions expiring between 2020 and 2029. You can then read any provisions in one of the Code services discussed

---

[45] In Cheetah the expiring provision Smart Charts can be accessed by clicking on Practice Tools in the upper menu bar and then typing "expiring" in the search box or looking under "F" for "Federal Tax Expiring Provisions Smart Charts."

[46] The Congressional Research Service also publishes information about extenders, generally focusing on a single year. See, e.g., MOLLY F. SHERLOCK ET AL., CONG. RESEARCH SERV., R46243, INDIVIDUAL TAX PROVISIONS ("TAX EXTENDERS") EXPIRING IN 2020: IN BRIEF (2020).

in this chapter. The JCT pamphlet is arranged in expiration year order; it does not have an overall Code section order listing.

H. Citators for Statutes

After Congress passes an act, litigation may ensue over the constitutionality or interpretation of individual Code sections. Constitutional litigation is discussed in Chapter 4, which includes examples of such claims. Litigation is more likely to involve disputes between the IRS and taxpayers over conflicting interpretations of statutory provisions.

Citators are an excellent tool for determining if a federal court has ruled on a statute's constitutionality. Because they are updated much more frequently, online citators are more useful search tools than are print citators. Online services also allow different types of searching. For example, if you use an online service, you may not even need its citator features. Instead, you can find constitutional challenges using a word search that includes the Code section and a variant of "constitutional."

Not only do print citators lack the frequency and word search advantages, they may also have coverage issues. The Shepard's print citators did not cover Tax Court decisions as extensively as electronic citators do. These limitations even applied to the earliest volumes of Shepard's Federal Tax Citations. The CCH and RIA print citators did not cover statutes at all. Citators are discussed in more detail in Chapter 11.

I. Problems

For any of the following problems involving Code sections, unless your instructor indicates otherwise, use only a print version of the Code.

1. Indicate the subtitle, chapter, subchapter, part, and subpart for the I.R.C. section listed below.

   a. 61

   b. 351

   c. 6601

2. Give the bill number for the Pub. L. No. listed below.

   a. 86–69

   b. 97–35

   c. 103–66

   d. 112–96

3. Indicate the popular name or short title for the Pub. L. No. listed below.

   a. 89–809

   b. 94–12

   c. 99–514

   d. 111–148

4. Indicate the full Statutes at Large citation, including Public Law or chapter number, for the act listed below.

a. Current Tax Payment Act of 1943

b. Payment-in-Kind Tax Treatment Act of 1983

c. Taxpayer Browsing Protection Act

d. Recovering Missing Children Act

5. For I.R.C. § 2010(c)(4)(B)(i),

   a. What was the most recent change?

   b. What act made this change (use the Public Law number)?

   c. What is the effective date for the change?

   d. What is the "popular name" of the Public Law that made this change?

6. Give the expiration date for the I.R.C. sections listed below.

   a. 40A

   b. 168(k)(5)(A)

   c. 263A(d)(2)(C)(i)

   d. 4271(a)

7. Indicate the scope limitations (e.g., subtitle, section, clause) for the I.R.C. sections listed below.

   a. 132(b)

   b. 163(c)

   c. 274(e)(2)(B)(ii)

   d. 317(a)

   e. 641(c)(1)

8. Your client Correos, Inc., is a corporation organized under the law of Spain.

   a. Is Correos a "foreign corporation"? What is the authority for your answer?

   b. Assume Correos is a foreign corporation subject to the tax imposed by I.R.C. § 881 and that it is wholly owned by a U.S. corporation, Good Enough Tax Planning, Inc. ("GETP"). GETP and one of GETP's wholly-owned U.S. subsidiaries constitute a "controlled group of corporations." Is Correos a "component member" of this controlled group? How did you obtain your answer?

   c. GETP sold a copyright to Correos for a substantial gain. Is the character of GETP's gain ordinary or capital? How did you obtain your answer?

Chapter 6

LEGISLATIVE HISTORIES

A. Introduction

This chapter continues the discussion of statutes begun in Chapter 5 by describing legislative history materials and indicating where they can be found. In addition to hearings, reports by tax-writing committees, and congressional floor debate, it includes reports by other committees and by entities such as the Government Accountability Office. This chapter also explains the process for tracing current statutes back to earlier versions. Legislative history documents for treaties are covered in Chapter 7.

Your goals for this chapter include familiarizing yourself with the documents comprising a statute's legislative history, learning where to find them, and understanding how judges view them when interpreting statutes. Refer to discussion in Chapter 5 as needed.

B. Groups Involved in Legislation[1]

1. Congressional Committees

The **House Committee on Ways and Means** and the **Senate Committee on Finance** have primary jurisdiction over revenue bills. Other relevant committees include each chamber's **Budget Committee** and committees with jurisdiction over other areas with tax implications.[2] Each of these committees has subcommittees that may act with respect to pending legislation. If the House and Senate pass different versions of a bill, a **Conference Committee** meets to resolve these differences.

Five members each from Ways and Means and Finance sit on the **Joint Committee on Taxation** (JCT).[3] JCT members are assisted by a staff of accountants, attorneys, and economists. The JCT may issue proposals and reports that the Ways and Means and Finance Committees rely on, but it is not charged with drafting legislation. Courts often treated its reports as having less interpretive significance than those issued by the tax-writing committees. The 2013 Supreme Court decision in *United States v. Woods*[4] further reduced the significance of these reports.

The JCT website lists reports by year or group of years, beginning with 1920–1929. These reports are in PDF format and are searchable. The JCT's **General Explanation** of legislation enacted by Congress (which has been referred to as the **Bluebook** or the

---

1 Table 6-A (*infra* page 67) provides website information for entities described in this section.

2 E.g., in the 116th Congress, the House Committee on Small Business has a Subcommittee on Economic Growth, Tax and Capital Access. Subcommittee names may change over time. This House committee previously had subcommittees on Finance and Tax and on Tax, Finance, and Exports.

3 I.R.C. §§ 8001–8023. The JCT is charged with investigating the operation and effects of the tax system, its administration, and means of simplifying it. I.R.C. § 8022. It also reviews tax refunds exceeding $2,000,000 ($5,000,000 in the case of a C corporation). I.R.C. § 6405(a). This committee was the Joint Committee on Internal Revenue Taxation between 1926 and 1975.

4 571 U.S. 31, 48 (2013) ("[w]e have held that such '[p]ost-enactment legislative history (a contradiction in terms) is not a legitimate tool of statutory interpretation.' ").

Blue Book) can be used as authority if a taxpayer is disputing the section 6662 substantial underpayment penalty discussed in Chapter 2.

The **Joint Economic Committee**, which is also comprised of members of each chamber, is tasked "to review economic conditions and to recommend improvements in economic policy."[5] It occasionally issues reports and other documents related to taxation.[6]

2. Congressional Support Entities

Three entities are organized as nonpartisan support services. Each issues reports on various tax administration and policy issues.

The **Government Accountability Office** is the investigative arm of Congress. The GAO audits the operation of federal agencies, investigates allegations of illegal and improper activities, reports on how well government programs and policies meet their objectives, performs policy analyses, and issues legal decisions and opinions.[7] The GAO issues reports on tax administration and on substantive tax topics. It is headed by the Comptroller General of the United States.

The **Congressional Budget Office** provides analyses to aid in economic and budget decisions.[8] Its chief responsibility is to the House and Senate Budget Committees. It also provides support to other committees, primarily Appropriations, Ways and Means, and Finance.[9]

The **Congressional Research Service** (known as the Legislative Reference Service between 1914 and 1970) provides policy and legal analysis to members of Congress. Until 2018, it treated its work as confidential, but it now makes CRS reports available at crsreports.congress.gov/.[10] Although the CRS now publishes its reports, including several older reports, you can also find older reports using other sources, several of which are listed in Section D.

3. The Executive Branch

a. Executive Office of the President

The **President** may propose legislation, which a member of Congress will introduce, in messages to Congress (e.g., the State of the Union Address) or in other

[5] "About Joint Economic Committee" webpage, J. ECON. COMM., https://www.jec.senate.gov/public/index.cfm/about (last visited July 18, 2020).

[6] See, e.g., *The Promise of Opportunity Zones: Hearing Before the Jt. Econ. Comm.*, 115th Cong. (S. Hrg. 115–297, May 17, 2018).

[7] "What GAO Does" webpage, U.S. GOV'T ACCOUNTABILITY OFFICE, https://www.gao.gov/about/what-gao-does/ (last visited July 18, 2020). The GAO was called the General Accounting Office until July 7, 2004.

[8] "About CBO" webpage, CONG. BUDGET OFFICE, https://www.cbo.gov/about/overview (last visited July 18, 2020).

[9] AN INTRODUCTION TO THE CONGRESSIONAL BUDGET OFFICE 1 (May 2019).

[10] Consolidated Appropriations Act, 2018, Pub. L. No. 115–141, § 154, 132 Stat. 348, 787 (2018). Although reports are now made public (including some from as early as 1993), the CRS website states "[a]ll queries and exchanges with Members of Congress are held in the strictest confidence. Legislators and congressional staff are free to access CRS experts and analysis, explore issues, dispute them, ask questions about them or float an unusual idea— all without question, challenge or disclosure. CRS employees do not discuss work undertaken for a Member or a committee with another congressional office or with anyone outside the organization." "About CRS: Values" webpage, CONG. RESEARCH SERV., https://www.loc.gov/crsinfo/about/values.html (last visited July 18, 2020). Pub. L. No. 115–141, § 154(a)(2)(B) exempts from disclosure reports that are not available for general congressional access on the CRS Congressional Intranet.

speeches. The **Office of Management and Budget** (OMB) is the implementation and enforcement arm of presidential policy throughout the government. It assists the President in formulating a budget, oversees agency performance, coordinates and reviews significant federal regulations, reviews and clears agency communications with Congress, and reviews and clears drafts of executive orders and presidential memoranda.[11]

The **Council of Economic Advisers** (CEA) provides analysis and advice on the formulation of economic policy. The OMB and CEA are part of the **Executive Office of the President**. Some administrations have listed other tax- or economics-related entities in the Executive Office, including the Office of the United States Trade Representative, the Domestic Policy Council, and the National Economic Council.

b. Other Executive Branch Agencies

Several other executive branch entities issue reports with respect to taxation. As discussed in Chapter 5, Congress often asks the **Treasury Department** or other agencies to study and report on issues. The **IRS National Taxpayer Advocate** issues two required reports to Congress each year. The first outlines objectives planned for the next year. The second discusses serious issues facing taxpayers and recommendations for solving them. The National Taxpayer Advocate may also issue recommendations for legislation.

c. URL Listings for Relevant Government Entities

Table 6-A lists current URLs for government entities involved in the legislative process. The table includes both legislative bodies and entities that provide analysis or suggestions before or after legislation is enacted. If you need a URL for another entity, you can access government sites in the Government Agencies and Elected Officials section of the USA.gov website (www.usa.gov).

4. Other Groups

Members of Congress regularly receive written input from constituents, professional societies, trade associations, and lobbyists. These groups also testify at hearings on proposed legislation.

Table 6-A. Entities That Enact, Suggest, or Analyze Legislation

Entity	*URL (http://)*
Congressional Budget Office (CBO)	www.cbo.gov
Congressional Research Service (CRS)	www.loc.gov/crsinfo/about/
Council of Economic Advisers (CEA)	www.whitehouse.gov/administration/eop/cea
Government Accountability Office (GAO)	gao.gov

11 OFFICE OF MGMT. & BUDGET, at https://www.whitehouse.gov/omb (last visited July 18, 2020).

Entity	*URL (http://)*
House of Representatives	www.house.gov/
Budget Committee	budget.house.gov/
Ways and Means Committee	waysandmeans.house.gov/
Internal Revenue Service (IRS)	www.irs.gov
IRS National Taxpayer Advocate	www.irs.gov/taxpayer-advocate
Joint Committee on Taxation (JCT)	www.jct.gov
Joint Economic Committee (JEC)	www.jec.senate.gov/
Office of Management and Budget (OMB)	www.whitehouse.gov/omb
Office of the United States Trade Representative (USTR)	www.ustr.gov/
President	www.whitehouse.gov
Senate	www.senate.gov
Budget Committee	www.budget.senate.gov/
Finance Committee	www.finance.senate.gov/
Treasury Department	home.treasury.gov/
Inspector General for Tax Administration (TIGTA)	www.treasury.gov/tigta/
Office of the Benefits Tax Counsel (BTC)	www.treasury.gov/about/organizational-structure/offices/Pages/Office-of-the-Benefits-Tax-Counsel.aspx
Office of the International Tax Counsel (ITC)	home.treasury.gov/about/offices/tax-policy/international-tax-counsel
Office of Tax Analysis (OTA)	www.treasury.gov/about/organizational-structure/offices/Pages/Office-of-Tax-Analysis.aspx
Office of the Tax Legislative Counsel (TLC)	www.treasury.gov/about/organizational-structure/offices/Pages/Office-of-the-Tax-Legislative-Counsel.aspx
Office of Tax Policy (OTP)	home.treasury.gov/policy-issues/tax-policy

→ If www appears in the table, the website would not open without it or it displayed www despite opening without it.

C. Legislative Process

The process for enacting tax legislation is almost identical to that used for other federal laws. The major difference relates to the constitutional limitation discussed in Chapter 4: revenue-raising bills must originate in the House of Representatives.[12] This section discusses the legislative process; Section D covers finding the documents discussed in this section.

1. Introduction of Bill

The sponsoring legislator may present remarks for inclusion in the **Congressional Record** at the bill's introduction. If the administration is proposing an item, a presidential message may accompany the proposal transmitted to Congress.

The bill receives a number when it is introduced. Similar bills may be introduced in the same chamber; each receives its own number. [See Illustration 6-1.] The same is true for bills introduced in both the House and Senate; they receive separate numbers in each chamber.

Illustration 6-1. Excerpt from Related Bills Introduced in 2019

Related Bills: H.R.748 — 116th Congress (2019-2020) All Information (Except Text)

A related bill may be a companion measure, an identical bill, a procedurally-related measure, or one with text similarities. Bill relationships are identified by the House, the Senate, or CRS, and refer only to same-congress measures.

Bill	Latest Title	Relationships to H.R.748	Relationships Identified by	Latest Action
H.R.1865	Further Consolidated Appropriations Act, 2020	Related bill	CRS	12/20/2019 Became Public Law No: 116-94.
H.R.1869	Restoring Investment in Improvements Act	Related bill	CRS	03/26/2019 Referred to the House Committee on Ways and Means.
H.R.1922	Restoring Access to Medication Act of 2019	Related bill	CRS	10/23/2019 Ordered to be Reported in the Nature of a Substitute (Amended) by Voice Vote.
H.R.2150	Home Health Care Planning Improvement Act of 2019	Related bill	CRS	04/10/2019 Referred to the Subcommittee on Health.
H.R.2452	Medicare for America Act of 2019	Related bill	CRS	05/31/2019 Referred to the Subcommittee on Courts, Intellectual Property, and the Internet.

→ There were 48 bills related to H.R. 748, which became the Coronavirus Aid, Relief, and Economic Security Act (CARES Act).

The Related Bills listed in Congress.gov are not necessarily identical. If they relate to a topic you are tracking, make sure you read each of them.

Bill numbers are sequential for each term of Congress (e.g., H.R. 1; S. 1); there is not a separate numbering system for each session within the two-year term. Occasionally, a bill number will be reserved for major legislation; that bill may be introduced after a bill with a higher number.

2. Referral to Committee and Committee Action

After its introduction, the bill is referred to the appropriate committee, generally the House Ways and Means Committee or the Senate Finance Committee. The

[12] "All Bills for raising Revenue shall originate in the House of Representatives . . . ." U.S. CONST. art. I, § 7, cl. 1.

committee (or a subcommittee thereof) may hold hearings, which will be published.[13] It may issue a committee report to accompany the bill that is reported out of committee. These reports are numbered by Congress. For example, the House Ways and Means Committee report that accompanied H.R. 1 in the 115th Congress (popularly known as the Tax Cuts and Jobs Act) is H.R. Rep. No. 115–409, 115th Cong., 1st Sess. (2017) [Illustration 6-2].

Illustration 6-2. Excerpt from H.R. Rep. No. 115–409, 115th Cong., 1st Sess. 166 (2017)

4. Repeal of deduction for personal casualty and theft losses (sec. 1304 of the bill and sec. 165 of the Code)

PRESENT LAW

A taxpayer may generally claim a deduction for any loss sustained during the taxable year, not compensated by insurance or otherwise. For individual taxpayers, deductible losses must be incurred in a trade or business or other profit-seeking activity or consist of property losses arising from fire, storm, shipwreck, or other casualty, or from theft.[132] Personal casualty or theft losses are deductible only if they exceed $100 per casualty or theft. In addition, aggregate net casualty and theft losses are deductible only to the extent they exceed 10 percent of an individual taxpayer's adjusted gross income.

REASONS FOR CHANGE

The Committee believes that the repeal of many existing tax incentives, including the deduction for personal casualty and theft losses, makes the system simpler and fairer for all families and individuals, and allows for lower tax rates. The Committee further believes that repeal of this provision is consistent with streamlining the tax code, broadening the tax base, lowering rates, and growing the economy.

→ The Senate Finance Committee did not issue a report for H.R. 1.

The version of the bill that the committee chair initially issues is referred to as the **chairman's mark.**[14] After committee deliberation, which may include input from committee, IRS, and Treasury staffs and from other groups described in Section B, the marked-up bill may differ significantly from its initial version. Its name may also change. For example, in 2011 H.R. 4 was introduced in the 112th Congress as the Small Business Paperwork Mandate Elimination Act of 2011. Its name was changed to the Comprehensive 1099 Taxpayer Protection and Repayment of Exchange Subsidy Overpayments Act of 2011 on the floor of the House of Representatives through the substitution of the text of a related bill (H.R. 705).

The bill, or a similar version, may have been simultaneously considered in the other chamber or considered after being passed in the first chamber. The process in the second chamber, generally the Senate, is comparable to that described above.

3. House and Senate Floor Debate

A bill sent to the floor by committee can die in one chamber, pass intact, or pass with amendments. Each chamber separately deliberates on the bill before voting. Although Senate rules permit more extensive debate and floor amendments than do

[13] Committees may hold hearings even if no bill is pending. They may also move a bill without holding hearings.

[14] As of July 2020, all tax-writing committee chairs have been male.

House procedures, each chamber can change the bill. A bill passed by one chamber and sent to the other is called an **engrossed** bill.

Questions and answers and other statements made during floor debate can illuminate the meaning of legislation.[15] Be aware, however, that statements can be made to an empty chamber or simply added as text. Note also that the speaker's identity is relevant. Comments made by the chair of the relevant committee, or by the bill's sponsor(s), are likely to be more informed than comments made by legislators who were not involved in the legislation's introduction or committee action. Colloquies between legislators may also be useful.

If both chambers pass the bill with identical terms, it can be sent to the President. If the versions differ, a Conference Committee is appointed.

4. Conference Committee Action

The Conference Committee meets to resolve House and Senate differences. It generates a third report, the **Conference Report**. That document is usually numbered as a House report. The Conference Report explains the resolution of House-Senate differences [Illustration 6-3].

[15] In *Ashburn v. United States*, 740 F.2d 843 (11th Cir. 1984), the court referred to committee reports and congressional debates as evidence of the meaning of a phrase in the Equal Access to Justice Act. See also *Commissioner v. Engle*, 464 U.S. 206 (1984), in which the Court's opinion on the meaning of I.R.C. § 613A cited to testimony at hearings, floor debate, and committee reports. Be aware that the Supreme Court has become less receptive to using legislative history materials in construing statutes.

Illustration 6-3. Excerpt from H.R. Rep. No 115–466, 115th Cong., 1st Sess. 261 (2017)

3. Repeal of deduction for personal casualty and theft losses (sec. 1304 of the House bill, sec. 11044 of the Senate amendment, and sec. 165 of the Code)

PRESENT LAW

A taxpayer may generally claim a deduction for any loss sustained during the taxable year, not compensated by insurance or otherwise. For individual taxpayers, deductible losses must be incurred in a trade or business or other profit-seeking activity or consist of property losses arising from fire, storm, shipwreck, or other casualty, or from theft.[173] Personal casualty or theft losses are deductible only if they exceed $100 per casualty or theft. In addition, aggregate net casualty and theft losses are deductible only to the extent they exceed 10 percent of an individual taxpayer's adjusted gross income.

HOUSE BILL

The House bill repeals the deduction for personal casualty and theft losses. However, notwithstanding the repeal of the deduction, the provision retains the benefit of the deduction, as modified by the Disaster Tax Relief and Airport and Airway Extension Act of 2017,[174] for those individuals who sustained a personal casualty loss arising from hurricanes Harvey, Irma, or Maria.

Effective date.—The provision is effective for losses incurred in taxable years beginning after December 31, 2017.

SENATE AMENDMENT

The Senate amendment temporarily modifies the deduction for personal casualty and theft losses. Under the provision, a taxpayer may claim a personal casualty loss (subject to the limitations described above) only if such loss was attributable to a disaster declared by the President under section 401 of the Robert T. Stafford Disaster Relief and Emergency Assistance Act.

5. Floor Action on Conference Report

Unlike the pre-conference bills, a bill that emerges from the Conference Committee cannot be further amended during floor debate. Each chamber must pass it or reject it as written.[16] That "final" version (the **enrolled** bill) is then prepared for submission to the President.

6. Correcting Drafting Errors

Unlike treaties, bills die when a Congress's second session ends.[17] Members work under extreme time pressure to pass pending legislation by that date. As a result, a Conference Report's version may contain errors, which Congress passes along with the rest of the bill. If both chambers agree, Congress can adopt a **concurrent resolution** making necessary changes before the act is enrolled for submission to the President. If they do not agree, or find the errors too late, the error may be corrected in a **technical**

[16] H.R. 1, which was enacted as Pub. L. No. 115–97, is an oddity. Before the Senate vote on the Conference agreement, the Senate Parliamentarian required that three provisions, including the bill's proposed short title (Tax Cuts and Jobs Act) be eliminated for failure to comply with rules governing reconciliation bills (which allow the Senate to pass the bill by a simple majority and avoid filibusters). After the Senate voted to accept the bill with those revisions, the House revoted and also accepted it.

[17] Chapter 7 discusses other differences between statutes and treaties.

corrections bill or in a technical corrections section of a later bill.[18] Some errors go uncorrected for years.[19]

7. Presidential Action

The bill becomes law if the President signs it within 10 days of its presentment. It also becomes law if the President does nothing and Congress remains in session during that period. Alternatively, the President can veto the bill; Congress can override a veto only by a two-thirds vote in each chamber.[20] If the President does nothing and the congressional session ends during the 10 days, the bill is "pocket-vetoed."[21] The President may issue a statement when signing or vetoing a bill.

D. Locating Legislative History Documents: Citations and Text

The process used for locating legislative history documents varies depending on whether you are using print materials or online services. If you are using print materials, your research may involve two steps. First you must obtain citations for the documents you need.[22] Then you must locate those documents. When researching online, you may be able to skip the first step and find your documents using word and Code section searches or by searching directly for the act or its history.

Many of the illustrations in this section are from government websites, which have excellent coverage of legislative history materials, particularly from the mid-1990s (and in some cases even earlier). Illustrations of commercial materials are provided for older legislative history materials.

1. Versions of the Bill

A bill that is enacted into law is often amended during the enactment process. Versions include the bill as introduced, as reported by a committee, as passed by one chamber of Congress (engrossed bill), as reported by a committee of the other chamber of Congress, as passed by the other chamber of Congress, and as reported by the Conference Committee, passed by both chambers, and sent to the President (enrolled bill). The enacted bill is the final version; it will include the notes added by the Office of the Federal Register. [See Illustration 5-1, *supra* page 29.]

Congress.gov currently includes PDF versions of each bill introduced since 1993 (the 103rd Congress). You can search Congress.gov by phrase [Illustrations 6-4 and 6-5] or bill number. Govinfo.gov has the same coverage dates and documents in its Congressional Bills collection.

---

18 See, e.g., H.R. Con. Res. 328, 98th Cong., 2d Sess. (1984), 98 Stat. 3454 (1984), making technical changes to the Tax Reform Act of 1984. Compare H.R. Con. Res. 395, 99th Cong., 2d Sess. (1986), which failed to pass, leaving flaws in the 1986 Act.

19 In 2007 and 2008, Congress enacted two provisions to which it assigned the number I.R.C. § 121(b)(4). The error was finally corrected in 2014 by Pub. L. No. 113–295, § 212(c).

20 Congress overrode President Franklin Roosevelt's veto of the Revenue Act of 1943, ch. 63, 58 Stat. 21 (1944).

21 "If any Bill shall not be returned by the President within ten Days (Sundays excepted) after it shall have been presented to him, the Same shall be a Law, in like Manner as if he had signed it, unless the Congress by their Adjournment prevent its Return, in which Case it shall not be a Law." U.S. CONST. art. 1, § 7, cl. 2.

22 Beginning in 1975, Statutes at Large includes citations to committee reports, Congressional Record items, and presidential messages immediately following the text of each act.

Illustration 6-4. Congress.gov Search for Bills by Phrase

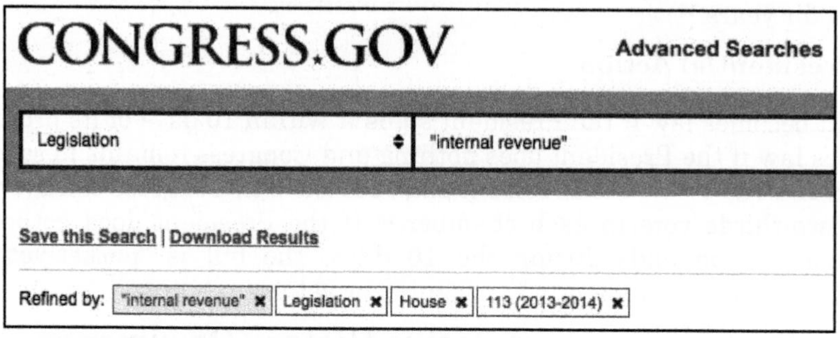

→ Congress.gov allows you to select a number of search parameters. These include Congress, Chamber of Origin, Bill Type, Committee, and Subject/Policy Area. You can also search by bill number or words and phrases.

→ This search covered the phrase "internal revenue," refined to limit results to the 113th Congress and bills originating in the House.

→ Congress.gov found 1,067 "hits." The search in Illustration 6-5 was further refined to cover only enacted bills.

If you need bills from earlier sessions of Congress, check to see if your library has the microfiche set entitled CIS Congressional Bills, Resolutions & Laws on Microfiche (1933–2010) (available from ProQuest).

Internal Revenue Acts of the United States: 1909–1950, and subsequent legislative history sets published by William S. Hein & Company, include different versions of enacted legislation. Many of these legislative histories are available in print or microform. They are included in the HeinOnline Taxation & Economic Reform in America database.

Fee-based services include the text of more recent bills in addition to older proposed legislation. When using these services, check the relevant database for coverage dates. Retrospective coverage in some databases does not begin earlier than the coverage in the government sites. The Lexis+ Congressional Full Text Bills files contain the full text of each version; coverage begins in 1989 with the 101st Congress. Cheetah provides full-text coverage of both enacted and unenacted legislation.

Illustration 6-5. Congress.gov Search for Enacted Bills by Phrase

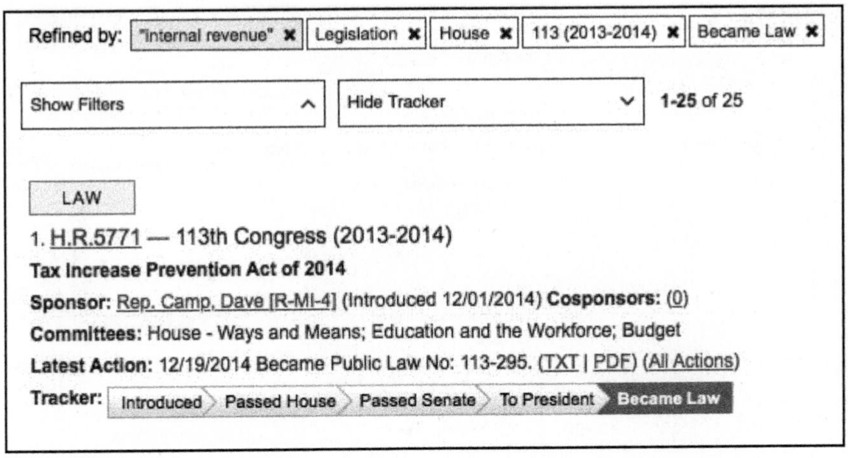

→ The revised search found 25 "hits." The first one listed appears above as sorted by date of introduction (newest to oldest).

2. Statements on the Floor of Congress

The Congressional Record prints introduced bills and statements made at their introduction. It also prints statements, questions, and answers made during floor debate. Make sure you check whether your citation is to the bound or daily version. Page numbers indicate H for House and S for Senate.

Congressional Record can be accessed through its indexes, but it is easier to search online. The service you use for this purpose will depend on the year involved.

The GPO makes the daily version of Congressional Record available online through govinfo.gov beginning with 1994.[23] Govinfo.gov also includes the Congressional Record Index since 1983. Congress.gov currently begins its coverage of the Congressional Record in 1995; archived versions for 1989 through 1994 can be browsed but not searched.

---

[23] As of July 2020, while govinfo.gov begins its coverage in 1994 in its Congressional Record file, its Congressional Record (Bound Edition) file begins in 1873.

Illustration 6-6. Congressional Record Search in govinfo.gov

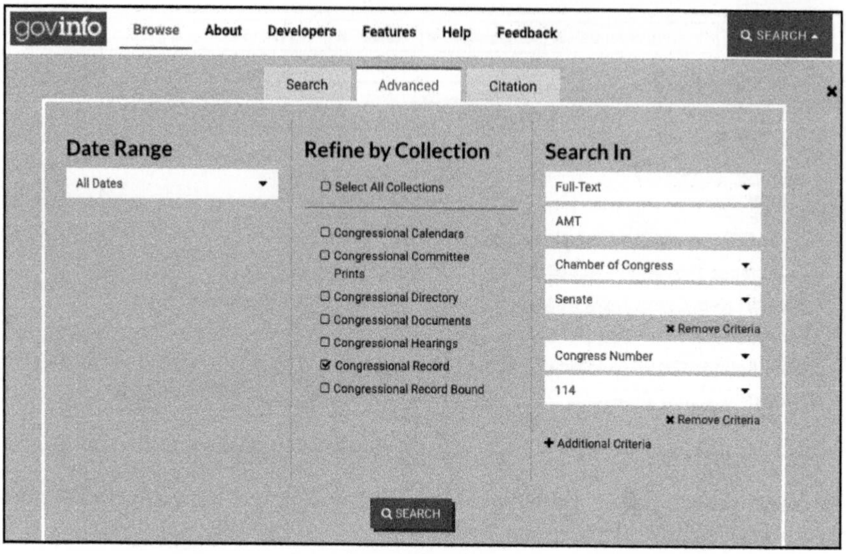

→ To search in govinfo.gov, you can include up to five items in the Advanced Search function. This search yielded the 4 "hits" shown in Illustration 6-7.

→ This search yielded the same 4 "hits" when we ran it using "AMT" instead of AMT. The first "hit" did not relate to the alternative minimum tax.

Illustration 6-7. Congressional Record Search Results in govinfo.gov

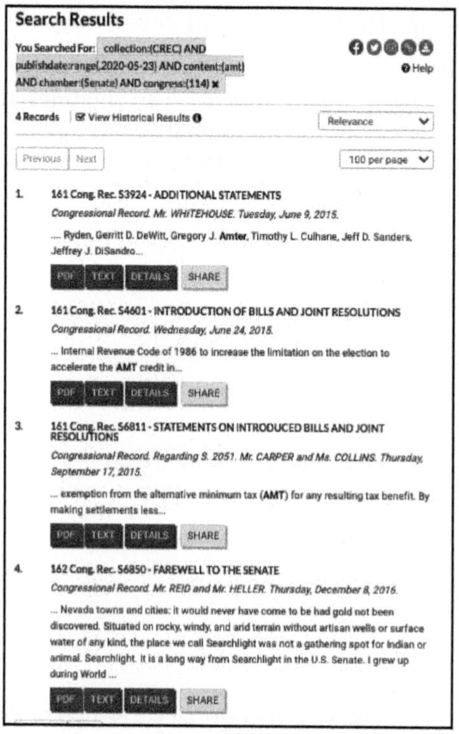

Illustration 6-8. Congressional Record Search in Congress.gov

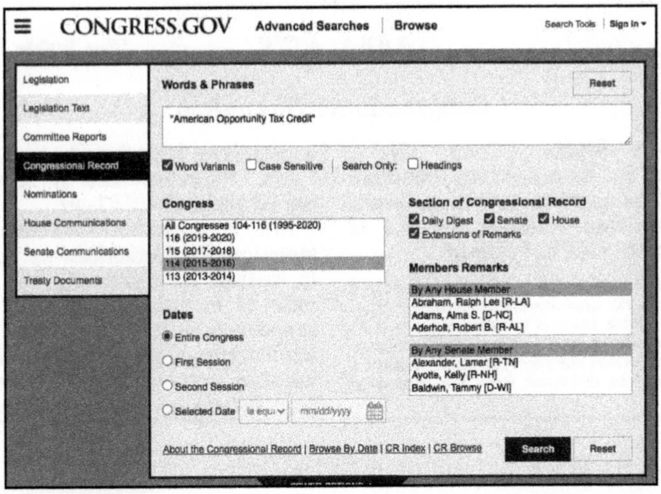

→ Above is the "more options" search screen on Congress.gov. We searched for "American Opportunity Tax Credit" and limited the search to the 114th Congress.

→ The search yielded 34 "hits" available in text or PDF format.

You can search Congressional Record online in Westlaw Edge (since 1985) and Lexis+ (since 1873).[24] ProQuest Congressional provides the bound Congressional Record (1873–2009) and the daily Congressional Record since 1985. HeinOnline currently carries the bound Congressional Record (1873–mid-2015) and the daily Congressional Record since 1980.[25] Bloomberg Law has two Congressional Record files (Congressional Record (since 1989) and Historical Congressional Record (1933–1988)) in its U.S. Legislative collection.[26] You may also be able to locate older volumes of Congressional Record in the library's microform collection.

Three services print excerpts from Congressional Record: Tax Management Primary Sources (1969–2003); Internal Revenue Acts—Texts and Legislative History (since 1954); and Seidman's Legislative History of Federal Income and Excess Profits Tax Laws (1861–1953). Barton's Federal Tax Laws Correlated provides page citations for the period from 1953 through 1969.[27]

---

24 Lexis+ carries the Congressional Record for 1873–1997 in its Congressional Record Retro file; that file is available only in PDF. A separate Congressional Record file begins in 1989.

25 HeinOnline also includes predecessor documents, e.g., the Congressional Globe.

26 You can reach many of Bloomberg's congressional materials using either its All Legal Content link or its Laws & Regulations link. The former link often gives more robust search options.

27 Seidman's and Barton's are also available in HeinOnline.

Illustration 6-9. Excerpt from Congressional Debate in Seidman's

1028 1864 ACT [See inside back cover

Congressional Discussion

Discussion—Senate (Cong. Globe, 38th Cong., 1st Sess.).—THE PRESIDING OFFICER. The question now is on inserting the following words at the end of section one hundred and fifteen[1]:

***And provided further*, That net profits realized by sales of property upon investments made within the year, for which income is estimated, shall be chargeable as income; and losses on sales of property purchased within the year, for which income is estimated, shall be deducted from the income of such year.**

accumulates from year to year.

MR. JOHNSON. Has it been so construed under the old law?

MR. FESSENDEN. That was the construction the Commissioner put upon it in writing. Our difficulty was to fix any ratio of income. If anything could be considered as income in such case, it is the increase of value for the year. If, for instance, you buy property one year and hold it, and by last year's accumulation

→ Seidman's prints excerpts from an act's legislative history.

3. Committee Hearings

Transcripts of hearings can be located in a library's government documents section or in its microform collection. Westlaw Edge includes hearings in its U.S. Congressional Testimony database (since 1993). Bloomberg Law has separate files for House and Senate Committee Transcripts beginning with the 104th Congress (1995). ProQuest Congressional includes published and unpublished hearings from 1824. HeinOnline includes Congressional Hearings since 1887.

Beginning with the 104th Congress (1995), govinfo.gov includes transcripts of hearings (including written submissions). The House Ways and Means Committee website Committee Activity tab includes hearings beginning with 2008; the Senate Finance Committee website Hearings tab includes hearings since 2001; its Library tab includes printed hearings since 1913.

4. Committee Reports

You can find committee reports in a library's government documents or microform collections if you have the appropriate citation. Reports are numbered sequentially by Congress, not by committee. The numbering does not restart when a term of Congress goes into its second session.

Citations include initials to indicate which chamber issued them, but they do not indicate which committee. Although omitted from the material appearing in Table 6-B, citations do indicate the number and session of Congress.

Table 6-B. Illustrative Committee Report Citations

	Taxpayer Relief Act of 1997, Pub. L. No. 105–34, 111 Stat. 788 (1997)	*Tax Increase Prevention and Reconciliation Act of 2005, Pub. L. No. 109–222, 120 Stat. 345 (2006)*
House	H.R. Rep. No. 105–148	H.R. Rep. No. 109–304
Senate	S. Rep. No. 105–33	None
Conference	H.R. Rep. No. 105–220	H.R. Rep. No. 109–455

→ The House report for Pub. L. No. 105–34 came from the Budget Committee, rather than from Ways and Means.

As the entry for Pub. L. No. 109–222 indicates, legislation may be enacted with fewer than three reports. Some legislation is enacted without any committee reports.

a. Citations for Reports

Online sources provide immediate access to reports even if you lack citations. Unfortunately, they rarely cover pre-1954 Code material. If you need a citation to an older report, several services provide that information.[28]

- Barton's Federal Tax Laws Correlated (through 1969) (print and HeinOnline) [Illustration 6-10]
- Legislative History of the Internal Revenue Code of 1954 (1954 through 1969)
- Standard Federal Tax Reporter—Citator (Cumulative Bulletin rather than report number citations for amendments to 1954 and 1986 Codes; listed in Code section order)
- TaxCite (citations to reports printed in the Cumulative Bulletin for commonly cited statutes enacted between 1913 and 1993)

If you know the act number, title, or subject matter, you may also be able to obtain citations from a source such as ProQuest Congressional or HeinOnline; each includes a government legislative history compilation known as the Serial Set. Your library microform collection may also have this set.

[28] The Joint Committee on Taxation published legislative history information in 1991. STAFF OF JT. COMM. ON TAX'N, 102D CONG., LISTING OF SELECTED FEDERAL TAX LEGISLATION REPRINTED IN THE IRS CUMULATIVE BULLETIN, 1913–1990 (JCS–19–91) (Jt. Comm. Print, Dec. 19, 1991). This study is available on the JCT website.

Illustration 6-10. Legislative History Citations in Barton's

TABLE E						Amendments — Legislative History				
Public Law						House of Representatives				
Number	Date	Cong.	Stats. at Large	Cum. Bull.	USCCAN	H. Rept.	Cong./Date	Cum. Bull.	USCCAN	Floor debate
87-293	9-22-61	87/1	75:612	61-2/336	87-1/683	1115	87-1/9-5-61	61-2/419	87-1/2842	107 CR 19238, 19490, 19536, 19803, 20027
87-312	9-26-61	87/1	75:674	61-2/339	87-1/758	939	87-1/8-15-61	61-2/425		107 CR 16521, 19539
87-321	9-26-61	87/1	75:683	61-2/341	87-1/768	425	87-1/5-24-61	61-2/442		107 CR 10371, 19537

→ The HeinOnline version has two pages for each act. The second page for each act covers the Senate and Conference Committees.

b. Text of Reports in Print

Once you have a citation, you can find full or partial text of committee reports in several publications. Print sources include the following:

- Cumulative Bulletin (1913–2003)[29]
- Rabkin & Johnson, Federal Income, Gift and Estate Taxation (1954 Code only)
- Seidman's Legislative History of Federal Income and Excess Profits Tax Laws (1861–1953) (print and HeinOnline)
- Standard Federal Tax Reporter (limited coverage)
- Tax Management Primary Sources (1969–2003)
- United States Tax Reporter (excerpts)

Each service has limitations. These include providing only partial texts, printing only one committee report rather than all reports for an act, or omitting original pagination. Seidman's omits estate and gift taxes altogether.

Internal Revenue Acts of the United States: 1909–1950 (and later series) provides full text with original pagination for all materials. It is available in print and HeinOnline. Because it omits pre-1909 material, you should consult Seidman's, which includes partial texts, for earlier reports.

c. Text of Reports Online

If you need reports published since the mid-1990s, online services provide the most comprehensive coverage and are the easiest to search. The government makes committee reports for the 104th and later Congresses available online through the Congress.gov and govinfo.gov websites. The Senate Finance Committee website has a library of Finance Committee and Conference Committee reports since 1913. Reports on these sites are usually published in PDF format.

---

[29] Committee reports for 1913 through 1938 appear in 1939–1 (pt. 2) C.B. With the exception of the 1954 Code, for which none are included, reports for most acts appeared in the Cumulative Bulletin, often in a separate volume. The government stopped including reports in the C.B. after 2003.

Bloomberg Law includes committee reports in its separate House and Senate Committee Reports files, with coverage beginning in 1995.

Checkpoint includes committee reports since the 104th Congress (1995) [Illustration 6-11].

Cheetah has several files that include reports. The Federal Tax-Major Tax Acts and Reports (1986–2020) folder covers major legislation beginning with the Tax Reform Act of 1986 and includes the current Congress. Additionally, you can find tax legislation listed under Tax-Federal>Tax Legislation & Analysis after selecting See All.

The Federal Research Library includes committee reports in its Tax Legislation database.

HeinOnline includes committee reports in its Taxation & Economic Reform in America library. Its retrospective coverage begins in 1909. It also includes committee reports in its U.S. Congressional Serial Set library.

ProQuest has committee reports beginning in 1789 for subscribers to the Serial Set Collection and beginning in 1990 for subscribers with a basic subscription.

The Westlaw Edge Federal Tax Legislative History database begins in 1948 with selective coverage and provides full coverage since 1990.

Illustration 6-11. Conference Committee Report in Checkpoint

Committee Report for conf109-455_2, pl109-222 , Conference

TAX INCREASE PREVENTION AND RECONCILIATION ACT OF 2005

Click here for a PDF of Conference Report 109-455 Click here for a PDF of the Estimated Revenue Effects of Conference Report 109-455

Contents

I. EXTENSION AND MODIFICATION OF CERTAIN PROVISIONS

A. Allowance of Nonrefundable Personal Credits Against Regular and Alternative Minimum Tax Liability (sec. 101 of the House bill, sec. 107 of the Senate amendment, and sec. 26 of the Code)

→ Checkpoint offers both PDF and hyperlink reading options for many of these reports.

5. Other Congressional Reports

a. Joint Committee on Taxation

One of the most important reports issued by the Joint Committee on Taxation's staff is the General Explanation ("Bluebook") of tax legislation.[30] That document can be used

[30] The relevant nomenclature can be confusing. First, although the JCT website currently uses the term Bluebook, these documents have also been referred to as the Blue Book, as is done in Treas. Reg. § 1.6662–4.

as authority if a taxpayer is disputing the substantial underpayment penalty discussed in Chapter 2.

Because the Joint Committee is not an official tax-writing committee, the General Explanation is not an official committee report. Services that cover committee reports may include General Explanations with other committee reports, cover them in a separate database, or not cover them at all. The same is true for other JCT staff reports and for reports of legislative subcommittees.

The JCT website includes both Bluebooks and other reports. Coverage currently begins with JCT–8–12, issued in August 1926. The numbering system includes the year of issue beginning in 1953. Documents first were classified as JCS in 1959 (JCS–10–59) and as JCX in 1979 (JCX–1–79). Be careful to use the prefix when searching for a JCT document. For example, JCS–4–13 (Dec. 20, 2013) covers a completely different topic than does JCX–4–13 (Feb. 11, 2013).[31]

Several subscription services carry JCT reports: Bloomberg Law: Tax (Bluebooks since the 104th Congress); Checkpoint (Bluebooks since the 104th Congress); Cheetah (Bluebooks since 1976 and limited coverage of other documents at least since 1985); Federal Research Library (Bluebooks since the Tax Reform Act of 1969); Lexis+ and Westlaw Edge (Bluebooks since 1976 and other documents since 1992). You can use these if the JCT site is down or if you prefer the search functions offered by commercial services.

Illustration 6-12. Document Categories on JCT Website

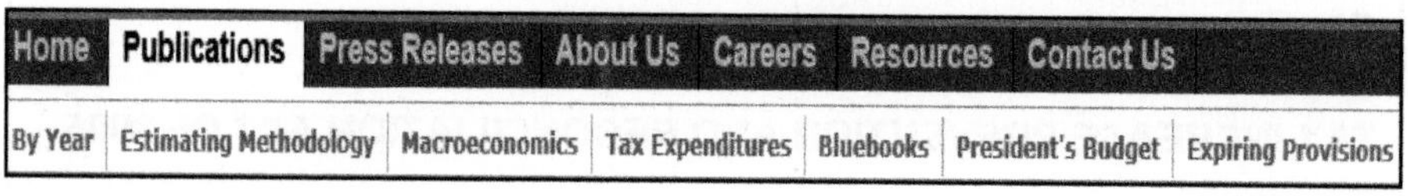

b. Joint Economic Committee

The JEC site lets you select between two tabs. When each house of Congress is controlled by a different party, the tabs are Republicans and Democrats. When both houses of Congress are controlled by the same party, the tabs are Majority and Minority. Both sites have links to charts, news, and analysis. The main committee page includes an Archives tab, which includes hearings and reports.

c. Congressional Support Entities

You may also want access to reports issued to Congress by congressional support entities, including the Congressional Budget Office, Congressional Research Service, and Government Accountability Office. You can find these items online, in microform

Second, the General Explanation issued by the JCT staff is not the only "Blue Book." Until 2009, the Treasury Department's General Explanation of the Administration's Fiscal [Year] Revenue Proposals was referred to as the Blue Book; it then became the Greenbook or Green Book. The most recent version, for fiscal 2017, was released in February 2016. Although the fiscal 2003 through 2010 documents include "Revenue Proposals" in their titles, the fiscal 2002 document uses the term "Tax Relief Proposals." Treasury General Explanations since fiscal 1999 are in the Tax Policy section of the Treasury Department website.

[31] With few exceptions, JCT documents currently use the JCX prefix.

collections, and in library government documents collections. Government websites are particularly likely to include documents generated after 1993.[32]

An important advantage of locating these documents online, whether through government websites or subscription services, is your ability to search for them based on concept rather than by document number.

Illustration 6-13. Topic Search on CBO Website

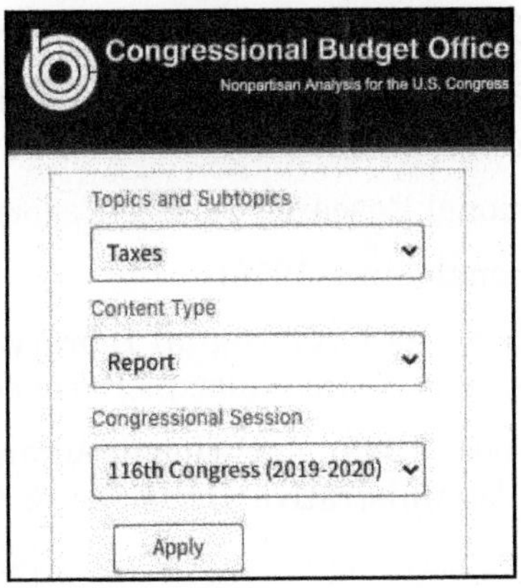

→ You can also search the website for such items as blog posts, cost estimates, data and technical information, graphics, podcasts, presentations, and working papers.

Illustration 6-14. Search Results on GAO Website

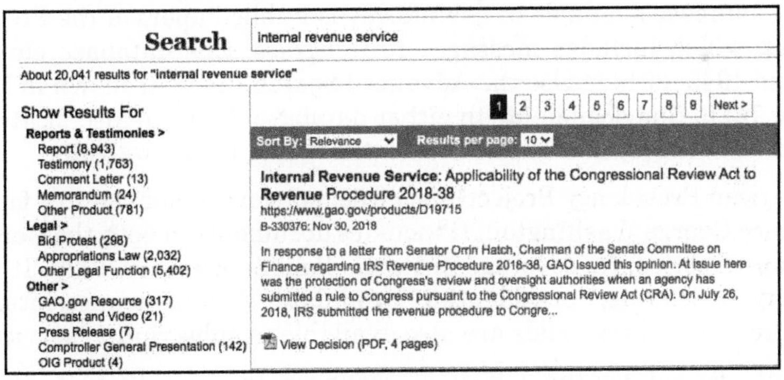

→ You can browse the GAO Reports & Testimonies page by date, topic, or agency. There is also an advanced search function that you can use to search on words and phrases.

As noted earlier, since being required to do so by Congress in 2018 the CRS posts its reports on its website, with older reports being included over time. Older reports are available online from the following sources:

---

[32] See Government Printing Office Electronic Information Access Enhancement Act of 1993, Pub. L. No. 103–40, 107 Stat. 112, codified at 44 U.S.C. § 4101.

- Bloomberg Law CRS Reports file (since December 2005) (in Laws & Regulations>Legislative Resources and in All Legal Content>U.S. Legislative>U.S. Congress)
- Cheetah (since 2003) (in CRS Reports and Other Studies)
- CRSReports.com (https://crsreports.com/)
- EveryCRSReport.com (www.everycrsreport.com)
- Federal Research Library (since 1987)
- HeinOnline (in U.S. Congressional Documents library; Taxation & Economic Reform in America library)
- Lexis+ (in Congressional Research Service Reports)
- ProQuest Congressional (since 1916)
- University of North Texas UNT Digital Library (1922 through January 2019) (https://digital.library.unt.edu/explore/collections/CRSR/)
- Westlaw Edge (since 1989) (in Home>Administrative Decisions & Guidance>Federal Administrative Decisions & Guidance) (listed under Tools & Resources)

6. Executive Branch Documents[33]

Presidential documents appear in the Compilation of Presidential Documents. This collection has been published daily since late January 2009; it previously was a weekly publication. It is available on the GPO's govinfo.gov website; coverage begins in 1992. Another GPO database available at govinfo.gov is Public Papers of the Presidents of the United States, which includes messages to Congress; this database currently covers 1929–1932 and 1945–2014.[34] Use the Advanced Search function shown in Illustration 6-6 (*supra* page 76) to find documents in either database. You can also locate presidential documents for the current administration on the White House website.

The American Presidency Project[35] is a free, nongovernment source for presidential documents since George Washington. It includes documents in both the Compilation and the Public Papers series. Its coverage of Public Papers begins in 1929. It also includes political party platforms, presidential candidate debate transcripts, and other documents. Presidential materials are also available in subscription services.[36]

Documents issued by the Office of Management and Budget, the Council of Economic Advisors, and other executive branch offices listed in Section B.3 (*supra* page 66) can be found at their websites [Table 6-A, *supra* page 67].

---

[33] Chapters 8 and 9 also include executive branch documents, particularly those related to interpreting or implementing legislation. Chapter 7 discusses documents related to treaties.

[34] Messages transmitting proposed legislation also appear in the Congressional Record.

[35] www.presidency.ucsb.edu.

[36] For example, the HeinOnline U.S. Presidential Library includes both the Daily (since 2009) and Weekly (1965–2009) Compilations of Presidential Documents and the Public Papers of the Presidents (1929–2014). Westlaw Edge has a Presidential Documents database (executive orders since 1936; other documents since 1984). Lexis+ has a Public Papers of the Presidents file (since 1981). You can search presidential documents on Bloomberg Law in the Federal Register Search file.

E. Unenacted Bills

Subscription and free services don't limit their coverage to enacted legislation. You can locate "legislative history" documents such as those described above even for bills that do not become law. For most unenacted legislation, the introduced bill may constitute the entire history: the bill may never emerge from the committee to which it is referred.

The following services provide at least partial legislative history documents for unenacted legislation:

- Bloomberg Law: Tax
- Checkpoint Pending & Enacted Legislation file
- Cheetah Tax Legislation and Analysis (various sub-files)
- Congress.gov [Illustration 6-15][37]
- Lexis+
- Westlaw Edge

Illustration 6-15. H.R. 4849, 111th Cong., 2d Sess., in Congress.gov

Actions Overview H.R.4849 — 111th Congress (2009-2010)

Bill History – Congressional Record References

Show Filters 3 results for Actions Overview

Date	Actions Overview
03/24/2010	Passed/agreed to in House: On passage Passed by recorded vote: 246 - 178 (Roll no. 182).(text: CR H2281-2285)
03/19/2010	Reported (Amended) by the Committee on Ways and Means. H. Rept. 111-447.
03/16/2010	Introduced in House

→ The Actions tab has three options: Actions Overview, All Actions Except Amendments, and All Actions.

F. Using Legislative History in Statutory Interpretation

After a bill becomes law, the interpretive process begins. Whether you are researching to determine the best way to structure a transaction, or because litigation is already in progress, you must locate authoritative interpretations of the law. In addition to locating legislative history materials issued for a current act, you may need to trace a Code section back to its original version.

1. In Lieu of Administrative Interpretations

Because Congress authorizes the Treasury Department to issue rules and regulations, you might start searching for interpretations in Treasury regulations (Chapter 8) or IRS documents (Chapter 9). These agencies cannot issue guidance as

[37] Govinfo.gov has separate collections for bills, reports, the Congressional Record, and hearings.

quickly as Congress enacts major legislation, and they invariably have a backlog of guidance projects.[38]

If no regulations are available, you can consult legislative history materials to ascertain congressional intent. Even after regulations appear, you can use legislative history to challenge their validity.[39] As discussed in Section H, courts vary in the degree of weight they grant legislative history.[40] Do not overlook this fact in doing your research.

2. Tracing Changes in Statutory Language

Legislative history necessarily includes the process by which a section evolved from its original version. Most 1986 Code provisions were continued from the 1954 Code using the same section numbering scheme. Although the 1939 Code's number system is quite different, you can easily trace current provisions to that Code or to earlier revenue acts.

Chapter 5 lists sources publishing the texts of prior laws. The materials below aid you in determining which sections of those laws are relevant.

a. 1986–1954–1939 Code Cross-Reference Tables

Code cross-reference tables provide cross-references between the 1939 and 1954 Codes. Although cross-references directly from the 1986 Code would also be helpful, the 1954 Code tables will suffice so long as the 1954 and 1986 section numbering systems remain substantially identical.

Certain limitations affect your use of cross-reference tables. First, Congress changed section numbers (adding new items and deleting or moving old ones) after enacting the 1954 Code and again in the 1986 Code. Cross-reference tables may not reflect these changes.[41] You must determine when each provision received its current section number. If the table has not been amended since then, use the previous section number in your tracing effort.

A second limitation is also worth noting. These tables reflect their compilers' opinions as to the appropriate cross-references. Different publishers' tables may yield different results. Illustrations 6-16 and 6-17 reflect this phenomenon for 1939 Code section 47.

Tables in these services cross-reference the 1954 and 1939 Codes:

- Barton's Federal Tax Laws Correlated (looseleaf volume) (print and HeinOnline)

---

[38] In a worst-case scenario, regulations lag several years behind statutes. For example, the regulations for I.R.C. § 501(c)(9) were issued in 1980 while the provision was enacted in 1928. Even if regulations do exist, they may not reflect amended Code language.

[39] See, e.g., *United States v. Nesline*, 590 F. Supp. 884 (D. Md. 1984), holding invalid a regulation that varied from the plain language of the statute and had no support in the committee reports; cf. *Tutor-Saliba Corp. v. Commissioner*, 115 T.C. 1 (2000), holding that a regulation comported with congressional intent.

[40] The Treasury Department and IRS cite to legislative history in administrative documents. See, e.g., T.D. 8810, 64 Fed. Reg. 3398 (1999) (conference report); Rev. Rul. 88–64, 1988–2 C.B. 10 (statement during floor debate).

[41] For example, Code cross-reference tables list 1939 Code § 23(aa)(1) as the predecessor of 1954 Code § 141. However, 1986 Code § 141 deals with an entirely different topic. 1954 Code § 141 corresponds to 1986 Code § 63(c). Bloomberg Law: Tax, Checkpoint, and Westlaw Edge have separate files for the initial versions of the 1939 and 1954 Codes. Cheetah shows the final versions of the 1939 and 1954 Codes in its Archived Tax Code file.

- Cumulative Changes (1954 Code volume I) (print)
- Joint Committee on Taxation, Derivations of Code Sections of the Internal Revenue Codes of 1939 and 1954 (JCS–1–92) (Jan. 21, 1992) (JCT website) (derived from tables in Statutes at Large, volumes 53 and 68A)
- Legislative History of the Internal Revenue Code of 1954 (print and HeinOnline)
- Mertens, Law of Federal Income Taxation—Code (1954–58 Code volume) (1954 to 1939 only) (print)
- Rabkin & Johnson, Federal Income, Gift and Estate Taxation (volume 7B) (print)
- Seidman's Legislative History of Federal Income and Excess Profits Tax Laws (1953–1939 volume II) (print and HeinOnline)
- Standard Federal Tax Reporter (Code volume I in print; in Cheetah in the Current Internal Revenue Code file under Finding Lists>Cross-Reference Table I (1939 to 1954) and II (1954 to 1939))
- United States Statutes at Large (Appendix in volume 68A following text of 1954 Code) (print and HeinOnline)

Illustration 6-16. Excerpt from Seidman's Code References Table I

1954 CODE REFERENCES

[1953 Code section index precedes subject index]

TABLE I

1953 CODE SEC.	1954 CODE SEC.	1953 CODE SEC.	1954 CODE SEC.	1953 CODE SEC.	1954 CODE SEC.
13(a)	—	23(n)	167	44	453, 7101
15(a)	11	23(o)(1)-(5)	170	45	482
15(c)	1551	23(p)	404	46	442
21	63	23(q)(1)-(3)	170	47(b)-(c)	443, 6011(a)
22(a)	61	23(r)(1)	591	48	441, 7701

→ Seidman's ceased publication when the 1954 Code was adopted. Its 1953–1954 table reflects the initial version of the 1954 Code. It does not reflect any section renumbered in a later year. This table is page 3005 of 1953–1939 volume II.

Illustration 6-17. Excerpt from Cheetah Cross Reference Table I

47(a)	443, 6011(a)
47(c)	443
47(e)	443
47(g)	443

b. Tracing Pre-1939 Statutes

You can use these tools to trace provisions that predate the 1939 Code:

- Barton's Federal Tax Laws Correlated (print and HeinOnline)
- Joint Committee on Taxation, Derivations of Code Sections of the Internal Revenue Codes of 1939 and 1954 (JCS–1–92) (Jan. 21, 1992) (JCT website)
- Seidman's Legislative History of Federal Income and Excess Profits Tax Laws (print and HeinOnline)
- United States Statutes at Large (Appendix in volume 53 (pt. 1) following text of 1939 Code) (separate tables trace sections predating the Revised Statutes of 1875 back to their origin) (print and HeinOnline) [Illustration 6-18]

Illustration 6-18. Derivation of 1939 Code in 53 Statutes at Large

Part I—Reference Tables

TABLE A.—*Derivation of Internal Revenue Code*

[*=Amending statute. †=Reenacting statute. ‡=Adding statute.]

I. R. C. section	Date	Volume	Page	Chapter	Section
1, page 4	1938, May 28	52	452	289	1.
2....do.	....do.	52	452	289	2.
3....do.	....do.	52	452	289	3.
4....do.	....do.	52	452	289	4.
11	....do.	52	452	289	11.
12	....do.	52	453	289	12.
13	....do.	52	455	289	13.
14	....do.	52	456	289	14.
15	....do.	52	457	289	15.
21	....do.	52	457	289	21.
22 (a)–(l)	....do.	52	457	289	22.
22 (l)					
23	1938, May 28	52	460	289	23.

→ This table is on the page v that follows page 504, not on the first page v.

G. Legislative History Collections

This section provides additional information about several legislative history services discussed at various points in this chapter. Each began as a bound or looseleaf print service. These collections are useful for researching material that predates the government's move to electronic access. Unfortunately, they are no longer being published.

1. Barton's Federal Tax Laws Correlated

Five hardbound volumes trace income, estate, and gift tax provisions from the Revenue Act of 1913[42] through 1952. A sixth looseleaf volume covers the 1954 Code, including amendments through the Tax Reform Act of 1969. Barton's is no longer being published, but it is available in HeinOnline.

a. 1909–1952

Barton's reproduces in Code or act section order the text of the various tax acts. Because the acts are lined up in several columns on each page, you can read across a

[42] The original second edition (vol. 1) also contained the text of the income tax laws from 1861 through 1909. The reproduced second edition omits this material.

page and see every version of a particular section for the period that volume covers.[43] Barton's often uses different typefaces to highlight changes.

Illustration 6-19. Tracing Statutory Changes in Barton's

INDIVIDUAL CREDITS AGAINST NET INCOME. 65

Act of 1932.	**Act of 1928.**	**Act of 1926.**
Sec. 25. Credits of individual against net income. There shall be allowed for the purpose of the normal tax, but not for the surtax, the following credits against the net income:	**Sec. 25. Credits of Individual Against Net Income.** There shall be allowed for the purpose of the normal tax, but not for the surtax, the following credits against the net income:	CREDITS ALLOWED INDIVIDUALS. **Sec. 216.** For the purpose of the normal tax only there shall be allowed the following credits:
Sec. 25. (a) Dividends.—The amount received as dividends—	**Sec. 25. (a) Dividends.**—The amount received as dividends—	**Sec. 216. (a)** The amount received as dividends (1) from a domestic corporation other than a corporation entitled to the benefits of section 262 [100], and other than a corporation organized under the
Sec. 25. (a) (1) from a domestic corporation which is subject to taxation under this title, or	**Sec. 25. (a) (1)** from a domestic corporation, or	

→ Congress changed the statutory language in both 1928 and 1932 and renumbered the section in 1928.

The first two volumes provide a citation to Statutes at Large for each act. Volume 1 includes case annotations, and each volume has a subject matter index. The volumes covering the 1939 Code include tables indicating amending acts and effective dates for 1939 Code sections. Volume 5 has a retrospective table cross-referencing sections to pages in the four previous volumes.

b. 1953–1969

The looseleaf sixth volume does not print the text of Code sections. Its tables instead provide citations to primary sources that print the desired material. Tables A–D are in Code section order; Table E is in Public Law number order.

Table A provides the history of the 1954 Act. It indicates Statutes at Large page; House, Senate, and Conference report page (official and U.S. Code Congressional & Administrative News); 1939 Code counterpart; Revenue Act where the provision originated; and relevant pages in volumes 1–5. Table C is similar to Table A, but it covers the 1939 Code. It gives the 1954 Code section, the origin of the 1939 Code provision, and cross-references to volumes 1 through 5.

Table B covers amendments to the 1954 Code. For each section, it provides Public Law number, section, and enactment date; Statutes at Large citation; House, Senate, and Conference report numbers and location in the Cumulative Bulletin; comment (e.g., revision, amendment); and effective date information. A Supplement to Table B covers the Tax Reform Act of 1969. Table D is the same as Table B, but it covers post-1953 changes to the 1939 Code.

Table E [Illustration 6-10, *supra* page 80] provides citations to legislative history for all acts from 1953 through 1969. It also provides the following information for each act: Public Law number; date of enactment; congressional session; Statutes at Large, Cumulative Bulletin, and USCCAN citations for the act; congressional sessions, dates,

[43] Volume 1 covers 1913–1925; volume 2 covers 1926–1938; volume 3 covers 1939–1943; volume 4 covers 1944–1949; volume 5 covers 1950–1953; volume 6 covers 1954–1969. Although volume 5 is entitled 1950–1953, it ends with 1952 legislation. Volume 6 includes 1953 legislation.

and Cumulative Bulletin and USCCAN citations for House, Senate, and Conference reports; and Congressional Record citations for floor debate. Acts are not cited by popular name.

2. Seidman's Legislative History of Federal Income and Excess Profits Tax Laws

Seidman's stops in 1953, but it remains useful for determining the legislative history of provisions that originated in the 1939 Code or even earlier.[44] The two volumes covering 1939 through 1953 include both taxes. Separate volumes for the income tax and the excess profits tax were used for the earlier materials, covering 1861 through 1938 and 1917 through 1946, respectively. Seidman's is no longer being published, but it is available in HeinOnline.

Seidman's follows each act, beginning with the most recent, presenting the text of Code sections, followed by relevant committee reports and citations to hearings and the Congressional Record. In some cases, Seidman's excerpts these documents. [See Illustrations 6-9 (*supra* page 78) and 6-20 (*infra* page 91).] Seidman's uses different typefaces to show where in Congress a provision originated or was deleted.

Seidman's prints proposed sections that were not enacted along with relevant history explaining their omission. This information can aid you in interpreting provisions Congress did enact.

Although its coverage has great breadth, Seidman's does not print every Code section. It omits provisions with no legislative history, items lacking substantial interpretive significance, and provisions the editor considered long outmoded. Seidman's does not cover gift, estate, or excise taxes.

Seidman's has three indexes. The Code section index lists each section by act and assigns it a key number. The same key number is assigned to corresponding sections in subsequent acts. The key number index indicates every act, by section number and page in the text, where the item involved appears. A subject index lists key numbers by topic. A table in Volume II of the 1953–1939 set cross-references 1953 and 1954 Code sections covered in Seidman's. [See Illustration 6-16, *supra* page 87.]

---

[44] I.R.C. § 263, for example, contains language taken almost verbatim from § 117 of the 1864 Act. See Act of June 30, 1864, ch. 173, 13 Stat. 223, 281–82.

Illustration 6-20. Statutory Language and History in Seidman's

460 **1932 ACT** [See inside back cover

Sec. 113(b)(1)(B)

[SEC. 113. ADJUSTED BASIS FOR DETERMINING GAIN OR LOSS.]

[(b) Adjusted Basis.—* * *]

[(1) **General Rule.**—Proper adjustment in respect of the property shall in all cases be made—]

(B) in respect of any period since February 28, 1913, for exhaustion, wear and tear, obsolescence, amortization, and depletion ~~(computed without regard to discovery value or percentage depletion)~~, to the extent allowed (but not less than the amount allowable) under this Act or prior income tax ~~laws;~~ *laws. Where for any taxable year prior to the taxable year 1932 the depletion allowance was based on discovery value or a percentage of income, then the adjustment for depletion for such year shall be based on the depletion which would have been allowable for such year if computed without reference to discovery value or a percentage of income;*

Committee Reports

Report—Ways and Means Committee (72d Cong., 1st Sess., H. Rept. 708).— The subparagraph lettered (B) in the prior act has been separated into two subparagraphs lettered (B) and (C), to ductions. While the committee does not regard the existing law as countenancing any such inequitable results, it believes the new bill should specifically preclude any such possibility. (p.22)

→ Note how Seidman's indicates changes in statutory language.

3. Internal Revenue Acts of the United States: 1909–1950; 1950–

The original series, edited by Bernard D. Reams, Jr., provides comprehensive coverage of the legislative history documents discussed in this chapter. In addition to each congressional version of revenue bills, the 144 original volumes (1909–1950) contain the full texts of hearings, committee reports, Treasury studies, and regulations. Official pagination is retained for relevant documents. In addition to income and excise taxes, this set includes estate and gift, social security, railroad retirement, and unemployment taxes. This set is available in print, microfiche, and HeinOnline.

An Index volume contains several indexes for locating relevant materials. A chronological index lists each act and every item comprising its legislative history. That index indicates the volume, but not the page, where each item is located.[45] Other indexes cover miscellaneous subjects, such as hearings on items that did not result in legislation; Treasury studies; Joint Committee reports; regulations; congressional reports; congressional documents; bill numbers; and hearings. Unfortunately, there is neither a Code section nor a subject matter index.

Full-text materials appear by type of document rather than by the act involved. All hearings are printed together, as are all bills, laws, studies, and regulations. If you use the print version, you will need to use several volumes to assemble all materials for a particular law or provision. This is by no means a substantial drawback to using this set;

[45] These volumes are not consecutively paginated, so neither a detailed table of contents nor an index will lead you to the correct page. Although you will have to page through the particular print volume to reach the material you seek, that is a minor inconvenience.

assembling the same materials from elsewhere in the collection (assuming they are all available) would be far more difficult.

Professor Reams subsequently compiled materials to extend this set's coverage to later years. The later volumes are similar in coverage and format to the 1909–1950 materials, but hearings receive less attention.

The 1954 volumes include committee reports, hearings, debates, and the final act. Revenue bills and Treasury studies do not appear. Because the IRS Cumulative Bulletins do not cover the 1954 Act, these materials are particularly valuable. A two-volume update published in 1993 includes 50 House and Senate bills missing from the original volumes.

Other sets cover 1950–51, 1953–72, 1969, 1971, 1975, 1976, 1980, 1984, 1985 (Balanced Budget), 1986, 1987 (Balanced Budget), 1988, 1990, and 1993. Additional sets were edited by William Manz. They cover the Balanced Budget Act of 1997, the Taxpayer Relief Act of 1997, the Internal Revenue Service Restructuring and Reform Act of 1998, the Economic Growth and Tax Relief Reconciliation Act of 2001, the Tax Relief, Unemployment Insurance Reauthorization, and Job Creation Act of 2010, the Foreign Account Tax Compliance Act, the American Taxpayer Relief Act of 2012, the Bipartisan Budget Act of 2013, the Protecting Americans from Tax Hikes Act of 2015, and the Alternative Minimum Tax. These sets and others, some of which are compiled by government agencies and others by law firms, are available in HeinOnline as part of its Taxation & Economic Reform in America library. The electronic versions are easier to navigate than their print counterparts.

4. Eldridge, The United States Internal Revenue Tax System

This reprint of early legislative materials includes texts of revenue acts passed through 1894. The book contains extensive textual material, annotations for the various acts, and a descriptive history of the various acts. Hein reprinted this volume in 1994. It is available online in The Making of Modern Law: Legal Treatises 1800–1926 and in HeinOnline.

Illustration 6-21. Excerpt from Internal Revenue Acts of the United States Index Volume

REVENUE ACTS OF 1926 AND 1928

Volume

1930 AMENDMENT TO THE REVENUE ACTS OF 1926 AND 1928

SLIP LAW

Public resolution No. 88, 71st Cong., (H.J.Res. 340): joint resolution extending the time for the assessment, refund, and credit of income taxes for 1927 and 1928 in the case of married individuals having community income. Approved June 16, 1930. 46 Stat. 589 98

REPORTS

Extension of period of limitation in case of community income. Report. H.Rpt. 71-1608. May 23, 1930 98

Extension of period of limitation in case of community income. Report. S.Rpt. 71-888. June 9, 1930 98

HEARINGS

Extension of period of limitation in case of community income. Hearings before the Committee on Ways and Means, House of Representatives, 71st Cong., 2d session on H.J.Res. 340. May 21, 1930 58

5. Legislative History of the Internal Revenue Code of 1954

Prepared for the Joint Committee on Internal Revenue Taxation in 1967, this volume tracks all changes to the 1954 Code through October 23, 1965. It is arranged in Code section order and provides full text of the original 1954 language and all changes. It also includes ancillary provisions (both in other parts of U.S.C. and not in U.S.C.) and citations to Statutes at Large. There are four tables: 1939 Code sources of each 1954 provision; corresponding sections of the two Codes; post-1954 amendments to the 1939 Code; and amendatory statutes. The last table includes the Public Law number; date enacted; bill number; congressional report numbers; Act name; and Statutes at Large citation. This volume is available in HeinOnline.

6. Cumulative Changes

This multivolume looseleaf service tracks changes in the Code and Treasury regulations. There are series for the 1939, 1954, and 1986 Codes and regulations; many libraries lack the 1939 Code series. The service covered employment taxes; it had limited coverage of excise taxes.

The Code and regulations materials appear separately, arranged in Code section order. The 1954 service includes parallel citation tables for the 1939 and 1954 Codes.

A chart for each Code section indicates its original effective date. The chart includes the Public Law number, section, and enactment and effective dates of each amendment and the act section prescribing the effective date. The chart covers Code section subdivisions (subsections, paragraphs, and even smaller subdivisions). It does not include Statutes at Large citations.

The format of Cumulative Changes changed slightly in the mid-1990s. The later format gives citations for dates rather than the dates themselves. Illustration 6-22 includes both formats for Code section 51.

Illustration 6-22. Excerpt from Cumulative Changes

[See definitions preceding chart on page 1 of this section.]

SEC. 51 '86 I.R.C.	SUBSECTIONS					
	(f)—(h)	(i)(1)	(i)(2)	(i)(3)	(j)	(k)
Pub. Law 99-514. 10-22-86				Added by 1701(c) 1701(e)* Note 1		Redesig. 1878(f)(1) 1881* Note 1
AMENDING ACTS						
Pub. Law 103-66 8-10-93		13302(d) 13303* 8-10-93				

Public Law	Law Sec.	IRC Sec.	Eff. Date
P.L. 104-188	1201(a)	51(a)	1201(g)*
	1201(e)(1)	51(a)	1201(g)*
	1201(f)	51(c)(1)	1201(g)*
	1201(d)	51(c)(4)	1201(g)*

The pages following each chart reproduce each version (except the most recent one enacted before RIA stopped updating the service) since the provision's original introduction in the relevant Code.

7. Primary Sources

Primary Sources presents legislative history information for 1954 and 1986 Code sections and the Employee Retirement Income Security Act (ERISA). Unfortunately, its usefulness is limited to the period from 1969 to 2003. Materials presented for each Code section include presidential messages, committee reports, Treasury Department testimony at hearings, and discussion printed in Congressional Record.

The legislative histories were published in several series, each of which covers several years. Series I begins with sections affected by the Tax Reform Act of 1969; Series II, with the 1976 Tax Reform Act; Series III, with the Revenue Act of 1978; Series IV, with the Economic Recovery Tax Act of 1981; Series V, with the Tax Reform Act of 1986. Series I includes the 1939 Code version for many Code sections. Material appears in Code section order. Each series contains a Master Table of Contents in Code section order; these tables cover the current series and all prior series.

Illustration 6-23. Excerpt from Primary Sources, Series IV

IV-26 §168 [1981] pg.(i)

SEC. 168 – ACCELERATED COST RECOVERY SYSTEM

Table of Contents

	Page
STATUTE — [As Added by the Economic Recovery Tax Act of 1981 (P.L. 97-34)]	§ 168 [1981] pg. 1
LEGISLATIVE HISTORY	
Background	
97th Congress, 1st Sess. (H.R. 3849)	
Treasury Dept. Tech. Explanation of H.R. 3849	§ 168 [1981] pg. 28
House of Representatives	
Ways and Means Committee	
Committee Hearings	
Statement of Donald Regan, Sec'y of Treasury	§ 168 [1981] pg. 34
Committee Report	§ 168 [1981] pg. 35

H. Judicial Deference

Although judicial opinions cite legislative history documents in deciding between conflicting statutory interpretations, many judges prefer to resolve cases based on the so-called "plain meaning" of the statute. Those judges may give more deference to Treasury regulations than to legislative history if the statute is deemed ambiguous.[46]

The following items illustrate judicial statements regarding the deference courts give legislative history. Several of these statements reiterate statements made in earlier cases.

- "Delving into the legislative history is unnecessary because the statutes' language is unambiguous." *United States v. Farley*, 202 F.3d 198, 210 (3d Cir. 2000).
- "While the court makes its holding under the plain meaning rule of statutory construction, the court's conclusion is supported by the predecessor to § 402(a) which was § 165(b) of the I.R.C. of 1939 which had its beginnings in § 219(f) of the Internal Revenue Act of 1921." *Shimota v. United States*, 21 Cl. Ct. 510, 518 (1990).
- "The language of the statute leaves us with uncertainty . . . . The Secretary has not issued any regulations under section 613(e)(3), that might have provided guidance. We look to the legislative history behind the statute for assistance." *Newborn v. Commissioner*, 94 T.C. 610, 627 (1990).
- "Indications of congressional intent contained in a conference committee report deserve great deference by courts because 'the conference report represents the final statement of terms agreed to by both houses, [and] next to the statute itself it is the most persuasive evidence of congressional

---

[46] Deference to administrative interpretations is discussed in Chapters 8 and 9. Even if not accorded deference for purposes of resolving an issue, committee reports, managers' statements in the conference report, pre-enactment floor statements by one of a bill's managers, and the Bluebook all constitute authority for purposes of avoiding the substantial understatement penalty discussed in Chapter 2.

intent.'" *RJR Nabisco, Inc. v. United States*, 955 F.2d 1457, 1462 (11th Cir. 1992).

- "Blue Books are prepared by the staff of the Joint Committee on Taxation as commentaries on recently passed tax laws. They are 'written after passage of the legislation and therefore d[o] not inform the decisions of the members of Congress who vot[e] in favor of the [law].' We have held that such '[p]ost-enactment legislative history (a contradiction in terms) is not a legitimate tool of statutory interpretation.' While we have relied on similar documents in the past, . . . our more recent precedents disapprove of that practice. Of course the Blue Book, like a law review article, may be relevant to the extent it is persuasive." *United States v. Woods*, 571 U.S. 31, 47–48 (2013) (citations omitted).
- "Congress conveys its directions in the Statutes at Large, not in excerpts from the Congressional Record, much less in excerpts from the Congressional Record that do not clarify the text of any pending legislative proposal." *Begier v. Internal Revenue Service*, 496 U.S. 53, 68 (1990) (Scalia, J., concurring).
- "While Congress's later view as to the meaning of pre-existing law does not seal the outcome when addressing a question of statutory interpretation, it should not be discounted when relevant." *Sorrell v. Commissioner*, 882 F.2d 484, 489 (11th Cir. 1989).
- "While headings are not compelling evidence of meaning in themselves, the corresponding section of the Senate report clarifies and reinforces this analysis. That section is headed 'Production, acquisition, and *carrying* costs' (emphasis added) and expresses the intent that 'a single, comprehensive set of rules should govern the capitalization of costs of producing, acquiring, and *holding* property' (emphasis added)." *Reichel v. Commissioner*, 112 T.C. 14, 18 (1999).
- "Surrounding sentences are context for interpreting a sentence, but so is the history behind the sentence—where the sentence came from, what problem it was written to solve, who drafted it, who opposed its inclusion in the statute." *Sundstrand Corp. v. Commissioner*, 17 F.3d 965, 967 (7th Cir. 1994).
- "We also find the Government's reading more faithful to the history of the statutory provision as well as the basic tax-related purpose that the history reveals." *O'Gilvie v. United States*, 519 U.S. 79, 84 (1996).
- "Legislative history that is inconclusive, however, should not be relied upon to supply a provision not enacted by Congress." *St. Laurent v. Commissioner*, T.C. Memo. 1996–150, at *13.

I. Problems

Unless instructed otherwise by your instructor, use any government website to answer Problems 1 through 4.

1. Who introduced the following bill? What I.R.C. section would it add or amend?

   a. H.R. 4902, 98th Cong.

b. H.R. 2445, 111th Cong.

c. H.R. 286, 113th Cong.

d. H.R. 6233, 116th Cong.

2. Indicate the proposed short title and the last action listed for the bill described below.

a. H.R. 8, 109th Cong.

b. H.R. 6410, 112th Cong.

c. H.R. 3894, 113th Cong.

d. H.R.6760, 115th Cong.

3. Indicate the bill number, any proposed short title, and congressional session for a bill that would

a. Require animal abusers to use the alternative depreciation system.

b. Provide tax rate parity for different types of tobacco products.

4. The following questions concern current I.R.C. § 162(e).

a. Was there a version of § 162(e) in the Internal Revenue Code of 1954?

b. When did the most recent amendment to § 162(e) take place, and what legislation made the change? Include the section of the Public Law that made the change.

c. Was there a report on the most recent amendment to § 162(e) issued by the House Ways and Means Committee? By the Senate Finance Committee? By a Conference of the House and Senate? For each report, give its number.

d. Locate the House Ways and Means Committee Report you identified in part (c) above. Examine the portion of the House Ways and Means Committee Report that explains the change to § 162(e). (Hint: to locate the discussion of the change in the Committee Report, go to the BUSINESS TAX REFORM section of the report's CONTENTS pages.) What change did Congress make in this most recent amendment to § 162(e), and what was its rationale for doing so?

5. Using any source, indicate the 1939 I.R.C. counterparts to the 1954 I.R.C. sections listed below.

a. 3

b. 1001

c. 1347

d. 5179

6. In the Tax Reform Act of 1986 (Pub. L. No. 99–514), Congress amended I.R.C. § 164 to eliminate the deduction by individuals of state and local general sales taxes. Using BNA's *Primary Sources*, answer the following questions.

a. What language in § 164 authorized the deduction of state and local general sales taxes prior to the 1986 amendment?

b. According to the Senate Finance Committee Report on the amendment, what was the primary reason for eliminating this deduction? Give a full citation for your authority.

7. Section 322(b)(2) of the 1939 I.R.C. is one of the predecessors of current § 6511(b)(2). Using *Seidman's Legislative History*, answer the following questions.

a. Provide the report numbers for the reports issued by the House Ways and Means Committee and the Senate Finance Committee in connection with the 1942 amendments to § 322(b)(2).

b. Was there any testimony concerning the 1942 changes in hearings before the Senate Finance Committee? If so, provide the name(s) of the person(s) who testified and the page numbers within the transcripts where the testimony appears.

8. You are researching the legislative history of I.R.C. § 1033(a) for business property. Assume that § 1033(a) was part of the 1954 I.R.C. Using *Barton's Federal Tax Laws Correlated* for the source of legislative history, answer the following questions.

a. In what Revenue Act did the first statutory predecessor of § 1033(a) originate?

b. What section of that Revenue Act was the first statutory predecessor, and where in *Barton's* could you find the language of that provision? (Hint: use Table A in Volume 6 of *Barton's*.)

Chapter 7

TREATIES AND OTHER INTERNATIONAL MATERIAL

A. Introduction

This chapter discusses treaties and other documents you can consult when researching the treatment of taxpayers with ties to both the United States and another country.

Treaties are agreements between two (bilateral) or more (multilateral) countries. If the United States has a tax treaty with another country, that document probably applies to your international research project, but it is not the only relevant document. You may also need to locate statutes; congressional, State Department, and presidential documents; regulations; rulings; and judicial opinions.

Treaties are not the only bilateral agreements to which the United States is a party. In certain cases, your research will involve agreements that do not require ratification by the Senate.

In addition to sources of relevant United States law, your research is likely to involve the treaty partner's internal law. In appropriate situations, you may also have to consult documents issued by international organizations, including the United Nations, the Organisation for Economic Co-operation and Development (OECD), and the World Trade Organization (WTO).

Your goals include locating all relevant documents, determining their relative hierarchy and validity, and updating your research to encompass pending items. In accomplishing these goals, you should become familiar with the process by which treaties and other international agreements enter into force and the terminology used to describe treaty documents. You must also take into account changes in sovereignty. Newly independent or merged countries are not always covered by a treaty between the United States and the country with which they were formerly (or are currently) affiliated.

B. Functions of Treaties

Although United States citizens residing abroad pay United States income tax on both domestic and foreign-source income, they may also be taxed in the foreign country of residence. Similar problems may arise with regard to property and transfer taxes. Several statutory mechanisms exist to reduce the burden of taxation by more than one country. These include credits or deductions for certain foreign taxes and exclusions for certain foreign-source income.[1] Treaties between the United States and other countries may also limit harsh tax consequences.

Treaties serve other tax-related purposes. These include promoting trade by reducing tariffs and reducing tax evasion through exchanges of information with other countries. Although the United States may have separate income, estate, gift, and other

[1] I.R.C. §§ 27, 164(a), 911, 912 & 2014.

tax treaties with a given country, in many instances the only tax treaty will be that covering income.

C. Relationship of Treaties and Statutes

1. Authority for Treaties

Treaties are authorized by the Constitution. Article II, section 2, clause 2, provides that the President "shall have Power, by and with the Advice and Consent of the Senate, to make Treaties, provided two thirds of the Senators present concur . . . ." Article VI, clause 2, includes both statutes and treaties as the "supreme Law of the Land."

2. Conflict Between Treaties and Statutes

In determining which governs a transaction, neither a treaty nor a statute automatically receives preferential treatment by virtue of its status. As noted, the Constitution includes both treaties and statutes as the "supreme Law of the Land." While normally the "last in time" rule applies to reconcile conflicts between a treaty and a statute, that rule does not always apply.

In enacting Code sections, Congress can decide that treaty provisions will override statutory rules governing income earned (or property transferred) abroad by a United States citizen or resident or transactions undertaken in this country by a foreign national.[2] Congress can also provide that statutory rules will apply instead of treaty language.

In addition, treaties can be overruled by a later statute, by a later treaty, or by treaty termination. Statutory repeal is an extraordinary step, taken in the 1986 Act for cases of treaty shopping.[3] Section J includes several judicial decisions discussing the interplay between statutes and treaties.

D. Terminology

1. Treaties

Treaties are often referred to as **conventions**. They are generally amended by documents called **protocols**. Because there may be a long delay before a signed treaty is actually ratified, a pending treaty may be amended several times before it goes into force. A treaty may also be amended after it **enters into force**. Congress may consider protocols along with the original treaty or at a later date.

The Senate can consent to the treaty as signed by the parties or it can express **reservations**. If the countries involved accept these reservations, the treaty process goes forward. If they do not, the treaty may be renegotiated or it may effectively die. A **ratified treaty** enters into force only after the governments exchange **instruments of**

---

[2] See I.R.C. §§ 894 & 7852(d). Disclosure requirements apply to taxpayers who claim that a tax treaty overrules or modifies an internal revenue law. I.R.C. § 6114; Treas. Reg. § 301.6114–1; IRS Form 8833. See also I.R.C. § 7701(b) (definition of resident alien and nonresident alien); Treas. Reg. § 301.7701(b)–7 (coordination with income tax treaties).

[3] Pub. L. No. 99–514, § 1241(a), 100 Stat. 2085, 2576 (1986), modified for income tax treaties in 1988 by Pub. Law. No. 100–647, § 1012(q)(2)(A), 102 Stat. 3342, 3523. I.R.C. § 884(e)(1) currently reads: "No treaty between the United States and a foreign country shall exempt any foreign corporation from the tax imposed by subsection (a) . . . unless—(A) such treaty is an income tax treaty, and (B) such foreign corporation is a qualified resident of such foreign country."

ratification. A treaty that has been signed but which has not undergone whatever actions are necessary to bring it into force is **unperfected**.

Each treaty partner designates a **competent authority** to resolve disputes that may arise over which country has jurisdiction to tax an item. The competent authorities may enter into a **memorandum of understanding**; it is not part of the treaty ratification process.

As was true for statutes, you must take note of **effective dates**. A treaty can become effective on the date it enters into force, at a later date, or even at an earlier date. Different treaty provisions may become effective at different dates. If a treaty is later amended by a protocol, the protocol is subject to the ratification process that applied to the original treaty and may have its own set of date limitations.

2. Executive Agreements

The United States also enters into agreements that do not require the advice and consent of the Senate for their validity. These so-called **international agreements other than treaties** are often referred to as **executive agreements**.[4] These agreements include competent authority agreements, tax information exchange agreements and, more recently, intergovernmental agreements implementing the Foreign Account Tax Compliance Act (FATCA).

Some types of international agreement are authorized by statute. For example, social security totalization agreements are authorized by 42 U.S.C. § 433. The President can enter into these agreements, which go into effect unless either the House of Representatives or the Senate adopts a resolution of disapproval within the time limit specified in the statute.

E. Treaty Numbering Systems

Treaties are numbered in a variety of ways, depending on which source is involved. Relevant numbering systems are those used by the State Department, the Senate, and the United Nations.

The State Department assigns treaties a Treaties and Other International Acts Series (T.I.A.S.) number.[5] T.I.A.S. began in 1945. The government previously published treaties in Treaty Series (T.S.) (1–994) and in Executive Agreement Series (E.A.S.) (1–506). T.I.A.S. numbering begins at 1501 to reflect that it continues the other series. [See Table 7-A, *infra* page 102.] The last treaty numbered in this format was 13179 in 2001. Treaties and other agreements are now numbered by year, month, and day (e.g., TIAS 14-627, which entered into force on June 27, 2014).

A treaty also receives a Senate Executive Document number or a Senate Treaty Document number. The Senate Executive Document system assigned each treaty a letter and a number based on the Congress that received the treaty for ratification. The Senate Treaty Document nomenclature began in the 97th Congress; this system gives each

4 "Frequently Asked Questions" home page, U.S. DEP'T OF STATE, https://2009-2017.state.gov/s/l/treaty/faqs/70133.htm (last visited May 23, 2020). This information appears on an archived page rather than on the current state.gov webpage.

5 Treaties in Force uses the letters NP (not printed in Treaties and Other International Acts Series) to indicate treaties that will not be covered by T.I.A.S. If a treaty is part of T.I.A.S. but does not yet have a number, Treaties in Force prints "TIAS" with no further explanation.

treaty a number and also indicates in which Congress the Senate Foreign Relations Committee published its recommendation to the full Senate.

The United Nations numbering system applies to treaties registered with that body (United Nations Treaty Series (UNTS)). The United States is party to some, but not all, of these treaties.

You will rarely need to know treaty numbers if your goal is limited to finding a treaty. The sources noted in Section G let you locate treaties by country. The T.I.A.S. number is important if you are using Shepard's Federal Statute Citations to find decisions interpreting treaties through 1995. The print Shepard's stopped covering treaties at that point.

Table 7-A. Treaty Numbers for the 1980 Estate Tax Convention Between the United States and Germany

Numbering System	*Number*
State Department	TIAS 11082 (entered into force 6/27/1986)
Senate	S. Treaty Doc. No. 97–1
United Nations	Reg. No. I–36888, 2120 UNTS 283[6]

F. Treaty History Documents

The treaty history discussed in this section is illustrated by excerpts from documents for the income tax treaty between the United States and Denmark. These documents were obtained from the websites listed in Table 7-B, *infra* page 112. Section G lists other sources for treaty documents.

Treaties, in common with statutes, involve both legislative and executive branches of government. However, the order in which each group acts is reversed. Treaties begin with the executive branch and are negotiated by representatives of each government. Unlike bills, pending treaties do not expire at the end of a Congress.

Although State Department representatives are consulted, the Treasury Office of Tax Policy has primary responsibility for negotiating a tax treaty.[7] The treaty signing process has two steps. Changes can be made after a treaty is **initialed** but not after it has been **signed**. The Treasury Department issues a press release after a tax treaty has been signed.

The State Department submits the treaty to the President, asking that the treaty be transmitted to the Senate.[8] The letter from the State Department to the President is a **letter of submittal**; the letter from the President to the Senate is a **letter of transmittal**. The Senate Foreign Relations Committee receives the treaty and both letters. It issues a **Senate Treaty Document**, which contains all three documents.

---

[6] Treaties in Force lists the United Nations Treaty Series volume and page but not the UNTS-assigned treaty number.

[7] The treaty will be signed by a State Department official, not a Treasury official.

[8] The House of Representatives plays no role in the treaty ratification process. As noted in Section D.2, some agreements, such as those regarding social security, are transmitted to both the House and Senate but do not require ratification.

The Treasury Department prepares a **Technical Explanation** for use by the Senate Foreign Relations Committee. The Joint Committee on Taxation also issues reports. The Foreign Relations Committee holds hearings. The Committee issues a **Senate Executive Report** transmitting the treaty to the full Senate for ratification. Debate by the full Senate appears in the Congressional Record.

After the treaty is ratified by the appropriate government entities in each country, the countries exchange **instruments of ratification** and announce that the treaty has **entered into force**. The Treasury Department issues a press release announcing this information.

Some treaties involve more documents than others. For example, they may have protocols, diplomatic notes, or memorandums of understanding. As Table 7-B (*infra* page 112) indicates, individual government websites often cover only a few of the relevant documents. As a result, a treaty service is a better source for determining which documents exist and often for accessing those documents. Unfortunately, as is true for government sources, many subscription treaty services limit the type of documents they carry. Government websites and other services carrying treaties and treaty history documents are covered in Section G.

Illustration 7-1. Press Release Announcing Treaty Signing

Home » Press Center » Press Releases » UNITED STATES AND DENMARK SIGN NEW INCOME TAX TREATY

UNITED STATES AND DENMARK SIGN NEW INCOME TAX TREATY

8/19/1999

FROM THE OFFICE OF PUBLIC AFFAIRS

LS-64

The Treasury Department announced Thursday that Assistant Secretary for Tax Policy Donald C. Lubick and Danish Charg� daffaires Lars M�ller signed a new income tax Treaty between the United States and Denmark at the State Department in Washington. This tax Treaty, if ratified, will replace the current Treaty that entered into force on December 1, 1948, and will represent an important step toward achieving Treasurys goal of updating the United States existing tax treaty network.

→ Lawrence Summers (LS) was Secretary of the Treasury in 1999.

→ This document can be found in the Press Center section of the Treasury Department website (Archived Press Releases). The first (�) symbol is supposed to be an é; the second should be an ø.

Illustration 7-2. Letter of Submittal

LETTER OF SUBMITTAL

DEPARTMENT OF STATE,
Washington, September 7, 1999.

The PRESIDENT,
The White House.

THE PRESIDENT: I have the honor to submit to you, with a view to its transmission to the Senate for advice and consent to ratification, the Convention Between the Government of the United States of America and the Government of the Kingdom of Denmark for the Avoidance of Double Taxation and the Prevention of Fiscal Evasion with Respect to Taxes on Income, signed at Washington on August 19, 1999 ("the Convention"), together with a Protocol.

This Convention replaces the current convention between the United States of America and the Government of the Kingdom of Denmark signed at Washington on May 6, 1948. This proposed Convention generally follows the pattern of the U.S. Model Tax Treaty while incorporating some features of the OECD Model Tax Treaty and recent U.S. tax treaties with developed countries. The proposed Convention provides for maximum rates of tax to be applied to various types of income, protection from double taxation of income and exchange of information. It also contains rules making

→ Note the references to model tax treaties and other U.S. treaties.

Illustration 7-3. President's Letter of Transmittal

LETTER OF TRANSMITTAL

THE WHITE HOUSE, *September 21, 1999.*

To the Senate of the United States:

I transmit herewith for Senate advice and consent to ratification the Convention Between the Government of the United States of America and the Government of the Kingdom of Denmark for the Avoidance of Double Taxation and the Prevention of Fiscal Evasion with Respect to Taxes of Income, signed at Washington on August 19, 1999, together with a Protocol. Also transmitted for the information of the Senate is the report of the Department of State concerning the Convention.

It is my desire that the Convention and Protocol transmitted herewith be considered in place of the Convention for the Avoidance of Double Taxation, signed at Washington on June 17, 1980, and the Protocol Amending the Convention, signed at Washington on August 23, 1983, which were transmitted to the Senate with messages dated September 4, 1980 (S. Ex. Q, 96th Cong., 2d Sess.) and November 16, 1983 (T. Doc. No. 98–12, 98th Cong., 1st Sess.), and which are pending in the Committee on Foreign Relations. I desire, therefore, to withdraw from the Senate the Convention and Protocol signed in 1980 and 1983.

→ Note how long the prior proposed treaty was pending.

Illustration 7-4. Treasury Technical Explanation

DEPARTMENT OF THE TREASURY TECHNICAL EXPLANATION OF THE CONVENTION BETWEEN THE GOVERNMENT OF THE UNITED STATES OF AMERICA AND THE GOVERNMENT OF THE KINGDOM OF DENMARK FOR THE AVOIDANCE OF DOUBLE TAXATION AND THE PREVENTION OF FISCAL EVASION WITH RESPECT TO TAXES ON INCOME SIGNED AT WASHINGTON, AUGUST 19, 1999

GENERAL EFFECTIVE DATE UNDER ARTICLE 29: 1 JANUARY 2001

INTRODUCTION

This is a Technical Explanation of the Convention and Protocol between the United States and Denmark signed at Washington on August 19, 1999 (the "Convention" and "Protocol"). References are made to the Convention between the United States and Denmark for the Avoidance of Double Taxation and the Prevention of Fiscal Evasion with Respect to Taxes on Income signed at Washington, D.C., on May 6, 1948 (the "prior Convention"). The Convention replaces the prior Convention.

Negotiations took into account the U.S. Treasury Department's current tax treaty policy, as reflected in the U.S. Treasury Department's Model Income Tax Convention of September 20, 1996 (the "U.S. Model") and its recently negotiated tax treaties, the Model Income Tax Convention on Income and on Capital, published by the OECD in 1992 and amended in 1994, 1995 and 1997 (the "OECD Model"), and recent tax treaties concluded by Denmark.

The Technical Explanation is an official guide to the Convention and Protocol. It reflects the policies behind particular Convention provisions, as well as understandings reached with respect to the application and interpretation of the Convention and Protocol. In the discussions of

Illustration 7-5. JCT Explanation (JCS–8–99)

INTRODUCTION

This pamphlet,[1] prepared by the staff of the Joint Committee on Taxation, describes the proposed income tax treaty, as supplemented by the proposed protocol, between the United States of America and the Kingdom of Denmark ("Denmark"). The proposed treaty and proposed protocol were both signed on August 19, 1999.[2] The Senate Committee on Foreign Relations has scheduled a public hearing on the proposed treaty and proposed protocol on October 13, 1999.

Part I of the pamphlet provides a summary with respect to the proposed treaty and proposed protocol. Part II provides a brief overview of U.S. tax laws relating to international trade and investment and of U.S. income tax treaties in general. Part III contains an article-by-article explanation of the proposed treaty and proposed protocol. Part IV contains a discussion of issues with respect to the proposed treaty and proposed protocol.

Illustration 7-6. Hearings, S. HRG. 106–356

BILATERAL TAX TREATIES AND PROTOCOL: ESTONIA—TREATY DOC. 105–55; LATVIA—TREATY DOC. 105–57; VENEZUELA—TREATY DOC. 106–3; DENMARK—TREATY DOC. 106–12; LITHUANIA—TREATY DOC. 105–56; SLOVENIA—TREATY DOC. 106–9; ITALY—TREATY DOC. 106–11; GERMANY—TREATY DOC. 106–13

WEDNESDAY, OCTOBER 27, 1999

U.S. SENATE,
COMMITTEE ON FOREIGN RELATIONS,
Washington, DC.

The committee met, pursuant to notice, at 3:05 p.m. in room SD–419, Dirksen Senate Office Building, Hon. Chuck Hagel presiding.

Present: Senators Hagel and Sarbanes.

Senator HAGEL. Good afternoon.

The committee meets today to consider bilateral income tax treaties between the United States and Estonia, Latvia, Lithuania, Venezuela, Denmark, Italy, and Slovenia as well as an estate tax protocol with Germany.[1]

The United States has tax treaties with 59 countries. This global network of treaties is designed to protect U.S. taxpayers from double taxation and to provide the IRS with information and data to prevent tax evasion and avoidance.

The treaties prevent international double taxation by setting down rules to determine what country will have the primary right to tax income and at what rates. These bilateral international tax treaties are important for America's economic growth.

Illustration 7-7. Senate Foreign Relations Committee Executive Report

106TH CONGRESS *1st Session*	SENATE	EXEC. RPT. 106–9

TAX CONVENTION WITH DENMARK

NOVEMBER 3, 1999.—Ordered to be printed

Mr. HELMS, from the Committee on Foreign Relations, submitted the following

REPORT

[To accompany Treaty Doc. 106–12]

The Committee on Foreign Relations, to which was referred the Convention between the Government of the United States of America and the Government of the Kingdom of Denmark for the Avoidance of Double Taxation and the Prevention of Fiscal Evasion with Respect to Taxes on Income, signed at Washington on August 19, 1999, together with a Protocol, having considered the same, reports favorably thereon, with one declaration and one proviso, and recommends that the Senate give its advice and consent to ratification thereof, as set forth in this report and the accompanying resolution of ratification.

→ This document is in the govinfo.gov and the Congress.gov Congressional Reports collections.

Illustration 7-8. Senate Executive Report 106–9, at 5

> **The Congressional tax-writing committees and this Committee have made it clear in the past that treaties are not the appropriate vehicle for granting credits for taxes that might not otherwise be creditable under the Code or Treasury regulations. The Committee believes that it would be more appropriate for the United States to address unilaterally problems of the sort raised by special oil and gas taxes imposed by foreign countries. The Committee believes that treaties should not be used in the future to handle foreign tax credit issues which are more appropriately addressed either legislatively or administratively. Nevertheless, the Committee believes that given the circumstances surrounding the Danish hydrocarbon tax, it is justifiable to provide a credit for such tax in this case.**

→ Note the discussion of using treaties to grant tax credits.

Illustration 7-9. 145 Cong. Rec. (Bound) 28857–58 (1999)

> TAX CONVENTION WITH DENMARK
>
> The resolution of ratification is as follows:
>
> *Resolved, (two-thirds of the Senators present concurring therein),* That the Senate advise and consent to the ratification of the Convention between the Government of the United States of America and the Government of the Kingdom of Denmark for the Avoidance of Double Taxation and the Prevention of Fiscal Evasion with Respect to Taxes on Income, signed at Washington on August 19, 1999, together with a Protocol (Treaty Doc. 106-12), subject to the declaration of subsection (a) and the proviso of subsection (b).
>
> (a) DECLARATION.—The Senate's advice and consent is subject to the following declaration, which shall be binding on the President:
>
> (1) TREATY INTERPRETATION.—The Senate affirms the applicability to all treaties of the constitutionally based principles of treaty interpretation set forth in Condition (1) of the resolution of ratification of the INF Treaty, approved by the Senate on May 27, 1988, and Condition (8) of the resolution of ratification of the Document Agreed Among the States Parties to the Treaty on Conventional Armed Forces in Europe, approved by the Senate on May 14, 1997.
>
> (b) PROVISO.—The resolution of ratification is subject to the following proviso, which shall be binding on the President:
>
> (1) SUPREMACY OF CONSTITUTION.—Nothing in the Convention requires or authorizes legislation or other action by the United States of America that is prohibited by the Constitution of the United States as interpreted by the United States.

→ Note the limitations on the President in the Declaration and Proviso.

Illustration 7-10. Treaty as Transmitted to Senate

The Government of the United States of America and the Government of the Kingdom of Denmark, desiring to conclude a Convention for the avoidance of double taxation and the prevention of fiscal evasion with respect to taxes on income, have agreed as follows:

ARTICLE 1
General Scope

1. Except as otherwise provided in this Convention, this Convention shall apply to persons who are residents of one or both of the Contracting States.

2. This Convention shall not restrict in any manner any benefit now or hereafter accorded:
   a) by the laws of either Contracting State; or
   b) by any other agreement between the Contracting States.

3. Notwithstanding the provisions of subparagraph 2b):
   a) the provisions of Article 25 (Mutual Agreement Procedure) of this Convention exclusively shall apply to any dispute concerning whether a measure is within the scope of this Convention, and the procedures under this Convention exclusively shall apply to that dispute; and
   b) unless the competent authorities determine that a taxation measure is not within the scope of this Convention, the non-discrimination obligations of this Convention exclusively shall apply with respect to that measure, except for such national treatment or most-favored-nation obligations as may apply to trade in goods under the General Agreement on Tariffs and Trade. No national treatment or most-favored-nation obligation under any other agreement shall apply with respect to that measure.

→ The letters of submittal and transmittal are included in Treaty Doc. 106–12. It is available in the govinfo.gov Congressional Documents collection and in the Congress.gov Treaty Documents collection.

Illustration 7-11. Press Release That Treaty Entered into Force

FROM THE OFFICE OF PUBLIC AFFAIRS

April 3, 2000
LS-521

TREASURY ANNOUNCES EFFECTIVE DATES OF NEW TAX AGREEMENT WITH DENMARK

The Treasury Department on Monday announced that a new income tax treaty with Denmark entered into force on March 31, 2000. The treaty, to which the U.S. Senate gave advice and consent to ratification in November, 1999, replaces the existing tax treaty between the United States and Denmark, which was signed in 1948.

On March 31, Denmark notified the United States that Denmark had complied with the constitutional requirements for entry into force of the bilateral income tax treaty between the two countries. The United States had previously provided reciprocal notification to the Denmark, and accordingly, the treaties entered into force on March 31. The treaties apply, with respect to taxes withheld at source, in respect of amounts paid or credited on or after May 1, 2000 and, with regard to other taxes, in respect of taxable years beginning on or after January 1, 2001.

→ Note the different effective dates.

Illustration 7-12. Press Release for Protocol to Treaty

May 3, 2006
JS-4231

United States and Denmark Sign Protocol to Income Tax Treaty

Washington – Today the Treasury Department announced that U.S. Ambassador James P. Cain and Danish Tax Minister Kristian Jensen signed a new Protocol to amend the existing bilateral income tax treaty, concluded in 1999, between the two countries. The Protocol was signed Tuesday.

The agreement significantly reduces tax-related barriers to trade and investment flows between the United States and Denmark. It also modernizes the treaty to take account of changes in the laws and policies of both countries since the current treaty was signed. The Protocol brings the tax treaty relationship with Denmark into closer conformity with U.S. treaty policy.

The most important aspect of the Protocol deals with the taxation of cross-border dividend payments. The Protocol is one of a few recent U.S. tax agreements to provide for the elimination of the source-country withholding tax on dividends arising from certain direct investments and on dividends paid to pension funds. The Protocol also strengthens the treaty's provisions preventing so-called treaty shopping, which is the inappropriate use of a tax treaty by third-country residents.

→ John Snow (JS) was Secretary of the Treasury in May 2006.

→ Note the comment about conformity with U.S. treaty policy.

Illustration 7-13. Exchange of Notes in Connection with Protocol

Copenhagen, May 2, 2006

Excellency:

I have the honor to refer to the Protocol signed today between the Government of the United States of America and the Government of the Kingdom of Denmark Amending the Convention for the Avoidance of Double Taxation and the Prevention of Fiscal Evasion with Respect to Taxes on Income, and to confirm, on behalf of the Government of the United States of America, the following understandings reached between our two Governments.

In reference to clause a) (iv) of paragraph 3 of Article 10 (Dividends) of the Convention, as amended by the Protocol, it is understood that the U.S. competent authority generally will exercise its discretion to grant benefits under such paragraph to a company that is a resident of Denmark if:

→ The reference to Article 10 (Dividends) refers to the article numbering system in the original treaty.

→ Note the reference to how the competent authority will act with respect to dividends.

Illustration 7-14. Protocol to Treaty

ARTICLE II

1. Article 10 (Dividends) of the Convention shall be omitted and the following shall be substituted:

"ARTICLE 10

Dividends

1. Dividends paid by a resident of a Contracting State to a resident of the other Contracting State may be taxed in that other State.

→ Article II of the protocol amends Article 10 of the original treaty.

There are additional documents available for the protocol to this treaty. These include the letters of submittal and transmittal, Treasury Technical Explanation, the Joint Committee on Taxation Technical Explanation, the Senate Foreign Relations Committee report, testimony at hearings, and the press release announcing that the protocol had entered into force.

G. Locating Treaties and Their Histories

When a treaty goes into force, it is added to the State Department's Treaties and Other International Acts Series (T.I.A.S.). T.I.A.S. is the treaty equivalent of Statutes at Large; the treaty equivalent of United States Code is United States Treaties and Other International Agreements (U.S.T.).[9] Because the print official treaty publications have not been updated for many years, you should use other sources to obtain the text of recent treaties.

Tax treaties and their revising protocols are published in various places, several of which are limited to tax treaties. Many sources also provide access to at least some treaty history documents. Unfortunately, few sources provide access to all relevant information.

The sources below discuss the formats in which you can locate treaties and other documents. Your library may also carry them in microform.

[9] The government stopped publishing T.I.A.S. and U.S.T. in print after the 1983–84 volume of U.S.T. Documents numbered by year, month, and day now appear on the State Department website at https://www.state.gov/bureaus-offices/treaty-affairs. There is also a link to Treaties and International Agreements in the Policy Issues section of the State Department website. This site includes treaties and agreements included in T.I.A.S. that entered into force since 1996.

1. United States Government Sources

The IRS website,[10] which is arranged by country, includes PDF versions of income tax treaties that are in force; it does not include ratified treaties until they go into force. The site also includes Treasury Technical Explanations for many of the treaties. The IRS site also links to Publication 901. Publication 901 lists current treaties and provides information about how each treaty affects specific categories of taxpayers. The IRS site does not include congressional action, Joint Committee explanations, or press releases.

The Tax Policy link on the Treasury Department website (under Policy Issues) has a direct link to a Treaties and Tax Information Exchange Agreements (TIEAs) page. Alternatively, you can use the International Tax link to reach the treaties page. The International Tax page has three components. The Treaties and Tax Information Exchange Agreements link provides access to recently signed proposed treaties, protocols, and information exchange agreements, to Treasury Technical Explanations, and to the Model Income Tax Convention. The Foreign Account Tax Compliance Act (FATCA) link provides access to Treasury documents related to FATCA implementation. The Additional International Tax Documents link provides access to letters, Treasury testimony at hearings, and White Papers. Although the website descriptions of these links do not list other documents, you may be able to find diplomatic notes, press releases, and other documents using the website's search function. The Treasury website does not include all these items for every treaty, and it does not include congressional action. In addition, it does not include documents issued before November 1996. The Treaties and Tax Information Exchange Agreements page arranges items by date; FATCA agreements are listed after other agreements. It also has a by-country selection option. Documents are available in PDF format.

Govinfo.gov offers access to hearings, congressional debate, a treaty's congressional history, and committee reports for treaties. It also includes the letters of submittal and transmittal and treaty language. JCT explanations are available on the JCT site, Congress.gov, and govinfo.gov. The Congress.gov Treaty Documents section includes the treaty text, letters of submittal and transmittal, and all Senate actions (including any Resolution of Ratification). Coverage begins for the 81st Congress.

The weekly Internal Revenue Bulletin contains recent material. I.R.B. material was reprinted in the Cumulative Bulletin at six-month intervals through volume 2008–2; the C.B. then ceased publication. Because of their arrangement, these publications are more useful for finding IRS material relating to treaties than for finding the treaties themselves.[11] The I.R.B. is available online at the IRS website and through subscription online services. Print publication ceased in early 2013.

---

[10] https://www.irs.gov/businesses/international-businesses/united-states-income-tax-treaties-a-to-z (last visited July 18, 2020).

[11] See STAFF OF JT. COMM. ON TAX'N, 102D CONG., LISTING OF SELECTED INTERNATIONAL TAX CONVENTIONS AND OTHER AGREEMENTS REPRINTED IN THE IRS CUMULATIVE BULLETIN, 1913–1990 (JCS–20–91) (Jt. Comm. Print, Dec. 31, 1991), for citations to older treaty documents and administrative guidance. This document is available on the JCT website.

Table 7-B. Government Sites Providing Treaty Documents

Document	*Website*
Congressional Record	Congress.gov govinfo.gov
Diplomatic Notes	Congress.gov Treasury.gov
Hearings	Congress.gov govinfo.gov Treasury.gov[12]
JCT Explanations	Congress.gov govinfo.gov JCT.gov
Letters of Submittal and Transmittal	Congress.gov govinfo.gov[13]
Press Releases	Treasury.gov
Senate Executive Report	Congress.gov govinfo.gov
Senate Treaty Document	Congress.gov govinfo.gov
Treasury Technical Explanation	IRS.gov Treasury.gov
Treaty and Protocol Texts	Congress.gov govinfo.gov IRS.gov Treasury.gov

2. Subscription Services

Subscription services that cover treaty materials are available in a variety of formats. In addition to online coverage of treaty documents, many services also provide a print or microform version of these documents. Other services are limited to a single format. The discussion below indicates available formats.

a. CCH Tax Treaties Reporter

The CCH Tax Treaties Reporter looseleaf service is available in print and on Cheetah.[14] It reproduces texts of United States income and estate tax treaties, exchange

[12] The Treasury website includes only Treasury Department testimony.

[13] These are included in the govinfo.gov Presidential Documents collection and the Senate Treaty Documents collection. The Senate Treaty Documents collection is part of the Congressional Documents collection.

[14] Cheetah offers an International Tax Suite, which includes the U.S. Tax Treaties Reporter, the World Tax Treaties Reporter, several international-focused treatises, and several practice tools. This material can be accessed on Cheetah's Tax-International tab. In Cheetah, the treaty information is nested under Tax-

of information agreements, shipping and air transport treaties, social security agreements, and FATCA agreements. It reproduces selected treaty documents, including letters of submittal and transmittal, diplomatic notes, and Treasury and congressional reports. CCH includes editorial comments and annotations, and it reproduces several relevant IRS publications. It also includes texts of model treaties. Supplementation is monthly.

Certain Cheetah subscriptions include full-text treaty history documents. Cheetah also provides links to texts of administrative documents (such as revenue procedures and letter rulings) and judicial decisions interpreting each treaty.

Illustration 7-15. Cheetah Documents: Material Under U.S.-Denmark

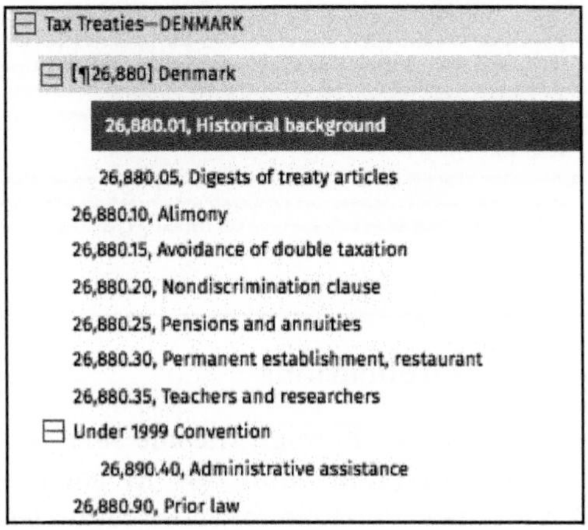

b. Federal Tax Coordinator 2d

The RIA Federal Tax Coordinator 2d looseleaf service is available in print, on Checkpoint, and on Westlaw Edge. Chapter O covers United States tax treaties.

The textual discussion in the Checkpoint version is linked to the treaty text in the Checkpoint U.S. Tax Treaties in Force library. U.S. Tax Treaties in Force includes the text of treaties, protocols, and diplomatic notes, but it does not include legislative history documents.

Federal>Standard Federal Tax Reporter>Foreign income and tax treaties-Secs. 861–999>Tax treaties and conventions.

Illustration 7-16. Federal Tax Coordinator 2d Discussion: U.S.-Denmark Income Tax Treaty

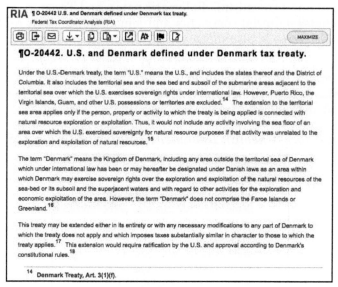

RIA ¶O-20442 U.S. and Denmark defined under Denmark tax treaty.
Federal Tax Coordinator Analysis (RIA)

MAXIMIZE

¶O-20442. U.S. and Denmark defined under Denmark tax treaty.

Under the U.S.-Denmark treaty, the term "U.S." means the U.S., and includes the states thereof and the District of Columbia. It also includes the territorial sea and the sea bed and subsoil of the submarine areas adjacent to the territorial sea over which the U.S. exercises sovereign rights under international law. However, Puerto Rico, the Virgin Islands, Guam, and other U.S. possessions or territories are excluded.[14] The extension to the territorial sea area applies only if the person, property or activity to which the treaty is being applied is connected with natural resource exploration or exploitation. Thus, it would not include any activity involving the sea floor of an area over which the U.S. exercised sovereignty for natural resource purposes if that activity was unrelated to the exploration and exploitation of natural resources.[15]

The term "Denmark" means the Kingdom of Denmark, including any area outside the territorial sea of Denmark which under international law has been or may hereafter be designated under Danish laws as an area within which Denmark may exercise sovereign rights over the exploration and exploitation of the natural resources of the sea-bed or its subsoil and the superjacent waters and with regard to other activities for the exploration and economic exploitation of the area. However, the term "Denmark" does not comprise the Faroe Islands or Greenland.[16]

This treaty may be extended either in its entirety or with any necessary modifications to any part of Denmark to which the treaty does not apply and which imposes taxes substantially similar in character to those to which the treaty applies.[17] This extension would require ratification by the U.S. and approval according to Denmark's constitutional rules.[18]

[14] Denmark Treaty, Art. 3(1)(f).

c. Bloomberg Law Publications

The Tax Management Portfolios—Foreign Income service is available in print and online.[15] This service covers individual countries in separate Portfolios (Business Operations in [Country]); there is a Portfolio for most countries with which the United States has an income tax treaty. The Detailed Analysis sections contain explanations, significant cases, and other annotations. The Working Papers include treaty texts. Other Portfolios cover general topics, such as the foreign tax credit and transfer pricing.

Other Bloomberg products include an online Treaties service (updated for new material), International Journal (monthly), International Tax Developments Tracker (weekdays), and Transfer Pricing Report (biweekly). There is also an online International Tax Treaty finding tool; it includes treaties to which the United States is not a signatory as well as those between the United States and another country.

d. Tax Notes Publications

Tax Notes covers treaty documents in its online Worldwide Tax Treaties service. Treaty documents include full texts of treaties (including treaties pending ratification) and all documents comprising each treaty's legislative history. You can search administrative documents and judicial interpretations.

In addition to treaties and their protocols, this service includes memorandums of understanding and competent authority agreements. A U.S. Treaty Summaries section covers each income tax treaty as amended by later documents. You can also use this service to compare the terms of different treaties. Tax Notes covers income, administrative assistance, estate and gift tax, transportation, and social security

[15] The Portfolios are no longer available to purchase in print for those without a subscription to Bloomberg Law.

treaties. It also includes United States, United Nations, and OECD model treaties. This service is not limited to treaties to which the United States is a signatory.

Tax Notes also covers international news in Tax Notes International (weekly) and Tax Notes Today International (daily).

Illustration 7-17. Worldwide Tax Treaties: Information About the U.S.-Denmark Income Tax Treaty

TREATY PARTNERS	Denmark; United States
SIGNED	August 19, 1999
IN FORCE	March 31, 2000
EFFECTIVE	Withholding taxes, from May 1, 2000; other provisions, from January 1, 2001. See Article 29.
STATUS	In Force
MLI INFORMATION	The treaty is subject to modification by the OECD Multilateral Instrument (MLI); one or more of the treaty partners have signed the MLI and included the treaty in their list of Covered Tax Agreements under Article 2(1)(a)(ii). Denmark MLI Reservations and Notifications. Compare MLI Reservations and Notifications to MLI.
AMENDMENTS	This convention, signed August 19, 1999, has been amended by a protocol signed May 2, 2006.
EDITOR'S NOTE	This version of the treaty incorporates changes made by the protocol signed May 2, 2006. The protocol entered into force December 28, 2007; its withholding tax provisions apply from February 1, 2008, and its other provisions apply from January 1, 2008.
OFFICIAL CITATIONS	Treaty Doc. 106-12
TAX ANALYSTS CITATIONS	Doc 1999-33612-I
U.S. Legislative History	
Extended Summary	

e. Legislative History of United States Tax Conventions (Roberts & Holland Collection)

This looseleaf service, introduced in 1986, updated and expanded a four-volume 1962 version prepared by the Joint Committee on Taxation staff. The 21 volumes contain the full text of treaties and legislative history documents, including presidential messages, Senate Executive Reports, floor debate, Joint Committee staff explanations, and hearings. Official pagination is retained.

This service focused on the treaty and treaty history documents rather than on subsequent judicial and administrative interpretations. Although the most recent supplement was from 2006, the print service remains a valuable source of compiled treaty history documents.

After this service was added to the HeinOnline database, William Manz began updating it. As of July 2020, the service had been updated through a 2020 supplement. Illustration 7-18 shows the PDF copy of the book; Illustration 7-19 shows the same contents listing in HeinOnline.

Illustration 7-18. Roberts & Holland Collection: Documents for U.S.-Denmark Income Tax Treaty

SECOND BASIC CONVENTION (signed Aug. 19, 1999).

Treasury News, LS-64, Aug. 19, 1999 385

Presidential Message of Transmittal to Senate, Senate Treaty Doc. 106-12, 106th Cong., 1st Sess., Sept. 21, 1999 386

Staff of Joint Comm. on Taxation, Explanation, JCS 8-99, Oct. 8, 1999 437

Testimony, Lindy Paull, Chief of Staff of the Joint Committee on Taxation, JCX-76-99. 497

Testimony, Philip R. West, Treasury International Tax Counsel, Treas. News, LS-177, Oct. 27, 1999. 501

Treasury Dept., Technical Explanation 526

Senate Executive Report, 106-9, 106th Cong., 1st Sess., Nov. 3, 1999 627

Treasury News, LS-521, April 2, 2000 680

Senate Resolution Ratifying Treaty 681

TIAS , entered into force March 31, 2000. (Not Available)

SUPPLEMENTARY PROTOCOL (signed May 2, 2006)

Treaties, hearing before the Senate Committee on Foreign Relations (July 17, 2007).

See: BELGIUM 661.

Diplomatic Notes Referring to the Denmark-United States Tax Protocol (May 2, 2006) 683

Protocol Amending Tax Convention with Denmark, Sen. Exec. Rep. 110-3 (Nov. 14, 2007) (includes Technical Explanation) 687

Protocol Amending Tax Convention with Denmark, Treaty Doc. 109-19

Illustration 7-19. U.S.-Denmark Treaty Documents from HeinOnline

Page DENMARK 385
Presidential Message of Transmittal to Senate, Senate Treaty Doc. 106-12, 106th Cong., 1st Sess., Sept. 21, 1999 *Second Basic Convention*
Page DENMARK 386
Staff of Joint Comm. on Taxation, Explanation, JCS 8-99, Oct. 8, 1999 *Second Basic Convention*
Page DENMARK 437
Testimony, Lindy Paull, Chief of Staff of the Joint Comm. on Taxation, JCX-76-99 *Second Basic Convention*
Page DENMARK 497
Testimony Philip R. West, Treasury International Tax Counsel, Treas. News, LS-177, Oct. 27, 1999 *Second Basic Convention*
Page DENMARK 501
Treasury Dept., Technical Explanation *Second Basic Convention*
Page DENMARK 526
Senate Executive Report, 106-9, 106th Cong., 1st Sess., Nov. 3, 1999 *Second Basic Convention*
Page DENMARK 627
Treasury News, LS-521, April 2, 2000 *Second Basic Convention*

f. Rhoades & Langer, U.S. International Taxation and Tax Treaties

This treatise covers the treaty and non-treaty aspects of both inbound and outbound transactions. Following the topical discussion in the main text sections, Appendix A prints the text of current, proposed, and terminated income tax treaties. It also includes text of estate and gift tax treaties, tax information exchange agreements, and transportation agreements; it includes links to text of social security totalization agreements. Appendix B includes United States model treaties and Technical Explanations. In addition to the print version, this treatise is available on Lexis+.

In addition to its T.I.A.S. citation, a brief legislative history accompanies each treaty. If a treaty no longer applies, the service still covers that country and indicates when the treaty went out of force. Cross-references to any pertinent revenue rulings and letter rulings follow each treaty article.

g. Kavass's Current Treaty Index; Kavass's Guide to the United States Treaties in Force

Kavass's Current Treaty Index is available in both print and in HeinOnline. Currently in its 65th edition, its volumes cover 1982 to 2019, and it is published twice per year. The index is just that, an index of all the treaties signed by the United States. The treaties are listed in various ways: chronologically; by country (bilateral and multilateral); by subject; and geographically by subject. The geographic subject index shows all the various treaties signed between the United States and a particular country.

Kavass's Guide to the United States Treaties in Force is a three-book set published yearly, and it is available in print and in HeinOnline. Book I lists U.S. bilateral and multilateral agreements by their official treaty number, starting with TS 3 (Navigation treaty with Argentina signed in 1854). Book II indexes the treaties and agreements by subject and geography, similarly to the Current Treaty Index. Book III contains an index listing treaties chronologically (by signature date) and another index listing U.S. bilateral/multilateral treaties in force by Country and International Organization.

Both Guides contain only lists of the various treaties signed, not the actual treaty texts. To find the actual treaties, you can use the other sources listed in this section.

h. Other Sources

Lexis+ includes country-specific information in a Doing Business in [Country] series. Westlaw Edge has a U.S. Tax Treaties and Conventions database. It also carries the Journal of International Taxation and many Warren Gorham & Lamont international tax treatises.

H. Pending Treaties

The government regularly announces the status of treaty negotiations. This information is carried in newsletters, in looseleaf services, and on government websites.

If you want to determine if a tax treaty has been signed and is pending before the Senate, you can locate this information in the Treaties Pending in the Senate section of the State Department website.[16] Congress.gov lets you narrow a treaty search to Taxation and further narrow it to the treaty's status; your options include committee consideration, floor consideration, and approved by the Senate.[17] There is a Treaties section on the Senate Foreign Relations Committee website. Looseleaf services such as those discussed in Section G are also a good source of information about pending treaties and treaties that are being negotiated.

I. Citators for Treaties

Two sources that formerly provided citations to judicial and administrative decisions regarding treaties are of use only for historical research. Shepard's Federal Statute Citations provides citations to court decisions involving treaties through 1995; you need the U.S.T. and T.I.A.S. citations to use this volume. Citations to IRS pronouncements (1954–1993/94) can be found in the Service's Bulletin Index-Digest System, currently available in HeinOnline.

In the absence of a formal citator, you can locate judicial and administrative rulings in looseleaf and online services that focus on treaties or that have extensive treaty coverage.

J. Interpreting Treaties

1. Administrative Interpretations

In many instances, the executive branch must issue guidance to implement or interpret treaty provisions. For example, Title 26, Chapter I, Subchapter G of the Code of Federal Regulations provides regulations regarding tax treaties. These regulations do

[16] As of July 18, 2020, the list of pending treaties on the State Department website (under Home>Bureaus/Offices Reporting Directly to the Secretary>Office of the Legal Adviser>Office of Treaty Affairs) (https://www.state.gov/treaties-pending-in-the-senate/) covered through October 22, 2019.

[17] For all the search options select "Search Tools" (upper right of the page), then expand "Treaty Documents." You can also access "Treaty Documents" directly from a link at the bottom of the Congress.gov home page.

not follow the regulations numbering system described in Chapter 8, and they cover only four treaty countries.[18]

The IRS issues revenue rulings and other guidance interpreting treaty provisions. You can locate these documents by using the treaty country as a search term instead of using a Code section. Chapter 9 discusses locating IRS documents.

2. Judicial Interpretations

Because treaties and statutes are both approved by Congress, many of the rules of interpretation applied to statutes apply to treaties. The list below illustrates interpretation rules applied to treaties, including in situations involving a conflict between a treaty and a statute.

- "[W]hen a treaty and an act of Congress conflict 'the last expression of the sovereign will must control'." *Lindsey v. Commissioner*, 98 T.C. 672, 676 (1992) (citations omitted).
- "Unless the treaty terms are unclear on their face, or unclear as applied to the situation that has arisen, it should rarely be necessary to rely on extrinsic evidence in order to construe a treaty, for it is rarely possible to reconstruct all of the considerations and compromises that led the signatories to the final document. However, extrinsic material is often helpful in understanding the treaty and its purposes, thus providing an enlightened framework for reviewing its terms." *Xerox Corp. v. United States*, 41 F.3d 647, 652 (Fed. Cir. 1994) (citation omitted).
- "The Government correctly notes that '[a]lthough not conclusive, the meaning attributed to treaty provisions by the Government agencies charged with their negotiation and enforcement is entitled to great weight.' Courts nevertheless 'interpret treaties for themselves.' ... Moreover, because we are to interpret treaties so as to give effect to the intent of both signatories, ... an agency's position merits less deference 'where an agency and another country disagree on the meaning of a treaty[.]' Finally, this court, when considering different provisions of the 1975 Treaty, has declined to defer to Treasury's contemporaneous interpretation where it conflicted with the contemporaneous intent of the Senate." *Westminster Bank, PLC v. United States*, 512 F.3d 1347, 1358 (Fed. Cir. 2008) (citations omitted).
- "Even where a provision of a treaty fairly admits of two constructions, one restricting, the other enlarging, rights which may be claimed under it, the more liberal interpretation is to be preferred." *North West Life Assurance Co. of Canada v. Commissioner*, 107 T.C. 363, 378 (1996) (citation omitted).
- "We construe a treaty like a contract." *Amaral v. Commissioner*, 90 T.C. 802, 813 (1988) (citations omitted).
- "It does appear, however, that in the case of treaties, courts have sometimes been more willing to resort to extra-textual, preparatory

[18] Denmark (Treas. Reg. §§ 521.101–.117), France (Treas. Reg. §§ 514.1–.10, 514.22), Ireland (Treas. Reg. §§ 513.2–.11), and Switzerland (Treas. Reg. §§ 509.101–.121).

material to determine meaning, and also to allow for more liberal interpretation of the words of a treaty. In such instances the decision of the courts to resort to sources beyond the treaty language and/or to a more liberal interpretation of the written word often has occurred because the treaty language is not completely clear and requires further explanation." *Snap-On Tools, Inc. v. United States*, 26 Cl. Ct. 1045, 1065 (1992) (citations omitted).

- "While neither a treaty nor U.S. revenue laws have preferential status, the Code's provisions nonetheless are to be applied with due regard to germane tax treaty provisions." *Zhongxia Ye v. Commissioner*, T.C. Memo. 2017–216, at *11 (citations omitted).
- "Thus, to the extent that a treaty can reasonably be interpreted to avoid conflict with a subsequent enactment, such an interpretation is to be preferred." *Norstar Bank of Upstate New York v. United States*, 644 F. Supp. 1112, 1116 (N.D.N.Y. 1986) (citations omitted).
- "Where a treaty and a statute 'relate to the same subject, the courts will always endeavor to construe them so as to give effect to both, if that can be done without violating the language of either.' " *Kappus v. Commissioner*, 337 F.3d 1053, 1056 (D.C. Cir. 2003) (citations omitted).

K. United Nations, OECD, and WTO

The United States belongs to several international organizations whose activities may affect U.S. tax legislation and administration. Relevant organizations include the United Nations, OECD, and WTO.

1. United Nations

As noted in Section E, the United Nations numbers treaties that are registered with it. Its website includes a searchable treaty database.[19] The United Nations model tax treaty, Model Double Taxation Convention between Developed and Developing Countries, is also available on its website. The most recent version is from 2017. United States treaty history documents indicate if the parties considered that model treaty.[20]

2. OECD

The Organisation for Economic Co-operation and Development was formed in December 1960 as a continuation of the Organisation for European Economic Co-operation. The 37 member states use the OECD as a forum to compare policies and work towards answers of common problems. Negotiations in the OECD have culminated in formal agreements on combating bribery, arrangements of export credits, and the

[19] https://treaties.un.org/Pages/AdvanceSearch.aspx?tab=UNTS&clang=_en (last visited July 18, 2020).

[20] See, e.g., STAFF OF JOINT COMM. ON TAX'N, EXPLANATION OF THE PROPOSED INCOME TAX TREATY BETWEEN THE UNITED STATES AND THE PEOPLE'S REPUBLIC OF BANGLADESH (JCX–04–06), at 2 (Jan. 26, 2006):

> The United States and the People's Republic of Bangladesh do not have an income tax treaty currently in force. The proposed treaty is similar to other recent U.S. income tax treaties, the 1996 U.S. model income tax treaty ("U.S. model"), the 1992 model income tax treaty of the Organization for Economic Cooperation and Development, as updated ("OECD model"), and the 1980 United Nations Model Double Taxation Convention Between Developed and Developing Countries, as amended in 2001 ("U.N. model").

treatment of capital movement. Many non-member countries have signed OECD agreements.

The United States is a signatory to the OECD Mutual Administrative Assistance in Tax Matters Convention, which entered into force in 1995 and was amended in 2010. As of May 2020, it had not signed (or indicated it will sign) the Multilateral Convention to Implement Tax Treaty Related Measures to Prevent Base Erosion and Profit Shifting. The OECD has published several model treaties, such as the OECD Model Tax Convention on Income and on Capital, which the United States takes into account in negotiating tax treaties.[21] Treaty explanations indicate variances from the OECD Model Convention. The Centre for Tax Policy and Administration page of the OECD website covers a wide array of tax-related projects.[22] The website also has hyperlinks to a variety of reports and news releases related to taxation.

3. WTO

The World Trade Organization was formed in 1995 to deal with the global rules of trade between nations. It succeeded the General Agreement on Tariffs and Trade (GATT). Trade disputes resolved by WTO panels extend beyond such traditional measures as tariffs. Its 2002 holding, that U.S. tax provisions favoring foreign sales corporations were invalid export subsidies, led to several changes in the Internal Revenue Code.[23] The WTO's Dispute Settlement page can be searched by country, subject, year, and WTO agreement.

L. Other International Material

1. General Information

If a transaction will take place in another country, you may need information about that country's tax laws and general business climate. Background material appears in sources such as the Tax Management Portfolios (Chapter 12). Pamphlets published by major accounting firms and other organizations also provide useful background information. Individual country websites are easy to access.[24] Many of them are available in English in addition to the country's official language.

Although background materials provide an introduction, they cannot substitute for primary source materials. Many United States law libraries have collections of materials from other countries, particularly countries that use English as their primary language. Subscription databases also carry relevant information.

---

[21] The most recent OECD Model Treaty was issued in 2017. The most recent U.S. Model Treaty was issued in February 2016.

[22] The OECD's Global Forum on Transparency and Exchange of Information for Tax Purposes publishes peer review reports on countries' practices with respect to transparency and effective exchange of information.

[23] World Trade Organization Appellate Body ruling (WT/DS108/AB/RW) (Jan. 14, 2002) on appeal from Panel Report, United States—Tax Treatment for "Foreign Sales Corporations"—Recourse to Article 21.5. of the DSU by the European Communities (the "Panel Report"). The WTO Dispute Settlement Body adopted the Appellate Body ruling on January 29, 2002 (WT/DS/108/25). The documents related to this dispute are available at https://www.wto.org/english/tratop_e/dispu_e/cases_e/ds108_e.htm.

[24] See, e.g., HM REVENUE & CUSTOMS, https://www.gov.uk/government/organisations/hm-revenue-customs (last visited July 18, 2020).

You can also find primary source material on other countries' websites.[25] In some cases, the material is available in English even if that is not the other country's official language. Material is likely to be dispersed among multiple websites—e.g., statutes, administrative interpretations, and judicial opinions. If the country has a Legal Information Institute, its website will include links to a variety of primary source material. The British & Irish Legal Information Institute (BAILII),[26] for example, provides links to LIIs for many other countries in addition to covering statutes and judicial decisions in the United Kingdom, England and Wales, Scotland, Northern Ireland, Jersey, Saint Helena, and Ireland. Older material is less likely to be included.

Illustration 7-20. Portion of U.K. Legislation Website

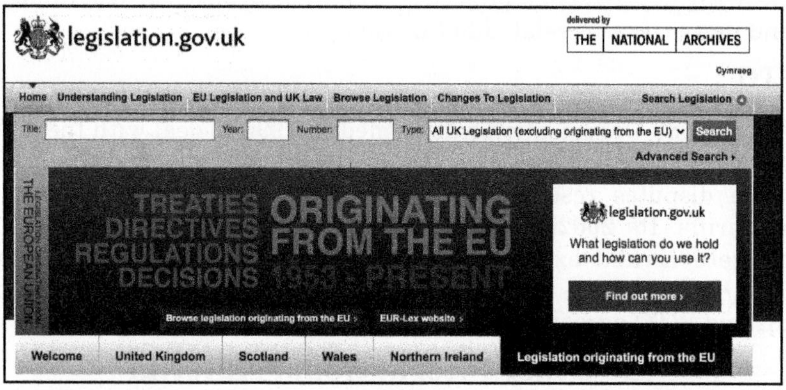

→ This site limits itself to legislation and statutory instruments. BAILII covers judicial decisions in addition to legislation.

Do not overlook extra-national law if the particular country is a member of the European Union or other multi-country union.[27]

2. Material in Other Languages

Although not limited to international taxation, a practitioner may need access to U.S. or foreign materials in a language other than English. Treaties to which the United States is a signatory are published in both English and the official language of the other country.

3. Treaties with Native American Tribes

Treaties the United States entered into with Native Americans are beyond the scope of this book. You should be aware that tax rules applied to Native Americans may involve claims of treaty-based exemptions.[28]

---

[25] See, e.g., LEGISLATION.GOV.UK, http://www.legislation.gov.uk (last visited July 18, 2020).

[26] BRITISH AND IRISH LEGAL INFO. INST., https://www.bailii.org (last visited July 18, 2020).

[27] See EUR-LEX, https://eur-lex.europa.eu/homepage.html (last visited July 18, 2020). It provides European Union legislation and case law in the languages used by EU member states.

[28] See, e.g., *Perkins v. Commissioner*, 150 T.C. 119 (2018); *Uniband, Inc. v. Commissioner*, 140 T.C. 230 (2013); *Cook v. United States*, 86 F.3d 1095 (Fed. Cir. 1996).

M. Problems

1. Which tax treaties are in force between the United States and the country listed?
   a. Finland
   b. Ireland
   c. Japan
   d. Malta
2. When did the following U.S.-(Country listed) income tax treaties enter into force?
   a. Bulgaria
   b. Egypt
   c. India
   d. Morocco
3. Provide a citation for and holding of the IRS document described below.
   a. 1999 Chief Counsel Advice memorandum concerning the classification of U.S.-source endorsement income of nonresident alien athletes under U.S. income tax treaties.
   b. 2001 Chief Counsel Advice memorandum concerning whether residents of East Timor are covered by the U.S.-Indonesia income tax treaty.
   c. 2009 letter ruling concerning whether the taxpayer satisfied the 12-month stock ownership requirement of the U.S.-United Kingdom income tax treaty.
   d. 2010 letter ruling concerning whether a taxpayer who resided in Russia, but who was a partner in a partnership that had offices in the United States, was exempt from U.S. tax on partnership income under the U.S.-Russian Federation income tax treaty.
4. Locate and give the holding and any appeals action for the decision described below.
   a. A Tax Court decision involving the gambling winnings of a South Korean national and the effect of the U.S.-Korea Income Tax Treaty.
   b. A Tax Court decision whether taking an IRA deduction for a contribution to a French pension plan was covered by the U.S.-France income tax treaty.
   c. A Tax Court decision whether wages paid to a medical resident were exempted from tax by the U.S.-Pakistan income tax treaty.
   d. A Court of Federal Claims decision about whether an Irish citizen who resided in Switzerland could take advantage of the U.S.-Ireland income tax treaty and exclude winnings from a three-day backgammon match in the United States.

5. Print out tax information from the country-specific website assigned by your instructor.

Chapter 8

TREASURY REGULATIONS

A. Introduction

This chapter discusses regulations, which Congress authorizes in the Internal Revenue Code and in other statutes. It explains the different categories of regulations—proposed, temporary, and final—and the difference between general authority and specific authority regulations. It also covers other terms used to describe regulations, judicial deference to administrative positions, and sources in which you can find relevant documents. This chapter's coverage of regulations is similar to the coverage in Chapters 5 and 6 for statutes and their legislative history.

Your goals for this chapter include locating all relevant documents, determining their relative importance, and updating your research to include projects that may result in proposed regulations.

B. Functions of Administrative Guidance

As discussed in Chapters 5 and 6, Congress enacted the Internal Revenue Code and other statutes governing income, transfer, and excise taxes. Taxpayers interpret those statutes in determining their liability for these taxes. Courts become involved when there is a controversy between the government and a taxpayer. In interpreting statutes, both taxpayers and courts must consider administrative interpretations.

The Treasury Department and IRS interpret and enforce internal revenue laws. In some areas, such as employee benefits, they share their authority with other administrative agencies. This chapter focuses on one form of administrative guidance, regulations—primarily those issued as Treasury regulations. Chapter 9 focuses on IRS pronouncements.

C. Terminology

1. Proposed, Temporary, and Final Regulations

You should expect to encounter regulations in three different stages. The citation format indicates whether the item is a Proposed Regulation (e.g., Prop. Treas. Reg. § 1.801–4), a Temporary Regulation (e.g., Temp. Treas. Reg. § 1.1041–1T), or a Final Regulation (e.g., Treas. Reg. § 1.106–1). Assuming the citation is correct, a regulation that does not include either a "Prop." or a "T" is a final regulation. Each type can be cited as authority for avoiding the substantial understatement penalty discussed in Chapter 2.[1]

a. Proposed Regulations

Proposed regulations offer guidance for taxpayers seeking to comply with statutory rules. Taxpayers generally receive an opportunity to submit written comments

1 I.R.C. § 6662(b).

or testify at hearings before proposed regulations become final. Unlike temporary regulations, proposed regulations do not automatically expire after a set time period.

The Internal Revenue Manual provides that taxpayers "generally may not rely on proposed regulations for planning purposes . . . ." It provides an exception for two situations. In the first situation, there are no applicable final or temporary regulations, and the Preamble expressly states that taxpayers can rely on the proposed regulations. In the second situation, there are applicable final or temporary regulations, but the Preamble expressly states that taxpayers can rely on the proposed regulations despite the existence of the temporary or final regulations. These are referred to as **reliance regulations**.[2]

b. Temporary Regulations

The IRS can simultaneously issue a proposed regulation as a **temporary regulation**. Unlike a proposed regulation, a temporary regulation is effective when it is published in the Federal Register. It provides immediate, binding guidance and receives more deference than a proposed regulation. It becomes operative without the benefit of public comment.

Code section 7805(e) mandates that temporary regulations issued after November 20, 1988, also be issued as proposed regulations; this ensures that there will be a notice and comment procedure before regulations are finalized.[3] Section 7805(e) also requires that temporary regulations expire no more than three years after they are issued. This limitation does not apply to temporary regulations issued on or before that date, and several older temporary regulations are still in effect.[4]

c. Final Regulations

Regulations issued after any necessary notice and comment period are referred to as final regulations. The **final regulations** may differ from the proposed or temporary regulations they replace for various reasons, including government response to taxpayer comments or judicial decisions. In addition to regulatory analysis information described in Section E, the Preamble accompanying the Treasury Decision will describe comments received and any changes made in response to comments.

2. General Authority, Specific Authority, Interpretive, and Legislative Regulations

Most regulations are issued pursuant to the Code section 7805(a) general mandate. You may see these referred to as **general authority regulations**. These contrast to regulations issued for Code sections in which Congress included a specific grant of authority.[5] The specific grant of authority allows IRS experts to write rules for technical areas. We refer to these as **specific authority regulations**.

---

2 IRM 32.1.1.2.2(2) (Aug. 2, 2018). If only proposed regulations have been issued, the IRM indicates that "the Office of Chief Counsel ordinarily should not take any position in litigation or advice that would yield a result that would be harsher to the taxpayer than what the taxpayer would be allowed under the proposed regulations." IRM 32.1.1.2.2(3) (Aug. 2, 2018).

3 Proposed regulations need not be issued as temporary regulations.

4 See, e.g., Treas. Reg. § 1.163–8T (T.D. 8145, 7/1/87).

5 See, e.g., I.R.C. § 469(*l*)(1) ("The Secretary shall prescribe such regulations as may be necessary or appropriate to carry out provisions of this section" for what constitutes an activity, material participation, or active participation for the passive activity loss rules).

You may encounter references equating general authority and **interpretive** (or **interpretative**) regulations and equating specific authority and **legislative regulations**. However, the IRS makes a further distinction in the Internal Revenue Manual. Interpretive regulations are exempt from notice and comment requirements. They are considered interpretive "because the underlying statute implemented by the regulation contains the necessary legal authority for the action taken and any effect of the regulation flows directly from that statute."[6] Regulations are considered to be legislative "when Congress simply provided an end result, without any guidance as to how to achieve the desired result or when a statutory provision does not provide adequate authority for the regulatory action taken."[7]

As noted in Section K, courts once gave specific authority regulations more deference than they accorded general authority regulations. The Supreme Court's decision in *Mayo Foundation for Medical Education and Research v. United States*[8] does not support that distinction.

Understanding terminology is important. General and specific authority relate to the Code section authority for a particular regulation; interpretive and legislative relate to whether notice and comment are required; and proposed, temporary, and final relate to steps in the process for issuing regulations. For example, a regulation can be both a final regulation, a general authority regulation, and a legislative regulation.

3. Federal Register and Code of Federal Regulations

The **Federal Register** contains the text of proposed, temporary, and final regulations, including their Preambles and other information about the regulation. Items appear in the order in which they are filed; they are not arranged by subject matter or by issuing agency. The Federal Register is the regulatory equivalent of Statutes at Large, which is discussed in Chapter 5. The Federal Register is published each weekday.

The **Code of Federal Regulations** (C.F.R.) is the regulatory equivalent of United States Code. Final and temporary regulations are classified by topic into the appropriate C.F.R. title. Title 26 covers most tax provisions. Each C.F.R. title is updated only once a year in the official C.F.R. publication; title 26 is updated as of each April 1. The government's e-CFR website is updated daily, but it is not an "official legal edition" of the C.F.R.[9]

4. Treasury and Other Agency Regulations

a. Treasury Regulations

Title 26 of the Code of Federal Regulations (C.F.R.) is the Internal Revenue title of C.F.R. It contains most of the regulations you will need for resolving tax problems. Instead of citing these regulations as 26 C.F.R. sections, you can cite them as **Treasury Regulations** (Treas. Reg.).

---

6 IRM 32.1.1.2.6(1) (Sept. 23, 2011). See also IRM 32.1.1.2.8(1), (3), (4) (Aug. 2, 2018).

7 IRM 32.1.1.2.7 (Aug. 2, 2018). See also IRM 32.1.1.2.8(1), (2) (Aug. 2, 2018).

8 562 U.S. 44 (2011).

9 You can reach e-CFR directly (www.ecfr.gov). It is also available as a link in the Browse by A to Z section of govinfo.gov.

Some Treasury-issued regulations appear elsewhere in C.F.R. Regulations in 31 C.F.R. (Money and Finance: Treasury) cover other Treasury Department functions, including Practice before the Internal Revenue Service (Circular 230).[10]

b. Other Agency Regulations

The Treasury Department is one of several Cabinet Departments, each of which may issue regulations. Regulations may also be issued by Independent Agencies (e.g., the Social Security Administration).[11] If another agency has authority for provisions affecting tax law, its regulations are also relevant. For example, the Department of Labor issues regulations in the employee benefits area. Those regulations appear in 29 C.F.R. Regulations related to the Affordable Care Act appear in titles 26 (Internal Revenue), 29 (Labor), and 45 (Public Welfare).

5. Numbering Systems

As was true for statutes, several numbering systems are relevant to regulations. In addition to the actual regulation number, these include the project number, Treasury Decision Number, Regulation Identifier Number (RIN), sequence number, and OMB Control Number. You can use these numbers to find regulations or information about their status in various government documents and websites. You can also use some of them to find information about compliance with government mandates discussed in Section E. Because most of the numbering systems are different, the only ones likely to cause confusion are the RIN and OMB numbers.

a. Regulation Number

The **regulation number** is the number used to cite a regulation. If it is a Treasury regulation, its number reflects the underlying Code section and whether it is a proposed, temporary, or final regulation. Examples of Treasury and other regulations numbers appear in Section F.

b. Project Number

When the IRS opens a regulations project, it assigns it a **project number.**[12] It uses those project numbers for its proposed regulations. Although the project numbering system has changed several times, certain parts have remained constant.

Before an IRS reorganization in 1988, most projects were drafted in the IRS Legislation and Regulations Division and began with the letters LR. Employee benefits and exempt organization projects were designated EE; international projects, INTL. Projects begun under this system received new letter designations but not new numbers after 1988.

Between 1988 and August 1996, project numbers indicated the IRS division with responsibility for the project. [See note 14, *infra* page 129.] The current numbering system began in August 1996. All project numbers now begin with REG, followed by a

---

[10] This group of sections begins at 31 C.F.R. § 10.0.

[11] The executive branch also includes numerous boards, committees, and commissions. These include the Office of Information and Regulatory Affairs (OIRA) and the Taxpayer Advocacy Panel (TAP). OIRA is part of the Office of Management and Budget; TAP is an advisory group.

[12] A single project number (or T.D.) can cover multiple regulations sections. For example, the proposed regulations covered by REG–137604–07 include changes to regulations interpreting Code sections 2, 3, 21, 32, 63, 151, 152, 6013, and 6109.

series of numbers, followed by the project's year. There is no indication of which IRS Chief Counsel division has authority for the regulations project. A recent example of this numbering system is REG–113295–18, covering proposed regulations to reflect deductions for estates and non-grantor trusts after the suspension of miscellaneous itemized deductions under I.R.C. § 67(g). The document appeared in the Federal Register in May 2020.[13] The –18 indicates it was a 2018 project.

Although the numbering system no longer indicates which division produced the regulation,[14] that information does appear in the Drafting Information section included in the regulation's Preamble.

c. Treasury Decision Number

Final and proposed regulations are issued as **Treasury Decisions** (T.D.). Treasury Decisions are numbered sequentially; the current numbering system began in 1900. It does not indicate the year of issue or the Code section involved. After the regulation text is added to the C.F.R., the most important information in the T.D. appears in the Preamble.

d. Regulation Identifier Number

The Regulatory Information Service Center (RISC) assigns **Regulation Identifier Numbers** to agency rulemaking projects. Each RIN begins with a four-digit agency code (1545 for tax regulations), followed by a four-character alphanumeric code. The alphanumeric part of the number is assigned in the order in which the project is entered in the government database tracking rulemaking projects.

The RIN does not change as the item advances from prerule to final rule. The RIN appears in the Unified Agenda and in the headings of proposed and final regulations published in the Federal Register.

e. Sequence Number

The **sequence number** is likely the least important number you will encounter. Regulatory Agendas printed in the Federal Register include sequence numbers for each document. The sequence numbers indicate where the document appears in that Agenda; they change from Agenda to Agenda. Since fall 2007, the standalone online Agendas omit the sequence numbers; the versions included in the Federal Register retain them.[15]

f. OMB Control Number

If a regulation involves collection of information and is therefore subject to the Paperwork Reduction Act, the OMB assigns an **OMB Control Number**. The OMB numbers for all the regulations are collected in Treas. Reg. § 602.101. Each OMB Control number begins with a four-digit agency code, followed by another four-digit numerical code. The relevant agency code for tax regulations is 1545.

---

[13] 85 Fed. Reg. 27693 (2020).

[14] The IRS operating divisions that followed the Internal Revenue Service Restructuring and Reform Act of 1998, Pub. L. No. 105–206, 112 Stat. 685, don't replace the Chief Counsel units. Between 1988 and August 1996 the IRS project designations were CO (Corporate), EE (Employee Benefits and Exempt Organizations), FI (Financial Institutions and Products), GL (General Litigation), IA (Income Tax and Accounting), INTL (International), and PS (Passthroughs and Special Industries).

[15] See, e.g., 84 Fed. Reg. 71182 (2019).

6. Additional Rulemaking Terminology

Regulations rarely appear immediately after a Code section is enacted or amended. Relevant stages include opening a regulations project, announcing a proposed rule (or making an advance announcement), and issuing proposed, temporary, or final regulations. Rules issued by agencies other than the IRS may use different names for their rulemaking projects even though the processes are much the same.

a. Advance Notice of Proposed Rulemaking

The IRS may publish an **Advance Notice of Proposed Rulemaking** (ANPRM). Advance notices indicate rules the IRS expects to propose. In the advance notice, the IRS may request public comment, which could influence the resulting NPRM. The ANPRM includes the project number and the RIN. ANPRMs are issued in what the Unified Agenda refers to as the prerule stage. The IRS does not issue an ANPRM for every project in this stage.

b. Notice of Proposed Rulemaking; Final Regulations

The IRS publishes the text of a proposed regulation and its accompanying Preamble as a **Notice of Proposed Rulemaking** (NPRM). Notices include the project number and the RIN. Neither number reflects the underlying Code section number or the year the proposal is filed with the Federal Register. The NPRM is issued at the end of prerule stage of the process. The IRS issues a final regulation at the end of the process. Its preamble responds to comments received in response to the NPRM.

7. Dates

a. Filing and Publication Dates

Because they are not statutes, regulations are not enacted. Instead they are issued or promulgated by being filed with the Federal Register. The **filing date** generally precedes the **publication date** by a day or two. The T.D. information following each temporary and final regulation includes the Federal Register date. That date is also listed before Preambles to proposed, temporary, and final regulations. The date is important because of the rules concerning retroactivity discussed in Section E.2.a (*infra* page 135).

b. Effective Date

The Preamble to the T.D. or NPRM includes the regulation's **effective date**, which can vary from its filing and publication dates. The Preamble may include an expected effective date. If a proposed regulation is involved, it might instead say: "These regulations are applicable to taxable years beginning after the date final regulations are published in the Federal Register."

c. Expiration Date and "Stale" Regulations

Final regulations generally continue in effect indefinitely. Temporary regulations issued after November 20, 1988, expire no later than three years after they are issued.[16]

---

[16] I.R.C. § 7805(e)(2).

Although a final regulation continues in effect until it is withdrawn, its validity is compromised if the Code section it interprets is amended or a judicial opinion rejects its reasoning. The T.D. date indicates when a regulation was issued or amended. If it contradicts its Code section, it probably has not been amended to reflect the most recent statutory change.[17] If it varies from a judicial holding, the IRS may have decided to continue litigating its position rather than withdraw it. Chapter 9 discusses administrative announcements regarding continuing litigation.

8. Preambles and Texts of Regulations

Preambles to T.D.s and NPRMs discuss the regulation and provide other useful information, much of which is discussed elsewhere in this chapter. Preambles appear in the Federal Register but not in the C.F.R.

Table 8-A. Preamble Supplementary Information Segments

Background
Explanation of Provisions
Effective/Applicability Date[18]
Availability of IRS Documents
Effect on Other Documents
Special Analyses
Comments and Requests for Public Hearing
Drafting Information
List of Subjects

Two items follow the Preamble. The first is the amendment to the authority provision in the affected C.F.R. subdivision. This amendment indicates the Code section authorizing each regulation, a concept discussed in Section C.2 (*supra* page 126). The second item is the regulation's text. That language is added to the C.F.R. if it is a temporary or final regulation. If it is a proposed regulation, the text appears in the Federal Register but not the C.F.R. Preambles are illustrated in Illustrations 8-1 and 8-2 (*infra* pages 132 and 137).

---

[17] Looseleaf services that print regulations often indicate that a regulation does not reflect a statutory change.

[18] A proposed applicability date is provided for proposed regulations.

Illustration 8-1. Preamble to T.D. 9884

Federal Register / Vol. 84, No. 228 / Tuesday, November 26, 2019 / Rules and Regulations **64995**

2. Musculoskeletal System (1.00 and 101.00): February 4, 2022.

* * * * *

5. Cardiovascular System (4.00 and 104.00): February 4, 2022.

6. Digestive System (5.00 and 105.00): February 4, 2022.

* * * * *

9. Skin Disorders (8.00 and 108.00): February 4, 2022.

* * * * *

15. Immune System Disorders (14.00 and 114.00): February 4, 2022.

* * * * *

[FR Doc. 2019–25635 Filed 11–25–19; 8:45 am]

BILLING CODE 4191–02–P

DEPARTMENT OF THE TREASURY

Internal Revenue Service

26 CFR Part 20

[TD 9884]

RIN 1545–BO72

Estate and Gift Taxes; Difference in the Basic Exclusion Amount

AGENCY: Internal Revenue Service (IRS), Treasury.

ACTION: Final regulations.

SUMMARY: This document contains final regulations addressing the effect of recent legislative changes to the basic exclusion amount allowable in computing Federal gift and estate taxes. The final regulations will affect donors of gifts made after 2017 and the estates of decedents dying after 2025.

DATES:

Effective Date: These final regulations are effective on and after November 26, 2019.

Applicability Date: For date of applicability, see § 20.2010–1(f)(2).

FOR FURTHER INFORMATION CONTACT: Deborah S. Ryan, (202) 317–6859 (not a toll-free number).

SUPPLEMENTARY INFORMATION:

Background

Section 11061 of the Tax Cuts and Jobs Act, Public Law 115–97, 131 Stat. 2504 (2017) (TCJA) amended section 2010(c)(3) of the Internal Revenue Code (Code) to provide that, for decedents dying and gifts made after December 31, 2017, and before January 1, 2026, the basic exclusion amount (BEA) is increased by $5 million to $10 million as adjusted for inflation (increased BEA). On January 1, 2026, the BEA will revert to $5 million as adjusted for inflation.

This document contains amendments to the Estate Tax Regulations (26 CFR part 20) relating to the BEA described in section 2010(c)(3) of the Code. On November 23, 2018, a notice of proposed rulemaking (proposed regulations) under section 2010 (REG–106706–18) was published in the **Federal Register** (83 FR 59343). No public hearing was requested or held. Written or electronic comments responding to the proposed regulations were received. After consideration of all the comments, this Treasury decision adopts the proposed regulations with certain revisions. Comments and revisions to the proposed regulations are discussed in the Summary of Comments and Explanation of Revisions.

The final regulations adopt the special rule provided in the proposed regulations in cases where the portion of the credit against the estate tax that is based on the BEA is less than the sum of the credit amounts attributable to the BEA allowable in computing gift tax payable within the meaning of section 2001(b)(2). In that case, the rule provides that the portion of the credit against the net tentative estate tax that is attributable to the BEA is based upon the greater of those two credit amounts. The rule thus would ensure that the estate of a decedent is not inappropriately taxed with respect to gifts that were sheltered from gift tax by the increased BEA when made.

Summary of Comments and Explanation of Revisions

1. Overview

Most commenters agreed that the special rule would avoid an unfair situation that otherwise could effectively vitiate the statutory increase in the BEA during the period January 1, 2018, through December 31, 2025 (increased BEA period). These commenters also acknowledged that the special rule would provide important clarification for taxpayers. However, one commenter suggested an alternate approach and two others disputed the regulatory authority to adopt the special rule. Some commenters suggested technical changes. All of the other comments were requests for clarification of the interaction of the special rule with the inflation adjustments to the BEA, the deceased spousal unused exclusion (DSUE) amount, and the generation-skipping transfer (GST) tax, and requests for additional examples. These comments are discussed in this preamble.

2. Inflation Adjustments

Several commenters noted that the example in the proposed regulations does not reflect the annual inflation adjustments to the BEA, and requested clarification of the effect of those adjustments on the application of the special rule. The inflation adjustments were not included in that example for purposes of more simply illustrating the special rule. However, by definition, the term BEA refers to the amount of that exclusion as adjusted for inflation, so the Department of the Treasury (Treasury Department) and the IRS agree that examples including inflation adjustments would be appropriate. Accordingly, the examples in the final regulations reflect hypothetical inflation-adjusted BEA amounts.

One commenter requested confirmation that under the special rule a decedent does not benefit from the increased BEA, including inflation adjustments, to the extent it is in excess of the amount of gifts the decedent actually made, and agreed that this is the appropriate interpretation of the statute. Specifically, the increased BEA as adjusted for inflation is a "use or lose" benefit and is available to a decedent who survives the increased BEA period only to the extent the decedent "used" it by making gifts during the increased BEA period. The final regulations include *Example 2* in § 20.2010–1(c)(2)(ii) to demonstrate that the application of the special rule is based on gifts actually made, and thus is inapplicable to a decedent who did not make gifts in excess of the date of death BEA as adjusted for inflation.

Commenters also sought confirmation that under the special rule a decedent dying after 2025 will not benefit from post-2025 inflation adjustments to the BEA to the extent the decedent made gifts in an amount sufficient to cause the total BEA allowable in the computation of gift tax payable to exceed the date of death BEA as adjusted for inflation. This is confirmed in *Example 1* of § 20.2010–1(c)(2)(i) of these final regulations. In computing the estate tax, the BEA, in effect, is applied first against the decedent's gifts as taxable gifts were made. To the extent any BEA remains at death, it is applied against the decedent's estate. Therefore, in the case of a decedent who had made gifts in an amount sufficient to cause the total BEA allowable in the computation of gift tax payable to equal or exceed the date of death BEA as adjusted for inflation, there is no remaining BEA available to be applied to reduce the estate tax. The special rule does not change the five-step estate tax computation required under sections 2001 and 2010 of the Code or the fact that, under that computation, only the credit that remains after computing gift tax payable may be applied against the estate tax.

→ Note the discussion of comments received.

9. Agendas and Guidance Plans

Agencies announce their regulatory plans twice a year in the Unified Agenda of Federal Regulatory and Deregulatory Actions.[19] The **Unified Agenda** appears as a

[19] This document is often referred to as the Semiannual Agenda.

searchable database on the Reginfo.gov (since fall 1995),[20] Regulations.gov (since fall 2007), and govinfo.gov (since spring 1994) websites. The fall issue of the Agenda includes the **Regulatory Plan**. The Plan provides information about the most significant actions each agency plans for the coming year.

In addition, the Treasury and IRS issue an annual **Priority Guidance Plan**, which lists guidance they hope to issue during the next 12 months. The Priority Guidance Plan covers both regulations and other types of guidance. The Unified Agenda and Priority Guidance Plan are discussed further in Section I (*infra* page 145).

D. Regulatory Process

1. IRS and Treasury

Regulations begin as projects assigned to drafters in the relevant division of the IRS Chief Counsel's office. The Unified Agenda or Priority Guidance Plan will generally list these items. The Unified Agenda lists the Code section and project number and indicates a target date by which action, such as publishing the proposed regulations, will occur. The Priority Guidance Plan currently lists particular acts for which guidance is needed and lists other topics (e.g., Exempt Organizations, Financial Institutions and Products) alphabetically under a "General Guidance" heading. Within each topic, it lists both regulations and other guidance the Treasury Department and IRS hope to issue; Code sections are included for most items. For example, the initial version of the 2019–2020 Plan includes as an item under Implementation of Tax Cuts and Jobs Act "Final regulations under § 2010 addressing the computation of the estate tax in the event of a difference between the basic exclusion amount applicable to gifts and that applicable at the donor's date of death."[21]

Because the IRS may issue advance notices regarding its proposals,[22] researchers interested in future regulations must also check IRS documents discussed in Chapter 9.

After a **notice and comment period**, the IRS has several options.[23] These include finalizing the proposed regulation without modifications, finalizing it with modifications, modifying it and asking for additional comments, or withdrawing it and starting the drafting process over again. Because proposed regulations—unlike temporary regulations—do not expire after three years, the IRS can also retain the proposal in its original form without further action.

2. Congress

In March 1996, Congress added a congressional review procedure (popularly referred to as the Congressional Review Act) for agency rules. This procedure allows Congress to disapprove a "major" rule by a **joint resolution of disapproval**. A disapproved rule does not become effective unless the President vetoes the disapproval

---

[20] Although the full Agenda previously appeared in the Federal Register, that is no longer the case. Coverage since fall 2007 is limited to the Regulatory Plan and agendas required by the Regulatory Flexibility Act.

[21] Final regulations were issued in November 2019 (T.D. 9884) [Illustration 8-1].

[22] See, e.g., Notice 2015–49, 2015–30 I.R.B. 79.

[23] For making comments to, or finding the comments of others, see Section I.5 (*infra* page 155).

and Congress fails to override the veto. Major rules are suspended for up to 60 days for the congressional review and for additional time if needed for the override process.[24]

Congress may intervene by imposing a moratorium on regulations in a particular area, as it did for "nonstatutory" fringe benefits before the enactment of Code section 132. Moratoria can include rulings as well as regulations.[25] Congress could also reject a regulation by changing the statute to produce a different outcome. One area of practitioner frustration relates to Code sections with no regulations despite statutory language saying the Secretary "shall" issue regulations.

E. Regulatory Authority

1. Entities Involved

The two most important entities involved in promulgating regulations are the IRS and the Treasury Department. Regulations are drafted by the IRS, but they are issued under the authority of the Secretary of the Treasury. Sections C and D describe various steps involved in issuing a regulation.

Code section 7805(a) authorizes the Secretary to "prescribe all needful rules and regulations for the enforcement" of the tax statutes. Other Code sections that refer to regulations also use the term "the Secretary." Section 7701(a)(11)(B) defines that term to mean "the Secretary of the Treasury or his delegate." If the statute instead says "the Secretary of the Treasury," section 7701(a)(11)(A) prohibits delegation.

The Secretary has delegated the regulations drafting function to the Commissioner of Internal Revenue.[26] For that reason, this book generally refers to the IRS role in the regulations process. Nevertheless, you must refer to them as Treasury regulations, not IRS regulations.

2. Code Limitations on Authority

Section 7805(a) authorizes issuing regulations, but it is not an absolute grant of authority. Several limitations apply to the IRS's authority to issue regulations. These relate to retroactivity and taxpayer burden. The government describes its compliance with these rules in the Preambles that accompany regulations.

---

[24] 5 U.S.C. §§ 801–808. A major rule is "any rule that the Administrator of the Office of Information and Regulatory Affairs of the Office of Management and Budget finds has resulted in or is likely to result in—(A) an annual effect on the economy of $100,000,000 or more; (B) a major increase in costs or prices for consumers, individual industries, Federal, State, or local government agencies, or geographic regions; or (C) significant adverse effects on competition, employment, investment, productivity, innovation, or on the ability of United States-based enterprises to compete with foreign-based enterprises in domestic and export markets." Id. § 804(2).

[25] "During fiscal year 2016—(1) none of the funds made available in this or any other Act may be used by the Department of the Treasury, including the Internal Revenue Service, to issue, revise, or finalize any regulation, revenue ruling, or other guidance not limited to a particular taxpayer relating to the standard which is used to determine whether an organization is operated exclusively for the promotion of social welfare for purposes of section 501(c)(4) of the Internal Revenue Code of 1986 (including the proposed regulations published at 78 Fed. Reg. 71535 (November 29, 2013)) . . . ." Consolidated Appropriations Act, 2016, Pub. L. No. 114–113, Div. E, § 127(1) (2015).

[26] Treas. Reg. § 301.7805–1(a). The Treasury Department's Office of Tax Policy is also involved. The Tax Policy website states "Tax Policy develops and implements tax policies and programs; reviews regulations and rulings to administer the Internal Revenue Code . . . ." https://home.treasury.gov/about/offices/tax-policy (last visited July 18, 2020).

a. Retroactivity

Code section 7805(b) imposes limits on issuing regulations with retroactive effect. Beginning with statutes enacted on July 30, 1996, a proposed, temporary, or final regulation cannot apply to any taxable period before the earliest of its filing with the Federal Register[27] or the date on which a notice substantially describing its expected contents is issued to the public. This rule does not apply to regulations filed or issued within 18 months of the statute's enactment, necessary to prevent abuse, or issued to correct procedural defects in previously issued regulations.[28]

b. Small Business

Code section 7805(f) requires the Treasury Department to submit proposed and temporary regulations to the Small Business Administration's Chief Counsel for Advocacy. The Chief Counsel for Advocacy is required to comment on the regulation's impact on small business. The Preamble accompanying the final regulations must discuss these comments.[29]

3. Other Limitations on Authority[30]

a. Administrative Procedure Act

Agencies must publish notices of proposed rulemaking in the Federal Register.[31] These notices include information about the time and place for a public rulemaking procedure, indicate the agency's legal authority for promulgating the regulation, and indicate the terms or substance of the proposed rule. Publication generally must precede the effective date by at least 30 days. After receiving and considering comments, the agency must include a concise general statement of the rule's basis and purpose. Interpretive rules are exempt from these requirements; the APA's definition of "rule" does not indicate whether regulations issued pursuant to Code section 7805 are necessarily interpretive.[32] Taxpayers can challenge a regulation for violating APA requirements in addition to challenging the regulation's interpretation of the underlying Code section.[33]

---

[27] A final regulation can be retroactive to the date its proposed version was filed. It might even relate back to an IRS notice, described in Chapter 9.

[28] Congress can legislatively waive section 7805(b). In addition, the IRS can authorize taxpayers to elect retroactive application. I.R.C. § 7805(b)(6)–(7).

[29] Comparable requirements apply to final regulations that are not based on proposed regulations; those submissions must occur before the regulation is filed.

[30] In addition to discussing the substance of a proposed or final regulation, the agency must also address relevant regulatory constraints. See, e.g., Preamble to T.D. 9889, 85 Fed. Reg. 1866 (2020), which addresses Executive Orders 12866, 13132, 13175, 13563, and 13711, the Paperwork Reduction Act, the Regulatory Flexibility Act, the Unfunded Mandates Reform Act, and the Congressional Review Act.

[31] 5 U.S.C. § 553.

[32] 5 U.S.C. § 551(4).

[33] See, e.g., *Altera Corp. v. Commissioner*, 145 T.C. 91 (2015), rev'd, 926 F.3d 1061 (9th Cir. 2019), cert. denied, 2020 WL 3405861 (S. Ct. 2020) (Tax Court invalidated regulation based in part on the government's failure to respond to significant comments before promulgating it); *Chamber of Commerce v. Internal Revenue Service*, 2017 WL 4682050 (W.D. Tex. 2017) (government failed to adhere "to the APA's notice-and-comment requirements").

b. Executive Orders

E.O. 12866. In 1993, President Clinton issued an order setting forth a statement of regulatory philosophy and principles and providing a regulatory planning and review process for proposed and existing regulations. The Office of Management and Budget is charged with ensuring that regulations follow the stated philosophy and principles. The order also requires that agencies submit their regulatory plans for the year for OMB review.[34] You can search for agency submissions governed by Executive Order 12866 on the Reginfo.gov website (Regulatory Review tab). You can also search directly in an online version of the Federal Register or in a service covering Preambles to regulations.

E.O. 13132. In August 1999, President Clinton issued Executive Order 13132. It generally prohibits an agency from publishing rules with federalism implications if there would be substantial, direct compliance costs for state or local governments unless the agency engages in consultation provided for in the Executive Order.[35]

E.O. 13175. In November 2000, President Clinton issued Executive Order 13175 to require each federal agency to have "an accountable process to ensure meaningful and timely input by tribal officials in the development of regulatory policies that have tribal implications."[36]

E.O. 13563. In January 2011, President Obama issued Executive Order 13563 to improve regulation and regulatory review and reduce burdens on the public.[37] Agencies are to develop a plan to periodically review significant regulations to determine if any should be "modified, streamlined, expanded, or repealed."

E.O. 13771. President Trump issued three Executive Orders in early 2017. Executive Order 13771, entitled "Reducing Regulation and Controlling Regulatory Costs," generally requires an agency to identify at least two existing regulations to be repealed whenever it "publicly proposes for notice and comment or otherwise promulgates a new regulation . . . ."[38]

E.O. 13777. Executive Order 13777, entitled "Enforcing the Regulatory Reform Agenda," looks to reducing "unnecessary regulatory burdens." It requires agency task forces to evaluate existing regulations and recommend regulations for "repeal, replacement, or modification."[39]

E.O. 13789. Executive Order 13789, entitled "Identifying and Reducing Tax Regulatory Burdens," directed the Treasury Department to review all significant tax regulations issued since January 1, 2016. The Department was to propose actions regarding regulations identified as unduly burdensome or complex or that exceeded the IRS's statutory authority.[40]

---

34 58 Fed. Reg. 51735 (1993).

35 64 Fed. Reg. 43255 (1999).

36 66 Fed. Reg. 67249 (2000).

37 76 Fed. Reg. 3821 (2011).

38 82 Fed. Reg. 9339 (2017).

39 82 Fed. Reg. 12285 (2017). The Executive Order applies to regulations issued since January 1, 2016.

40 82 Fed. Reg. 19317 (2017). In Notice 2017–38, 2017–30 I.R.B. 147, the IRS identified eight significant regulations that either imposed an undue financial burden on U.S. taxpayers or added undue complexity to the federal tax laws. The Treasury Department later indicated that it would withdraw two proposed regulations, revoke in substantial part three temporary or final regulations, and substantially revise three other regulations. 82 Fed. Reg. 48013 (2017).

Section 6(b) of E.O. 12866 provides that the OMB's Office of Information and Regulatory Affairs will give "meaningful guidance and oversight" regarding significant regulatory actions so that the agency's actions are consistent with applicable law. For years, the IRS and Treasury Department argued that many regulations projects were exempt from OIRA review based on a 1983 Memorandum of Agreement. Following the issuance of Executive Order 13789, Treasury and OMB entered into a new 2018 Memorandum of Agreement. OIRA will now review tax regulatory actions that are likely to create a serious inconsistency with or otherwise interfere with another agency's action; raise novel legal or policy issues; or have a non-revenue effect on the economy of at least $100 million.[41]

The 2017 Executive Orders slowed the pace of issuing new regulations, and several proposed, temporary, or final regulations have been withdrawn or modified.[42]

Illustration 8-2. Preamble Discussion of Regulatory Constraints

Special Analyses

Certain IRS regulations, including these, are exempt from the requirements of Executive Order 12866, as supplemented and reaffirmed by Executive Order 13563. Therefore, a regulatory impact assessment is not required. It is hereby certified that these regulations will not have a significant economic impact on a substantial number of small entities. This certification is based on the fact that few, if any, small entities will be affected by these regulations. The regulations primarily will affect multinational financial institutions, which tend to be larger businesses, and foreign persons. Therefore, a Regulatory Flexibility Analysis is not required. Pursuant to section 7805(f) of the Code, the notice of proposed rulemaking preceding this regulation was submitted to the Chief Counsel for Advocacy of the Small Business Administration for comment on their impact on small business.

→ This excerpt is from T.D. 9815, 82 Fed. Reg. 8144, 8155 (2017).

c. Paperwork Reduction Act of 1995[43]

One of this act's goals is reducing duplication and burden on the public. The OMB performs this function by reviewing information requests. An agency that wants to require information submissions from the private sector must obtain OMB approval.

The Reginfo.gov website lets you search for agency submissions involving information collection. A significant number of the results are tax return forms.

---

41 https://www.whitehouse.gov/wp-content/uploads/2018/04/OIRA-TreasuryMOA_4.11.18.pdf. Certain exceptions apply for guidance to implement the Tax Cuts and Jobs Act.

42 The IRS proposed repealing 298 unnecessary, duplicative, or obsolete regulations in REG–132197–17. 83 Fed. Reg. 6806 (2018).

43 The Paperwork Reduction Act begins at 44 U.S.C. § 3501.

d. Regulatory Flexibility Act

Federal agencies that are required to publish notices of proposed rulemaking must prepare and publish for comment an initial regulatory flexibility analysis. This requirement also applies to notices of proposed rulemaking for interpretive rules involving the internal revenue laws that impose information collection requirements on small business.[44] The analysis includes information about the agency's objectives, the small entities affected, and the type of compliance requirements involved.

You can use the search feature on the Reginfo.gov site to search for such items. Alternatively, you can search in an online service covering the Federal Register (including govinfo.gov) or covering Preambles to Treasury Regulations.

e. Unfunded Mandates Reform Act of 1995[45]

The goal of this act is to prevent the federal government from imposing unfunded mandates that might interfere with other priorities held by state, local, and tribal governments. In appropriate cases, the Special Analyses section of the Preamble will address this act.

F. Working with Regulations

1. Title 26, C.F.R.

a. Format

Title 26 of the C.F.R. has no subtitles and only one chapter (Chapter I—Internal Revenue Service, Department of the Treasury). Chapter I is divided into seven subchapters and numerous parts.

Table 8-B. List of Subchapters and Partial List of Parts

Subchapter/Part	*Title*
Subchapter A	Income Tax
Part 1	Income Taxes
Part 2	Maritime Construction Reserve Fund
Part 3	Capital Construction Fund
Part 4	Temporary Income Tax Regulations Under Section 954 of the Internal Revenue Code
Part 5	Temporary Income Tax Regulations Under the Revenue Act of 1978
Subchapter B	Estate and Gift Taxes
Part 20	Estate Tax; Estates of Decedents Dying After August 16, 1954
Part 25	Gift Tax; Gifts Made After December 31, 1954

[44] See 5 U.S.C. § 603. A final regulatory flexibility analysis, including a description of public comments and the agency's response, accompanies the final regulation. Id. § 604.

[45] Pub. L. No. 104–4, 109 Stat. 48 (1995), codified in 2 U.S.C.

Subchapter/Part	*Title*
Part 26	Generation-Skipping Transfer Tax Regulations Under the Tax Reform Act of 1986
Subchapter C	Employment Taxes and Collection of Income Tax at Source
Subchapter D	Miscellaneous Excise Taxes
Subchapter F	Procedure and Administration
Part 300	User Fees
Part 301	Procedure and Administration
Subchapter G	Regulations Under Tax Conventions
Subchapter H	Internal Revenue Practice
Part 601	Statement of Procedural Rules
Part 602	OMB Control Numbers Under the Paperwork Reduction Act

→ Subchapter E is currently Reserved.

There are subdivisions within each part, but they are not separately numbered and often lack formal titles (e.g., subpart). For example, one subdivision of Subchapter A, Part 1, is Normal Taxes and Surtaxes. Two of its subdivisions are Determination of Tax Liability and Computation of Taxable Income. Those units are themselves further subdivided.

Other titles of C.F.R. label more of their subdivisions. For example, title 31 (Money and Finance: Treasury) includes subtitles, chapters, parts, and subparts.

b. Tables of Contents

Title 26 of the C.F.R. has an overall table of contents, which lists parts, at the beginning of the title. It has a regulations section table of contents at the beginning of each part. A third type of table of contents exists for certain series of regulations within title 26. Regulations that merely list the contents use the numbering system discussed in Section F.2 and end in –0.

Illustration 8-3. Table of Contents for I.R.C. § 2056 Regulations

§ 20.2056–0 Table of contents.

This section lists the captions that appear in the regulations under §§ 20.2056(a)–1 through 20.2056(d)–3.

§ 20.2056(a)–1 Marital deduction; in general.

(a) In general.
(b) Requirements for marital deduction.
(1) In general.
(2) Burden of establishing requisite facts.
(c) Marital deduction; limitation on aggregate deductions.
(1) Estates of decedents dying before 1977.

→ Govinfo.gov offers PDF and XML versions.

c. Authority for Regulations

When a proposed, temporary, or final regulation is published in the Federal Register, the authority (Code section 7805 or another section) precedes the regulation text. When a temporary or final regulation is published in C.F.R., the authority information is omitted, but it is available elsewhere in C.F.R. Authority information in C.F.R. appears immediately after a listing of sections in a particular part.

Illustration 8-4. Partial Authority Listing for Gift Tax Regulations (Part 25)

> AUTHORITY: 26 U.S.C. 7805.
> Section 25.2505–2 also issued under 26 U.S.C. 2010(c)(6).
> Section 25.2512–5 also issued under 26 U.S.C. 7520(c)(2).
> Section 25.2512–5A also issued under 26 U.S.C. 7520(c)(2).
> Section 25.2518–2 is also issued under 26 U.S.C. 2518(b).
> Section 25.6060–1 also issued under 26 U.S.C. 6060(a).
> Section 25.6081–1 also issued under the authority of 26 U.S.C. 6081(a).
> Section 25.6109–2 also issued under 26 U.S.C. 6109(a).

2. Regulations Numbering Scheme

a. Subdivisions

Most regulations have three segments. The first segment, called the prefix, indicates where the regulation appears; prefixes use the part numbers illustrated in Table 8-B (*supra* page 138).

The second segment generally indicates the Code section being interpreted. Thus, Treas. Reg. § 1.106–1 interprets Code section 106. The third segment is similar to the subdivisions used for Code subsections and is discussed in Section F.4 and illustrated in Table 8-C (*infra* page 141).

Each regulations section is further subdivided into

- paragraphs (e.g., Treas. Reg. § 20.2010–2(a));
- subparagraphs (e.g., Treas. Reg. § 20.2010–2(a)(3)); and
- subdivisions (e.g., Treas. Reg. § 20.2010–2(a)(3)(ii)).

The regulations do not uniformly follow the nomenclature above. For example, Treas. Reg. § 1.61–2(d)(1) contains the following language: "Except as otherwise provided in paragraph (d)(6)(i) of this section . . . ."

Smaller units exist but do not receive formal names. For example, Treas. Reg. § 1.274–2(b)(1)(iii)*(a)* says: "Except as otherwise provided in *(b)* or *(c)* of this subdivision . . . ." The subdivision referred to is (iii); *(a)*, *(b)*, and *(c)* are smaller units of (iii).[46]

b. Examples

Regulations frequently contain examples illustrating how the regulation applies to particular facts. These may appear in a separate Examples subdivision (e.g., Treas. Reg.

[46] Tax Notes offers nonsubscription access to tax regulations. It indicates the full citation for each regulation. This tool is highly beneficial for lengthy, complex regulations.

§ 1.119–1(f)) or as part of a subdivision to which the example applies (e.g., Treas. Reg. § 1.162–5(b)(3)(ii)). In some cases, a regulations section will be titled Examples (e.g., Treas. Reg. § 1.1368–3).

3. Significance of Regulations Prefixes

The prefix is critical for finding the correct regulation. First, regulations in different parts may interpret the same Code section. For example, Treas. Reg. §§ 1.7520–1, 20.7520–1, and 25.7520–1 all interpret Code section 7520. Minor differences in their texts reflect their application to different taxes.

Second, regulations in some parts don't interpret a Code section but the number following the prefix is a Code section number. For example, Treas. Reg. § 1.1–1 is an income tax regulation for Code section 1. Treas. Reg. § 2.1–1 is a definition section dealing with the maritime construction reserve fund; it has nothing to do with Code section 1.[47] Although its prefix (2) indicated it related to the maritime construction reserve fund [Table 8-B, *supra* page 138], that information alone would not have told you that the regulation had nothing to do with Code section 1.

4. Relationship of Code and Regulations Subdivisions

The third segment of the regulation does not indicate the Code subsection involved. In fact, there may be significantly more regulations sections than Code subsections. Table 8-C illustrates the relationship of Code and regulations sections for Code section 61(a).

Table 8-C. Relationship of Code and Regulations Subdivisions

Code Subsection/Paragraph	*Regulations Section(s)*
61(a)	1.61–1, –14, –22[48]
61(a)(1)	1.61–2, –15, –21
61(a)(2)	1.61–3, –4, –5
61(a)(3)	1.61–6
61(a)(4)	1.61–7
61(a)(5)	1.61–8
61(a)(6)	1.61–8
61(a)(7)	1.61–9
61(a)(8)	1.61–10
61(a)(9)	1.61–10
61(a)(10)	1.61–11
61(a)(11)	1.61–12
61(a)(12)	1.61–13

[47] Regulations in Part 601 follow this pattern. Treas. Reg. § 601.101, for example, has nothing to do with I.R.C. § 101.

[48] The relationship between Treas. Reg. § 1.61–22, issued in 2003, and paragraphs in I.R.C. § 61(a) varies based on how the particular split-dollar life insurance arrangement is analyzed.

Code Subsection/Paragraph	*Regulations Section(s)*
61(a)(13)	1.61–13
61(a)(14)	1.61–13

5. Letters in Second Segment of Section Number

a. Formats

Most section numbers follow this format: Treas. Reg. § 1.61–1. Two other formats include a capital or lower case letter before the third segment.

The regulation number includes a capital letter if the underlying Code section includes a capital letter. For example, Treas. Reg. § 1.263A–1 is a regulation for Code section 263A. Capital letters may also appear even though the Code section does not include a capital letter. Treas. Reg. § 1.170A–1 is an example of this situation.

Some regulations include lower case letters before the third segment. Treas. Reg. § 1.672(a)–1 illustrates that format. The letter in parentheses may indicate the relevant Code subsection but does not necessarily do so.

b. Location in C.F.R.

If a section number includes a letter before the third segment, it follows the regulations for the Code section that don't include a letter. If more than one letter is used, those regulations appear in alphabetical order. Temporary regulations always include a capital T, which appears at the end of the regulation. Temporary regulations appear in the normal number order in C.F.R.

Illustration 8-5. Order of I.R.C. § 448 Regulations in C.F.R.

Regulation	*Title*
§ 1.448–1	Limitation on the use of the cash receipts and disbursements method of accounting.
§ 1.448–1T	Limitation on the use of the cash receipts and disbursements method of accounting (temporary).
§ 1.448–2	Nonaccrual of certain amounts by service providers.

Illustrations 8-6 through 8-8 show the regulations order for Code section 142 in C.F.R., the Standard Federal Tax Reporter (SFTR), and Lexis+. Each uses a different order.

Illustration 8-6. Order of I.R.C. § 142 Regulations in C.F.R.

Regulation	*Title*
§ 1.142–0	Table of contents.
§ 1.142–1	Exempt facility bonds.
§ 1.142–2	Remedial actions.
§ 1.142–3	Refunding Issues. [Reserved]

Regulation	*Title*
§ 1.142–4	Use of proceeds to provide a facility.
§ 1.142(a)(5)–1	Exempt facility bonds: Sewage facilities.
§ 1.142(a)(6)–1	Exempt facility bonds: solid waste disposal facilities.
§ 1.142(f)(4)–1	Manner of making election to terminate tax-exempt bond financing.

Illustration 8-7. Order of I.R.C. § 142 Regulations in SFTR/Cheetah

Standard Federal Tax Reporter (2020), §1.142-0. Table of contents

Standard Federal Tax Reporter (2020), §1.142-1. Exempt facility bonds

Standard Federal Tax Reporter (2020), §1.142-2. Remedial actions

Standard Federal Tax Reporter (2020), §1.142-3. Refunding issues

Standard Federal Tax Reporter (2020), §1.142-4. Use of proceeds to provide a facility

Standard Federal Tax Reporter (2020), §1.103-7. Industrial development bonds

Standard Federal Tax Reporter (2020), §1.103-8. Interest on bonds to finance certain exempt facilities

Standard Federal Tax Reporter (2020), §1.103-8. Interest on bonds to finance certain exempt facilities. LR-190-78, 8/22/84.

Standard Federal Tax Reporter (2020), §1.103-8. Interest on bonds to finance certain exempt facilities. LR-269-84, 11/7/85.

Standard Federal Tax Reporter (2020), §1.103-9. Interest on bonds to finance industrial parks

Standard Federal Tax Reporter (2020), §1.103-11. Bonds held by substantial users

Standard Federal Tax Reporter (2020), §1.142(a)(5)-1. Exempt facility bonds: Sewage facilities

Standard Federal Tax Reporter (2020), §1.142(a)(6)-1. Exempt facility bonds: solid waste disposal facilities

Standard Federal Tax Reporter (2020), §1.142(f)(4)-1. Manner of making election to terminate tax-exempt bond financing

→ Standard Federal Tax Reporter includes regulations that are not strictly tied to section 142.

Illustration 8-8. Order of I.R.C. § 142 Regulations in Lexis+

○ § 1.142-0 Table of Contents.

○ § 1.142-1 Exempt facility bonds.

○ § 1.142(f)(4)-1 Manner of making election to terminate tax-exempt bond financing.

○ § 1.142-2 Remedial actions.

○ § 1.142-3 Refunding issues. [Reserved]

○ § 1.142-4 Use of proceeds to provide a facility.

○ § 1.142(a)(5)-1 Exempt facility bonds: Sewage facilities.

○ § 1.142(a)(6)-1 Exempt facility bonds: solid waste disposal facilities.

6. Regulations Issued for Prior Internal Revenue Acts and Codes

Regulations issued for 1954 Code sections also apply to the 1986 Code to the extent Code sections (or their numbers) remained unchanged. Regulations interpreting the 1939 Code (and pre-1939 Code acts) followed a different numbering system. Unless otherwise indicated, you can assume that references in this book cover regulations interpreting the 1986 Code.

Illustration 8-9. Excerpt from 26 C.F.R. (1938)

TITLE 26—INTERNAL REVENUE

CHAPTER I—BUREAU OF INTERNAL REVENUE
DEPARTMENT OF THE TREASURY

Subchapter A—Income and Excess-Profits Tax

PART 3—INCOME TAX UNDER THE REVENUE ACT OF 1936

§ 3.22 (a)-14 *Cancelation of indebtedness*—(a) *In general.* The cancelation of indebtedness, in whole or in part, may result in the realization of income. If, for example, an individual performs services for a creditor, who in consideration thereof cancels the debt, income in the amount of the debt is realized by the debtor as compensation for his services. A taxpayer realizes income by the payment or purchase of his obligations at less than their face value. (See § 3.22 (a)-18.) If a shareholder in a corporation which is indebted to him gratuitously forgives the debt, the transaction amounts to a contribution to the capital of the corporation.

(3) an "arrangement" or a "real property arrangement" confirmed under Chapter XI or XII, respectively, of the Bankruptcy Act, as amended; or

(4) a "wage earner's plan" confirmed under Chapter XIII of the Bankruptcy Act, as amended.

If, however, such plan of corporate reorganization or agreement of composition referred to in (1) to (4) above had for one of its principal purposes the avoidance of income tax, the cancelation or reduction of indebtedness, under such plan or agreement confirmed under section 12, 74 or 77B or under Chapter X, XI, XII or XIII of the Bankruptcy Act, as amended, may result in the realization of income.

→ Each act had its own set of regulations and its own part of 26 C.F.R. As is the case for current regulations, the number to the right of the decimal point represented the corresponding act section number.

→ The C.F.R. began publication in 1938.

7. Regulations for Other C.F.R. Titles

Each C.F.R. title has its own numbering system. The most common difference between Treasury regulations in 26 C.F.R. and other regulations relates to material following the decimal point. Table 8-D illustrates tax-related section numbers from four other C.F.R. titles.

Table 8-D. Regulation Numbers in Other C.F.R. Titles

Citation	*Caption*
27 C.F.R. § 53.61	Imposition and rates of tax.
29 C.F.R. § 2510.3–2	Employee pension benefit plan.
31 C.F.R. § 10.1	Offices.
41 C.F.R. § 302–17.2	Why does relocation affect personal income taxes?

G. Definitions in Regulations

As was true for the Code itself, the regulations frequently define terms within individual sections, and a definition in one section may apply in interpreting another section. Some groups of regulations include a definitions section.[49] Other regulations sections enlarge upon definitions found in Subtitle F, Chapter 79, of the Code.[50] Finally, because several Code sections defer to other statutes or agency interpretations, you may have to find definitions in Statutes at Large, United States Code, or other titles of C.F.R.[51]

[49] See, e.g., Treas. Reg. § 1.179–4 Definitions.

[50] See, e.g., Treas. Reg. § 301.7701–1.

[51] See, e.g., I.R.C. § 4064(b)(1)(B): "The term 'automobile' does not include any vehicle which is treated as a nonpassenger automobile under the rules which were prescribed by the Secretary of Transportation . . . ."

H. Rules Affecting Multiple Regulations Sections

As is the case for the Code, rules appearing in a regulation section may apply only to that section, to a subdivision thereof, or to several sections. See, for example, Treas. Reg. § 1.414(r)–3(c)(5)(iii)(A):

> Solely for purposes of the separateness rules of this section and the assignment rules of § 1.414(r)–7, if an employee changes status as described in paragraph (c)(5)(iii)(B) of this section, an employer may, for up to three consecutive testing years after the base year (within the meaning of paragraph (c)(5)(iii)(B)*(1)* or *(2)* of this section), treat the employee as providing the same level of service to its lines of business as the employee provided in the base year.

I. Locating Regulations Documents

The first step in locating administrative documents is determining which items you need. The following paragraphs divide documents by type rather than by where you can find them.

Many of the items covered in this section can be located on government websites. Some items are included on more than one such site. These sites do not have identical coverage dates or search functions. Several items, particularly those of historical interest, are likely to be available only in print or microform or from subscription-based websites.

1. Unified Agenda and Priority Guidance Plan

The Unified Agenda of Federal Regulatory and Deregulatory Actions and the Priority Guidance Plan relate to planned regulatory action. Unless you are tracking agency plans over time, you probably need only the most recent versions of each. Documents for the current year (and several prior years) are available on government websites.

a. Unified Agenda

The Unified Agenda is issued twice a year and is available at govinfo.gov, Regulations.gov, and Reginfo.gov. You might hear it referred to as the Semiannual Agenda or the Semiannual Regulatory Agenda.

The Treasury Department and agencies[52] within its umbrella are grouped together in the Agenda. In addition to the IRS, agencies include the Alcohol and Tobacco Tax and Trade Bureau, the Bureau of the Fiscal Service, the Financial Crimes Enforcement Network, and the Office of the Comptroller of the Currency.

In some instances, such as projects involving employee benefits, you may also need to consult the Agendas produced by other government agencies. For example, some regulations covering the Affordable Care Act are jointly issued by the Departments of Labor, Health and Human Services, and Treasury (and their respective sub-agencies, Employee Benefits Security Administration, Centers for Medicare & Medicaid Services, and IRS).[53]

---

[52] Although this book refers to these entities as agencies, they are actually bureaus.

[53] See, e.g., T.D. 9624, 78 Fed. Reg. 39870 (2013), announcing regulations affecting 26 C.F.R., 29 C.F.R., and 45 C.F.R. Each agency has its own RIN.

Although the Agenda is issued semiannually, a Regulatory Plan is required in the fall Agenda. That plan indicates the most important items that should be issued within the fiscal year. Since fall 2007, only the Regulatory Plan and rules that are subject to the Regulatory Flexibility Act appear in the Federal Register.

Illustration 8-10. Partial Listing of IRS Proposed Rule Stage Items on Reginfo.gov

TREAS/IRS	Proposed Rule Stage	Mark to Market for Dealers in Securities	1545-AS85
TREAS/IRS	Proposed Rule Stage	Mark-to-Market Accounting for Dealers in Commodities and Traders in Securities or Commodities	1545-AW06
TREAS/IRS	Proposed Rule Stage	Special Rules Relating to Transfers of Intangibles to Foreign Corporations	1545-AY41
TREAS/IRS	Proposed Rule Stage	Below-Market Loans	1545-BC78
TREAS/IRS	Proposed Rule Stage	Reduction of Fuel Excise Tax Evasion	1545-BE03
TREAS/IRS	Proposed Rule Stage	Further Guidance on the Application of Section 409A to Nonqualified Deferred Compensation Plans	1545-BF50
TREAS/IRS	Proposed Rule Stage	Determination of Governmental Plan Status	1545-BG43
TREAS/IRS	Proposed Rule Stage	Rules for Home Construction Contracts	1545-BG70
TREAS/IRS	Proposed Rule Stage	Interest on Deferred Tax Liability for Contingent Payment Sales Under Section 453(A)	1545-BH10

→ Regulations projects are listed by stage, in RIN number order. Click on the RIN to reach detailed information.

Illustration 8-11. Detailed Information for RIN 1545–AS85

TREAS/IRS **RIN:** 1545-AS85 **Publication ID:** Fall 2019
Title: Mark to Market for Dealers in Securities
Abstract:

The regulations will provide guidance on the mark-to-market method of accounting for securities dealers.

Agency: Department of the Treasury(TREAS)
RIN Status: Previously published in the Unified Agenda
Major: No
EO 13771 Designation: Other
CFR Citation: 26 CFR 1.475(a)-1 26 CFR 1.475(a)-2 26 CFR 1.475(b)-3
Legal Authority: 26 U.S.C. 475 26 U.S.C. 7805
Legal Deadline: None
Priority: Substantive, Nonsignificant
Agenda Stage of Rulemaking: Proposed Rule Stage
Unfunded Mandates: No

Timetable:

Action	Date	FR Cite
NPRM	01/04/1995	60 FR 397
NPRM Comment Period End	04/04/1995	
Second NPRM	06/00/2020	

Additional Information: REG-209724-94 (NPRM) Drafter attorney: Marsha Sabin (202) 317-6945 Reviewer attorney: William E. Blanchard (202) 317-3900 Treasury attorney: N/A CC:FIP Section 1.475(a)-3 finalized in TD 8700. Section 1.475(b)-4 finalized in TD 8700. Section 1.475(c)-2 finalized in TD 8700.
Regulatory Flexibility Analysis Required: No
Small Entities Affected: No
Included in the Regulatory Plan: No
RIN Data Printed in the FR: No
Related RINs: Related to 1545-AW06
Government Levels Affected: None
Federalism: No
Agency Contact:
Marsha A. Sabin
Department of the Treasury
Internal Revenue Service
1111 Constitution Avenue NW., Room 3547,
Washington, DC 20224
Phone:202 317-6945
Fax:855 574-9025
Email: marsha.a.sabin@irscounsel.treas.gov

The Agendas for the Treasury Department available at Regulations.gov can be sorted by agency, project title, RIN, stage of rulemaking, and whether the project appears in the Regulatory Plan. The stages of rulemaking are Prerule, Proposed Rule, Final Rule, Long-term Action, and Completed Action.[54] Reginfo.gov also allows sorting, but only by agency, project title, RIN, and stage of rulemaking. Its Agency Rule List indicates three stages of rulemaking—Prerule, Proposed Rule, and Final Rule. It also has a search function [Illustration 8-12, *infra* page 147].

If you know a project's RIN but not the actual project number, you can easily find it online in the Agenda. You can also search by project number or Code section. If you are unsure whether a project exists, you can search for projects by agency.

---

[54] In early August 2020, Regulations.gov was in the process of migrating to its beta site (https://beta.regulations.gov). The beta site would use the original website URL after the migration is complete and the original Regulations.gov is retired. Using this website has been challenging during the transition.

The Regulations.gov website currently includes Agendas since fall 2007; the Reginfo.gov website currently includes Agendas and Regulatory Plans since fall 1995. Despite their similar names and some overlapping content, the Reginfo.gov and Regulations.gov sites differ in their primary focus. Reginfo.gov lets you search for regulations projects based on a variety of criteria [Illustration 8-12]. Regulations.gov lets you search for pending regulations projects, comment on them, and read comments submitted by others. A comments search is illustrated in Section I.5. [See Illustration 8-20, *infra* page 156.]

Illustration 8-12. Advanced Search in Reginfo.gov

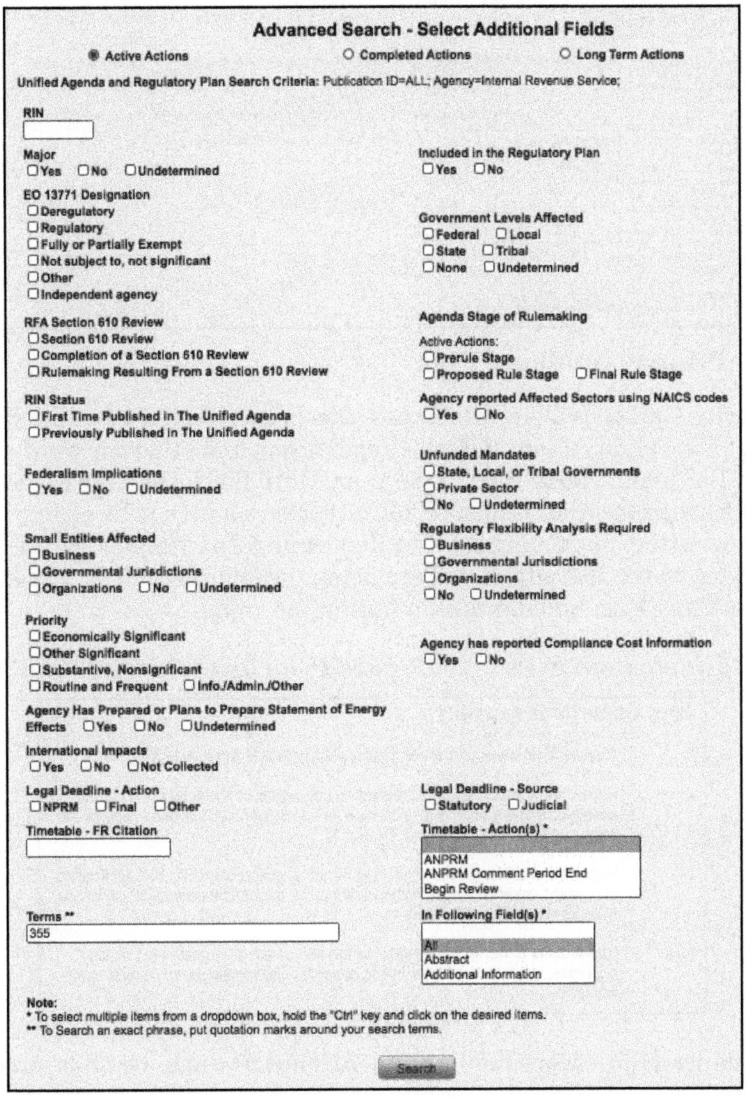

Advanced Search - Select Additional Fields

Active Actions — Completed Actions — Long Term Actions

Unified Agenda and Regulatory Plan Search Criteria: Publication ID=ALL; Agency=Internal Revenue Service;

RIN

Major: Yes / No / Undetermined

Included in the Regulatory Plan: Yes / No

EO 13771 Designation: Deregulatory / Regulatory / Fully or Partially Exempt / Not subject to, not significant / Other / Independent agency

Government Levels Affected: Federal / Local / State / Tribal / None / Undetermined

RFA Section 610 Review: Section 610 Review / Completion of a Section 610 Review / Rulemaking Resulting From a Section 610 Review

Agenda Stage of Rulemaking — Active Actions: Prerule Stage / Proposed Rule Stage / Final Rule Stage

RIN Status: First Time Published in The Unified Agenda / Previously Published in The Unified Agenda

Agency reported Affected Sectors using NAICS codes: Yes / No

Federalism Implications: Yes / No / Undetermined

Unfunded Mandates: State, Local, or Tribal Governments / Private Sector / No / Undetermined

Small Entities Affected: Business / Governmental Jurisdictions / Organizations / No / Undetermined

Regulatory Flexibility Analysis Required: Business / Governmental Jurisdictions / Organizations / No / Undetermined

Priority: Economically Significant / Other Significant / Substantive, Nonsignificant / Routine and Frequent / Info./Admin./Other

Agency has reported Compliance Cost Information: Yes / No

Agency Has Prepared or Plans to Prepare Statement of Energy Effects: Yes / No / Undetermined

International Impacts: Yes / No / Not Collected

Legal Deadline - Action: NPRM / Final / Other

Legal Deadline - Source: Statutory / Judicial

Timetable - FR Citation

Timetable - Action(s) *: ANPRM / ANPRM Comment Period End / Begin Review

Terms **: 355

In Following Field(s) *: All / Abstract / Additional Information

Note:
* To select multiple items from a dropdown box, hold the "Ctrl" key and click on the desired items.
** To Search an exact phrase, put quotation marks around your search terms.

Search

→ You reach this search screen after selecting the Unified Agenda>Search>Advanced Search, then the desired publications (most current, all available, selected), and then Department of the Treasury>Internal Revenue Service on the previous screens.

→ This search looks for anything relating to I.R.C. § 355 in All Fields.

Illustration 8-13. Agenda Search Results

View Rule

View EO 12866 Meetings   Printer-Friendly Version   Download RIN Data in XML

TREAS/IRS   **RIN:** 1545-BN47   **Publication ID:** Spring 2017
Title: Guidance Under Section 355 Concerning Device and Active Trade or Business
Abstract:

Proposed regulations under section 355 of the Internal Revenue Code that would clarify the application of the device prohibition and the active business requirement of section 355.

Agency: Department of the Treasury(TREAS)   **Priority:** Substantive, Nonsignificant
RIN Status: Previously published in the Unified Agenda   **Agenda Stage of Rulemaking:** Final Rule Stage
Major: No   **Unfunded Mandates:** No
EO 13771 Designation: uncollected
CFR Citation: 26 CFR 1
Legal Authority: 26 U.S.C. 7805
Legal Deadline: None
Timetable:

Action	Date	FR Cite
NPRM	07/15/2016	81 FR 46004
NPRM Comment Period End	10/13/2016	
Final Action	12/00/2017	

Additional Information: REG-134016-15 (NPRM) Drafting attorney: Stephanie Floyd (202) 317-5081 Reviewing attorney: Russell Subin (202) 317-5368 Treasury attorney: Brett York (202) 622-1285 CC:CORP:3
Regulatory Flexibility Analysis Required: No   **Government Levels Affected:** None
Federalism: No
Included in the Regulatory Plan: No
RIN Data Printed in the FR: No
Agency Contact:
Stephanie D. Floyd
Attorney
Department of the Treasury
Internal Revenue Service
1111 Constitution Avenue NW., Room 5040,
Washington, DC 20224
Phone:202 317-5081
Fax:855 561-0293
Email: stephanie.d.floyd@irscounsel.treas.gov

b. Priority Guidance Plan

The Priority Guidance Plan, which has also been referred to as the Business Plan and the Guidance Priority Plan, includes regulations and other forms of guidance that Treasury and IRS plan to issue during the year. Until 2002, the Plan covered a calendar year. Beginning with the plan issued in 2002, it covers a plan year ending June 30. It is covered by newsletters such as Daily Tax Report and Tax Notes Federal. You can also find all the Plans on the IRS site. If you are using the Guidance Plan to track IRS action, be sure to check any Plan updates issued during the year.

Illustration 8-14. 2019–2020 Priority Guidance Plan

GIFTS AND ESTATES AND TRUSTS

1. Guidance on basis of grantor trust assets at death under §1014.
2. Regulations under §2032(a) regarding imposition of restrictions on estate assets during the six month alternate valuation period. Proposed regulations were published on November 18, 2011.
3. Regulations under §2053 regarding personal guarantees and the application of present value concepts in determining the deductible amount of expenses and claims against the estate.
4. Regulations under §7520 regarding the use of actuarial tables in valuing annuities, interests for life or terms of years, and remainder or reversionary interests.

→ The Guidance Plan covers regulations, revenue rulings, revenue procedures, and other guidance.

2. Proposed, Temporary, and Final Regulations

a. Federal Register

The Federal Register includes the text, including Preambles, of proposed, temporary, and final regulations. It also includes corrections that are filed after the initial publication. Because it includes the Preambles, you may prefer reading a new regulation in the Federal Register even if it also appears in C.F.R. If the IRS is simply amending an existing regulation, the Federal Register version includes only the amendment and not the full text. Illustration 5-3 (*supra* page 31) illustrates an analogous situation for amendments to the Code.

The GPO's govinfo.gov site carries the Federal Register, with separate daily access to each agency, beginning with the 1994 volume; earlier volumes (currently beginning in 1936) are also available but do not offer separate daily agency access. You can search the Federal Register by project number, Federal Register date, RIN, or underlying Code section.

There are other places you can access the Federal Register. Your library may have it in print or microform. It is also available in subscription services. Bloomberg Law, HeinOnline, Lexis+, and Westlaw Edge all begin coverage in 1936.

b. Code of Federal Regulations

The C.F.R. includes the text of temporary and final regulations. It also includes T.D. numbers, dates, and Federal Register citations for each regulation.[55] The beginning of each C.F.R. part lists the authority (I.R.C. § 7805 or another Code section) for regulations in that part. [See Illustration 8-4, *supra* page 140.] The C.F.R. does not include proposed regulations or Preambles.

Because the C.F.R. section numbers generally correspond to Code section numbers, it is easier to find temporary and final regulations in the C.F.R. than in the Federal Register.[56] As noted above, you might choose to use the Federal Register because it includes Preambles.

Although many libraries carry the print softbound C.F.R. volumes, they are best used for historical purposes. The government does not update C.F.R. volumes every time an agency promulgates a new regulation. Instead it republishes C.F.R. titles on an annual basis; several titles are replaced each calendar quarter. The annual reissue of Title 26 includes regulations issued as of April 1. Searching C.F.R. print updates for later material is a tedious process.[57]

---

[55] If a 1954 Code regulation was originally published before 1960, the IRS may have republished it that year in T.D. 6498, 6500, or 6516. The C.F.R. begins the regulation's history at that point.

[56] The method for issuing regulations in the Federal Register makes that publication analogous to Statutes at Large for revenue acts. Each T.D. is listed separately by publication date rather than by Code section. The Code of Federal Regulations, which is in section number order, is analogous to United States Code for statutes.

[57] There is also an electronic version of the C.F.R.'s List of Sections Affected (LSA), but it only gives a citation to the Federal Register. You will need to locate the actual change there. Basic legal research texts discuss using LSA. Because it is easier to use e-CFR, this book ignores the LSA search process.

The GPO's govinfo.gov site carries the C.F.R. beginning with the 1997 volume; there is partial coverage for 1996 (but it does not cover Title 26).[58] If you know the regulation section number, you can go to it directly because C.F.R. is arranged in regulations section order. If you know the Code section number only, you can browse the regulations for that Code section until you find the relevant regulation. Alternatively, you can use the Advanced Search function to search the C.F.R. by citation, date, or phrase.

The government does not update the online C.F.R. any more often than it updates the print version. To avoid missing temporary and final regulations issued since the last C.F.R. update, use e-CFR (www.ecfr.gov) instead of C.F.R. You can also use a subscription service, such as Bloomberg Law, Federal Research Library, Lexis+, or Westlaw Edge, which updates its C.F.R. database as new regulations are issued.

If you need a volume of C.F.R. that precedes the date on which the government began publishing it electronically, you may be able to find it in the library's print or microform collection. It is also available in subscription services, such as HeinOnline (since 1938).

Illustration 8-15. Search in C.F.R. on govinfo.gov for Disregarded Entity

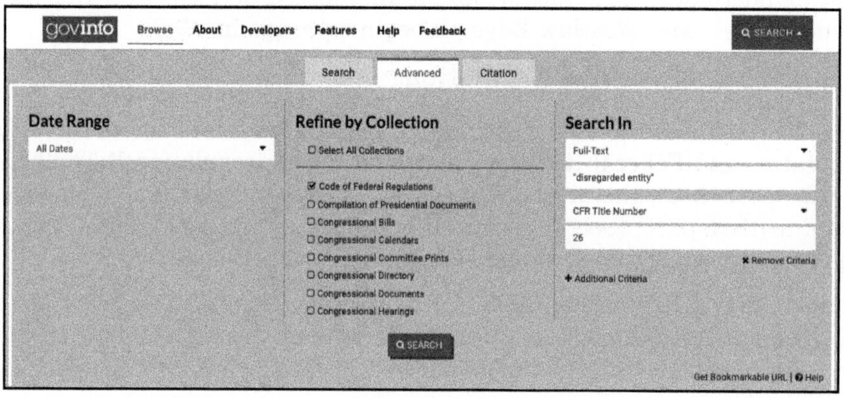

→ The search could have also been restricted by date.

[58] The govinfo.gov Browse option lists "Code of Federal Regulations (CFR), 1996 to Present." It also includes four listings that start with "CFR," but those do not include the actual regulations.

Illustration 8-16. Disregarded Entity Regulations

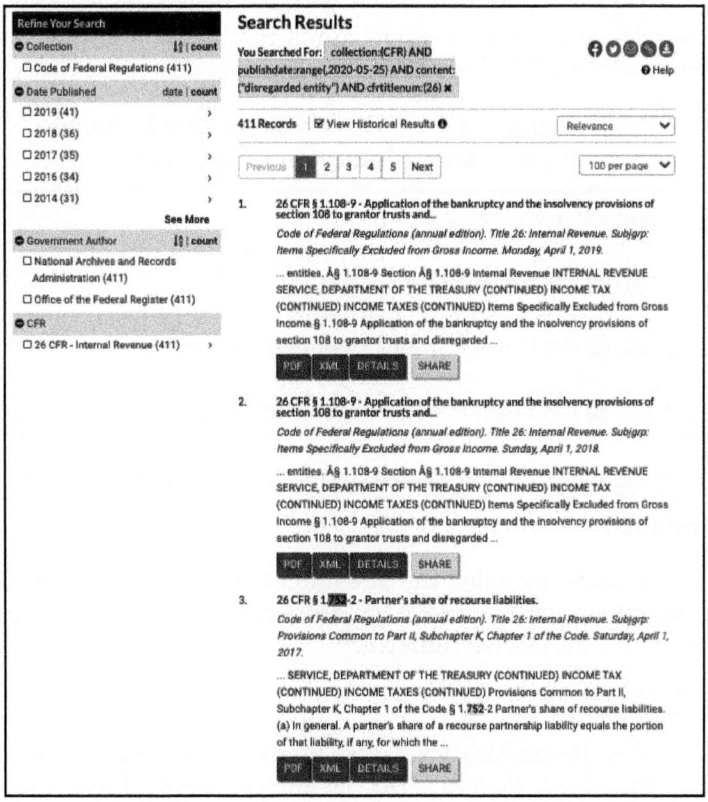

→ You can sort results by relevance, alphabetical order (A–Z or Z–A), or date (forward or reverse). Date is particularly relevant if you are searching multiple years' volumes at once.

→ You can also restrict the results to a particular year (or years).

c. Subscription Services That Include Regulations

Bloomberg Law, Checkpoint, Cheetah, Federal Research Library, HeinOnline, Lexis+, ProQuest, Westlaw Edge, and other online services have databases covering regulations. These services also include access to Preambles that accompany regulations.

Looseleaf services, in particular United States Tax Reporter (USTR) and Standard Federal Tax Reporter (SFTR), include regulations text in their compilation volumes; Preambles are in separate volumes. USTR is available in print and on Checkpoint and Westlaw Edge; SFTR is available in print and on Cheetah. Other tax-oriented services provide print versions of tax regulations. These include Mertens, Federal Tax Regulations, published in annual softbound volumes with updating throughout the year in a looseleaf Current Developments binder.

Looseleaf services frequently include proposed regulations in their compilation volumes along with temporary and final regulations. [See Illustration 8-17.] If a service instead files proposed regulations in a separate volume, it may arrange them by Federal Register date. Those services generally include a table that cross-references from the underlying Code or regulations section to the appropriate page, paragraph, or section in the looseleaf service. They are unlikely to have tables cross-referencing project numbers. If you use the service's electronic version, filing method is less important as you can reach regulations using hyperlinks.

Illustration 8-17. United States Tax Reporter Regulations Listing on Checkpoint

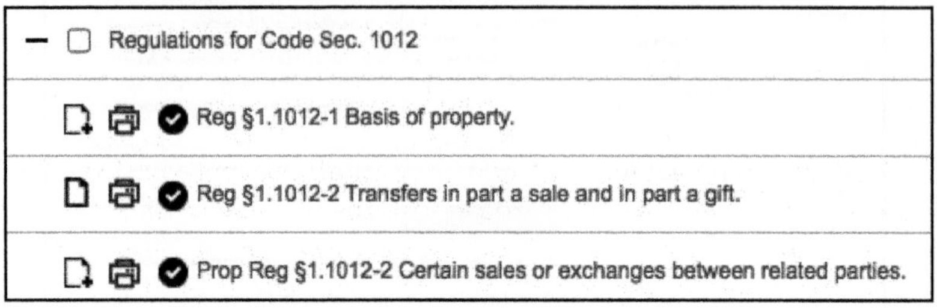
Regulations for Code Sec. 1012
Reg §1.1012-1 Basis of property.
Reg §1.1012-2 Transfers in part a sale and in part a gift.
Prop Reg §1.1012-2 Certain sales or exchanges between related parties.

→ The proposed regulation follows the existing final regulation in USTR.

3. Preambles

The Federal Register includes the Preambles for each proposed, temporary, and final regulation with the regulation text. Excerpts or full text also appear in the Internal Revenue Bulletin and Cumulative Bulletin.[59]

Tax-oriented looseleaf services don't publish Preambles with the regulations text. If they print the Preambles, they do so in separate volumes.[60] Mertens, Federal Tax Regulations, publishes Preambles for tax regulations in looseleaf volumes. Coverage begins in 1985. Standard Federal Tax Reporter prints Preambles for proposed regulations in its U.S. Tax Cases Advance Sheets volume; it includes current year Preambles for T.D.s in the Regulations Status Table in its New Matters volume. United States Tax Reporter prints Preambles to proposed regulations in a separate volume for Preambles; it prints current year Preambles for T.D.s in the IRS Rulings section of its Recent Developments volume.

Cheetah includes the SFTR service, and Checkpoint includes USTR. If you use these looseleaf services online, simply use their Preamble option. Other electronic services may include Preambles as a separate database or in their Federal Register coverage. Illustrations 8-1 and 8-2 (*supra* pages 132 and 137) show excerpts from a Preamble.

4. Earlier Versions of Regulations

The discussion of the Federal Register and C.F.R. in this section listed services that covered earlier versions of those documents. This subsection continues that discussion.

a. 1954 and 1986 Codes

Prior language may be important for evaluating recent changes in a regulation or for research involving a completed transaction. If you need the language of a 1954 or 1986 Code regulation, you can find it in United States Code Congressional &

---

[59] Preambles for proposed regulations were added to the C.B. in 1981.

[60] If a regulation was issued in both proposed and temporary format, a looseleaf service may carry only the Preamble to the temporary regulation.

Administrative News—Federal Tax Regulations. This service has separate volumes for each year since 1954 and prints regulations in effect on January 1 of the particular year. Electronic services such as Westlaw Edge have "Prior" or "Historical" links that give access to versions of the C.F.R. going back to the early 1980s.

If you need a regulation that was both issued and withdrawn within a single calendar year and thus might be omitted from a USCCAN search for a single year, you may be able to find it by searching in both the C.F.R. and Federal Register collection on govinfo.gov. Two other services—Cumulative Changes and Mertens, Law of Federal Income Taxation—may also be useful for older material. They are described later in this subsection.

If you lack access to a service that tracks regulations, make a list of T.D. numbers for the regulation you are tracing. Those numbers appear immediately after the particular regulation in C.F.R. and in most other versions of the regulations. The T.D.s are published in the Cumulative Bulletins, which your library is likely to carry.[61] The Cumulative Bulletin is also available online. Lexis+ has coverage from 1954; Westlaw Edge and HeinOnline include all volumes from 1919 through the final C.B. (2008–2).

Note one limitation in using T.D. numbers to find older versions of regulations. The IRS republished many 1954 Code regulations that were issued before 1960 in T.D. 6498, 6500, or 6516. The USCCAN service ignores the pre-1960 publication in its history notes; Cumulative Changes omits the 1960 T.D. numbers but includes the pre-1960 T.D.s. If you use any service to find T.D. numbers, be sure you know how that service treats those early items.

(1) e-CFR/eCFR

The version of e-CFR in effect in July 2020 does not allow tracing regulations language over time. The beta version of e-CFR will offer a Point-in-Time option. Users will be able to determine how a regulation looked over time. Color-coding and strike-outs will indicate specific changes in a regulation's language.[62]

(2) Cumulative Changes

Tables of amendments cover all regulations sections for each tax; individual sections do not have their own charts. Each table indicates the original and all amending T.D. numbers and filing dates and provides a Cumulative Bulletin or Internal Revenue Bulletin citation. Unfortunately, this service is no longer current.

The 1986 service also includes cross-references to United States Tax Reporter. A numerically ordered Table of Amending TDs indicates the purpose, date, and C.B. or I.R.B. citation for each regulation issued.[63]

---

[61] Finding Lists in the CCH and RIA citators indicate which volume of the I.R.B. or C.B. contains each T.D. Since 2007, RIA cites to the paragraph in United States Tax Reporter instead of the bulletins.

[62] The system currently covers changes beginning in 2017 but additional historical data is planned. The beta version can be viewed at ecfr.federalregister.gov. It appears that the new site will be called eCFR with no hyphen.

[63] Although T.D. 6500, a 1960 republication of existing income tax regulations is not formally included, Cumulative Changes does list the original pre-1960 T.D. A cautionary note warns the user to remember that pre-1960 regulations were republished in T.D. 6500. T.D. 6498 (procedure and administration) and T.D. 6516 (withholding tax) receive similar treatment. These T.D.s do not appear in the Cumulative Bulletin.

The tables follow the regulations part designations. As a result, they do not follow a strict Code section numerical sequence. The 1954 series includes tables for regulations that have been redesignated or replaced.

Immediately following the tables, the editors print prior versions of each regulation. Older materials note changes in italics and use footnotes to indicate stricken language; later materials do not use this format. Cumulative Changes includes the T.D. number and the dates of approval and of filing for each version of a regulation.

(3) Mertens, Law of Federal Income Taxation

Until the mid-1990s, Mertens, Law of Federal Income Taxation, published a Regulations series. That series published all income tax regulations issued or amended within a given time span (two or more years per volume).

b. 1939 Code and Earlier

Early regulations don't follow the regulations format used elsewhere in this book. Initially they were issued with respect to individual revenue acts [Illustration 8-9, *supra* page 144]. They were often divided into articles rather than section numbers. The first named set of regulations (Regulations Number 33) was issued in 1914.[64] Unlike the regulation shown in Illustration 8-9, article numbers in regulations did not correspond to act section numbers.

The Federal Register is available online on govinfo.gov, beginning in 1994, and in print, beginning in 1936. Thus, the online versions are not good sources for finding early regulations. Even for years it covers, it is tedious to search in print. In many libraries, the best source for 1939 Code and earlier regulations will be the Cumulative Bulletin. It began publication in 1919; the first T.D. it includes is 2836.

The GPO published Treasury Decisions Under Internal Revenue Laws of the United States from 1899 until 1942. It covers 1898 through July 9, 1942. The current T.D. numbering system began in 1900 with the third volume. Many early T.D.s look less like regulations and more like "public" private letter rulings.[65]

HeinOnline lets you browse the C.F.R. back to its 1938 edition. Its Title/Part/Section Quick Locator lets you search by year, title, part, and section; you do not have to specify a section if you want to read the entire title and part. Because the Locator uses drop-down menus for year, title, and part, it won't let you search for a non-existent set of regulations.

---

[64] See HENRY CAMPBELL BLACK, A TREATISE ON THE LAW OF INCOME TAXATION UNDER FEDERAL AND STATE LAWS § 71 (2d ed. 1915). This treatise is available online in HeinOnline and The Making of Modern Law: Legal Treatises 1800–1926.

[65] "SIR: In reply to a letter of inquiry addressed to this office on the 29th ultimo by Frederick D. Howe, treasurer and manager of the Warren Specialty Company, Auburn, N.Y., will you please inform him that the beverage (liqueur) called creme de menthe being, as it is understood, a compound of distilled spirits with other materials, any person manufacturing it for sale must be required to pay special tax as a rectifier . . . ." T.D. 33, 3 TREASURY DECISIONS UNDER INTERNAL REVENUE LAWS OF THE UNITED STATES, 32–33 (1900). This series is available in HeinOnline.

Illustration 8-18. Searching C.F.R. in HeinOnline

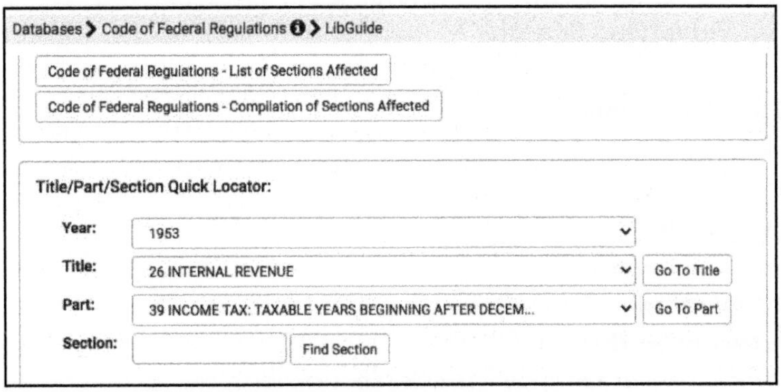

Illustration 8-19. Portion of 1953 Income Tax Regulations in HeinOnline

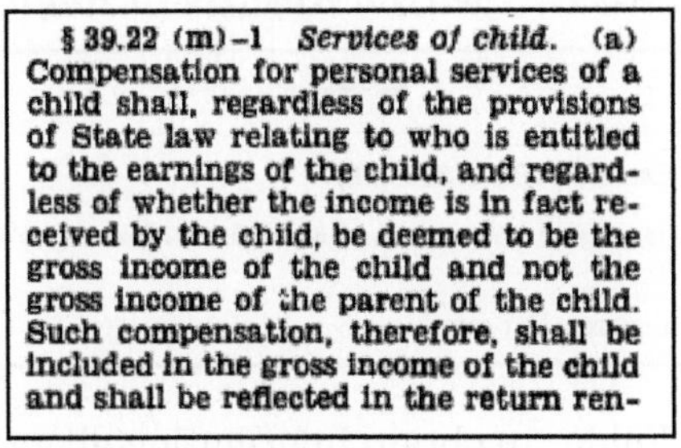

§ 39.22 (m)-1 *Services of child.* (a) Compensation for personal services of a child shall, regardless of the provisions of State law relating to who is entitled to the earnings of the child, and regardless of whether the income is in fact received by the child, be deemed to be the gross income of the child and not the gross income of the parent of the child. Such compensation, therefore, shall be included in the gross income of the child and shall be reflected in the return ren-

→ Compare the 1953 regulation to current I.R.C. § 73.

5. Hearings Transcripts and Other Taxpayer Comments

The Treasury Department does not hold a hearing for every proposed regulation. Even when it schedules a hearing, it may end up canceling it because no one requests the opportunity to comment in person. Newsletters such as Daily Tax Report and Tax Notes Federal report on testimony at hearings and taxpayer written comments.

The Regulations.gov website lets you search for proposed and final rules and submit comments on proposed rules. It also gives you access to comments made by other taxpayers and their representatives.[66] Illustrations 8-20 through 8-22 cover written comments submitted with respect to the proposed regulation (REG–113295–18) mentioned in Section C.5 (*supra* page 128). If you don't know the project number or RIN, you can search for projects by keyword or by agency (Treasury, in this case). The site also includes options for narrowing your search by date.

[66] There may be a lag of several weeks before comments submitted through this website are actually posted.

Illustration 8-20. Search for Comments in Regulations.gov

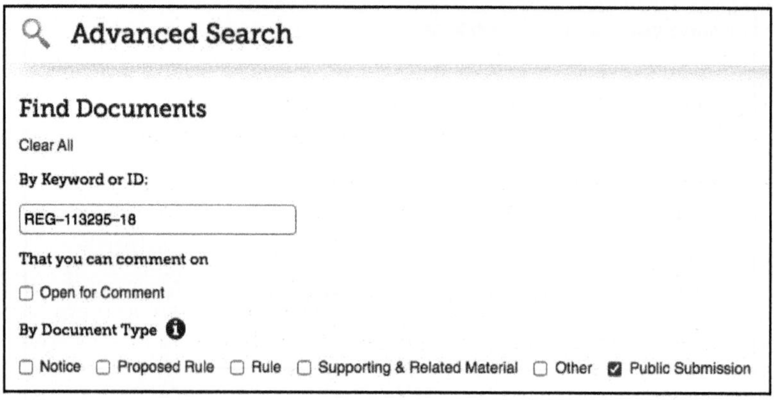

Illustration 8-21. Search Results in Regulations.gov

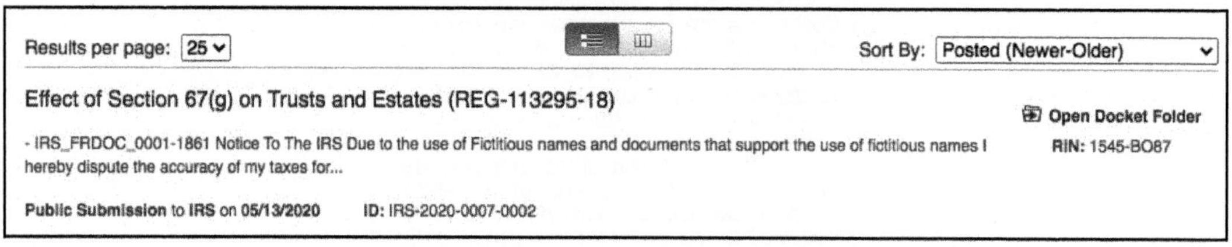

→ Click on Open Docket Folder to obtain information about any comments.

Illustration 8-22. Partial List of Comments Received

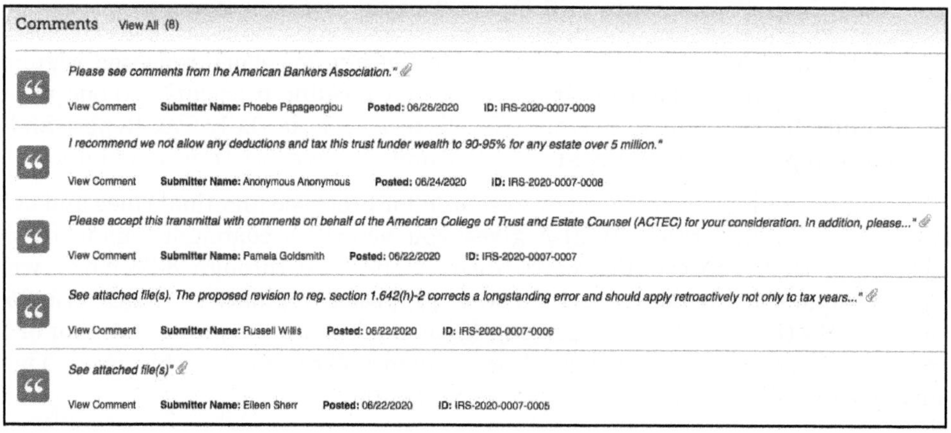

You can also comment on proposed regulations at the IRS page on the Federal Register website.[67] The site links to Regulations.gov to make or show any comments.

When the IRS issues final regulations, the Preamble summarizes taxpayer comments made in response to the NPRM. The Preamble also indicates if the IRS acted in response to those comments.

---

[67] FED. REG., www.federalregister.gov/agencies/internal-revenue-service (last visited July 18, 2020).

J. Citators for Regulations

Regulations rarely keep pace with new legislative activity. Whenever a Code section changes, researchers must review existing regulations. They may no longer be relevant. They may even be totally invalid. If a regulation appears to contradict statutory language, check the date of its most recent T.D. to see if it predates the statutory change.

When an existing regulation affects a transaction, that regulation's success or failure in litigation is certainly relevant. The government is bound nationally by adverse decisions in the Supreme Court. It is effectively bound within a particular circuit by an adverse circuit court decision because trial courts follow the law of their circuit. The IRS is not bound in its dealings with taxpayers in circuits that have not addressed the regulation. Because the Supreme Court hears relatively few tax cases, the government may decide not to withdraw a regulation merely because the Tax Court or a single circuit court invalidates it.[68]

A citator indicating judicial action on regulations is extremely useful for determining how courts ruled on challenges to particular regulations. KeyCite (Westlaw Edge), Shepard's (Lexis+), and Smart Code (Bloomberg Law) serve that purpose. They allow you to check a particular regulation. The citators provided by CCH and RIA are not as useful because they are based on T.D. number rather than regulation number. Because T.D.s often involve more than one regulation section, citators based on regulations section numbers are more likely to provide the desired information.

You can also search electronic services without using a citator by using the regulations section number and a variant of valid (or invalid) as your search terms. For example, there are two options for researching Treas. Reg. § 1.752–6 in Westlaw Edge. You may enter either of the following searches: "kc treas reg 1.752–6" or "kc 26 cfr 1.752–6."[69] Another option is going directly to the regulation. When you see the regulation, you will know there are problems because a red flag appears on the screen.

Illustration 8-23. Westlaw Edge Flag for Treas. Reg. § 1.752–6

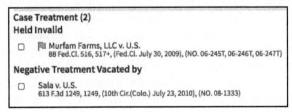

Case Treatment (2)
Held Invalid

☐ Murfam Farms, LLC v. U.S.
88 Fed.Cl. 516, 517+, (Fed.Cl. July 30, 2009), (NO. 06-245T, 06-246T, 06-247T)

Negative Treatment Vacated by

☐ Sala v. U.S.
613 F.3d 1249, 1249, (10th Cir.(Colo.) July 23, 2010), (NO. 08-1333)

→ The next step would be to read these and any other cases discussing the regulation's validity.

---

[68] Compare *Western Nat. Mut. Ins. Co. v. Commissioner*, 65 F.3d 90 (8th Cir. 1995), invalidating Treas. Reg. § 1.846–3(c), with *Atlantic Mut. Ins. Co. v. Commissioner*, 111 F.3d 1056 (3d Cir. 1997), holding the regulation valid. The Supreme Court upheld the Third Circuit. See 523 U.S. 382 (1998). See also the *Altera Corp. v. Commissioner* litigation discussed in note 33, *supra* page 135.

[69] "kc" stands for KeyCite, the Westlaw Edge cite-checking service. To find decisions that use the term "validity," refine the search by adding root expanders. Remember to check search terminology options when you use an electronic service.

Illustration 8-24. Westlaw Edge Options for Treas. Reg. § 1.752–6

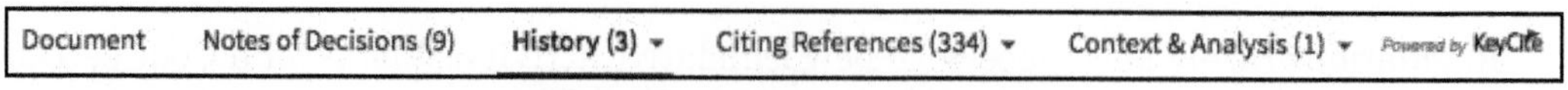

→ Under Citing References, you can further refine your research by selecting particular types of citing references (e.g., cases or regulations).

If you are using a service that lacks a citator (or that has a citator that uses T.D. instead of regulation numbers), you can simply use the regulation as your search term.

K. Judicial Deference

In determining the degree of deference they should give to regulations, courts are guided by several Supreme Court decisions, the best-known of which is *Chevron*.[70] The *Chevron* Court held

> When a court reviews an agency's construction of the statute which it administers, it is confronted with two questions. First, always, is the question whether Congress has directly spoken to the precise question at issue. If the intent of Congress is clear, that is the end of the matter; for the court, as well as the agency, must give effect to the unambiguously expressed intent of Congress. If, however, the court determines Congress has not directly addressed the precise question at issue, the court does not simply impose its own construction on the statute, as would be necessary in the absence of an administrative interpretation. Rather, if the statute is silent or ambiguous with respect to the specific issue, the question for the court is whether the agency's answer is based on a permissible construction of the statute.[71]

Although *Chevron* is not a tax decision, it is cited in many tax cases and therefore appears if you enter *Chevron* into an electronic service. There are also tax cases involving the same company. This situation will also occur for other taxpayers that have been involved in significant nontax litigation.

The excerpts below illustrate judicial approaches to deference. Taxpayers may challenge a regulation if its promulgation failed to satisfy provisions in the statutes and Executive Orders discussed in Section E. They may also challenge its substance. In the latter situation, three statements apply irrespective of the approach taken. First, the degree of deference accorded specific authority regulations is no longer higher than that accorded general authority regulations. Second, proposed regulations receive much less deference than do temporary or final regulations. Third, an agency cannot issue a regulation that contradicts an earlier judicial decision if the Supreme Court held that its original interpretation was the only interpretation of the statute.

---

[70] *Chevron U.S.A. Inc. v. Natural Resources Defense Council, Inc.*, 467 U.S. 837 (1984). Other decisions that courts may cite when discussing deference include *National Muffler Dealers Association v. United States*, 440 U.S. 472 (1979), and *National Cable & Telecommunications Association v. Brand X Internet Services*, 545 U.S. 967 (2005).

[71] *Chevron*, 467 U.S. at 842–43 (footnotes omitted). The Court added: "If Congress has explicitly left a gap for the agency to fill, there is an express delegation of authority to the agency to elucidate a specific provision of the statute by regulation. Such legislative regulations are given controlling weight unless they are arbitrary, capricious, or manifestly contrary to the statute. Sometimes the legislative delegation to an agency on a particular question is implicit rather than explicit. In such a case, a court may not substitute its own construction of a statutory provision for a reasonable interpretation made by the administrator of an agency." Id. at 843–44 (footnotes omitted).

- "The preamble to the final regulations discusses seven major groups of comments and the changes Treasury made in response to them. But an agency cannot reasonably be expected to address every comment it received. The APA 'has never been interpreted to require the agency to respond to every comment, or to analyse every issue or alternative raised by the comments, no matter how insubstantial.'" *Oakbrook Land Holdings, LLC v. Commissioner*, 154 T.C. No. 10, at *20 (2020) (citation omitted).[72]

- "It may be that judges today would use other methods to determine whether Congress left a gap to fill. But that is beside the point. The question is whether the Court in *Colony* concluded that the statute left such a gap. And, in our view, the opinion (written by Justice Harlan for the Court) makes clear that it did not.

  Given principles of *stare decisis*, we must follow that interpretation. And there being no gap to fill, the Government's gap-filling regulation cannot change *Colony's* interpretation of the statute. We agree with the taxpayer that overstatements of basis, and the resulting understatement of gross income, do not trigger the extended limitations period of § 6501(e)(1)(A)." *United States v. Home Concrete & Supply, LLC*, 566 U.S. 478, 489–90 (2012) (overruled by I.R.C. § 6501(e)(1)(B)(ii)).

- "The principles underlying our decision in *Chevron* apply with full force in the tax context . . . . We have held that *Chevron* deference is appropriate 'when it appears that Congress delegated authority to the agency generally to make rules carrying the force of law, and that the agency interpretation claiming deference was promulgated in the exercise of that authority.' Our inquiry in that regard does not turn on whether Congress's delegation of authority was general or specific." *Mayo Foundation for Medical Education and Research v. United States*, 562 U.S. 44, 55, 57 (2011) (citation omitted).

- "While we do not defer to the trial court, an agency's interpretation of its own regulation is entitled to a level of deference even 'broader than deference to the agency's construction of a statute, because in the latter case the agency is addressing Congress's intentions, while in the former it is addressing its own.' That being said, 'an agency's inconsistent interpretation of its regulation detracts from the deference we owe to that interpretation.'" *Abbot Laboratories v. United States*, 573 F.3d 1327, 1330 (Fed. Cir. 2009) (citations omitted).

- "Agency inconsistency is not a basis for declining to analyze the agency's interpretation under the *Chevron* framework." *National Cable & Telecomm. Association v. Brand X Internet Services*, 545 U.S. 967, 981 (2005).

- "To invoke these passages from our decisions for the general proposition that regulations may not add rules not found in the statute and not precluded by the statute is to misread them. Indeed, supplementation of a

---

72 The Tax Court also held the regulation was substantively valid.

statute is a necessary and proper part of the Secretary's role in the administration of our tax laws." *Hachette USA, Inc. v. Commissioner*, 105 T.C. 234, 251 (1995).

- "If the regulations constituted a reasonable interpretation of [the statute], we would be compelled to uphold them even if [the taxpayer's] interpretation were more reasonable." *Estate of Bullard v. Commissioner*, 87 T.C. 261, 281 (1986).
- "The reasonableness of each possible interpretation of the statute can also be measured against the legislative process by which [it] was enacted." *Commissioner v. Engle*, 464 U.S. 206, 220 (1984).
- "[Proposed regulations] carry no more weight than a position advanced on brief. . . ." *F.W. Woolworth Co. v. Commissioner*, 54 T.C. 1233, 1265 (1970).

L. Problems

1. What type of a regulation (general authority/specific authority; interpretive/legislative) is Treas. Reg. § 1.666(a)–1A, as contrasted with one such as Treas. Reg. § 1.469–4? Is there a difference in the standard for judicial determination of validity between the two regulations?

2. List all the T.D.s issued for the regulation below. Use a print source if one is available.

   a. § 1.165–1

   b. § 1.513–1

   c. § 1.817–2

   d. § 1.1272–1

3. You were completing a research project in June 2020 on I.R.C. § 385 and wanted to know if there were any new regulations. Were any proposed, temporary, or final regulations for that section issued shortly before June 2020? If there were, what do(es) the regulation(s) address?

4. Who drafted each T.D. listed below? In which IRS Chief Counsel division did that attorney work?

   a. 9600

   b. 9400

   c. 9200

   d. 9000

5. Determine the Code section to which T.D. 8602 pertains. Use a print source if one is available.

6. What are the most recent regulations in progress under I.R.C. § 67? What do they address? What is their current status?

7. In the course of a research project concerning the rules of I.R.C. § 179(b), you came across Treas. Reg. § 1.179–2. Explain why you must be particularly cautious in looking to this regulation for guidance. (Do not discuss the substance of these provisions.)

8. Assume that, in order to enhance your understanding of Treas. Reg. § 1.752–2, you decide to research the history of that regulation. Use a print source if one is available.

a. Where can you find the Preamble to the initial final version of the regulation? (Hint: use the T.D. number and the *Cumulative Bulletin*.)

b. Examine the first page or two of the Preamble. Did the IRS previously issue a Temporary Regulation? If so, what is the T.D. number assigned to that Temporary Regulation, and where could you find that Temporary Regulation?

c. What is the most recent T.D. for this regulation?

9. Using online sources, locate the court decision described below and indicate which regulation is involved. These decisions involve whether a regulation is valid. Use the materials in Chapter 11 as necessary.

a. 2019 Court of Appeals decision involving whether exceptions to the physical delivery rule in regulations displaced the common law "mailbox rule."

b. 2012 Court of Appeals decision involving the associated-property regulations and the avoided-cost rule.

c. 2011 Bankruptcy Court decision involving the inconsistency between regulations under I.R.C. § 597 and regulations under I.R.C. § 1504.

d. 2006 Tax Court decision involving the grandfathered provisions of the generation-skipping transfer tax and a transfer by general power of appointment.

10. Your instructor will select a regulations project from the most recent Priority Guidance Plan. Find that project in the most recent Unified Agenda and indicate all relevant dates for guidance.

11. Find comments submitted on a proposed regulation selected by your instructor.

12. Draft comments on a proposed regulation selected by your instructor.

Chapter 9

INTERNAL REVENUE SERVICE DOCUMENTS

A. Introduction

This chapter discusses guidance, other than regulations, issued by the Internal Revenue Service. These documents can be issued more quickly than regulations, in part because they do not undergo notice and comment procedures. In addition to describing the different types of guidance, this chapter indicates which can be cited as precedential and which constitute "substantial authority," concepts discussed in Chapter 2. It also discusses sources in which you can find these documents, the role of the Freedom of Information Act and other statutes affecting the release of IRS documents, and judicial deference to various IRS pronouncements.

Your goals for this chapter include learning which documents are available and where they can be found, determining their relative importance, and locating IRS and judicial action with respect to them.

B. Types of IRS Documents

There are several methods for categorizing IRS documents. Three such methods are their means of publication, their initial audience, and their status as precedent or as substantial authority.

1. Means of Publication

The IRS publishes several documents in the weekly Internal Revenue Bulletin. The most important of these are revenue rulings, revenue procedures, notices of acquiescence and nonacquiescence, notices, and announcements. Items currently included in the I.R.B. were cumulated every six months and appeared in the Cumulative Bulletin, but the IRS ceased publishing the C.B. after the 2008–2 volume. The I.R.B. and C.B. are discussed in Section K.

The IRS issues other types of guidance, such as private letter rulings, and actions on decisions, which it does not publish in the I.R.B. Many of these items were released to the public following Freedom of Information Act (FOIA) litigation; others have been exempted from release by statute.

The discussion in Sections C through H categorizes IRS documents by their publication status: officially published in the I.R.B. or in other IRS publications; available because of FOIA or other release-related litigation; or exempted from release by statute. Section I discusses items issued before the FOIA Library came into existence.

Sections C through G loosely track the documents' placement in the FOIA Library, which is part of the IRS website. There are some exceptions. First, forms and related publications are officially published, but they are not part of the five types of documents with links on that page. There is a Forms & Instructions tab at the top of the FOIA Library page; it takes you to a Forms, Instructions & Publications page on which you can search for these documents. Second, several documents were discontinued before the IRS began electronic publication or have been subsumed into other document titles. Discussion in this chapter indicates those exceptions.

Illustration 9-1. Portion of IRS Website Home Page

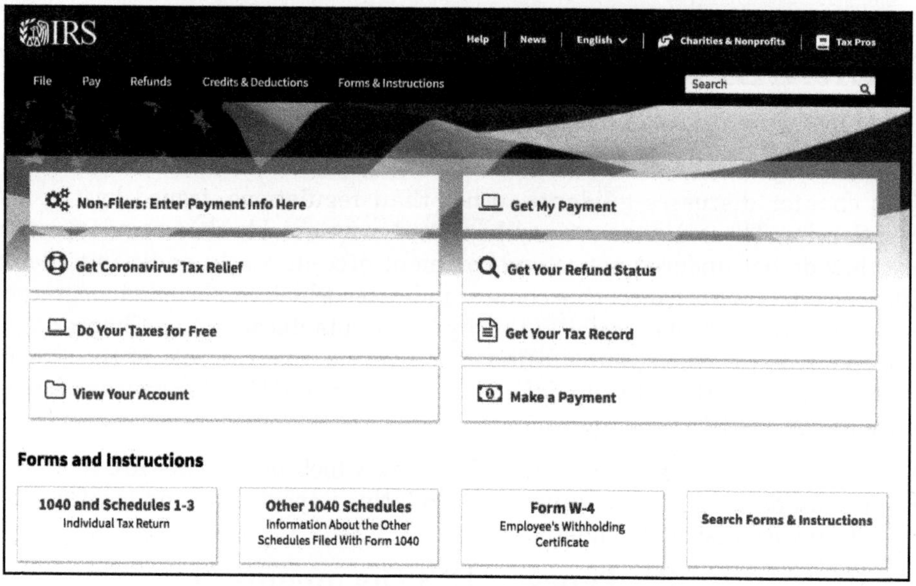

→ A link at the bottom of the home page takes you to the Freedom of Information Act (FOIA) page.

Illustration 9-2. FOIA Page Link to IRS FOIA Library

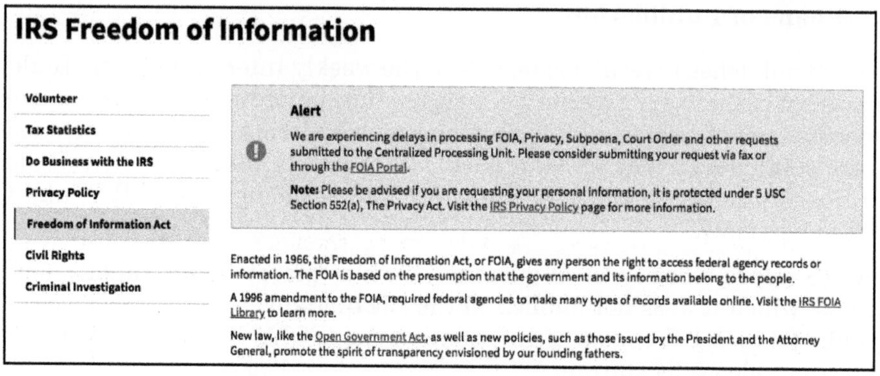

→ Click on IRS FOIA Library to reach the page shown in Illustration 9-3.

Illustration 9-3. IRS FOIA Library

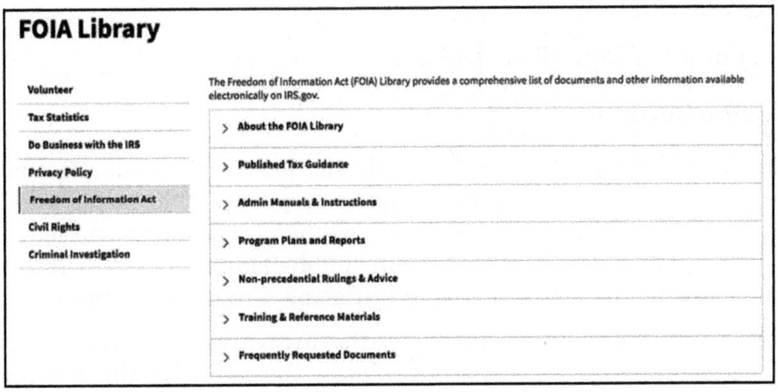

→ Each section has a dropdown menu listing the various IRS materials.

2. Initial Audience[1]

Documents published in the Internal Revenue Bulletin are directed to all taxpayers and their representatives. Forms, instructions, publications, Frequently Asked Questions (FAQs), and Fact Sheets (FS) are often geared to taxpayers seeking information on their own. Although not published in the I.R.B., they are available on the IRS website.

Private letter rulings are directed to a specific taxpayer; the IRS makes them available to other readers after deleting identifying material. Still other documents are written for government personnel. Many of them, such as Legal Advice Issued by Associate Chief Counsel, are publicly available.

3. Status as Precedent or Substantial Authority

Items printed in the I.R.B. constitute authority for avoiding the substantial understatement penalty discussed in Chapter 2.[2] These documents can be cited as precedent, and the IRS considers itself bound by them in its dealings with taxpayers whose facts are substantially the same as those discussed in the documents. As discussed in Section O, the degree of deference they receive from courts is mixed.

Items that are not published in the I.R.B. fall into two categories. A few of them are not precedential but nevertheless constitute authority for avoiding the substantial understatement penalty. Others are neither precedential nor authority for avoiding the penalty. Even though these documents are not precedential, courts occasionally cite them.

C. Documents Published in the IRS FOIA Library

The first four items discussed below are published in the weekly Internal Revenue Bulletins, which are found in the Published Tax Guidance section of the FOIA Library. Each constitutes authority for avoiding the substantial understatement penalty. Each is

---

1 See Stephanie Hunter McMahon, *Classifying Tax Guidance According to End Users*, 73 TAX LAW. 245 (2020).

2 I.R.C. § 6662(b).

currently numbered by year; the numbering system does not indicate the Code or regulations section involved.

1. Revenue Rulings (Rev. Rul.)

a. Background

The IRS issues rulings designed to apply the law to particular factual situations. Unlike regulations, rulings do not first appear in proposed form for public comment. Rulings fall into two categories—revenue rulings and letter rulings. If the IRS determines a topic is of general interest, it may publish guidance in the Internal Revenue Bulletin as a **revenue ruling** rather than initiating a regulations project.

Although a revenue ruling is not as authoritative as a Treasury regulation, any taxpayer whose circumstances are substantially the same as those described in the ruling can rely upon it.[3] Code section 7805(b)(8) provides that revenue rulings can apply retroactively unless their text indicates otherwise. They are not subject to the section 7805(b)(1) limitations on retroactivity applied to regulations. [See Illustration 9-4 for an excerpt from a revenue ruling.]

Although the number varies from year to year, there have been relatively few revenue rulings issued in recent years.[4] Many of those issued represent regularly scheduled guidance rather than rulings on new topics.[5]

---

[3] Although it happens rarely, the IRS has issued adverse rulings based on a set of facts encountered in an audit and then asserted the ruling as authority when the taxpayer litigated. See Rev. Rul. 79–427, 1979–2 C.B. 120, discussed in *Niles v. United States*, 710 F.2d 1391, 1393 (9th Cir. 1983). The IRS occasionally issues pro-taxpayer revenue rulings or revenue procedures based on analogies to statutory authority. For example, Rev. Proc. 2017–24, 2017–7 I.R.B. 916, allowed an exclusion for debt discharged pursuant to the Department of Education's "Defense to Repayment" and "Closed School" programs. The relevant Higher Education Act provided an exclusion only for loans discharged under the "Closed School" program.

[4] The IRS issued more than 763 revenue rulings in 1955; it issued 26 in 2019 (although the Finding Lists include only 24 of them and number the final one as 28). See Jasper L. Cummings, Jr., *Our Guidance Drought*, TAX NOTES, Oct. 23, 2017, at 565.

[5] The Appendix to the Priority Guidance Plan includes a month-by-month listing of Regularly Scheduled Publications. This list includes notices and revenue procedures in addition to revenue rulings.

Illustration 9-4. Excerpt from Rev. Rul. 2019–24

Part I

26 CFR 1.61-1: Gross income.
(Also §§ 61, 451, 1011.)

Rev. Rul. 2019-24

ISSUES

(1) Does a taxpayer have gross income under § 61 of the Internal Revenue Code (Code) as a result of a hard fork of a cryptocurrency the taxpayer owns if the taxpayer does not receive units of a new cryptocurrency?

(2) Does a taxpayer have gross income under § 61 as a result of an airdrop of a new cryptocurrency following a hard fork if the taxpayer receives units of new cryptocurrency?

BACKGROUND

Virtual currency is a digital representation of value that functions as a medium of exchange, a unit of account, and a store of value other than a representation of the United States dollar or a foreign currency. Foreign currency is the coin and paper money of a country other than the United States that is designated as legal tender, circulates, and is customarily used and accepted as a medium of exchange in the country of issuance. *See* 31 C.F.R. § 1010.100(m).

Cryptocurrency is a type of virtual currency that utilizes cryptography to secure transactions that are digitally recorded on the legacy distributed ledger. Following a hard fork, transactions involving the new cryptocurrency are recorded on the new distributed ledger and transactions involving the legacy cryptocurrency continue to be recorded on the legacy distributed ledger.

An airdrop is a means of distributing units of a cryptocurrency to the distributed ledger addresses of multiple taxpayers. A hard fork followed by an airdrop results in the distribution of units of the new cryptocurrency to addresses containing the legacy cryptocurrency. However, a hard fork is not always followed by an airdrop.

Cryptocurrency from an airdrop generally is received on the date and at the time it is recorded on the distributed ledger. However, a taxpayer may constructively receive cryptocurrency prior to the airdrop being recorded on the distributed ledger. A taxpayer does not have receipt of cryptocurrency when the airdrop is recorded on the distributed ledger if the taxpayer is not able to exercise dominion and control over the cryptocurrency. For example, a taxpayer does not have dominion and control if the address to which the cryptocurrency is airdropped is contained in a wallet managed through a cryptocurrency exchange and the cryptocurrency exchange does not support the newly-created cryptocurrency such that the airdropped cryptocurrency is not immediately credited to the taxpayer's account. ... tributed ledger for *Crypto R* experiences a hard fork, resulting in the creation of *Crypto S*. On that date, 25 units of *Crypto S* are airdropped to *B*'s distributed ledger address and *B* has the ability to dispose of *Crypto S* immediately following the airdrop. *B* now holds 50 units of *Crypto R* and 25 units of *Crypto S*. The airdrop of *Crypto S* is recorded on the distributed ledger on *Date 2* at *Time 1* and, at that date and time, the fair market value of *B*'s 25 units of *Crypto S* is $50. *B* receives the *Crypto S* solely because *B* owns *Crypto R* at the time of the hard fork. After the airdrop, transactions involving *Crypto S* are recorded on the new distributed ledger and transactions involving *Crypto R* continue to be recorded on the legacy distributed ledger.

LAW AND ANALYSIS

Section 61(a)(3) provides that, except as otherwise provided by law, gross income means all income from whatever source derived, including gains from dealings in property. Under § 61, all gains or undeniable accessions to wealth, clearly realized, over which a taxpayer has complete dominion, are included in gross income. *See Commissioner v. Glenshaw Glass Co.*, 348 U.S. 426, 431 (1955). In general, income is ordinary unless it is gain from the sale or exchange of a capital asset or a special rule applies. *See, e.g.*, §§ 1222, 1231, 1234A.

b. Numbering System

The IRS numbers revenue rulings chronologically.[6] The ruling number has two segments; the first indicates the year and the second indicates the ruling number for the year. Beginning in 2000, the IRS began using all four digits to indicate the year; it previously used only the last two digits.

The IRS began issuing numbered revenue rulings in 1953 and adopted the current numbering system in 1954. Earlier rulings, with different names, appeared in pre-1953 Cumulative Bulletins.

Table 9-A. Pre-1953 Titles of Published Rulings

Designation	*Official Name*
A.R.M.	Committee on Appeals and Review Memorandum
A.R.R.	Committee on Appeals and Review Recommendation
A.T.	Alcohol Tax Unit; Alcohol and Tobacco Tax Division
C.L.T.	Child-Labor Tax Division
C.S.T.	Capital-Stock Tax Division
C.T.	Carriers Taxing Act of 1937; Taxes on Employment by Carriers

6 The first ruling issued in 2020 was Rev. Rul. 2020–1. Each week's rulings are numbered sequentially.

Designation	*Official Name*
D.C.	Treasury Department Circular
Dept. Cir.	Treasury Department Circular
E.P.C.	Excess Profits Tax Council Ruling or Memorandum
E.T.	Estate and Gift Tax Division or Ruling
Em.T.	Employment Taxes
G.C.M.	Chief Counsel's Memorandum; General Counsel's Memorandum; Assistant General Counsel's Memorandum
I.T.	Income Tax Unit or Division
L.O.	Solicitor's Law Opinion
MS.	Miscellaneous Unit or Division or Branch
M.T.	Miscellaneous Division or Branch
Mim.	Mimeographed Letter; Mimeograph
Mim.	Solicitor's Law Opinion
O.	Office Decision
Op. A.G.	Opinion of Attorney General
P.T.	Processing Tax Decision or Division
S.	Solicitor's Memorandum
S.M.	Solicitor's Memorandum
S.R.	Solicitor's Recommendation
S.S.T.	Social Security Tax and Carriers' Tax; Social Security Tax; Taxes on Employment by Other than Carriers
S.T.	Sales Tax Unit or Division or Branch
Sil.	Silver Tax Division
Sol. Op.	Solicitor's Opinion
T.	Tobacco Division
T.B.M.	Advisory Tax Board Memorandum
T.B.R.	Advisory Tax Board Recommendation
Tob.	Tobacco Branch

c. Format

Revenue rulings begin by indicating the Code or regulations section involved. Most recent revenue rulings contain five segments: Issue; Facts; Law; Analysis; and Holding. Other sections that may appear include Background, Effect on Other Documents (for rulings that revoke, modify, obsolete, or otherwise affect a prior holding), and Effective Date. Rulings also indicate the IRS employee who drafted them or who can be contacted if the taxpayer has questions; Cumulative Bulletins issued before 1998 omit drafting information.

2. Revenue Procedures (Rev. Proc.) and Procedural Rules

a. Background

Revenue procedures are published statements of IRS practices and procedures that are published in the Internal Revenue Bulletin. Procedures of general applicability may also be added to the IRS Statement of Procedural Rules and published in the Code of Federal Regulations.

Several revenue procedures are issued each year to provide guidance on how to obtain rulings and other IRS advice. [See Table 9-B.] For example, the first procedure each year (e.g., Rev. Proc. 2020–1) provides procedures for obtaining rulings, determination letters, and closing agreements. It also includes a sample ruling request format and a schedule of user fees.

Table 9-B. Annual Revenue Procedures for Obtaining Guidance

Number	*Subject*
2020–1	Procedures for issuing private letter rulings, closing agreements, information letters, and determination letters on issues under the jurisdiction of listed Chief Counsel subdivisions
2020–2	Procedures for furnishing technical advice on issues under the jurisdiction of listed Chief Counsel subdivisions
2020–3	Areas for which the IRS will not issue a letter ruling or determination letter on issues under the jurisdiction of listed Chief Counsel subdivisions
2020–4	Procedures for obtaining rulings and other information for exempt organizations and employee plans from the Office of the Commissioner, Tax Exempt and Government Entities Division, Employee Plans Rulings and Agreements Office
2020–5	Procedures for furnishing determination letters on issues under the jurisdiction of the Director, Exempt Organizations Rulings and Agreements
2020–7	Areas under the jurisdiction of the Associate Chief Counsel (International) for which the IRS will not issue a ruling

b. Numbering System

Revenue procedures have been numbered chronologically since 1955. Beginning in 2000, the Service began using all four digits to indicate the year. The procedure number does not indicate the Code or regulations section involved.

Items included in the IRS Statement of Procedural Rules are part of 26 C.F.R. and are numbered as Treasury regulations. Their prefix is 601.

c. Format

Revenue procedures include several subdivisions. The number of subdivisions generally reflects the procedure's scope and complexity. The following subdivisions are commonly used: Purpose; Background; Scope; Effective Date; Effect on Other Documents; and Drafting Information. In appropriate cases, the procedure will also include sections such as Record Keeping, Request for Comments, and Paperwork Reduction Act.

3. Notices

The IRS issues **notices** to provide guidance before revenue rulings, revenue procedures, and regulations are available. [See Illustration 9-5.] As noted in Chapter 8, notices may describe future regulations in a manner that will pass muster under the Code section 7805(b) rules on retroactivity.

Notices are numbered by year in the same manner as revenue rulings and revenue procedures. Notices may be subdivided into parts similar to those used for revenue rulings and procedures. Shorter notices may not have subdivisions.

Illustration 9-5. Excerpt from Notice 2020–26

> **Extension of Time to File Application for Tentative Carryback Adjustment**
>
> **Notice 2020-26**
>
> SECTION 1. PURPOSE
>
> This notice provides relief for certain taxpayers to allow them to take advantage of amendments made to the net operating loss (NOL) provisions set forth in § 172 of the Internal Revenue Code (Code) by section 2303 of the Coronavirus Aid, Relief, and Economic Security Act (CARES Act), Public Law 116-136, 134 Stat. 281 (March 27, 2020). Specifically, this notice extends the deadline for filing an application for a tentative carryback adjustment under § 6411 of the Code with respect to the carryback of an NOL that arose in any taxable year that began during calendar year 2018 and that ended on or before June 30, 2019.
>
> SECTION 2. BACKGROUND
>
> Section 2303(b) of the CARES Act amends § 172(b)(1) to carry back any NOL arising in a taxable year beginning after December 31, 2017, and before January 1, 2021, to each of the five taxable years preceding the taxable year in which the NOL arises (carryback period). As a

4. Announcements

Announcements alert taxpayers to a variety of information but are somewhat less formal than revenue rulings, revenue procedures, and notices. Information provided in announcements includes corrections to previously published regulations and IRS guidance,[7] lists of organizations classified as private foundations and organizations that have lost tax-exempt status, and extensions of time to file forms. Announcements did not appear in the Cumulative Bulletin until 1998.

5. Other Documents Published in the Internal Revenue Bulletin

The weekly Bulletins contain other information, much of which is issued by the IRS. IRS information includes disbarment notices, delegation orders (Del. Order) announcing delegations of authority to various IRS offices, and **notices of acquiescence** and **nonacquiescence** (acq.; nonacq.).[8] The last two mentioned notices are important because they indicate if the IRS will continue to litigate an issue it has lost in a judicial proceeding. IRS litigation plans are discussed further in Section D.3 (*infra* page 173).

Non-IRS material has included Executive Orders issued by the President, Treasury regulations, new treaty documents, and Supreme Court decisions. These materials can also be found in sources other than the I.R.B. and are discussed in other chapters.

6. Non-Internal Revenue Bulletin Documents

Although the IRS website home page can appear somewhat cluttered, it has a clear link to tax return forms and accompanying instructions (Forms & Instructions); that link also covers explanatory booklets (Publications). These documents contain few, if any, citations to authority, and they do not indicate if the IRS position has been disputed. Even if they are misleading, taxpayers who rely on them cannot cite them as authority against a contrary IRS position.[9] These documents are not authority for avoiding the substantial understatement penalty.

The numbering system for tax return forms and publications does not indicate the underlying Code or regulations section number. In addition, the relevant numbering systems are not coordinated. For example, Code section 280A provides the rules governing deductions for an office in the taxpayer's home. Taxpayers compute the deduction on IRS Form 8829. The IRS explains the deduction rules in Publication 587.

The IRS Statistics of Income Bulletin may be of interest if you are doing research on taxpayer characteristics. It is available on the Tax Stats, Facts & Figures section at the bottom of the website's home page under "Our Agency."

The IRS also publishes Frequently Asked Questions (FAQ) and Fact Sheets (FS) for various topics. As is the case for forms and publications, taxpayers cannot cite these documents as authority against a contrary IRS position or for avoiding the substantial underpayment penalty.[10] Many FAQs can be reached by way of the home page's Interactive Tax Assistant ("Get Answers to Your Tax Questions"). If you are looking for information and the home page does not have a link, use the Search feature.

---

7 For example, Ann. 2016–29, 2016–34 I.R.B. 272, announced a correction of an error in Notice 2016–44.

8 Most, but not all, I.R.B. items were cumulated every six months in the Cumulative Bulletin. Between 1998 and its cessation after 2008, the C.B. reprinted all I.R.B. items. See Section K for a discussion of the C.B.

9 See *Bobrow v. Commissioner*, T.C. Memo. 2014–21.

10 "In our review of IRS guidance, we found that in recent years, IRS has issued information for taxpayers in the form of FAQs. This does not fall under IRS's definition of official guidance and cannot be relied upon as precedent by taxpayers to support a position if it has not been published in the IRB. However, limitations on using this information are not always communicated clearly to taxpayers or their advisors." U.S. GOV'T ACCOUNTABILITY OFFICE, GAO–16–720, REGULATORY GUIDANCE PROCESSES: TREASURY AND OMB NEED TO REEVALUATE LONG-STANDING EXEMPTIONS OF TAX REGULATIONS AND GUIDANCE 12 (2016).

D. Non-Precedential Rulings & Advice

Many of the documents discussed in this section are useful for determining the IRS position on relevant issues. Others provide information but are not informative about IRS positions. Code section 6110(k)(3) prevents you from citing the documents described in this section as precedent. You can use several of them as authority for avoiding the substantial underpayment penalty discussed in Chapter 2. Litigation resulted in their release and in the enactment of statutes requiring or restricting taxpayer access. Documents issued since the IRS began electronic release appear in the Non-precedential Rulings & Advice section of the FOIA Library.

1. FOIA Litigation and Section 6110

The lawsuit that first resulted in disclosure of unpublished documents involved private letter rulings and was brought under the Freedom of Information Act (FOIA).[11] That lawsuit resulted in the disclosure of rulings issued after October 31, 1976, and led to the enactment of Code section 6110, an IRS-specific disclosure statute.

Section 6110, which has been amended several times since its 1976 enactment, requires the release of written determinations and of background file documents related to those written determinations. The Code defines written determination as a ruling, determination letter, technical advice memorandum, or **Chief Counsel advice**.[12]

Chief Counsel advice (CCA; C.C.A.) is defined in Section 6110(i)(1)(A):

> (A) In general
>
> For purposes of this section, the term "Chief Counsel advice" means written advice or instruction, under whatever name or designation, prepared by any national office component of the Office of Chief Counsel which—
>
> (i) is issued to field or service center employees of the Service or regional or district employees of the Office of Chief Counsel; and
>
> (ii) conveys—
>
> (I) any legal interpretation of a revenue provision;
>
> (II) any Internal Revenue Service or Office of Chief Counsel position or policy concerning a revenue provision; or
>
> (III) any legal interpretation of State law, foreign law, or other Federal law relating to the assessment or collection of any liability under a revenue provision.

---

[11] *Tax Analysts and Advocates v. Internal Revenue Service*, 405 F. Supp. 1065 (D.D.C. 1975) (brought under 5 U.S.C. § 552).

[12] I.R.C. § 6110(a) & (b)(1). Background file documents for a written determination include "the request for that written determination, any written material submitted in support of the request, and any communication (written or otherwise) between the Internal Revenue Service and persons outside the Internal Revenue Service in connection with such written determination . . . received before issuance of the written determination." Id. § 6110(b)(2).

The IRS makes written determinations available in its FOIA Reading Room and on its website. It releases background documents only on written request; there are fees for finding these items, deleting confidential information, and duplicating them. I.R.C. § 6110(e) & (k); Rev. Proc. 2012–31, 2012–33 I.R.B. 256; IRM 1.35.19.8 (July 19, 2016).

A revenue provision is "any existing or former internal revenue law, regulation, revenue ruling, revenue procedure, other published or unpublished guidance, or tax treaty . . . ."[13]

Section 6110 provides timetables for disclosure by the IRS. The disclosure date is later than the document's actual issue date to allow time for notifying taxpayers that rulings they have requested are being made public and redacting taxpayer-identifying information. Taxpayers have the opportunity to dispute whether redaction is sufficient but cannot prevent disclosure altogether.[14]

2. Numbering Systems

Unless a different system is indicated, the publicly released documents discussed in this section use a common numbering system. The system is based on a multi-digit number (e.g., 84–37–084 or 200203010). Although citation manuals may use the dashes, the IRS does not use them for these documents. Abbreviations preceding the numbers indicate the type of document (e.g., private letter ruling, technical advice memorandum).

The dashes are useful because they call attention to what the document number means. The digits preceding the first dash reflect the year the document was released; the next two digits indicate the week of release; the final digits are the document number for that week.

Although the document number does not reflect the underlying Code section, many documents also include Uniform Issue List Code (UILC) numbers, which are sometimes listed as UIL. UILC numbers, which do reflect the underlying Code section, are discussed in Section M (*infra* page 191). The IRS website lets you sort many documents by UILC number.

3. Items Categorized as Non-Precedential Rulings & Advice[15]

Of the items discussed in this section, those in 3.a (Actions on Decisions) and 3.e (IRS Written Determinations) are most likely to be of interest.

a. Actions on Decisions (AOD; A.O.D.; Action on Dec.; Action on Decision)

The IRS uses several means for announcing future litigation information. One mechanism is the notice of acquiescence or nonacquiescence in cases it has lost. Those notices appear in the I.R.B. Until early 1993, the Service issued those notices only for Tax Court regular decisions. It now issues them for all trial and circuit courts.[16] These notices summarize the decision that appears in an action on decision.

---

[13] I.R.C. § 6110(i)(1)(B).

[14] *Anonymous v. Commissioner*, 134 T.C. 13 (2010).

[15] Although general counsel memoranda issued after March 12, 1981, constitute authority for avoiding the substantial underpayment penalty, the IRS stopped issuing these in the 1990s, ultimately revoked prior GCMs, and eliminated them from this section of the FOIA Library. These documents, which provided the reasoning and authority used in revenue rulings, private letter rulings, and technical advice memoranda, may still be available on subscription services.

[16] Although these notices should be the primary means of publishing this information in the Bulletin, the IRS may use other guidance for this purpose. See, e.g., Rev. Rul. 94–47, 1994–2 C.B. 18; Notice 95–57, 1995–2 C.B. 337; Notice 96–39, 1996–2 C.B. 309.

An **action on decision** indicates why the Service recommends (1) not appealing an adverse decision and (2) acquiescing or not acquiescing in that decision.[17] These are separate recommendations. The Service may recommend not acquiescing and continue to litigate an issue even though it does not appeal a particular case it lost.[18] That is the case in AOD 2020–01 in the illustration below. The opposite can also occur. The IRS may acquiesce and indicate it will no longer litigate the issue.

Illustration 9-6. AOD 2020–01

ACTION ON DECISION

Subject: Paychex Business Solutions, LLC, et al., v. United States of America, 2017 WL 2692843 (M.D. Fla. 2017).

Issue: Whether control over the bank account from which wage payments are made is sufficient for an entity to be a section 3401(d)(1)[1] statutory employer.

Discussion: For the years at issue, Paychex Business Solutions, LLC. et al. (Plaintiffs) were professional employer organizations (PEOs) headquartered in Florida and licensed by the State of Florida. Plaintiffs entered into a client service agreement (CSA) with each client company (client) in order to provide employer payroll functions and certain human resource functions. The CSAs provided that Plaintiffs assumed full responsibility for the reporting, collection, and payment of employment taxes[2] to the Internal Revenue Service (IRS) with respect to the clients' employees. With respect to payroll processes, typically, Plaintiffs obtained certain payroll information from clients two days prior to the date on which the clients' employees were paid. The clients would

Unlike notices of acquiescence, AODs were never limited to Tax Court regular decisions. As is true for acquiescence notices, the IRS does not issue an AOD for every case it loses. Taxpayers can use AODs issued after March 12, 1981, as authority for avoiding the substantial understatement penalty.

AODs are numbered sequentially by year. The numbering system provides no information about the underlying case name or issue involved. The IRS website search function [Illustration 9-11, *infra* page 189] numbers each AOD by year and number within the year (e.g., 2021–01). Internally, several of these documents have slightly different numbering formats.[19]

Although the IRS refers to these documents as AOD without periods, citation systems use other formats. For example, you might encounter "action on dec." or "action on decision."

---

[17] "An Action on Decision is issued at the discretion of the Service only on unappealed issues, decided adverse to the government." I.R.M. 4.10.7.2.9.8.1 (Jan. 1, 2006).

[18] Because Department of Justice attorneys litigate appeals, an IRS recommendation following a trial court defeat will not necessarily result in appellate court litigation.

[19] For example, some documents include CC (Chief Counsel) in their number (e.g., CC–2002–02), while others have no number at all (e.g., the document numbered 2001–07 on the search wheel). In addition, sometimes a document uses two digits and sometimes three for the item number (e.g., CC–1997–005 versus 2000–05). Beginning with 2007–03, the document simply lists the I.R.B. in which the notice of acquiescence or nonacquiescence appears; the AOD number appears only in the search wheel.

If a later AOD revokes an earlier one, the IRS may remove the earlier item from its website; subscription services generally retain these items.

b. Appeals Settlement Guidelines (ASG)

In addition to documents entitled **Appeals Settlement Guidelines**, this section includes older documents referred to as **Industry Specialization Program Coordinated Issue Papers** or **Industry Specialization Program Settlement Guidelines**. These documents "represent Appeals position regarding the potential hazards of litigation for proper resolution of an Appeals Coordinated Issue by providing guidance to ensure consistent treatment of the issue." Items are categorized by topic and contain extensive discussion and citations to authority. These documents are not numbered.

c. Chief Counsel Bulletins

The FOIA Library currently includes links to three types of Chief Counsel Bulletins: Criminal Tax Bulletins; Collection, Bankruptcy and Summonses Bulletins; and Disclosure Litigation Bulletins. These documents provide information to IRS employees about litigation in a variety of areas. None of them constitutes authority for avoiding the substantial understatement penalty.

Criminal Tax Bulletins (CTB; C.T.B.; CT Bulletin) compile cases pertaining to criminal tax matters. The IRS has used several numbering systems for these documents. In some cases, it uses one set of numbers on the website, but the document itself is numbered using a different system.

Documents issued between December 1998 and October 2001 have nine-digit numbers; the first four digits represent the year, the second two digits represent the week, and the last three digits represent the number for that week (e.g., 200202063).[20] This system is used on both the website and the documents.

The next numbering system generally reflects the year and month that begins each compilation (e.g., 2001–12 and 2006–12).[21] The Bulletins themselves either don't show any numbers or are numbered using the nine-digit system described in the preceding paragraph. The nine-digit number is based on the document's release date, which may be in a later year than the year covered by its contents.

Between November 2007 and May 2018, website Bulletin numbering shows the first and last month covered by each Bulletin (e.g., 201605–201701 for May 2016 through January 2017). The actual Bulletins don't show any numbers. The two most recent Bulletins (2019–09 and 2020–06) reflect the year and month of issue.

Collection, Bankruptcy and Summonses Bulletins (CBS; C.B.S.; CBS Bulletin) summarized general litigation developments. These documents were called **General Litigation Bulletins** (GL) from 1998 through June 2000 (Bulletins 458 through 477 on the website). Although numbered in a separate series, these bulletins

---

[20] The number for this October 2001 item begins with 2002 because October 2001 is the first month of the government's fiscal year 2002.

[21] The Bulletin covering June through August 2006 is numbered 2006–2, which is inconsistent with the other Bulletins for that year—2006–1 (January 2006 through April 2006) and 2006–12 (December 2006 through February 2007).

also share the common nine-digit numbering system. For example, Bulletin No. 490 is also numbered 200139029. The last bulletin was issued in January 2002 (Bulletin 496).

Disclosure Litigation Bulletins (DLB; D.L.B.) discussed litigation and other developments concerning FOIA and related litigation. They are numbered by year. The most recent bulletin posted on the IRS website was DLB 2000–3.

Tax Litigation Bulletins (TLB; T.L.B.) summarized recent court decisions and briefs. They also included recommendations for appellate action. These bulletins are numbered by year (e.g., TLB 96–5). They are not included on the IRS website, but may be included in subscription service databases. Westlaw Edge, for example, includes them in its IRS Litigation Bulletins database.

d. Information Letters (IIL; I.I.L.)

The national office issues information letters to taxpayers (and to members of Congress who request them) that provide statements of well-defined law; they do not apply these statements to particular facts.[22] These letters are numbered by year (e.g., 2020–0004). You can search for them by subject, letter number, or Uniform Issue List Code.

e. IRS Written Determinations

This category currently includes three items: letter rulings (and determination letters), technical advice memoranda, and Chief Counsel advice. As discussed below, several items currently included within the Chief Counsel advice umbrella had their genesis in documents that were previously issued under other names.

(1) Private Letter Rulings (PLR; P.L.R.; Ltr. Rul.; Priv. Ltr. Rul.)

Private letter rulings are written in response to taxpayer requests for guidance as to a proposed transaction's tax consequences. In addition to the underlying facts, issues raised, and legal analysis, these rulings indicate which Chief Counsel's office division produced them.

Some private letter rulings are eventually formally published as revenue rulings, but most are available to the public only through the section 6110 disclosure procedure. Although the IRS is not bound by them in its dealings with other taxpayers,[23] letter rulings that were issued after October 31, 1976, constitute authority for avoiding the substantial understatement penalty.

(2) Determination Letters

Determination letters are similar to letter rulings but emanate from IRS district offices rather than the national office. District office personnel issue them only if they can be based on well-established rules that apply to the issues presented. Otherwise, the matter is appropriately handled by the national office.

---

[22] For example, IIL 2009–0255 responds to a request for the IRS to publish a standard mileage rate for business use of a motorcycle.

[23] But see *Ogiony v. Commissioner*, 617 F.2d 14, 17–18 (2d Cir. 1980) (Oakes, J., concurring). Although commenting that they had no precedential force, the Supreme Court has cited private letter rulings as evidence of IRS inconsistent interpretation. See *Rowan Cos., Inc. v. United States*, 452 U.S. 247, 261 n.17 (1981).

(3) Technical Advice Memoranda (TAM; T.A.M.; Tech. Adv. Mem.)

Technical advice memoranda are issued by the national office in response to IRS requests arising out of tax return examinations. Unlike letter rulings, which focus on proposed transactions, technical advice memoranda cover completed transactions. In contrast to field service advice, discussed below, technical advice requests generally involve both the taxpayer and the IRS. Memoranda issued after October 31, 1976, constitute authority for avoiding the substantial understatement penalty.

(4) Other Chief Counsel Advice Items

(a) Field Service Advice (FSA; F.S.A.)

IRS field attorneys, revenue agents, and appeals officers requested national office advice if a case presented a significant legal question of first impression and no guidance existed as to the Chief Counsel's legal position or policy. Field personnel could seek **field service advice** instead of a technical advice memorandum and could do so without the taxpayer's knowledge. Field service advice does not constitute authority for avoiding the substantial understatement penalty. Field service advice has not been issued as a separately titled item since December 2003.

(b) Service Center Advice (SCA; S.C.A.)

The national office issued **service center advice** with regard to tax administration responsibilities. The Service began using the common numbering system for these documents in 1999. It used a separate numbering system in 1997 and 1998. SCAs do not constitute authority for avoiding the substantial understatement penalty.

(c) IRS Legal Memoranda (ILM; I.L.M.)

Legal memoranda provide information about taxpayers to IRS field or service center personnel. These documents may respond to a field office query or they may provide information to the field (e.g., notice that a taxpayer's request to change accounting method has been denied). These documents do not constitute authority for avoiding the substantial understatement penalty. Although these documents use the common numbering system, some subscription services call them by different names. Searching by number yields the same results irrespective of system; searching by title may not.[24]

(d) Litigation Guideline Memoranda (LGM; L.G.M.)

Litigation guideline memoranda discuss variations on fact patterns and tactical approaches that IRS field personnel might use in litigation; the last one was prepared in 1999. Because litigation guidance is issued currently through other IRS work products (e.g., Chief Counsel Notices), the IRS stated in November 2016 that "to the extent that existing LGMs have not been formally obsoleted or withdrawn, they may now be considered obsolete."[25]

---

[24] Depending on the publisher, these documents may be referred to as Chief Counsel advice, Chief Counsel advisories, or IRS legal memoranda (ILM).

[25] CC–2017–001 (Nov. 2, 2016).

(e) IRS Technical Assistance (ITA; I.T.A.)

The national office provides **technical assistance** to other IRS offices. Technical assistance issued to district and regional offices, Chief Counsel field offices, and service centers is subject to disclosure. These documents are not authority for avoiding the substantial understatement penalty.

Technical assistance documents use the common numbering system (e.g., 200211042 dealt with whether the recipient of a transferable state remediation tax credit had gross income). Although Tax Notes indexes these documents as ITAs, the IRS website classifies them as Chief Counsel advice or advisory.

(f) Additional Items

Guidance is subject to disclosure even if it takes relatively little time to produce. For example, even advice prepared in less than two hours and transmitted by email is subject to disclosure.[26] Since 2003, redacted versions of revocations and denials of tax-exempt status have also been subject to release.[27]

The name given the particular item is generally unimportant because most Chief Counsel advice uses a common numbering system, can be searched based on Code sections, and with few exceptions does not constitute substantial authority for avoiding the section 6662(b) penalty.

f. Legal Advice Issued by Associate Chief Counsel

These documents are issued to IRS national program executives and managers to assist them in administering their programs; they are signed by executives in the national office of Chief Counsel. The legal advice in these documents often relates to industry-wide issues. These items are often referred to as generic legal advice[28] or non-taxpayer specific legal advice.

This series begins in 2006. Documents are numbered by year and begin with the prefix AM (e.g., AM–2019–002, Qualified Plan Adoption Requirements). These documents are arranged in reverse chronological order. The website indicates the subject but does not include a search or sorting feature.

g. Legal Advice Issued by Field Attorneys

These documents are issued to assist field or service center employees. Their numbering reflects the year and week of release and ends with an F (e.g., 20200801F, "Statute of Limitations for IRC § 4980H"). Some publishers refer to these documents as field attorney advice or Non Docketed Service Advice Reviews.

This series begins in 2003. Documents are arranged in reverse chronological order. The website indicates the subject but does not include a search or sorting feature.

h. Legal Advice Issued to Program Managers

These documents are similar in purpose to legal advice issued by Associate Chief Counsel; they are signed by attorneys in the national office of Chief Counsel. These

[26] *Tax Analysts v. Internal Revenue Service*, 495 F.3d 676 (D.C. Cir. 2007).

[27] *Tax Analysts v. Internal Revenue Service*, 350 F.3d 100 (D.C. Cir. 2003).

[28] Practitioners may refer to a generic legal advice memorandum as a GLAM.

documents are numbered by year and begin with the prefix PMTA (program manager technical assistance). For example, PMTA–2020–05 concerns whether restored back pay to exonerated military service members is included in gross income or excluded under I.R.C. § 139F.

This series begins in 2007. The website listing includes UIL numbers and subject for PMTA documents, but it does not have a search or sorting feature.

E. Admin Manuals & Instructions

1. Appeals Coordinated Issues (ACI)

Issues were selected for **appeals coordinated issue** status because they required uniformity of treatment on a national basis. Items selected could apply to an entire industry, a large number of partners, shareholders, or creditors, or a nationwide tax avoidance scheme. Although the Admin Manuals & Instructions section still lists Appeals Coordinated Issues, its hyperlink sends you to Appeals Settlement Guidelines for the latest information.

2. Chief Counsel Notices (CCN; C.C.N.)

These documents notify personnel of changes in policies or procedures, litigating positions, or other administrative information. Many of them are eventually added to the **Chief Counsel Directives Manual** (CCDM) and deleted as separate entries on the IRS website. Chief Counsel Notices do not constitute authority for avoiding the substantial understatement penalty.

Since fiscal 2001, these documents are numbered by year with CC as a prefix; they can be searched by number and subject. For example, CC–2017–005 provides procedures for Chief Counsel attorneys to follow to obtain approval to disclose the existence or identity of a whistleblower in civil tax cases. A notice will be cancelled when the information is incorporated into the CCDM.[29]

3. Internal Revenue Manual (IRM; I.R.M.)

Your research may involve IRS operating policies. For example, you may want to determine IRS procedures for appeals or for dealing with rewards to informants. The **Internal Revenue Manual** is an excellent source of information about IRS policies. It does not constitute authority for avoiding the substantial understatement penalty.

Illustration 9-7. Excerpt from IRM Table of Contents

Part 30	Administrative
Part 31	Guiding Principles
Part 32	Published Guidance and Other Guidance to Taxpayers
Part 33	Legal Advice
Part 34	Litigation in District Court, Bankruptcy Court, Court of Federal Claims, and State Court

29 The Chief Counsel Directives Manual is parts 30 through 39 of the IRM.

The IRM uses numerous decimals for subdivisions. Illustration 9-8 shows a portion of Part 36. The number after the first decimal is the chapter (3). The next number is the section (1). Items 1 through 11 are the next level.[30]

Illustration 9-8. Excerpt from IRM Subdivisions

- 36.3.1 Actions on Decision
  - 36.3.1.1 Actions on Decision
  - 36.3.1.2 Standards Governing Issuance of AODs
  - 36.3.1.3 Procedures for Determining Whether to Issue an AOD
  - 36.3.1.4 Drafting an AOD
  - 36.3.1.5 Format of AOD
  - 36.3.1.6 Coordination of AODs
  - 36.3.1.7 Approval and Issuance of AODs
  - 36.3.1.8 Distribution and Publication of Approved AODs
  - 36.3.1.9 Inquiries from the Public
  - 36.3.1.10 Chief Counsel Notices to Announce Changes in Service Litigating Positions
  - 36.3.1.11 Reconsideration of Actions

Part 36. Appellate Litigation and Actions on Decision

Chapter 3. Actions on Decision

Section 1. Actions on Decision

36.3.1 Actions on Decision

Manual Transmittal

March 14, 2013

Purpose

(1) This transmits revised CCDM 36.3.1, Appellate Litigation and Actions on Decision; Actions on Decision.

Material Changes

(1) CCDM 36.3.1.1 was revised to clarify that actions on decision (AODs) are published in the Internal Revenue Bulletin to expeditiously alert Service personnel and the public to the Office's current litigating position. It also clarifies that Counsel attorneys are required to follow the litigating positions announced in AODs in future litigation or dispute resolution.

4. Recent Delegation Orders/Policy Statements

The Recently Approved Delegation Orders and Policy Statements page contains documents covering recent delegation orders within the IRS and policy statements that have been approved but not yet added to the IRM. It also includes redelegations of authority by office heads. A separate page lists all current Commissioner Delegation Orders and their IRM locations.

5. Recent Interim Guidance to Staff

The documents in this section are arranged by Internal Revenue Manual part. Because they often supplement the IRM, you should check this part of the website when you work with a particular IRM section.

6. LB&I Industry Director Guidance

These documents are issued to provide guidance to LB&I (Large Business and International) examiners to ensure consistent tax administration. Documents are listed in reverse chronological order and include references to IRM sections.

7. Taxpayer Advocate Service Level Agreements (SLA)

The documents in this series cover agreements between the Taxpayer Advocate Service (TAS) and operating units within the IRS (e.g., Appeals, Criminal Investigation, LB&I). They cover the procedures and responsibilities for processing TAS casework when the authority to complete a case transaction lies with the other unit.

---

[30] Chapter 3 of Part 36 has relatively few levels. Some chapters have significantly more (e.g., IRM 36.2.1.1.5.5.1 (Nov. 14, 2006)).

8. Tax Exempt and Government Entities Directives

This section is for directives from the Tax Exempt and Government Entities Division. It is supposed to provide administrative guidance to the examiners and ensure consistent tax administration on matters relating to internal operations. Currently there is only one directive, from June 2015, on the treatment of uniforms issued to fire and police employees. The webpage also includes several Interim Guidance items.

9. Freedom of Information Act Obligations and Transparency Memo

This section consists of a memo stating the IRS's commitment "to openness in government" and describing "every employee's responsibility to promote transparency under the Freedom of Information Act (FOIA)." The memo states that federal agencies must respond to the requester within 20 days, that certain information should be made public proactively, and what other information may be provided to the public.

F. Program Plans & Reports

This section includes documents issued by the IRS or other entities within the Treasury Department. They are:

- IRS Annual Performance Plan (a lengthy summary of IRS goals and accomplishments; as of July 2020, the only document is for fiscal 2004);
- Annual Report to the Joint Committee on Taxation, which the Committee discloses to the public,[31] regarding requests for disclosure of taxpayer information;
- A link to a webpage describing Art Appraisal Services; it includes links to other relevant documents;
- Emailed CCA Reports (links to annual reports on the number of emailed Chief Counsel advice items disclosed and withheld from disclosure);
- FOIA Annual Reports (covering requests that were received and processed by agencies within the Treasury Department);
- Internal Revenue Service Progress Update Fiscal Year 2019 (discussing six IRS goals and plans for the next fiscal year);
- IRS Strategic Plan (Fiscal Year 2018–2022);
- Office of Chief Counsel Report on Professionalism (annual report to inform employees about the procedures followed and actions taken with respect to allegations of misconduct or unprofessional conduct); website currently covers 2008 through 2018);
- Priority Guidance Plans (this series begins in 1999 and is discussed in Chapter 8);
- Privacy Impact Assessments (covering information the IRS collects from the public); and
- Treasury Inspector General for Tax Administration (TIGTA) Annual Audit Plans (the website currently includes audit plans for fiscal 2010

[31] The JCT publishes these reports; the IRS site links to the relevant JCT reports.

through fiscal 2020; the TIGTA page includes links to audit reports for the same period).[32]

G. Training & Reference Materials

The documents in this section are training materials for IRS personnel. They include the following items:

- Audit Techniques Guides;

  The **Audit Technique Guides** are prepared to assist auditors who examine companies in a particular market segment (e.g., child care, farming, retail). Many of these documents include glossaries of terms a researcher can use to become familiar with a particular industry.[33]
- CCA Check Training Material (training related to a program that captures emailed Chief Counsel advice that may be subject to disclosure);
- Chief Counsel Advice Training Materials (information about redaction and disclosure of Chief Counsel advice);
- Chief Counsel Collection Due Process Desk Guide (summary of collection due process law);
- Disclosure & Privacy Law Reference Guide (history and discussion of disclosure and privacy statutes related to taxpayer information);
- EO Tax Law Training Articles (materials to help the public understand how the IRS administers the tax law provisions applied to exempt organizations);[34]
- Global Awareness Training for International Tax Examiners (training provided at an OECD meeting by the U.S. competent authority to promote awareness of global tax administration goals);
- IRS Chief Counsel Procedure & Administration Desk Guide (basic explanations of Procedure & Administration's primary subject areas);
- IRS FOIA Logs (information about FOIA requests processed by the IRS);
- IRS Records Control Schedules (lists of record types maintained by IRS offices and their destruction cycle);
- IRS Records Schedules (records disposition instructions);
- Practice Units (LB&I-produced training materials on tax issues);
- Tax Crimes Handbook (a resource for criminal tax attorneys to use in advising their clients);

---

[32] The Treasury Inspector General for Tax Administration's audit reports may give rise to changes in IRS procedures or even to legislation.

[33] For example, a Glossary of Terms in the Guide for the fishing industry explains the terms "pers" ("traditional flat amount paid to some crewmembers for certain duties, such as cook, mate, engineer, etc.") and "lay(s)" ("share of the catch").

[34] Documents include continuing education program (CPE) materials (1979–2004) and 2009 training materials.

- Tax Exempt and Government Entities Issue Snapshots (providing employees with analysis and resources for technical tax issues); and
- Tax Reform Training Material (current training materials are focused on the Tax Cuts and Jobs Act).

H. Unreleased Documents

1. Advance Pricing Agreements (APA)

Advance pricing agreements are made between taxpayers and the IRS regarding income allocation between commonly controlled entities. Companies that segment their operations between countries with different tax rates and structures can enter into APAs with both the United States and the other country if the two countries have a tax treaty. Code section 6110(b)(1)(B) exempts APAs from release to the public. The IRS does issue an annual report concerning APAs.[35]

In 2013, the oversight of the APA program moved from the Office of Chief Counsel to the Director, Transfer Pricing Operations, in LB&I. The program is now called the APA and Mutual Agreement Program.

2. Closing Agreements

Closing agreements memorialize the parties' agreement regarding specific taxpayer-IRS disputes. As a condition of the agreement, the IRS has occasionally forced publication of certain closing agreements with exempt organizations. Code section 6110(b)(1)(B) exempts closing agreements from release to the public.

I. Documents That Are Not Available on IRS Website

If a document was released before the FOIA Library began, you probably will not find it on the IRS website. This is true for older I.R.B. items and documents that reflect Freedom of Information Act or other statutory disclosure requirements. Some documents have never appeared on the IRS website because they were eliminated before there was a FOIA Library. Technical Memoranda (TM; T.M.; Tech. Mem.) fall into this category. These documents provided background information on regulations. Much of their content is reflected in the Preambles to T.D.s and NPRMs.

Although you can find current documents on the IRS website, you will have to locate earlier documents from other sources. Services such as Bloomberg Law, Checkpoint, Cheetah, Federal Research Library, Lexis+, and Westlaw Edge carry both I.R.B. items and other documents.

J. IRS Operating Division Documents

The Chief Counsel's office is not the only source of guidance that taxpayers and their representatives might research. Items are also issued by the IRS operating divisions: Large Business & International (LB&I); Small Business/Self-Employed (SB/SE); Wage & Investment (W&I); and Tax-Exempt and Government Entities (TE/GE). Guidance issued by the operating divisions includes the LB&I Directives discussed in Section E

---

[35] Ann. 2020–2, 2020–15 I.R.B. 609, covers calendar year 2019.

and Field Directives issued by various divisions. Each operating division has an "At-a-Glance" page on the IRS website.[36]

K. Print Internal Revenue Bulletin and Cumulative Bulletin

The IRS website is convenient because it includes information that the IRS publishes in the Internal Revenue Bulletin, other information that is available in the FOIA Library, and miscellaneous information (e.g., publications and tax forms). But, as is true for most government websites, coverage before the mid-1990s is virtually nonexistent.

Although you may have to obtain non-I.R.B. items from subscription services, you can probably find print versions of the I.R.B. or at least of its semiannual compilation—the Cumulative Bulletin. Even if your library has retained only the semiannual C.B.s, you will have print access to most pre-2009 I.R.B. material.

This section covers the I.R.B. and C.B. The IRS stopped compiling the C.B. after the 2008–2 volume, and it stopped printing a paper version of the I.R.B. in 2013.[37] The I.R.B. is still available online.

Illustration 9-9. Internal Revenue Bulletin Cover Page

INTERNAL REVENUE BULLETIN

IRS

HIGHLIGHTS OF THIS ISSUE

These synopses are intended only as aids to the reader in identifying the subject matter covered. They may not be relied upon as authoritative interpretations.

Bulletin No. 2020–30
July 20, 2020

INCOME TAX

Notice 2020-53, page 151.
In response to the ongoing Coronavirus Disease 2019 (COVID–19) pandemic, this notice provides temporary relief from certain requirements under § 42 of the Internal Revenue Code (Code) for qualified low-income housing projects and under §§ 142(d) and 147(d) of the Code for qualified residential rental projects.

REG-112339-19, page 155.
This document contains proposed regulations regarding the credit for carbon oxide sequestration under section 45Q of the Internal Revenue Code (Code). These proposed regulations will affect persons who physically or contractually ensure the capture and disposal of qualified carbon oxide, use of qualified carbon oxide as a tertiary injectant in a qualified enhanced oil or natural gas recovery project, or utilization of qualified carbon oxide in a manner that qualifies for the credit.

REG-117589-18, page 184.
These proposed regulations provide rules under section 1031 of the Internal Revenue Code relating to the non-recognition of gain or loss on exchanges of certain property for other property of like kind. The proposed regulations amend the existing regulations under section 1031 to add a definition of real property to reflect statutory changes limiting section 1031 to exchanges of real property. The proposed regulations also provide a rule addressing a taxpayer's receipt of personal property that is incidental to real property the taxpayer receives in the exchange.

REG-125716-18, page 197.
This document contains proposed regulations under section 1502 of the Internal Revenue Code (the Code). The proposed regulations would update existing regulations under section 1.1502-21 to reflect statutory changes made to section 172 of the Code by the Tax Cuts and Jobs Act, P.L. 115-97 (Dec. 22, 2017) and the Coronavirus Aid, Relief, and Economic Security Act, P.L. 116-36 (Mar. 27, 2020). The proposed regulations would affect taxpayers that file consolidated returns.

T.D. 9900, page 143.
Section 2303 of the "Coronavirus Aid, Relief, and Economic Security Act," Pub. L. No. 116-136, 134 Stat. 281 (March 27, 2020) (the "CARES Act"), amended the carryback provisions related to net operating losses. As a result of the CARES Act amendments, which specifically extended the carryback period for certain net operating losses, these temporary regulations permit certain acquiring consolidated groups to elect to waive all or a portion of the pre-acquisition portion of the extended carryback period under section 172 for certain losses attributable to certain acquired members.

---

[36] See, e.g., https://www.irs.gov/about-irs/small-business-self-employed-division-at-a-glance (last visited July 18, 2020).

[37] Ann. 2013–12, 2013–11 I.R.B. 651.

1. Internal Revenue Bulletin

The weekly **Internal Revenue Bulletin** (I.R.B.) has four parts. Part I prints the text of all revenue rulings and final regulations issued during the week; publication is in Code section order. It included Supreme Court tax decisions (Ct.D.) through 2008. Part II covers treaties, including Treasury Department Technical Explanations (Subpart A), and previously included tax legislation (Subpart B). Items rarely appear in Part II.

Part III contains notices and revenue procedures, while Part IV, "Items of General Interest," is varied in content. Its coverage includes disbarment notices, announcements, and notices of proposed rulemaking. Federal Register dates and comment deadlines are provided in addition to the Preambles and text of proposed regulations. The I.R.B. also includes notices of IRS acquiescence or nonacquiescence for judicial decisions against the government.

Each I.R.B. was separately paginated until mid-1999. The I.R.B. is now paginated successively over a six-month period. Each issue contains a Numerical Finding List for each type of item. [See Illustration 9-10, *infra* page 186.] A Finding List of Current Action on Previously Published Items indicates IRS (but not judicial) action; it was last published in 2018. The Finding Lists lack any tie-in to Code sections and cover no more than six months. The subject indexes (eliminated after 2014) also lack Code section information. The Bulletin is best used to locate material for which you already have a citation[38] or as a tool for staying abreast of recent developments.

2. Cumulative Bulletin (1919–2008)

From 1919 to 2008, the material in the I.R.B. was republished every six months in a hardbound Cumulative Bulletin (C.B.). Volumes initially were given Arabic numerals (1919–1921). Although volume spines may show Arabic numerals, the IRS used Roman numerals for the 1922 through 1936 volumes. Beginning in 1937, volumes were numbered by year (e.g., 1937–1). With the exception of 1943–1945, there were two volumes annually since 1920 (with occasional extra volumes for extensive legislative history material).[39] The –1, –2 numbering system for each year began in 1922.

The C.B. format varied over time. Before 1998, it largely followed that of the weekly service, but with four exceptions. First, major tax legislation and committee reports generally appeared in a third volume rather than in the two semiannual volumes.[40] Second, only disbarment notices and proposed regulations appeared from Part IV.[41] Third, it omitted drafting information for rulings. Finally, rulings appeared in the C.B. in semiannual Code section order; this bore no relation to their numerical order.

In 1998, the IRS ceased recompiling items in the C.B. The C.B. became simply a bound version of the individual I.R.B.s. Successive pagination for the I.R.B.s began in mid-1999.

---

38 You can locate citations in citators, looseleaf services, periodical articles, and newsletters.

39 The I.R.S. stopped publishing the –3 volume after 2003–3 C.B. You can obtain the legislative history material previously included in these volumes using the services covered in Chapter 6.

40 Committee reports for 1913 through 1938 appear in 1939–1 (pt. 2) C.B. Committee reports for the 1954 Code's enactment never appeared in the C.B.

41 These were printed in Part III or immediately following it through 1997. Proposed regulations, which appear as a separate category, were added in the 1981–1 volume. The C.B.'s format differed from the above description until the 1974–2 volume.

When the C.B. changed format, it added a Code Sections Affected by Current Actions listing. Although this provided additional assistance in using six-month's worth of material, it did not make searching over longer periods of time any easier. The other C.B. indexes and finding lists are as difficult to use as are their counterparts in the I.R.B.

Illustration 9-10. Numerical Finding List from 2020–19 I.R.B.

Numerical Finding List[1]

Bulletin 2020–19

AOD:

2020-1, 2020-12 I.R.B. *521*
2020-2, 2020-14 I.R.B. *558*
2020-3, 2020-17 I.R.B. *663*

Announcements:

2020-1, 2020-5 I.R.B. *552*
2020-2, 2020-15 I.R.B. *609*
2020-3, 2020-15 I.R.B. *655*
2020-4, 2020-17 I.R.B. *667*
2020-5, 2020-19 I.R.B. *796*

Notices:

2020-1, 2020-2 I.R.B. *290*
2020-2, 2020-3 I.R.B. *327*
2020-3, 2020-3 I.R.B. *330*
2020-4, 2020-4 I.R.B. *380*
2020-5, 2020-4 I.R.B. *380*
2020-6, 2020-7 I.R.B. *411*
2020-7, 2020-7 I.R.B. *411*
2020-8, 2020-7 I.R.B. *415*
2020-9, 2020-7 I.R.B. *417*

Revenue Procedures:

2020-1, 2020-01 I.R.B. *1*
2020-2, 2020-01 I.R.B. *107*
2020-3, 2020-01 I.R.B. *131*
2020-4, 2020-01 I.R.B. *148*
2020-5, 2020-01 I.R.B. *241*
2020-7, 2020-01 I.R.B. *281*
2020-9, 2020-02 I.R.B. *294*
2020-10, 2020-02 I.R.B. *295*
2020-11, 2020-06 I.R.B. *406*
2020-8, 2020-08 I.R.B. *447*
2020-12, 2020-11 I.R.B. *511*
2020-13, 2020-11 I.R.B. *515*
2020-17, 2020-12 I.R.B. *539*
2020-18, 2020-15 I.R.B. *592*
2020-14, 2020-16 I.R.B. *661*
2020-22, 2020-18 I.R.B. *745*
2020-23, 2020-18 I.R.B. *749*
2020-24, 2020-18 I.R.B. *750*
2020-26, 2020-18 I.R.B. *753*
2020-25, 2020-19 I.R.B. *785*
2020-28, 2020-19 I.R.B. *792*

Revenue Rulings:

2020-1, 2020-3 I.R.B. *296*
2020-2, 2020-3 I.R.B. *298*
2020-3, 2020-3 I.R.B. *409*

Table 9-C. Cumulative Bulletin Format Changes

Year	*Numbering*	*Other Major Changes*
1919	1, 2, 3	
1922	I–1, I–2, II–1	Rulings divided by type of tax
1937	1937–1, 1937–2	
1939		Committee reports added
1953		End of separate table of contents by type of tax
1974		End of separate sections for 1939 Code
1981		Proposed regulations added
1993		Acquiescences no longer limited to Tax Court regular decisions
1998		Six-month rearrangement of I.R.B. items ceased
2003		Last C.B. to include legislative materials
2008		Last edition of C.B. (2008–2 C.B.)

L. Locating IRS Documents

1. Documents Published in the Internal Revenue Bulletin

a. Finding Lists

You can find citations to these documents using print or online sources. Print sources include Code-based looseleaf services, such as Standard Federal Tax Reporter and United States Tax Reporter. You can also use topic-based looseleaf services such as Federal Tax Coordinator 2d and Rabkin & Johnson, Federal Income, Gift and Estate Taxation. Both types of looseleaf service are discussed in Chapter 12.

Because revenue rulings and procedures, notices, and announcements carry numbers that don't correspond to Code or regulations sections, electronic services are excellent tools for locating them. You can search many of their databases by topic, Code or regulations section, or prior ruling. Use case citators to find acquiescences and nonacquiescences.

b. Digests

Unlike finding lists, digests provide descriptions that help you decide if an item is likely to be useful. Keep in mind that a digest's usefulness is a function of its compiler's expertise and its frequency of supplementation.

You can locate digests in a looseleaf service such as United States Tax Reporter and in newsletters such as Tax Notes Today Federal.

c. Texts

Several services provide texts of I.R.B. items. Many of those listed below are available in print and online.

Looseleaf services such as Standard Federal Tax Reporter and United States Tax Reporter include the text of current year rulings in their print services; online services may include older rulings or provide links to them on other databases. The Rulings volumes of Mertens, Law of Federal Income Taxation include full text of revenue rulings and procedures since 1954 but do not carry other Internal Revenue Bulletin documents. Online databases associated with daily newsletters (e.g., Daily Tax Report) include I.R.B. items.

The print versions of the I.R.B. and C.B. (Section K, *supra* page 184) included text of all items issued for a particular week (or six-month period). Online services that carry the full I.R.B. or C.B. or that have databases of individual Bulletin items include the following:

- Bloomberg Law (I.R.B. items since 1919)
- Checkpoint (I.R.B. items since 1996)
- Cheetah (I.R.B. items since 1954)
- Federal Research Library (I.R.B. items since 1954)
- govinfo.gov (C.B. from 1919 through 2008)
- HeinOnline (C.B. from 1919 through 2008; semiannually cumulated I.R.B. since 2009)

- IRS.gov (I.R.B. since 1996)
- Lexis+ (I.R.B. items since 1954)
- Westlaw Edge (C.B. from 1919 through 2008; I.R.B. since 2009)

d. A Note on Searching in Online Sources

In using online sources, you must differentiate between those that allow searching by topic and those that include the relevant information but do not provide a means to find it using word or Code section searches. If you can't find the item without knowing its citation, the source is less valuable than one that allows access based on Code sections or phrases.

2. Other IRS Website Documents

You can also find IRS forms, instructions, and explanatory publications, FAQs, and fact sheets using the IRS website. You can use a word search similar to that shown in the preceding illustrations if you don't know the name or number of the form or publication you seek. The IRS site includes these documents in full text. Commercial services may also make them available.

3. Publicly Released Documents

Because the IRS issues so many of these documents, your library is more likely to provide access to them electronically than through a print service. If your library has a print service, you may prefer to find items electronically even if you ultimately read them in print.

Although the IRS website provides free access to publicly released documents, its home page does not indicate where to find them. To find most publicly available documents, click on Freedom of Information Act, which appears on the bottom of the home page. Then click on IRS FOIA Library. You will reach a screen that shows the types of documents currently available for you to search. [See Illustrations 9-2 and 9-3, *supra* pages 164–165.]

The link for IRS Written Determinations covers those documents discussed in Section D that follow a common numbering system. Documents such as AODs, which have their own numbering system, have their own search tools. Many items listed in the other FOIA Library categories do not have search screens on the IRS site.

Texts of publicly released documents are included in numerous online research sources. You can search these services by Code section or by phrases describing the issue you are researching.

With one exception, online services operate the same way for publicly released documents as they do for documents published in the I.R.B. That exception relates to descriptive initials used in the numbering system. As noted in Section D, commercial services may assign their own names to documents issued by the Chief Counsel's office. If you are not sure what name a particular service uses for Chief Counsel items, search across all possible databases rather than limiting yourself to a single database. Fortunately, all publishers use the same names for the most common items: letter rulings, technical advice memoranda, and actions on decisions.

The illustrations below contrast search tools on the IRS website with options available in commercial services. Remember that the IRS website does not include items before the mid-1990s; commercial services generally begin their coverage with each item's first public release.

When using a commercial service, consider two important questions. First, does it have the most recent items? Second, does it include all types of Chief Counsel advice?

Illustration 9-11. IRS Website AOD Finding List

Find [ ] in [Number] [Find] Find Help

1 - 25 of 122 files Show per page: 25 50 100 200 « Previous | 1 2 3 4 5 | Next »

Number	Decision	Issue	Released
2020-03	Rothkamm v. United States, 802 F.3d 699 (5th Cir. 2015), rev'g 2014 WL 4986884 (M.D. La. Sept. 15, 2014)	Whether section 7811(d) of the Code suspends the running of the limitations periods for filing a wrongful levy claim and a wrongful levy suit.	04/20/2020
2020-02	Feigh v. Commissioner, 152 T.C. No. 15 (2019) T.C. Docket No. 20163-17	Whether certain Medicaid waiver payments that are treated as excludable from gross income under § 131 pursuant to Notice 2014-7 may be earned income for purposes of the credits under § 32 and § 24.	03/30/2020
2020-01	Paychex Business Solutions, LLC, et al., v. United States of America, 2017 WL 2692843 (M.D. Fla. 2017)	Whether control over the bank account from which wage payments are made is sufficient for an entity to be a section 3401(d)(1)1 statutory employer.	03/16/2020
2019-03	GreenTeam Materials Recovery Facility PN, GreenWaste Recovery, Inc., Tax Matters Partner, et al. v. Commissioner	Whether the transfer of a non-capital asset is treated under § 1253 as the sale or exchange of a capital asset if the transferor does not retain any significant power, right, or continuing interest.	10/15/2019
2019-02	Union Pacific Railroad Company v. United States, 865 F.3d 1045 (8th Cir. 2017), rev'g No. 8:14CV237 (D. Neb. July 1, 2016)	Whether lump-sum payments made to unionized employees upon ratification of collective bargaining agreements are taxable compensation under the Railroad Retirement Tax Act ("RRTA").	10/09/2019

→ The IRS finding list sorts by AOD Number, Decision, Issue, and Release Date. This Finding List covers AODs issued since 1997.

Illustration 9-12. Checkpoint Listing of AODs

- Actions on Decisions (1967 to Present)
  - 2020
    - AOD 2020-01 – IRC Sec(s). 3401, 03/18/2020
    - AOD 2020-02 – IRC Sec(s). 24; 32; 131, 04/01/2020
    - AOD 2020-03 – IRC Sec(s). 6532; 7426; 7701; 7811, 04/24/2020

→ The Table of Contents indicates the Code section(s). Searching by key word or taxpayer name is also possible.

Commercial services often include documents that predate release mandated by litigation. For example, Checkpoint covers AODs issued since 1967. Lexis+ includes documents from 1963. Both predate the year (1981) for which the IRS was required to release these documents to the public.

Illustration 9-13. Partial List of IRS Databases in Lexis+

IRS Actions on Decisions
IRS Appeals Settlement Guidelines
IRS Around the Nation
IRS Chief Counsel Advice
IRS Chief Counsel Notices
IRS Criminal Tax Bulletin
IRS Cumulative Bulletin and Internal Revenue Bulletin
IRS Disclosure Litigation Bulletin (Archive)
IRS Exempt Organization Field Memoranda
IRS Fact Sheets
IRS Field Service Advice Memorandums (Archive)
IRS General Counsel Memoranda (Archive)
IRS General Litigation Bulletins (Archive)
IRS Generic Legal Advice Memoranda
IRS LBnI Coordinated Issue Papers[42]
IRS LBnI Industry Director Guidance

→ You can search databases by Code section or key word.

Illustration 9-14. IRS Website Written Determinations Finding List

Find [ ] in Number Find Find Help

1 - 25 of 66,632 files Show per page: 25 50 100 200 « Previous | 1 2 3 4 5 6 7 8 9 10 | Next »

Number	UILC	Subject	Released
202021026	501.00-00	Exemption From Tax on Corporations, Certain Trusts, etc. (Exempt v. Not Exempt)	05/22/2020
202021026	501.36-01	Section 501(c)(3) Organizations	05/22/2020
202021026	501.33-00	Private v. Public Interest Served	05/22/2020
202021026	501.03-30	Organizational and Operational Tests	05/22/2020
202021025	501.03-00	Religious, Charitable, etc., Institutions and Community Chest	05/22/2020
202021025	501.33-00	Private v. Public Interest Served	05/22/2020
202021024	501.04-00	Civic Leagues and Social Welfare Groups (See Also 0501.03-25)	05/22/2020
202021023	4945.04-04	Grants to Individuals	05/22/2020
202021022	4945.04-04	Grants to Individuals	05/22/2020
202021021	501.03-30	Organizational and Operational Tests	05/22/2020
202021021	501.35-00	"Exclusively" Test	05/22/2020

→ You can sort documents classified as written determinations based on Document Number, UILC, Subject, or Release Date.

42 "LBnI" is really "LB&I" ("Large Business and International").

→ The website does not indicate whether the document is a letter ruling, technical advice memorandum, or other Chief Counsel document.

M. Uniform Issue List (UIL/UILC)

The **Uniform Issue List** is a Code-section-based index of issues. The IRS assigns UIL numbers to documents released to the public pursuant to Code section 6110, which is discussed in Section D (*supra* page 172). This list is prepared by Chief Counsel Office personnel.[43] The IRS issued a UIL list in Publication 1102; its listing in the Catalog of U.S. Government Publications shows a November 1998 revision date. Some libraries may have retained this publication in their government documents section.

The IRS varies in the terminology used for UIL numbers. The terms UIL, UILC, or Index may precede the actual UIL number in a document.

N. Citators for IRS Documents

The IRS reviews its pronouncements for continued relevance. In addition, some IRS rulings have been subjected to judicial scrutiny. The status of these items can be determined from online services and from the citators illustrated in Chapter 11.[44] You can also use Mertens, Law of Federal Income Taxation—Rulings (since 1954).

Citators include judicial action and cover both I.R.B. documents and publicly available IRS determinations. They are better-suited for determining continued relevance than is the Mertens service. The Mertens service includes only IRS action and covers only revenue rulings and procedures. There is a risk that a revoked item was removed from the database. The I.R.B. includes a Current Actions on Previously Published Items section. It is not cumulated over multiple years and has not been updated since the end of 2018.

O. Judicial Deference

The items discussed in this chapter receive less government and public review than do Treasury regulations. As indicated by the excerpts below, judges vary in the amount of deference paid these pronouncements. Although items released as a result of FOIA litigation are not precedential, many courts take note of their holdings.

Decisions giving deference to rulings and other IRS documents must be judged in light of the Supreme Court's *Mead* decision, which involved a Customs Service ruling letter. The Court held: "We agree that a tariff classification has no claim to judicial deference under *Chevron*, there being no indication that Congress intended such a ruling to carry the force of law, but we hold that under *Skidmore v. Swift & Co.*, 323 U.S. 134 (1944), the ruling is eligible to claim respect according to its persuasiveness."[45]

In addition to judicial deference issues, the IRS must also take its own published guidance into account. In *Rauenhorst v. Commissioner*, the Tax Court criticized the IRS

---

43 IRM 30.7.1.4 (Oct. 5, 2005).

44 BCite (Bloomberg Law), the CCH Citator, KeyCite (Westlaw Edge), RIA Citator 2nd, and Shepard's (Lexis+) all cover IRS documents.

45 *United States v. Mead Corp.*, 533 U.S. 218, 221 (2001). See Chapter 8 for a brief discussion of *Chevron*. You may also encounter citations to *Bowles v. Seminole Rock & Sand Co.*, 325 U.S. 410 (1945), *Auer v. Robbins*, 519 U.S. 452 (1997), and *Kisor v. Wilkie*, 139 S. Ct. 2400 (2019). These decisions involve deference to an agency's interpretation of its own rules.

for taking a litigating position that conflicted with a published revenue ruling.[46] In *Barnes Group Inc. v. Commissioner*, the Tax Court held that taxpayers could not rely on a ruling because the transactional facts exceeded the scope of the facts in the ruling.[47]

1. Internal Revenue Bulletin Documents

- "[T]hree factors—the timing of the Notice, the lack of authority, and the Notice's inconsistency with prior IRS advice—mean that Notice 2015–56 is not entitled to deference under *Skidmore*. In short, Notice 2015–56 is merely another vehicle through which the Government conveyed its position in this case." *Sunoco, Inc. v. United States*, 128 Fed. Cl. 345, 348 (2016).
- "Respondent argues that we should give *Skidmore* deference to Rev. Proc. 99–43. . . . The revenue procedure was promulgated 16 months after the special rule's enactment .... The pronouncement in the revenue procedure is not supported by any analysis of text or legislative history or any other relevant guidance. It is not an interpretation but a litigation position." *Exxon Mobil Corp. v. Commissioner*, 136 T.C. 99, 117 (2011).
- "Revenue rulings are not binding precedent, but are entitled to some weight, as reflecting an interpretation of the law by the agency entrusted with its interpretation. Such rulings, however, do not require this court to apply a mistaken view of the law to a particular taxpayer. In particular, Supreme Court precedent makes clear that if a revenue ruling is found to be unreasonable or contrary to law, it is binding neither on the Commissioner nor this court, based on the rationale that the Congress, and only the Congress, has the power to make law." *Vons Companies, Inc. v. United States*, 51 Fed. Cl. 1, 12 (2001).[48]
- "We note that, in any event, revenue rulings are not entitled to any special deference." *Bhatia v. Commissioner*, T.C. Memo. 1996–429, at *10 n.5 (1996).
- "Revenue rulings represent the official IRS position on application of tax law to specific facts. . . . They relate to matters as to which the IRS is the 'primary authority.' . . . Revenue rulings are accordingly entitled to precedential 'weight.' " *Salomon Inc. v. United States*, 976 F.2d 837, 841 (2d Cir. 1992).

---

[46] 119 T.C. 157 (2002). IRM 32.2.2.10(4) (Aug. 11, 2004) (Force and Effect of Revenue Rulings, Revenue Procedures, Notices, Announcements, and News Releases) provides: "Chief Counsel attorneys must follow legal positions established by publications in papers filed in Tax Court or in defense letters or suit letters sent to DOJ. Chief Counsel attorneys may not rely on case law to take a position that is less favorable to a taxpayer in a particular case than the position set forth in a publication."

[47] T.C. Memo. 2013–109.

[48] The court later revised the first two sentences to read as follows: "Taxpayers generally may rely on a revenue ruling to support their interpretation of a provision of the Code, provided the ruling is unaffected by subsequent legislation, regulations, cases or other revenue rulings. Such rulings do not require this court to apply a mistaken view of the law to a particular taxpayer." 89 A.F.T.R.2d 2002–301 (2001). The court also stated its view regarding letter rulings, technical advice memoranda, and general counsel memoranda.

2. Other IRS Documents

- "Nor are we persuaded by the preamble or technical advice memorandum upon which petitioners rely. In addition to the obvious fact that these documents also are not items of legislative history, these documents are afforded little weight in this Court." *Allen v. Commissioner*, 118 T.C. 1, 17 n.12 (2002).
- "The interpretation of Rev. Proc. 71–21 contained in the General Counsel Memorandum and the IRS decision under the Revenue Procedure is not reflected in a regulation adopted after notice and comment and probably would not be entitled to *Chevron* deference. See *Mead* . . . . Here, however, as noted above, we are not dealing with an agency's interpretation of a statute and issues of *Chevron* deference, but with the IRS's interpretation of an ambiguous term in its own Revenue Procedure. In such circumstances, substantial deference is paid to an agency's interpretations reflected in informal rulings. In the context of tax cases, the IRS's reasonable interpretations of its own regulations and procedures are entitled to particular deference." *American Express Co. v. United States*, 262 F.3d 1376, 1382–83 (Fed. Cir. 2001) (citations omitted).
- "Such private letter rulings 'may not be used or cited as precedent,' § 6110(j)(3), and we do not do so. It does not follow that they are not relevant here." *Transco Exploration Co. v. Commissioner*, 949 F.2d 837, 840 (5th Cir. 1992).
- "Although this ruling cannot be cited as precedent under 26 U.S.C. § 6110(J)(3) [sic], it highlights the confusion this section has engendered at the IRS. More importantly, the fact that the IRS has done an about face since 1986 makes us even more reluctant to adopt their interpretation of this statute without an understandable articulation of a tax policy supporting it." *Estate of Spencer v. Commissioner*, 43 F.3d 226, 234 (6th Cir. 1995).
- "In *Herrmann*, the court would not rely on the GCM to interpret the plan involved because the GCM was fact specific to the plan for which it was written. The court, however, did rely on its interpretation of the Code section involved because it assumed the IRS would insist upon a uniform interpretation of the section. Here, where there is no case law in point, it is arguably permissible to use GCMs to instruct the court on how the IRS itself interprets § 501(c)(5), since they constitute the only real guidance as to what the IRS considers a labor organization for the purposes of a § 501(c)(5) exemption." *Morganbesser v. United States*, 984 F.2d 560, 563 (2d Cir. 1993).
- "While recognizing that the IRM does not represent law and is in no way binding upon this court, the court believes that the manual reflects the more reasonable interpretation of the Revenue Code's mandate in this instance. Thus, the manual's agreement with the court's own independent reading of the statute bolsters the court's conclusion." *Anderson v. United States*, 71 A.F.T.R.2d 93–1589, 93–1591, 93–1 U.S.T.C. ¶ 50,249, at 87,958 (N.D. Cal. 1993), rev'd, 44 F.3d 795, 799 (9th Cir. 1995) ("But the IRS

correctly concedes that its internal agents' manual does not have the force of law, and makes no *Chevron* argument for deference to this language from its manual, not promulgated as a regulation.") (citation omitted).

- "While the IRM does not have the force of law, the manual provisions do constitute persuasive authority as to the IRS's interpretation of the statute." *Ginsberg v. Commissioner*, 127 T.C. 75, 87 (2006).

3. IRS Litigating Positions

- "We now hold that the IRS' position in the amicus brief was an informal agency policy pronouncement not entitled to *Chevron* deference." *Matz v. Household International Tax Reduction Investment Plan*, 265 F.3d 572, 574 (7th Cir. 2001).

P. Problems

1. Use only print sources to determine who drafted the IRS document listed below.

   a. Rev. Rul. 96–11

   b. Notice 2002–59

   c. Notice 2005–58

   d. Rev. Proc. 2007–23

2. What is the most recent revenue ruling referring to the I.R.C. section listed?

   a. 42

   b. 172

   c. 280A

   d. 1244

3. What is the most recent revenue ruling referring to the Treasury regulation section listed?

   a. 1.213–1

   b. 1.165–11

   c. 1.483–1

   d. 1.1001–3

4. What is the status of the item listed? What later pronouncement effectuated the status change?

   a. Rev. Rul. 71–533

   b. Rev. Rul. 78–330

   c. Rev. Rul. 95–6

   d. Rev. Proc. 2003–61

5. Assume that you are concerned about the possible application of I.R.C. § 269 to your client's contemplated acquisition of another corporation. In the current year, will the IRS issue a private letter ruling on this question? What is the authority for your answer?

6. What is the most recent I.R.B. document listing all countries treated as being within the North American area for purposes of I.R.C. § 274(h)?

7. Using the Cumulative Bulletin, answer the following questions.

   a. What is the C.B. citation for Rev. Rul. 87–102?

   b. List all the decisions to which the IRS did not acquiesce in 1987.

   c. What revenue ruling appears at 2008–2 C.B. 166? What does it deal with?

8. Use online sources to find any AOD for each decision below. Indicate the IRS recommendation in each AOD you find.

   a. *Jacobs v. Commissioner* (Tax Court 2017)

   b. *Rothkamm v. United States* (5th Cir. 2015)

   c. *Voss v. Commissioner* (9th Cir. 2015)

   d. *Beatty v. Commissioner* (Tax Court 1996)

   e. *Xerox Corp. v. United States* (Fed. Cir. 1994)

9. Use only IRS.gov (and any other government sites you find while using IRS.gov) to determine the per diem meal and incidental expenses amount for anyone traveling to Houston, Texas, on an overnight business trip on September 1, 2017.

10. You are preparing to meet with an IRS auditor regarding a client's gift to charity. Use only the Internal Revenue Manual (available on the IRS.gov website) to determine a taxpayer's rights at initial contact.

11. Using the IRS.gov website, locate the non-I.R.B. document involving the following facts. Provide the citation and holding.

   a. Generic legal advice memorandum regarding whether an amount paid by the wrongdoer to compensate the government for the relator fee it paid in connection with an action against the wrongdoer under the False Claims Act is a nondeductible fine or penalty

   b. Program manager technical assistance regarding whether the IRS can remove the cents column from Form 941

   c. Information letter regarding child tax benefits for Amish taxpayers who have religious objections to obtaining Social Security Numbers for their children.

12. You have been assigned several clients for whom you expect to do tax controversy work. Indicate the URL for the Audit Technique Guide covering the profession or topic listed below.

   a. Architects and landscape architects

   b. Conservation easements

   c. Structured settlement factoring

   d. Veterinary medicine

13. Donald was thrilled when he was accepted into American Career Institute's program for information technology. He borrowed $30,000 in student loans to pay for his tuition, books, and supplies. Unfortunately, before he could graduate, the U.S.

Department of Education closed the school. The loans were forgiven under the Department of Education's "Defense to Repayment" or "Closed School" discharge process. At all times, Donald was solvent. Use only IRS materials to determine if Donald will have any gross income from the discharge of indebtedness.

14. What is the topic of Chief Counsel Advice 202020002?

Chapter 10

JUDICIAL REPORTS

A. Introduction

This chapter discusses the courts that decide tax cases, both initially and on appeal, and the reporter services in which you can locate judicial opinions. It also lists name changes for several courts and indicates when each court began hearing tax cases.

Your goals for this chapter include locating pertinent decisions, judging their relevance in a particular jurisdiction, and updating your research to include cases that are working their way through the litigation and appeals processes. Because Congress can usually "overrule" a judicial decision it dislikes by amending the statute, remember to check recently enacted and pending legislation before deciding that you can rely on a particular case as precedent. In addition, you must also check IRS litigating positions because the IRS may announce it will not follow an adverse lower court decision.

B. Court Organization

1. Trial Courts

Four courts serve as trial courts for most tax disputes: District Courts; the Court of Federal Claims; the Tax Court; and Bankruptcy Courts. Other bodies may also be relevant. The United States Court of International Trade hears cases involving tariffs and related tax matters.[1] In addition, as indicated in Chapter 7, disputes between governments may be heard by the World Trade Organization or other international tribunal. This chapter focuses on the four primary trial courts.

If litigation is contemplated, you must consider two questions. Which trial courts have jurisdiction over the matter?[2] If more than one court has jurisdiction, what factors are relevant in deciding where to litigate?

a. United States District Courts

Because District Courts are courts of general jurisdiction, their judges rarely develop as high a level of expertise on tax law questions as do judges of the Tax Court or even of the Court of Federal Claims. Taxpayers must pay the amount in dispute and sue for a refund as a condition to litigating in District Court, the only tribunal where a jury trial is available.

A significant number of District Court decisions are not published in Federal Supplement. You may be able to find them in other reporter services.[3]

---

1 See, e.g., *Princess Cruises, Inc. v. United States*, 22 Ct. Int'l Trade 498 (1998), rev'd, 201 F.3d 1352 (Fed. Cir. 2000). Many, but not all, CIT cases also appear in Federal Supplement. Appeals go to the Court of Appeals for the Federal Circuit.

2 Rules concerning jurisdiction appear in the Internal Revenue Code and in other titles of United States Code, particularly Title 28.

3 These include American Federal Tax Reports (A.F.T.R.) and U.S. Tax Cases (U.S.T.C.), discussed in Section D.2 (*infra* page 206), and various online services. Freedom of Information Act litigation forced the Justice Department to make all District Court tax opinions available to the public. *U.S. Dep't of Justice v. Tax Analysts*, 492 U.S. 136 (1989).

b. United States Court of Federal Claims

Although the Court of Federal Claims does not hear tax cases exclusively, the percentage of such cases it hears is likely to be greater than that heard in the average District Court. As in the District Court, a taxpayer must first pay the disputed amount before bringing suit.

Before October 1, 1982, this court was called the United States Court of Claims and the Court of Claims of the United States. Trials were conducted by a trial judge (formerly called a commissioner), whose decisions were reviewed by Court of Claims judges. Only the Supreme Court had jurisdiction over appeals from its decisions. Between October 1, 1982, and October 28, 1992, this court was called the United States Claims Court.

Table 10-A. Names Used by Tax Court and Court of Federal Claims in Published Decisions

Tax Court	*Court of Federal Claims*
United States Tax Court (since 1970)	United States Court of Federal Claims (since Oct. 29, 1992)
Tax Court of the United States (Oct. 22, 1942–1969)	United States Claims Court (Oct. 1, 1982–Oct. 28, 1992)
Board of Tax Appeals (1924–Oct. 21, 1942)	United States Court of Claims (1948–Sept. 30, 1982)
	Court of Claims of the United States (1863–1948)

c. United States Tax Court

Because Tax Court judges hear only tax cases, their expertise is substantially greater than that of judges in the other trial courts. Tax Court cases are tried by one judge, who submits an opinion to the chief judge for consideration. The chief judge can allow the decision to stand or refer it to the full court for review.[4] The published decision indicates if it has been reviewed; dissenting opinions, if any, are included.

In some instances, special trial judges hear disputes and issue opinions.[5] When the amount in dispute exceeds $50,000, the special trial judge does not issue the final opinion. The opinion is issued by a Tax Court judge. Before rule changes in 2005, the judge writing the opinion indicated that he or she adopted the special trial judge's report. The Tax Court did not separately release the trial judge's report to taxpayers. In 2005,

---

[4] "Court review is directed if the report proposes to invalidate a regulation, overrule a published Tax Court case, or reconsider, in a circuit that has not addressed it, an issue on which we have been reversed by a court of appeals." Mary Ann Cohen, *How to Read Tax Court Opinions*, 1 HOUS. BUS. & TAX L.J. 1, 5–6 (2001). The chief judge has 30 days in which to decide whether to direct that the report be reviewed. I.R.C. § 7460(b).

[5] The Supreme Court upheld this practice in *Freytag v. Commissioner*, 501 U.S. 868 (1991). The special trial judges were called commissioners until 1984. Plaintiffs have raised other constitutional issues involving the Tax Court's status. Although appeals from the Tax Court are heard by Article III (judicial branch) courts, the Tax Court is not an Article III court; it is authorized by Article I of the Constitution (legislative branch). See, e.g., *Kuretski v. Commissioner*, 755 F.3d 929 (D.C. Cir. 2014); *Battat v. Commissioner*, 148 T.C. 32 (2017). Both cases involve whether the presidential power to remove Tax Court judges is an unconstitutional violation of separation of powers. Since 2015, Code section 7441 has included the following sentence: "The Tax Court is not an agency of, and shall be independent of, the executive branch of the Government."

the United States Supreme Court held that withholding the trial judge's report violated the Tax Court's own rules.[6]

There are three main types of written Tax Court decisions.[7] Two of those types can result in appeals. The Government Publishing Office publishes **Regular** (or **Reported**) **Opinions**; these present important legal issues. If a Regular Opinion has been reviewed by the court, it is a **Reviewed Opinion**; if not, it is a **Division Opinion**. Other publishers print **Memorandum Opinions**, which involve well-established legal issues and are primarily fact-based.[8]

The Tax Court also has a **Small Case** division that taxpayers can elect to use for disputes of $50,000 or less. The **Summary Opinions** issued in those cases cannot be appealed or used as precedent. Until 2001, they were not published in any reporter service or on the Tax Court website.[9] Although Tax Court judges do hear cases brought in the Small Case division, these cases are likely to be heard by special trial judges.

A taxpayer can sue in the Tax Court without paying the amount in dispute prior to litigating. Taxpayers also had this privilege in the Tax Court's predecessor, the Board of Tax Appeals.

d. United States Bankruptcy Courts

Bankruptcy Courts came into existence in 1979. Before that, bankruptcy trustees appointed by District Court judges administered bankruptcy cases.[10] In addition to deciding priority of liens and related matters, United States Bankruptcy Courts issue substantive tax rulings.

District Court judges, Bankruptcy Appellate Panels, or Courts of Appeals review Bankruptcy Court decisions.[11] As a general rule, each circuit decides if it will use a Bankruptcy Appellate Panel (BAP) and whether the BAP will hear all cases. Direct appeal to a Court of Appeals has been authorized since 2005, but only in limited situations.[12]

Bankruptcy cases often have two captions. One caption begins with "In re." The other follows the format used for most cases "Plaintiff v. Defendant." If you are looking for a particular bankruptcy case, note both the debtor and the trustee's names so that

---

6 See *Ballard v. Commissioner*, 544 U.S. 40 (2005). The taxpayers in this case had reason to believe the special trial judge's report varied significantly from the Tax Court's published opinion. The Tax Court has since modified its Rule 183.

7 The Tax Court can also issue Bench Opinions. The judge's oral findings of fact and conclusions are recorded in the transcript of the case's proceedings. These cases generally involve legal issues that the court has repeatedly rejected or factual issues such as substantiation of deductions. Keith Fogg, *The United States Tax Court: A Court for All Parties*, BULL. INT'L TAX'N, Jan./Feb. 2016, at 78–79.

8 Memorandum decisions have been appealed as far as the Supreme Court. See, e.g., *Commissioner v. Duberstein*, 363 U.S. 278 (1960).

9 I.R.C. § 7463(b). The increase to $50,000 occurred in 1998; the previous limit was $10,000. A typical citation is *Serrano v. Commissioner*, T.C. Summ. Op. 2020–15.

10 Court of Appeals judges appoint Bankruptcy judges. 28 U.S.C. § 152(a).

11 See, e.g., *In re Michaud*, 199 B.R. 248 (Bankr. D.N.H. 1996), aff'd, *Michaud v. United States*, 206 B.R. 1 (D.N.H. 1997); *In re Mosbrucker*, 220 B.R. 656 (Bankr. D.N.D. 1998), aff'd, 227 B.R. 434 (B.A.P. 8th Cir. 1998), aff'd, 99–2 U.S.T.C. ¶ 50,883, 84 A.F.T.R.2d 99–6457 (8th Cir. 1999) (unpublished opinion).

12 28 U.S.C. § 158(d)(2).

you can find the case no matter which case reporter or citator service you are using. Table 10-B shows how three reporter services captioned a Bankruptcy Court case.[13]

Table 10-B. Case Captions for Bankruptcy Court Decisions

Reporter Service	*Caption*
Bankruptcy Reporter	*In re Guardian Trust Co.*, 242 B.R. 608 (Bankr. S.D. Miss. 1999)
U.S. Tax Cases	*In re Guardian Trust Company*, 99–2 U.S.T.C. ¶ 50,819 (Bankr. S.D. Miss. 1999)
American Federal Tax Reports	*Henderson v. United States*, 84 A.F.T.R.2d 99–5940 (Bankr. S.D. Miss. 1999)

e. Other Courts

The courts listed above can determine tax liability. But they are not the only courts that interpret the Code or administrative rulings. For example, parties to a contract governed by state law may have incorporated a federal tax provision. A state trial court may have to interpret that provision if a dispute between the parties arises.

2. Courts of Appeals

When your research uncovers trial court decisions, you should trace them to the appellate court level. This is particularly important if decisions conflict with each other and none comes from your jurisdiction.

Decisions of District Courts and the Tax Court are appealed to the Court of Appeals for the taxpayer's geographical residence[14] and from there to the Supreme Court. Even if the Tax Court disagrees with a particular circuit court precedent, it will follow it if that court would hear the appeal. This is the *Golsen* rule.[15] After appellate reversal in several circuits, the Tax Court is likely to change its position for future litigation.[16]

The District Court for the District of Columbia and the Court of Appeals for the D.C. Circuit review a significant number of challenges to agency action. This includes successful challenges to provisions of Circular 230, Regulations Governing Practice before the Internal Revenue Service.[17]

Two Courts of Appeals were established in the early 1980s. The Eleventh Circuit was carved out of the Fifth Circuit in 1981. If you represent a taxpayer who lives in the Eleventh Circuit, you should also consider Fifth Circuit decisions issued before October

[13] Even if each reporter uses the same case caption for the initial proceeding, they may use different captions for appellate decisions. See, e.g., *In re Harvard Industries, Inc.*, 568 F.3d 444 (3d Cir. 2009); *Harvard Secured Creditors Liquidation Trust v. Internal Revenue Service*, 103 A.F.T.R.2d 2009–2701 (3d Cir. 2009). Each reporter service lists the other name as a second name.

[14] From 1924 to 1926, appeals from the Board of Tax Appeals (the Tax Court's predecessor) were heard in District Court. Revenue Act of 1924, ch. 234, § 900(g), 43 Stat. 253, 336; Revenue Act of 1926, ch. 27, § 1001(a), 44 Stat. 9, 109.

[15] *Golsen v. Commissioner*, 54 T.C. 742 (1970), aff'd, 445 F.2d 985 (10th Cir. 1971).

[16] See, e.g., *Fazi v. Commissioner*, 102 T.C. 695 (1994).

[17] *Loving v. Internal Revenue Service*, 742 F.3d 1013 (D.C. Cir. 2014); *Ridgely v. Lew*, 55 F. Supp. 3d 89 (D.D.C. 2014).

1, 1981.[18] The Court of Appeals for the Federal Circuit was formed in 1982 to review decisions of what is now the Court of Federal Claims. Because the Supreme Court reviews so few Court of Appeals decisions, the Court of Federal Claims-Federal Circuit route offers a forum-shopping opportunity. Taxpayers can avoid adverse appellate court decisions from their "home" circuits by suing in the Court of Federal Claims.[19]

3. Supreme Court

As noted above, decisions from the circuit courts can be appealed to the United States Supreme Court. The Supreme Court hears cases involving both constitutional challenges and those involving statutory interpretation. The Court is unlikely to grant certiorari in a case involving only statutory interpretation unless there is a conflict between two or more circuits.

C. Locating Decisions

Your strategy for locating decisions depends on whether you are compiling a list of decisions to read or whether you are simply trying to locate a decision whose caption or citation you already have.

1. Compiling Finding Lists

If you need to find judicial decisions involving a particular statute, treaty, regulation, or ruling, you can compile a preliminary reading list using one of the annotated looseleaf services discussed in Chapter 12 or a treatise. You can also use one of the citators discussed in Chapter 11. You can also simply use the item as a search term in an online database.

2. Locating Cases by Party Name

If you know the name of a party, but not the reporter citation, you have several options for locating the decision. Online services are particularly helpful because you can include facts and issues in your search request. These services may include screens in which you can enter party names, judge names, or other information and retrieve a case. [See Illustrations 3-1 and 3-5 (*supra* pages 14 and 16) and 10-1 and 10-2 (*infra* pages 202 and 203).] In addition to subscription services, your options include court websites, free websites maintained by law schools and other entities, and Google Scholar.[20]

You also have print service options for locating case citations. If you know the taxpayer's first name and last name, you can use the RIA and CCH print citators; both list taxpayers alphabetically. The United States Tax Reporter looseleaf service also includes a Table of Cases. If you lack the taxpayer's first name, but do know the jurisdiction, you might instead consult the alphabetical list of parties in the most recent edition of West's Federal Practice Digest. That service does not include the Tax Court.

If you know who the other party is, you can narrow your search among various tax reporter services. As a general rule, cases that began in Tax Court are captioned

---

[18] See, e.g., *Estate of Kosow v. Commissioner*, 45 F.3d 1524, 1529 (11th Cir. 1995), citing a 1972 Fifth Circuit decision. Splitting the Ninth Circuit into two or even three circuits has been proposed many times. See, e.g., Judicial Administration and Improvement Act of 2019, H.R. 78, 116th Cong. (2019).

[19] See *Ginsburg v. United States*, 396 F.2d 983 (1968), for a discussion of this phenomenon in the court's predecessor, the Court of Claims.

[20] Google Scholar's Case law Search function lets you select all federal courts or select one or more federal courts of your choice.

"Taxpayer v. Commissioner," and cases that arose in District Court or Court of Federal Claims are captioned "Taxpayer v. United States."[21] Cases whose captions include "In re" often began in Bankruptcy Court, but reporter services differ in their captioning of bankruptcy cases. [See Table 10-B, *supra* page 200.]

Illustration 10-1. Initial Search Screen in Lexis+

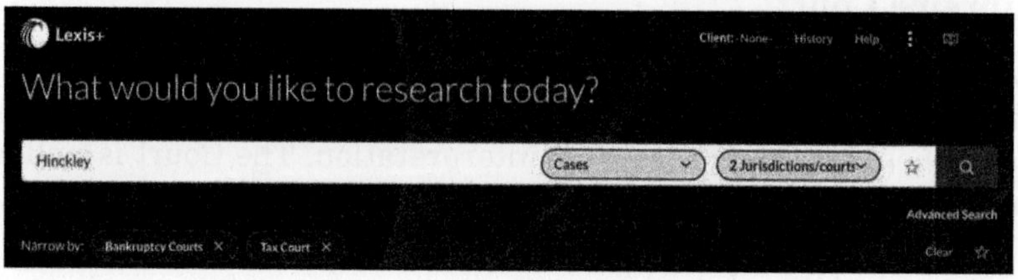

→ For this search we are looking for a case, but only know the taxpayer's last name and that it is a bankruptcy or tax case. Because you don't know which Bankruptcy Court, you can't narrow your search to that specific court. So here the search is restricted to Bankruptcy Court or Tax Court cases. If we knew the citation or docket number, we could run the search using those features instead of searching by name.

If you have a citation, you can retrieve the case in Westlaw Edge by entering the citation in the search box. Alternatively, you can enter the party's name in the search box. You can limit your search to specific courts or to all courts. Westlaw Edge includes the Supreme Court, Courts of Appeals, District Courts, Bankruptcy Courts, the Tax Court, and the Court of Federal Claims as options.

---

[21] Knowing where to start is particularly useful if you use print reporter services and lack access to the CCH and RIA citators and electronic services. If the case arose in the Tax Court, you can use the CCH Tax Court Reporter's Table of Decisions, including the Current and Latest Additions supplements to ascertain the CCH Decision Number. You can obtain a citation by cross-referencing those numbers to the official reports or the CCH Tax Court Memoranda service using cross-reference tables in Volume 2 of this service. You can locate cases originating in other trial courts, as well as all appeals court decisions, through A.F.T.R.'s Table of Cases, which is cumulated throughout each five-year period in the A.F.T.R. volumes.

Illustration 10-2. Using Find a Case by Citation in Checkpoint

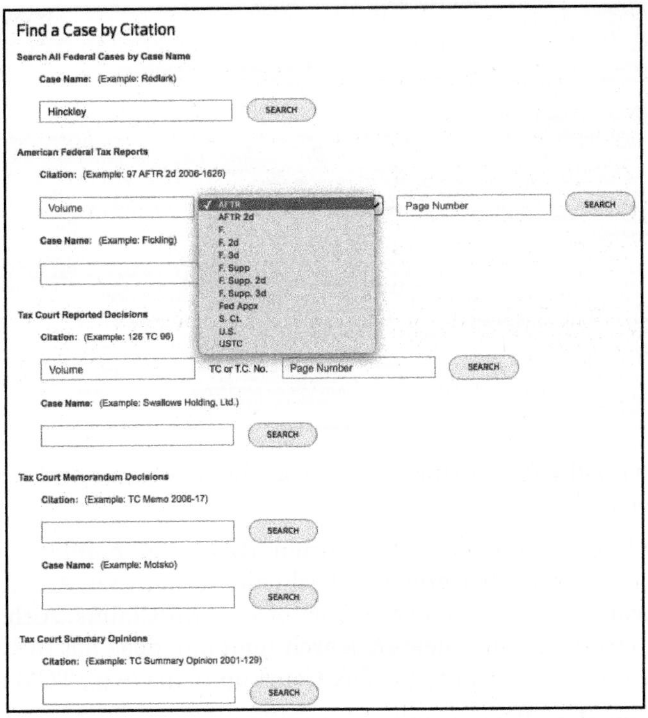

→ Checkpoint includes search by name and search by citation functions in one screen. If you don't know which court decided the case, place the taxpayer's name in the top box.

→ The box for searching AFTR has a pull-down menu allowing searches in several federal court reporter services. Neither Bankruptcy Reporter nor Federal Claims is a listed option, so you would need a parallel citation to A.F.T.R. or U.S.T.C.

Cheetah lets you enter a party's name in the Search Selected Content box; you can select "Cases" or you can limit your search to cases appearing in U.S.T.C. or to different Tax Court decisions (Regular, Memorandum, Small Tax Cases, Board of Tax Appeals). The search of Cases produces federal courts' written opinions that deal with the Internal Revenue Code or a tax-related issue.

Searching by name in Cheetah, you will initially retrieve all cases that include the name you entered, whether or not the case involved that party. You can narrow your results by court after you perform the search; for example, you may be interested only in cases from the Tax Court or from a particular district or appellate court.

Illustration 10-3. Results from a Case-Name Search in Cheetah

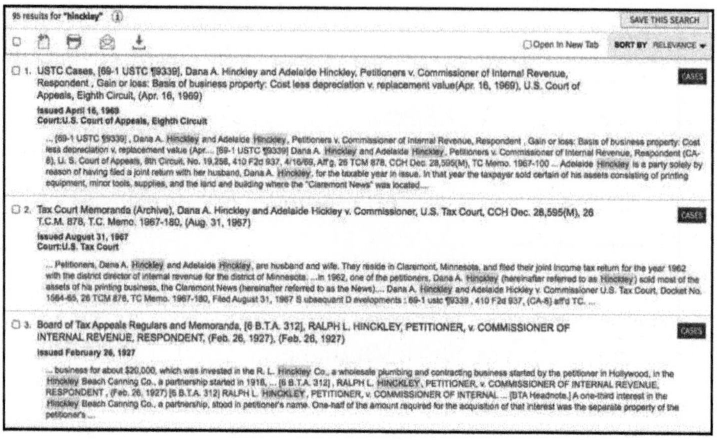
95 results for "hinckley"

SAVE THIS SEARCH

Open In New Tab SORT BY RELEVANCE

1. USTC Cases, [69-1 USTC ¶9339], Dana A. Hinckley and Adelaide Hinckley, Petitioners v. Commissioner of Internal Revenue, Respondent , Gain or loss: Basis of business property: Cost less depreciation v. replacement value(Apr. 16, 1969), U.S. Court of Appeals, Eighth Circuit, (Apr. 16, 1969) CASES

Issued April 16, 1969
Court:U.S. Court of Appeals, Eighth Circuit

... [69-1 USTC ¶9339] , Dana A. Hinckley and Adelaide Hinckley, Petitioners v. Commissioner of Internal Revenue, Respondent , Gain or loss: Basis of business property: Cost less depreciation v. replacement value (Apr.... [69-1 USTC ¶9339] Dana A. Hinckley and Adelaide Hinckley, Petitioners v. Commissioner of Internal Revenue, Respondent (CA-8), U. S. Court of Appeals, 8th Circuit, No. 19,258, 410 F2d 937, 4/16/69, Aff'g. 26 TCM 878, CCH Dec. 28,595(M), TC Memo. 1967-100 ... Adelaide Hinckley is a party solely by reason of having filed a joint return with her husband, Dana A. Hinckley, for the taxable year in issue. In that year the taxpayer sold certain of his assets consisting of printing equipment, minor tools, supplies, and the land and building where the "Claremont News" was located...

2. Tax Court Memoranda (Archive), Dana A. Hinckley and Adelaide Hickley v. Commissioner, U.S. Tax Court, CCH Dec. 28,595(M), 26 T.C.M. 878, T.C. Memo. 1967-180, (Aug. 31, 1967) CASES

Issued August 31, 1967
Court:U.S. Tax Court

... Petitioners, Dana A. Hinckley and Adelaide Hinckley, are husband and wife. They reside in Claremont, Minnesota, and filed their joint income tax return for the year 1962 with the district director of internal revenue for the district of Minnesota. ...In 1962, one of the petitioners, Dana A. Hinckley (hereinafter referred to as Hinckley) sold most of the assets of his printing business, the Claremont News (hereinafter referred to as the News).... Dana A. Hinckley and Adelaide Hickley v. Commissioner U.S. Tax Court, Docket No. 1564-65, 26 TCM 878, TC Memo. 1967-180, Filed August 31, 1967 S ubsequent D evelopments : 69-1 ustc ¶9339 , 410 F2d 937, (CA-8) aff'd TC. ...

3. Board of Tax Appeals Regulars and Memoranda, [6 B.T.A. 312], RALPH L. HINCKLEY, PETITIONER, v. COMMISSIONER OF INTERNAL REVENUE, RESPONDENT, (Feb. 26, 1927), (Feb. 26, 1927) CASES

Issued February 26, 1927

... business for about $20,000, which was invested in the R. L. Hinckley Co., a wholesale plumbing and contracting business started by the petitioner in Hollywood, in the Hinckley Beach Canning Co., a partnership started in 1918, ... [6 B.T.A. 312] , RALPH L. HINCKLEY , PETITIONER, v. COMMISSIONER OF INTERNAL REVENUE, RESPONDENT , (Feb. 26, 1927) [6 B.T.A. 312] RALPH L. HINCKLEY , PETITIONER, v. COMMISSIONER OF INTERNAL ... [BTA Headnote.] A one-third interest in the Hinckley Beach Canning Co., a partnership, stood in petitioner's name. One-half of the amount required for the acquisition of that interest was the separate property of the petitioner's ...

→ These are the results from using Hinckley as the case name and searching in Cases. The results are sorted by relevancy.

Cheetah also lets you find a case by citation. Its search template covers citations to U.S.T.C., the reporter services covered by Checkpoint (other than A.F.T.R.), and reporter services for Bankruptcy Courts and the Court of Federal Claims. Although Checkpoint includes U.S.T.C. citations, the Cheetah search template does not include A.F.T.R. The Cheetah template includes variants for Tax Court opinions (e.g., TCM and TC Memo).

Bloomberg Law also allows searches by name or citation. A search by name can be restricted to the court (e.g., Supreme Court, Court of Appeals (and any district), Tax Court, or Court of Federal Claims) and/or in the tax and accounting topic area.

The Tax Notes Federal Research Library allows searches by case name, citation, or docket number. It covers the following courts: Supreme Court; Courts of Appeals; District Courts; Bankruptcy Appellate Panels; Bankruptcy Courts; Court of Federal Claims; Tax Court; Board of Tax Appeals; and Court of International Trade.

3. Locating Cases by Citation

Online services let you find decisions by citation. In many cases, you don't need to worry about periods or spacing in reporter service abbreviations.[22] Checkpoint [Illustration 10-2, *supra* page 203] and Cheetah (under Citation Search) use templates for citation format.

Tax Court Regular and Memorandum Opinions can present problems. The Government Publishing Office officially publishes Regular Opinions, but it does not paginate them successively until it compiles them into a volume. If you have a citation to a fairly recent Tax Court Regular Opinion, be sure to note whether your citation is to a page number or a decision number.

The CCH and RIA services discussed in Section D do not use the same format for citing Tax Court Memorandum Opinions. For example, *Alber v. Commissioner* is reported on the Tax Court website as T.C. Memo. 2020–20; CCH cites it as 119 T.C.M.

[22] You may also be able to search by docket number, which could be preferable to searching by name if the taxpayer has a common name (e.g., Smith).

1126 (2020) and as CCH Dec. 61,625(M) in addition to using the Tax Court's citation; RIA cites it as 2020 RIA TC Memo ¶ 2020–020 in addition to using the Tax Court's citation. Table 10-D (*infra* page 208) contains more information about CCH and RIA citation formats for the Tax Court and other courts covered by their reporter services.

The Tax Court began using pinpoint citations for Memorandum Opinions in August 2012. Each page now begins with [*]. For example, *Alber v. Commissioner*, T.C. Memo. 2020–20, at *2, is a citation to material on the second page of that opinion.

4. Digests of Decisions

Digests are useful for locating decisions and for deciding which of them to read first. They may be less important if you are using online services that give an overview of each "hit" or if you search online services by key number.

Warren, Gorham & Lamont publishes several specialized digests; recent editions carry the Thomson Reuters Checkpoint imprint. Digests include Estate and Gift Tax Digest, International Tax Digest, Pass-Through Entity Tax Digest, Tax Procedure Digest, and Tax Valuation Digest. The start of coverage varies by digest. Several of the digests begin as early as 1954.

Services such as Standard Federal Tax Reporter and United States Tax Reporter digest cases in their compilation and updating volumes or in their newsletters. Newsletters include a limited number of case digests, which are not cumulated over time.

D. Case Reporters

Discussion in this section covers print reporter services that focus on taxation because you may not have encountered them in the basic legal research course. You can generally find the same materials electronically using subscription and free services. In some instances, electronic services will be your only option; Tax Court Summary Opinions are an example of that category.

Online services may have limited retrospective coverage; remember to check when each service began including a court's decisions. Your library may also carry microform services that include judicial decisions; these services may have extensive retrospective coverage but lag other services in covering current material.

1. Tax Court Decisions

Coverage of Tax Court decisions varies.[23] The government published Regular decisions by the Tax Court's predecessor, the Board of Tax Appeals, in the Board of Tax Appeals Reports (B.T.A.). The government did not publish B.T.A. Memorandum decisions. Prentice-Hall printed both Regular and Memorandum decisions. RIA, which acquired the Prentice-Hall services, also makes Tax Court decisions available.

The government publishes Tax Court Regular decisions in Tax Court of the United States Reports and United States Tax Court Reports; both are cited as T.C. It does not officially publish Tax Court Memorandum decisions or Tax Court Summary decisions. The Tax Court website includes Regular and Memorandum Opinions since September

[23] Table 10-A (*supra* page 198) lists relevant dates and court names for the Tax Court and Board of Tax Appeals. Although the Board began in 1924, it did not issue Memorandum decisions until 1928.

25, 1995 and Summary Opinions since January 10, 2001. It includes Regular Opinions in published format since January 11, 2010.

HeinOnline includes Tax Court and Board of Tax Appeals Regular Opinions (but not Memorandum or Summary Opinions) in its U.S. Federal Agency Documents, Decisions, and Appeals Library. These series are listed as Reports of the United States Tax Court and Reports of the United States Board of Tax Appeals. HeinOnline includes the original volumes in PDF format. Through a partnership with Fastcase, HeinOnline also provides access to Tax Court Memorandum Opinions; the HeinOnline Case Law tab includes Search Fastcase and Fastcase Lookup links.

Bloomberg Law: Tax includes Tax Court Regular, Memorandum, and Summary Opinions. The Tax Notes Federal Research Library also includes all three types of decisions.

2. Decisions of Other Courts

With the exception of Tax Court decisions, you can locate federal court decisions involving taxation in the sets listed in Table 10-C. Most of those sets are published by the GPO or by Thomson Reuters and are used the same way for tax research as for nontax research.

Table 10-C. Print Reporter Services Other than Tax Court[24]

Court/ Service	*Supreme Court*	*Court of Appeals*	*District Court*	*Bankruptcy Court*	*Federal Claims*
U.S.	1796–				
S. Ct.	1882–				
L. Ed.	1796–				
A.F.T.R.	1796–	1880–	1882–	1979–	1876–
U.S.T.C.	1913–	1915–	1915–	1979–	1924–
F.		1880–	1882–1932		1929–1932 1960–1982
Fed. Appx.		2001–			
F. Supp.			1932–		1932–1960
Ct. Cl.					1863–1982
Cl. Ct.					1982–1992
Fed. Cl.					1992–
B.R.				1979–	

→ Several reporters are in second or third series (e.g., F., F.2d, F.3d; F. Supp., F. Supp. 2d, F. Supp. 3d).

[24] The Cumulative Bulletin began including Supreme Court decisions in 1920; it calls them Court Decisions (Ct. D.). Early Bulletins included lower federal court decisions either as Ct. D.s or as Miscellaneous Rulings. Because the disparate labels make these items virtually impossible to locate, they are omitted from the table and from the discussion of case reporter services.

→ Only A.F.T.R. and U.S.T.C. print cases from all these courts.

→ A.F.T.R. volumes 1–4 reprint cases by reporter service (e.g., Federal Reporter, United States Reports) and not in strict chronological order.

→ Until 1912, so-called circuit courts decided cases; reports are found in Federal Cases and Federal Reporter.

The sets published by Research Institute of America (American Federal Tax Reports) and Commerce Clearing House (U.S. Tax Cases) differ enough from the others to warrant further discussion. These sets are available in print and as part of their respective publishers' online services: Checkpoint and Cheetah.

You can use these sets alone or in conjunction with each publisher's looseleaf reporting service, A.F.T.R. with RIA United States Tax Reporter and U.S.T.C.[25] with CCH Standard Federal Tax Reporter. Each service publishes decisions from all courts except the Tax Court, and each includes "unpublished" decisions omitted from Federal Supplement and Federal Reporter.[26]

a. Locating Decisions

A.F.T.R. and U.S.T.C. first include decisions in an Advance Sheets volume of the related looseleaf reporting service. This initial publication in conjunction with the looseleaf services results in recent decisions being available in print on a weekly basis. While both services are supplemented weekly, each occasionally prints decisions before the other does.

These cases also appear in the listings of new material in New Matters for Standard Federal Tax Reporter. The listings appear in Code section order and are cross-referenced to discussions in the compilation volumes. As a result, you can locate a recent case when you know the Code section involved but not the taxpayer's name, and you can immediately find a discussion of the topic in the compilation volumes. Daily and weekly newsletters, which are probably the only more current print source of these cases, often print only partial texts or digests and don't provide full-year cumulative indexes.

The reference method is important if you use these services. CCH cites decisions in the U.S.T.C. advance sheets and bound volumes by paragraph number (e.g., 88–1 U.S.T.C. ¶ 9390). RIA cites to decisions in A.F.T.R. by page number (e.g., 62 A.F.T.R.2d 88–5228).

The bound volumes include all types of tax cases—income, estate and gift, and excise; the individual Advance Sheets volumes do not. The different types of cases appear in Advance Sheets sections accompanying each publisher's looseleaf service for the particular area of tax law.

---

[25] The earliest volumes of this service print all Supreme Court decisions and those lower court decisions of "genuine precedent value . . . ." Foreword to 1 U.S.T.C. (1938). When CCH began issuing two volumes per year, it expanded coverage.

[26] See, e.g., *Alexander v. United States*, 88–1 U.S.T.C. ¶ 9390, 62 A.F.T.R.2d 88–5228 (N.D. Ga. 1988); *Estate of McLendon v. Commissioner*, 96–1 U.S.T.C. ¶ 60,220, 77 A.F.T.R.2d 96–666 (5th Cir. 1995) (unpublished opinion), rev'g and remanding T.C. Memo. 1993–459. The appellate court did issue a published opinion when it reversed the second Tax Court opinion. *McLendon v. Commissioner*, 135 F.3d 1017 (5th Cir. 1998), rev'g T.C. Memo. 1996–37.

b. Citation Format

Citation formats for the services published by CCH and RIA vary depending upon whether you follow the guidelines in a general citation manual or rules provided by the court, agency, or publication to which you are submitting a document.[27] You are likely to encounter any of the Table 10-D citation formats.

Table 10-D. Citation Formats for CCH and RIA Reporters

Reporter Service	*Possible Citation Formats*[28]
American Federal Tax Reports	AFTR; A.F.T.R.; A.F.T.R. (P-H); A.F.T.R. (RIA); AFTR2d; A.F.T.R.2d; A.F.T.R.2d (RIA)
U.S. Tax Cases	USTC; USTC para.; U.S.T.C. ¶; U.S. Tax Cas. (CCH)
Tax Court Reports	T.C.R. (CCH) Dec.; T.C.R. Dec. (P-H) ¶; T.C.R. Dec. (RIA) ¶; Tax Ct. Rep. (CCH); Tax Ct. Rep. Dec. (P-H); Tax Ct. Rep. Dec. (RIA) ¶
Tax Court Memorandum Decisions	T.C. Memo; T.C.M.; para. #, P-H memo T.C.; T.C.M. (CCH); T.C.M. (P-H) ¶; T.C.M. (RIA) ¶; T.C.M. (P-H); T.C.M. (RIA); RIA TC Memo ¶
Board of Tax Appeals Memorandum Decisions	B.T.A. Mem. Dec. (P-H) ¶; B.T.A.M. (P-H)

3. Parallel Citations

Electronic services make cases accessible without regard to reporter service. If you use bound volumes for your research, you may find that the volume for which you have a citation is not on the library shelf. Because so many case reporters cover each court level, you may be able to find that case in another set. All you need is the correct citation for the other reporter service.

Because general reporter services print nontax as well as tax decisions, numerous volumes cover each year's cases. Looking up the case name in several volumes is a tedious method of finding another printing. You can accomplish this task more quickly by locating the case citation in a citator and obtaining a parallel citation to the same decision in another reporter.

E. Briefs and Petitions

Briefs are relevant in determining which arguments the taxpayers and government have raised for court consideration. Westlaw Edge allows you to search briefs filed in the Supreme Court, circuit courts, and the Tax Court. If you type Tax Briefs in the search box, it offers you a Tax Briefs database. Judicial decisions available on Westlaw Edge often include links to the relevant briefs; you can find them in the Filings tab that

---

27 Although the ABA Section of Taxation is one of TAXCITE's participants, ABA publications often use formats other than those listed in TAXCITE. Because TAXCITE has not been updated since 1995, it omits many of the IRS documents discussed in Chapter 9. The IRS includes citation formats in the Internal Revenue Manual 4.10.7.2 (Jan. 1, 2006).

28 The citation formats in Table 10-D omit volume, page, and paragraph number formatting.

accompanies the decision. Lexis+ and Bloomberg Law also have separate files for Pleadings, Briefs, and Motions for most U.S. courts.

F. Evaluating Decisions

1. In General

Courts must determine how much weight to give opinions in cases cited by the taxpayer or government. An individual court, whether Tax Court, District Court, or Court of Federal Claims, will give its own decisions far more deference than it will give decisions of the other trial courts.

If a Court of Appeals has ruled, that opinion is binding precedent for District Court, Bankruptcy Court, and Tax Court cases that will be appealed in that circuit. Otherwise, the opinion is only persuasive precedent. Supreme Court decisions are binding precedent for all courts.

Although tax professionals evaluate judicial decisions when litigating, they also consider these decisions when advising clients about proposed transactions. Obviously they and their clients prefer that a transaction's tax consequences avoid government challenge.

2. Headnotes and Syllabus Numbers

Judicial decisions often include headnotes or syllabus numbers, which relate to the points of law involved. Publishers use these numbers in compiling digests and in other case-finding tools, including citators. You should not be surprised that publishers don't use the same numbering systems for these items. If you read a case in one publisher's reporter, you are likely to have problems using its headnote numbers in another publisher's digest or citator system.

3. Unpublished Opinions

There is a difference between an unpublished opinion and an opinion to which you cannot get access. Many services include decisions issued under no-publication rules. You may want to find these decisions, as they shed light on the court's thinking. In the past, some circuits allowed citations to those opinions; other circuits barred the citations. On April 12, 2006, the Supreme Court approved Federal Rule of Appellate Procedure 32.1, allowing citation to those opinions in all circuits. Note that the Court's ruling relates to citing the opinions; it does not mandate whether a court must treat them as precedent.

4. Officially Published Opinions

There is also a difference, as noted earlier in this chapter, between an officially published opinion and one available through other reporter services. Unless it was designated by court or statute as not precedential, you can cite any opinion as precedential or persuasive authority.

Unofficial reporters may include official pagination, but they do not have to do so. If you need to cite official pagination, you must use reporters that provide that information. If courts abandon the requirement of citing to print page numbers, and more decisions are posted online, the distinction between official and other publication sources will diminish for items other than headnotes.

5. Government Litigation Plans

If a court ruled against the government position, and the IRS issued a notice of acquiescence, the precedential value of the decision is further enhanced. Instead of acquiescing, the IRS may issue a notice of nonacquiescence, an action on decision [Illustration 9-6, *supra* page 174], or other document to indicate it will continue litigating and why it will do so. These IRS documents are discussed in Chapter 9.

Keep geographical limitations in mind; the government might indicate that it will continue to litigate only in courts outside the circuit in which it lost on appeal.

6. Changes in Code or Regulations

If Congress disagrees with a particular court decision, it may amend the Code and change the result for future years.[29] The IRS may also issue a new regulation, or amend an existing one, for the same purpose.[30] If you find a decision that appears relevant, make sure that the Code and regulations applied in that case are still in effect.

7. Statements Regarding Deference

If no appeals have been taken, you may be tempted to accord greater weight to a Tax Court decision than to a decision of another trial court. Although the Tax Court judges have specialized knowledge, the degree of deference their decisions receive is not necessarily greater than that given decisions from other trial courts.[31]

The items below illustrate statements regarding deference to decisions.

- "We review decisions of the Tax Court 'in the same manner and to the same extent as decisions of the district courts in civil actions tried without a jury.'" *Byers v. Commissioner*, 740 F.3d 668, 675 (D.C. Cir. 2014) (citations omitted).
- "We review the Tax Court's construction of the tax code de novo. Although we presume that the Tax Court correctly applied the law, we give no special deference to the Tax Court's decisions." *Best Life Assur. Co. of Calif. v. Commissioner*, 281 F.3d 828, 830 (9th Cir. 2002) (citations omitted).
- "The Commissioner also argues that a sufficient explanation had been provided, relying upon an older body of case law that purports to grant great deference to the Tax Court. . . . In these cases, however, the Tax Court provided some justification for its conclusions in a manner that allowed us to understand and reconstruct the Tax Court's rationale. In the case at hand, the Tax Court merely announced the discount it applied to

---

[29] Examples involving the Supreme Court's decisions in *Gitlitz v. Commissioner* and *United States v. Home Concrete & Supply, LLC,* appear in Chapter 5, Section F (*supra* page 50, note 33).

[30] See, e.g., Preamble to Prop. Treas. Reg. § 1.104–1, 74 Fed. Reg. 47152 (2009). The proposed regulations (which were later finalized) provided for excluding damages from personal physical injuries not defined as torts under statute or common law, reversing the emphasis on tort-like rights in *United States v. Burke*, 504 U.S. 229 (1992).

Administrative agencies can change their interpretations (even without the need to override a judicial decision), and thus change the outcome of future litigation, if the ruling in the *Brand X* case (cited to in Chapter 8, Section K, *supra* page 158), applies. But see *United States v. Home Concrete & Supply, LLC*, 566 U.S. 478, 489–90 (2012).

[31] The judge's identity may also be relevant. The statements of a judge whose opinions are regularly affirmed may be more valuable than those of a judge with a mixed record on appeal.

the Estate's stock without any explanation." *Estate of Mitchell v. Commissioner*, 250 F.3d 696, 703 n.6 (9th Cir. 2001).

- "A finding is clearly erroneous when, although there is evidence to support it, a review of the entire record leaves the reviewing court with the definite and firm conviction that a mistake has been made. This standard of review requires that we accord great deference to the values established by the tax court, but it does not render us a mere rubber stamp." *Gross v. Commissioner*, 272 F.3d 333, 343 (6th Cir. 2001) (citations omitted).
- "For the following reasons, pursuant to 28 U.S.C. § 1334(c)(1), we voluntarily ABSTAIN: (1) This adversary proceeding involves a classic two-party dispute, the outcome of which will have little or no effect on the estate; (2) there is litigation currently pending before the United States Tax Court, Docket # 4516–88; (3) the litigation requires the resolution of complex issues of tax law, some of which are unsettled or are questions of first impression; (4) there is a specialized forum for hearing this kind of dispute (i.e., the United States Tax Court); and (5) resolution of the issues would require this Court to interpret decisions of the United States Tax Court. In the circumstances, and in deference to its expertise in the subject matter of the litigation, this adversary proceeding is transferred to the United States Tax Court for hearing and adjudication." *In re Williams*, 209 B.R. 584, 585 (Bankr. D.R.I. 1997) (citation and footnotes omitted).

G. Citators

1. Subsequent Judicial Action

There are four commonly used citators for judging the relative authority of any tax decision, and many libraries own or have online access to all of them. The four are Shepard's, KeyCite, RIA Citator, and CCH Citator. A relatively new service is BCite, used by Bloomberg Law. KeyCite and BCite are online-only services. The others are available in print and online (but the RIA Citator has more retrospective coverage in its print version). All of these citators are discussed in detail in Chapter 11.

You can use a citator for several purposes. First, you can determine if a trial court decision has been affirmed or reversed on appeal. Second, you can find other decisions that approve of, or disagree with, the earlier case but do not affirm or reverse it. The later cases may be from the same jurisdiction, but distinguishable in some particular, or they may be from another jurisdiction altogether. Third, you can find IRS citations to the decision. Fourth, some citators list treatises, law review articles, and other secondary sources that discuss the decision.

If you are using an online reporter service, you don't have to leave the case to use its citator function. You may be able to click an accompanying link to find the decision's subsequent history [Illustrations 10-4 and 10-5, both of which involve the *Mitchell* decision from Table 10-E, *infra* page 212].

Illustration 10-4. Case Status Information in Westlaw Edge

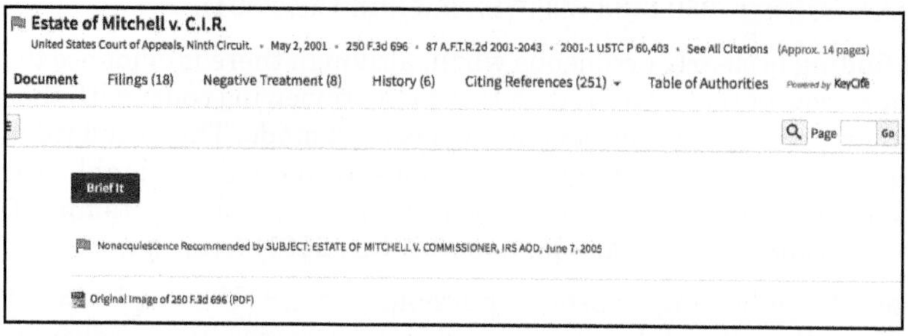

→ Check the flag indicating that nonacquiescence was recommended and the Negative Treatment tab, which indicates eight items.

Illustration 10-5. Case Status Information in Lexis+

● ESTATE OF PAUL MITCHELL v. COMMISSIONER OF INTERNAL REVENUE, 250 F.3d 696

→ If you click the hexagon, Lexis+ Shepardizes the decision.

2. Headnotes and Syllabus Numbers

As noted in Section F.2 (*supra* page 209), each reporter service makes its own decision regarding the headnotes or syllabus numbers it assigns a case. If you read a case in one service and are interested in a particular issue, make sure the citator you use is keyed to that service.

Table 10-E indicates how many headnotes appear in various reporter services for *Estate of Mitchell.* Illustrations 10-6 through 10-9 show excerpts from the headnotes in four reporter services.

Table 10-E. Headnote Numbers in Estate of Mitchell

Service	*Citation*	*Headnotes*
Federal Reporter	250 F.3d 696	10
Westlaw Edge	250 F.3d 696	10
Lexis+	250 F.3d 696; 2001 U.S. App. Lexis 7990	9
A.F.T.R.	87 A.F.T.R.2d 2001–2043	2
U.S.T.C.	2001–1 U.S.T.C. ¶ 60,403	0
Bloomberg Law	250 F.3d 696	0
Federal Research Library	250 F.3d 696	0

Illustration 10-6. Federal Reporter Headnotes

1. Internal Revenue ⚷4708

Whether notice of tax deficiency is timely presents mixed question of law and fact, which is reviewed de novo. 26 U.S.C.A. § 6501(a).

2. Internal Revenue ⚷4474

Statute under which postmark stamped on return, claim, or statement mailed to Internal Revenue Service (IRS) is deemed to be date of delivery applies only when document would otherwise be considered untimely filed. 26 U.S.C.A. § 7502(a).

Although Federal Reporter and Westlaw Edge are commonly owned, the print and electronic services differ in format. Westlaw Edge includes a PDF link to the decision in F.3d.

Illustration 10-7. Westlaw Edge Headnotes

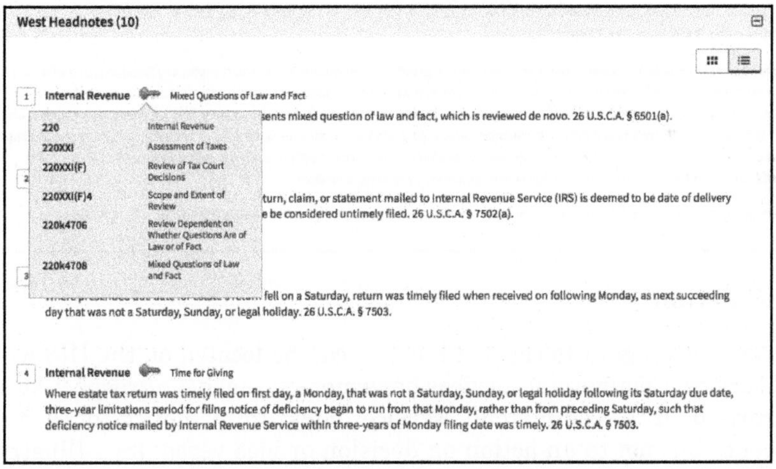

→ Click on a key to see a more-detailed list of topics. Alternatively, click on the Grid View link (upper right corner), and the list opens to the right of the headnote.

Illustration 10-8. Lexis+ Headnotes

Civil Procedure > Appeals > Standards of Review > De Novo Review
Governments > Legislation > Statute of Limitations > General Overview

HN1 Standards of Review, De Novo Review
Mixed question of law and fact are reviewed de novo. More like this Headnote

Shepardize - Narrow by this Headnote (0)

Tax Law > ... > Administration > Place & Time for Filing Returns > General Overview

HN2 Administration, Place & Time for Filing Returns
See 26 U.S.C.S. § 7502(a)(1). More like this Headnote

Shepardize - Narrow by this Headnote (0)

Tax Law > ... > Administration > Place & Time for Filing Returns > General Overview

HN3 Administration, Place & Time for Filing Returns
See 26 U.S.C.S. § 7503. More like this Headnote

Shepardize - Narrow by this Headnote (0)

Illustration 10-9. A.F.T.R.2d Headnotes on Checkpoint

HEADNOTE

1. Timely-mailing-as-timely-filing rules—application to return due on Saturday—effect on assessment limitations period. Tax Court properly rejected estate's claim that **Code Sec. 7502** 's timely-mailing provisions applied to establish return's filing date, and corresponding 3-year assessment limitations period's trigger, as early mailing date: **Code Sec. 7502** wasn't applicable to timely-mailed return; and, because statutory deadline fell on Saturday, **Code Sec. 7503** applied to extend due date, and thus limitations period's trigger, to following Monday. Also, even if **Code Sec. 7502** applied, **Code Sec. 6501** 's early return filing rules established filing date as last day of statutory period; so, deficiency notice sent within 3 years of return's Saturday deadline and Monday *delivery* dates was timely under either statutory scheme.

Reference(s): USTR Estate & Gift Taxes ¶75,085.01(10). **¶ 75,025.01(45);¶ 65,015.03(40);¶ 75,035.01Code Sec. 6501;Code Sec. 7502;Code Sec. 7503;Code Sec. 7508**

2. Gross estate—valuation—closely-held stock—burden of proof—expert opinions. Tax Court improperly failed to shift burden of proving estate tax deficiency to IRS where IRS own experts' testimony and valuations showed assessment was arbitrary and excessive, and thus not entitled to presumption of correctness. Also, propriety of Court's valuation of decedent's stock in closely-held co. wasn't determinable where Court didn't adequately clarify how it arrived at valuation, which widely diverged from experts on which it allegedly relied: Court didn't explain use of contradictory acquisition and publicly traded values as start values; or how it arrived at 35% combined lack-of- [pg. 2001-2044] marketability and minority-interest discount that wasn't supported by experts' estimates.

Reference(s): USTR Estate & Gift Taxes ¶20,315.12(5); 20,315.06(10); 66,625.01 **¶ 74,536.1426(90);¶ 74,536.1428(37)Code Sec. 2031;Code Sec. 6662**

3. IRS Action

IRS action with regard to cases it has lost can be located on the IRS website or in a commercial service. Commercial services have more extensive retrospective coverage. Do not be surprised if a commercial service cites to a notice of acquiescence or nonacquiescence but not to an action on decision or vice versa. [See Illustrations 10-10 through 10-14.] You can easily find both by searching in the service's database covering the I.R.B. (or C.B.) and its database covering actions on decisions.

Illustration 10-10. KeyCite Results for Mitchell Decision

Treatment	Title	Date	Type	Depth	Headnote(s)
Distinguished by NEGATIVE	1. Transupport, Inc. v. Commissioner of Internal Revenue 882 F.3d 274, 280+, 1st Cir.	Feb. 14, 2018	Case		7 8 F.3d
Distinguished by NEGATIVE	2. McCall v. Commissioner of Internal Revenue 2009 WL 910656, *3+, U.S.Tax Ct.	Apr. 06, 2009	Case		7 8 F.3d
Discussed by	3. Estate of Trompeter v. C.I.R. 279 F.3d 767, 770+, 9th Cir.	Jan. 30, 2002	Case		9 10 F.3d
Discussed by	4. Multi-Pak Corp. v. C.I.R. 2010 WL 2721409, *4+, U.S.Tax Ct.	June 22, 2010	Case		7 8 F.3d
Discussed by	5. Harper v. C.I.R. 2002 WL 992347, *22+, U.S.Tax Ct.	May 15, 2002	Case		7 8 F.3d
Distinguished by NEGATIVE	6. Wycoff v. Commissioner of Internal Revenue 2017 WL 4677657, *12, U.S.Tax Ct.	Oct. 16, 2017	Case		8 F.3d
Distinguished by NEGATIVE	7. Transupport, Incorporated v. Commissioner of Internal Revenue 2016 WL 6900913, *11, U.S.Tax Ct.	Nov. 23, 2016	Case		–
Distinguished by NEGATIVE	8. Cavallaro v. Commissioner of Internal Revenue 842 F.3d 16, 22, 1st Cir.	Nov. 18, 2016	Case		7 8 F.3d
Cited by	9. Blodgett v. C.I.R. 394 F.3d 1030, 1035, 8th Cir.	Jan. 12, 2005	Case		5 F.3d

→ You can sort the KeyCite Citing References results by Depth, Date, or Court Level.

→ KeyCite included 18 cases, more than 100 trial and appellate documents, and 121 secondary sources listed in the Citing References tab.

→ KeyCite cites to both the AOD and the nonacquiescence in the History tab (not illustrated above).

Illustration 10-11. Shepard's Citator Results for Mitchell Decision

Sort by: Analysis (red-blue)

1. Action on Dec. CC-2005-01, 2005 AOD LEXIS 1

Nonacquiescence by Commissioner at

... Estate of Mitchell v. Commissioner US Internal Revenue Service 2005 AOD LEXIS 1 Action on Decision CC-2005-01 Action on Dec. CC-2005-01 **SUBJECT:Estate of Mitchell v. Commissioner,250 F.3d 696(9th Cir. 2001)**, aff'g in part, rev'g in part, and remanding T.C. Memo. 1997-461 ; on remand, T.C. Memo. 2002-98 . Issue: Whether the Court of Appeals erred in shifting the burden of proving the valuation of stock to the Commissioner on the basis that the Commissioner's determination of the value of ...

Court: Internal Revenue Service
Date: June 3, 2005

2. Transupport, Inc. v. Comm'r, 882 F.3d 274, 2018 U.S. App. LEXIS 3426, 121 A.F.T.R.2d (RIA) 2018-788, 2018-1 U.S. Tax Cas. (CCH) P50161, 2018 WL 852078

Distinguished by: 882 F.3d 274 p.280

Based on Estate of Mitchell v. Commissioner, 250 F.3d 696 (9th Cir. 2001). Transupport argues that the burden should shift because the notice of deficiency was based on a valuation disavowed by the Commissioner. See 250 F.3d at 702. This case is unhelpful for three reasons. (HN8)

Court: 1st Cir.
Date: February 14, 2018
Headnotes: HN8

3. Cavallaro v. Comm'r, 842 F.3d 16, 2016 U.S. App. LEXIS 20713, 118 A.F.T.R.2d (RIA) 2016-6684, 2016-2 U.S. Tax Cas. (CCH) P60697, 2016 WL 6820367

Distinguished by: 842 F.3d 16 p.22

The two circuit cases cited by the Cavallaros do not persuade us otherwise. In Caracci v. Commissioner, 456 F.3d 444, 447, 456 (5th Cir. 2006), the Commissioner expressly conceded that the excise tax deficiency, which was grounded on a "brief, intermediate internal [valuation] analysis," was "excessive and erroneous." No such concession exists here, nor are we convinced on this record that the Bello report, standing alone, compels one. In Estate of Mitchell v. Comm'r, 250 F.3d 696, 702 (9th Cir. 2001), the estate tax deficiency notice rested on a stock valuation that the appraiser had altered according to the Commissioner's instructions, and that the IRS expert disavowed. The circumstances in the instant case are not analogous.

Discussion
Court: 1st Cir.
Date: November 18, 2016

4. Wycoff v. Comm'r, T.C. Memo 2017-203, 2017 Tax Ct. Memo LEXIS 203, 114 T.C.M. (CCH) 427

Distinguished by

Discussion

→ You can sort Shepard's on Lexis+ by Analysis, Discussion, Court, or Date. Shepard's found 17 citing case and 2 IRS citations (including the AOD).

Illustration 10-12. RIA Citator Results for Mitchell Decision

Related case: **AOD 2005-001, 2005 USTR ¶86,273**

Cited In

Cited favorably: **Trompeter, Emanuel, Est of v. Com., 89 AFTR 2d 2002-736, 279 F3d 770** *(CA9, 1/30/2002) [See 87 AFTR 2d 2001-2049, 250 F3d 703-704]*

Cited favorably: **Blodgett, Diane S. v. Com., 95 AFTR 2d 2005-451, 394 F3d 1035** *(CA8, 1/12/2005) [See 87 AFTR 2d 2001-2047, 250 F3d 701]*

Cases distinguished : **Cavallaro, William v. Com., 118 AFTR 2d 2016-6688, 842 F3d 22** *(CA1, 11/18/2016) [See 87 AFTR 2d 2001-2048, 250 F3d 702]*

Cases distinguished : **Transupport, Inc., v. Com., 121 AFTR 2d 2018-791, 2018-792, 882 F3d 280** *(CA1, 2/14/2018) [See 87 AFTR 2d 2001-2048, 250 F3d 702]*

Cited favorably: **Chapman Glen Limited, 140 TC 314, 140 TCR 178** *(5/28/2013) [See 87 AFTR 2d 2001-2047-2001-2048, 250 F3d 701-702]*

→ The RIA Citator on Checkpoint cites to AOD 2005–001. Shepard's cites to Action on Dec. CC–2005–01 [Illustration 10-11]. The IRS website search function uses 01 rather than 001.

→ You can enter the RIA Citator directly by citation or by taxpayer name. You can also enter it by clicking on the Citator link in the cited decision.

→ KeyCite (flagged) and RIA (Cited favorably) seem to view the *Blodgett* case differently.

Illustration 10-13. CCH Citator Results for Mitchell Decision

ANNOTATED AT . . . FEGT¶3220.076, ¶3220.079, ¶3220.362, ¶3220.379, ¶3220.83, ¶21,375.40, ¶21,790.30, ¶22,501.44, ¶22,520.50

• CA-9-- (aff'g TC in an unpublished memorandum) 2004-1 USTC ¶60,475 , 8

• TC-- (supplemental opinion) Dec. 54,715(M) , 83 TCM 1524 , TC Memo. 2

Zarlengo TC, Dec. 59,988(M) , 108 TCM 155 , TC Memo 2014-161

TC, Dec. 59,453(M) , 105 TCM 1330 , TC Memo 2013-51

Hess TC, Dec. 55,274(M) , 86 TCM 303 , TC Memo. 2003-251

• CA-9-- (aff'g, vac'g and rem'g TC) 2001-1 USTC ¶60,403 , 250 F3d 696

Trompeter Est. CA-9, 2002-1 USTC ¶60,428 , 279 F3d 767

Dunia Est. TC, Dec. 55,643(M) , 87 TCM 1353 , TC Memo. 2004-123

Harper Est. TC, Dec. 54,745(M) , 83 TCM 1641 , TC Memo. 2002-121

Sp. Rul. 6-7-2005, June 7, 2005Sp. Rul. 6-7-2005, June 7, 2005

→ The CCH Citator on Cheetah refers to a "Sp. Rul." dated June 7, 2005, which might be a citation to the AOD, but it does not provide a link. Westlaw also uses June 7 in its Direct History tree.

→ Shepard's lists a June 3, 2005, date for the AOD. That is the release date on the IRS website search wheel; the posted AOD is undated.

Illustration 10-14. BCite Results for Mitchell Decision

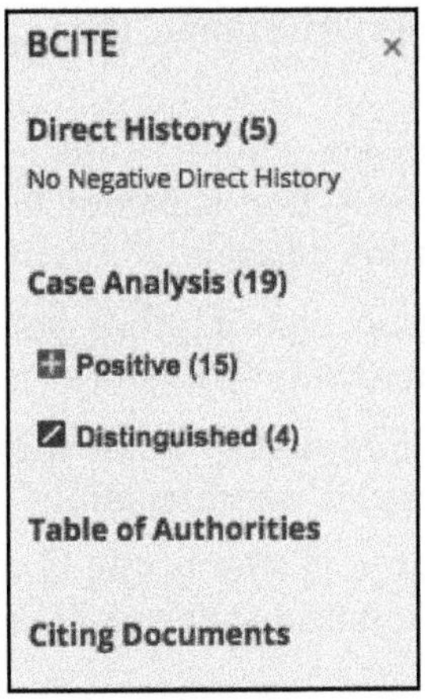

→ Bloomberg Law BCite Analysis considers only cases, not IRS documents, in determining negative history. The nonacquiescence is not listed under any of the BCite Analysis links on the *Mitchell* case page. The AOD is listed under the Citing Documents link (Administrative Orders & Decisions subfolder on Bloomberg Law; Agency Documents on Bloomberg Law: Tax).

H. Problems

1. For all parts of this problem except questions asking about other reporter services, use only U.S. Tax Cases.

   a. Indicate the name of the parties, court involved, and year for the decision found at 2014–1 U.S.T.C. ¶ 50,276. Is the decision published elsewhere (in another reporter)? If so, give the citation.

   b. What is the U.S.T.C. citation for a 2012 case involving Thomas Freeman?

   c. What is the U.S.T.C. citation for 562 F.3d 839? Give the names of the parties, court involved, and year for the decision. How many headnotes does the case have in U.S.T.C.? How many does it have in any other services you are asked to check?

2. Give the preferred citation for any decisions involving the taxpayer listed below. Use a citation to an unofficial service (e.g., A.F.T.R.2d, Lexis+, Westlaw Edge) only if you cannot locate a citation to an official reporter service.

   a. Joel Beeler

   b. Sandra Peppers

   c. Mario Boeri

   d. James Huntsman

3. Use online sources to determine whether the Tax Court was affirmed or reversed on appeal in the following cases. Cite to any appellate court opinions.

a. 62 T.C. 377

b. 139 T.C. 390

c. T.C. Memo. 2017–150

4. Use online sources and provide a citation to the case in which the following language appears.

a. "The owner of the cookie jar may dole out his treats as he wishes, but it does not follow that he may raid someone else's jar to feed a hungry tax collector, even if that be his desire and intent."

b. "The transaction at issue was a mere paper chase compelled by tax avoidance features rather than by business realities."

c. "Their refusal to be intimidated by what they may have considered to be legislative sound and fury, is commendable."

d. "As this appeal illustrates, § 6700(a)(2)(A) and (B) stand as Scylla and Charybdis, traps to the left and to the right for the promoter of an abusive tax shelter."

5. Locate judicial decisions involving the following issues.

a. A 2000 Tax Court decision involving whether a taxpayer's beekeeping, tree-farming, and rental activities were engaged in for profit.

b. A 2010 Tax Court decision involving whether a taxpayer's sperm bank was entitled to tax-exempt status as a private operating foundation.

c. A 2013 Tax Court decision involving the country to which a professional golfer's income was sourced.

d. A 2014 Tax Court decision involving deductions for an alleged business, the activities of which included planning, and accompanying models on, overnight trips to a clothing-optional beach for suntanning.

6. Provide the citation for a judicial decision involving taxation of futures contracts, in which the court quotes Dorothy's famous line to Toto.

Chapter 11

CITATORS

A. Introduction

This chapter discusses features of citators that were illustrated in earlier chapters. It makes references to specific illustrations in Chapter 10 (dealing with judicial decisions).

As illustrated in other chapters, you can use citators to determine if a particular statute, regulation, ruling, or judicial decision has been affected by, criticized, approved, or otherwise commented upon in a more recent proceeding. And as shown in Chapter 13, Shepard's and KeyCite let you determine if a judicial opinion has cited a particular periodical article or if an article has cited a particular decision.[1]

Goals for this chapter include determining coverage and format differences for each citator. The chapter focuses primarily on online versions of each citator. The online versions are easier to use, are generally updated more frequently, and provide hyperlinks to the citing material.

B. Terminology

This chapter discusses five citator services. Print citators group cited items in a particular format (for example, by year of decision, alphabetically, or by type of tax). Each item is followed by a list of later items that cite to it. Online versions of some citators also group cited items, but format for cited items is irrelevant when using an online citator.

A later item may merely cite the earlier item as authority or it may discuss the earlier item and indicate agreement or disagreement with its holding. The discussion may center on the earlier item as a whole or on a particular issue involved in that item.

In this chapter, the earlier material is referred to as the **cited** item; any later material that refers to it is a **citing** item. Subdivisions such as headnote or syllabus numbers, which refer to issues, are referred to by either term throughout this book.

C. Citator Format and Coverage Overview

Three of the five citators described in this chapter are available in both print and online formats. Because of updating frequency and the ability to search the equivalent of multiple print citator volumes, electronic citators are superior if you can find the same material in both formats. As noted above, this chapter focuses primarily on online citators.

---

[1] In a study comparing citators for negative results on cases the author concludes the results were inconsistent and "troubling." Paul Hellyer, *Evaluating Shepard's, KeyCite, and BCite for Case Validation Accuracy*, 110 LAW LIBR. J. 449 (2018).

1. Arrangement

a. Cited Items in Print Citators

The manner in which cited items are arranged is relevant only if you use a print citator and need to locate the correct citator volume.

Print citators follow a variety of format conventions, the most important of which relate to judicial decisions. The major distinction is between citators that arrange cases by reporter service citation and those that arrange them alphabetically. A second distinction relates to the overall arrangement of multivolume services.

The Shepard's print citators arrange cited cases by numerical reporter citations. The Commerce Clearing House (CCH) and Research Institute of America (RIA) citators arrange them by taxpayer name. Noting the taxpayer's first name can make your search easier, particularly if the taxpayer has a common last name. Alphabetization rules, particularly for names that begin with numbers are also important (e.g., 21 West Lancaster precedes Twenty Mile Joint Venture in RIA but not in CCH).

Each service uses a different method for classifying items into citator volumes. CCH divides its citator service to correspond to its separate income, estate and gift, and excise tax services. Shepard's uses separate volumes for different courts and reporter services. RIA does neither.

b. Citing Items in Online Citators

The arrangement for citing items is important no matter what type of citator you use. Some of the online citators give you more control than others over how citing material is arranged. In addition, citators change their ordering rules and presentation methods from time to time. It is important to keep distinctions in mind if you use more than one citator so that you don't overlook an item because you are used to a different arrangement.

2. Headnote/Syllabus Number and Judicial Commentary

Shepard's and KeyCite use headnote numbers to indicate issues and words or symbols to indicate commentary (e.g., distinguished, explained) or depth of treatment. BCite only uses symbols (called Indicators). CCH does neither. If you use CCH, you avoid the risk of an editor's coding error,[2] but you also receive no guidance as to whether citing references tend to be positive or negative. Although RIA uses headnote numbers in cases, its citator does not always refer to them. [See Illustration 10-12, *supra* page 216.]

3. Miscellaneous Differences

CCH uses fewer citing cases than do the others; it has limited its coverage to citing cases that affect the cited case's "effectiveness as precedent." The online Shepard's, KeyCite, and BCite include secondary sources as citing items. All services (including the online Shepard's) are more likely than the general Shepard's print service to include Tax Court (particularly Memorandum decisions) and IRS material as citing items.

Only Shepard's, KeyCite, and Bloomberg Law's Smart Code use statutes as cited material. Because the 1939 Code (and pre-1939 Revenue Acts) numbered statutes

---

[2] See, e.g., Hellyer, *supra* note 1.

differently, you should expect some extraneous results when you use a citator for a current Code provision.[3]

D. Shepard's Citations

Because of its long history, Shepard's is the best-known citator. It is available in print and electronically through Lexis+.

Table 11-A. General Shepard's Volumes

Cited Item	*Shepard's Volumes*
Constitution	Federal Statute Citations
Statutes	Federal Statute Citations
Treaties	Federal Statute Citations (until 1995)
Regulations	Code of Federal Regulations Citations
Revenue Rulings	Not Covered
District Court	Federal Citations
Federal Claims	Federal Citations
Bankruptcy Court	Bankruptcy Citations
Court of Appeals	Federal Citations
Supreme Court	United States Citations

Shepard's publishes a general print version and several specialty versions, including the Shepard's Federal Tax Citator. The print versions of Shepard's, both the general and the tax services, are divided both chronologically and by cited authority into hardbound and softbound volumes [Table 11-A]. As a result, searches using the print Shepard's take longer than those using another system. Note that your library may have print Shepard's available even if it has discontinued its subscription.

Shepard's online uses color-coded signals to alert you to treatment of the cited item [Table 11-B]. It also indicates, for each citing item, how it treated the cited item. That treatment uses much the same color coding[4] but uses small squares instead of different shapes. Shepard's also indicates the depth of discussion by the number of blue rectangles (Analyzed, Discussed, Mentioned, or Cited).

3 For example, KeyCiting, Shepardizing, or using Smart Code for 26 USC 213 (medical expenses) yields decisions citing section 213 of pre-Code revenue acts.

4 The blue treatment square is darker if the citation is in a dissenting opinion than if it is in the court's opinion.

Table 11-B. Shepard's Analysis Definition Codes

Color	*Symbol*	*Meaning*
Red	●	Warning: Negative treatment indicated
Red	(!)	Warning: Negative case treatment indicated for statute
Orange	Q	Questioned: Validity questioned by citing references
Yellow	▲	Caution: Possible negative treatment indicated
Green	◆	Positive treatment indicated
Blue	A	Neutral: Citing references with analysis indicated
Blue	I	Cited by: Citing information without history or treatment analysis (e.g., law review articles)
Orange	(!) At Risk	Case is at risk of being overruled because the cases cited within have been negatively treated by other decisions in the same jurisdiction

You can Shepardize directly by entering "shep:" before the citation in the search box. You can also click on the Shepardize link from an item you are reading.

The online Shepard's lets you sort citing items in a variety of ways. If the cited item is a judicial decision, for example, you can sort citing decisions by analysis (criticized, distinguished, etc.), court, publication status (reported, unreported), depth of discussion, particular headnote in the case, or date. If the cited item is a constitutional provision or statute, you can sort citing decisions by analysis, court, or date.

Citing items you can select from include citing decisions (judicial and agency) and a tab that includes law reviews, treatises, statutes, and regulations. If you want to review citing authorities in a particular category, you can refine your results to show decisions from a particular court level or to show only judicial decisions or only agency materials. Shepard's has tabs for appellate history and for a table of authorities.

Shepard's provides pinpoint citations to the exact page. It also has hyperlinks to the cited items, so that you can read them online. If a cited statute may be amended, Shepard's indicates that legislation is pending.

Shepard's includes the following cited items:

- Constitutional provisions [Illustration 11-1]
- Statutes [Illustration 11-2]
- Regulations and IRS documents
- Judicial decisions [Illustration 10-11, *supra* page 215]
- Law review articles [Illustration 11-3]

Illustration 11-1. Shepard's Citations to 16th Amendment of the Constitution

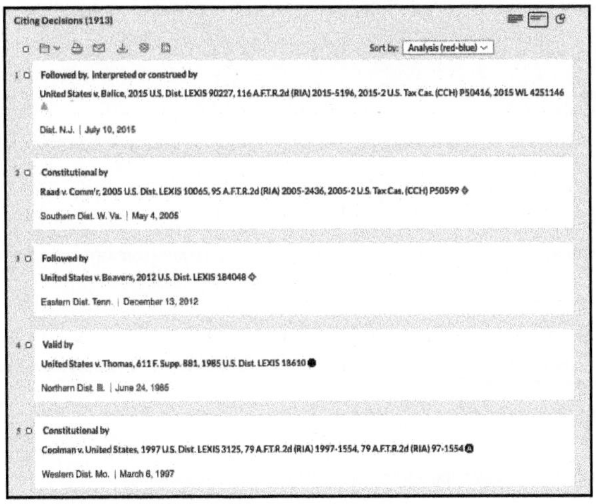
Citing Decisions (1913)

Sort by: Analysis (red-blue)

1 Followed by, Interpreted or construed by

United States v. Balice, 2015 U.S. Dist. LEXIS 90227, 116 A.F.T.R.2d (RIA) 2015-5196, 2015-2 U.S. Tax Cas. (CCH) P50416, 2015 WL 4251146

Dist. N.J. | July 10, 2015

2 Constitutional by

Raad v. Comm'r, 2005 U.S. Dist. LEXIS 10065, 95 A.F.T.R.2d (RIA) 2005-2436, 2005-2 U.S. Tax Cas. (CCH) P50599

Southern Dist. W. Va. | May 4, 2005

3 Followed by

United States v. Beavers, 2012 U.S. Dist. LEXIS 184048

Eastern Dist. Tenn. | December 13, 2012

4 Valid by

United States v. Thomas, 611 F. Supp. 881, 1985 U.S. Dist. LEXIS 18610

Northern Dist. Ill. | June 24, 1985

5 Constitutional by

Coolman v. United States, 1997 U.S. Dist. LEXIS 3125, 79 A.F.T.R.2d (RIA) 1997-1554, 79 A.F.T.R.2d (RIA) 97-1554

Western Dist. Mo. | March 6, 1997

→ The materials are sorted by Analysis (red to blue).

Illustration 11-2. Shepard's Citations to I.R.C. § 163

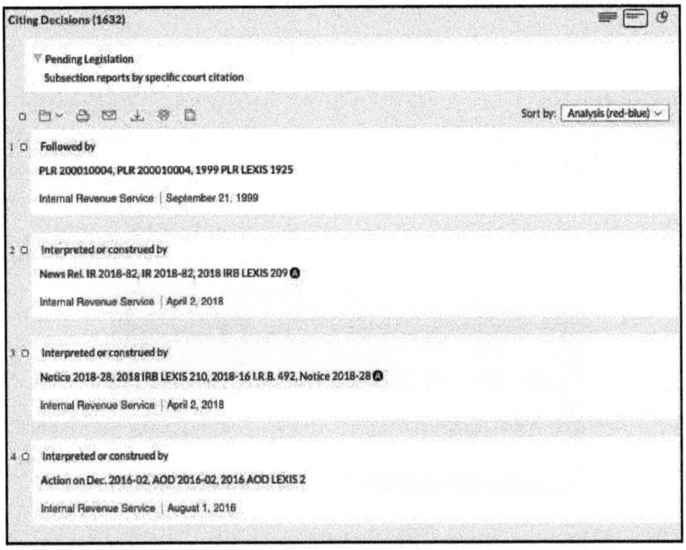
Citing Decisions (1632)

Pending Legislation

Subsection reports by specific court citation

Sort by: Analysis (red-blue)

1 Followed by

PLR 200010004, PLR 200010004, 1999 PLR LEXIS 1925

Internal Revenue Service | September 21, 1999

2 Interpreted or construed by

News Rel. IR 2018-82, IR 2018-82, 2018 IRB LEXIS 209

Internal Revenue Service | April 2, 2018

3 Interpreted or construed by

Notice 2018-28, 2018 IRB LEXIS 210, 2018-16 I.R.B. 492, Notice 2018-28

Internal Revenue Service | April 2, 2018

4 Interpreted or construed by

Action on Dec. 2016-02, AOD 2016-02, 2016 AOD LEXIS 2

Internal Revenue Service | August 1, 2016

→ We limited the results to IRS Agency Materials, and we sorted by Analysis (red to blue).

→ Note the warning that there is pending legislation. Clicking on the link brings up all bills introduced in Congress that would amend, repeal, or enact a change to section 163.

Illustration 11-3. Shepard's Citations to 67 Vand. L. Rev. 1581

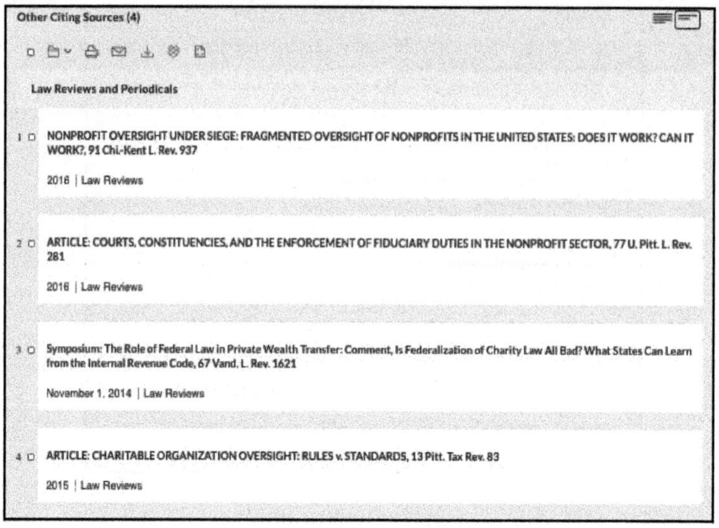

→ We limited the results to Other Citing Sources. You can also select Appellate History, Citing Decisions, or Table of Authorities.

E. KeyCite

Westlaw created the KeyCite system in 1997, and it was the first online-only citator. Like the Bloomberg Law citators, KeyCite is available only online. After you locate a primary source in Westlaw Edge, you click on the various tabs to read citing references. Alternatively, if you have a citation, you can KeyCite it directly in the search box.

Illustration 11-4. Using KeyCite Directly

You can use KeyCite to obtain all references (neutral, positive, and negative along with secondary materials) to the cited item, or you can limit yourself to negative references. KeyCite provides hyperlinks to the citing material.

KeyCite uses color-coded flags to indicate how the citing item treated the cited item. It uses green "depth of treatment" bars (▮▮▮▮) to indicate how extensively a cited case or administrative decision has been discussed by the citing case. A green quotation mark (") indicates a direct quote in the citing material.

Table 11-C. KeyCite Citing Reference Codes

Color	*Symbol*	*Meaning*
Red		The case is no longer good law for at least one point. For statutes/regulations it means the provision was amended, repealed, superseded, or held unconstitutional or preempted in whole or in part
Yellow		The case, statute or regulation has some negative treatment
Blue striped		The case has been appealed
Orange		The case may have been overruled for at least one point of law because it relies on an overruled or otherwise invalid prior decision

You can select how you want citing material displayed—by depth of treatment or by date. KeyCite also indicates whether the cited material was distinguished by, discussed by, cited by, or mentioned by the citing material. KeyCite indicates both the first page and the citing page for later material.

KeyCite includes the following cited items:

- Constitutional provisions
- Statutes
- Regulations and IRS documents
- Judicial decisions [Illustration 10-10, *supra* page 215]
- Law review articles [Illustration 11-5]

Illustration 11-5. KeyCite Citing References to 67 Vand. L. Rev. 1581

1. FRAGMENTED OVERSIGHT OF NONPROFITS IN THE UNITED STATES: DOES IT WORK? CAN IT WORK? 2016
91 Chi.-Kent L. Rev. 937 , 963

Previously Brendan Wilson and I concluded that oversight of nonprofit governance would be most effective if it remained the responsibility of the states, although it would benefit...

2. ARTICLES OF INTEREST... 2015
42 Est. Plan. 40 , 40

Is the Private Annuity Really Dead? Alexander A. Bove Jr. 29 Prob. & Prop. 46-48 (March/April 2015). A Fresh Look at State Asset Protection Trust Statutes. Ronald J. Mann. 67 Vand....

3. CHARITABLE ORGANIZATION OVERSIGHT: RULES v. STANDARDS 2015
13 Pitt. Tax. Rev. 83 , 149

Congress has traditionally utilized standards as a means of communicating charitable tax law in the Code. In the past fifteen years, however, Congress has increasingly turned to...

→ We limited the results to law reviews. Note that the results are slightly different from those for Shepard's in Illustration 11-3 (*supra* page 224).

F. BCite/Smart Code

Bloomberg Law has two different citator services. BCite covers judicial opinions and IRS documents; Smart Code covers constitutional provisions, statutes, and regulations.

1. BCite

Access to BCite is from the case; there is no direct access to the materials. As with the other citator services above, BCite uses color-coded symbols and shapes to alert you to treatment of the cited item [Table 11-D]. It also indicates for each citing item the depth of discussion by placing blue squares next to the cited material [Illustration 11-7, *infra* page 228].

Table 11-D. BCite Analysis Definition Codes

Color	*Symbol*	*Meaning*
Red	▬	Opinion has been reversed, vacated, or depublished within Direct History, or overruled in full or in part by a subsequent decision
Orange	◘	Opinion has been superseded, displaced, or rendered obsolete by statute, rule, or regulation
Yellow	▲	Caution: Opinion has either been modified/clarified/amended in Direct History or criticized by another court
Blue	✎	Subsequent court opinion differentiated either on law or facts
Green	✚	Positive treatment: Court cites, discusses, or follows this opinion with approval
Grey	✚	Opinion has no negative direct history and has not been cited by other courts

BCite has different elements available for each case: Direct History; Case Analysis; Table of Authorities; and Citing Documents. These can be accessed on the BCite Analysis toolbar to the right of the case [Illustration 11-6].

Illustration 11-6. Bloomberg Law Case Illustration

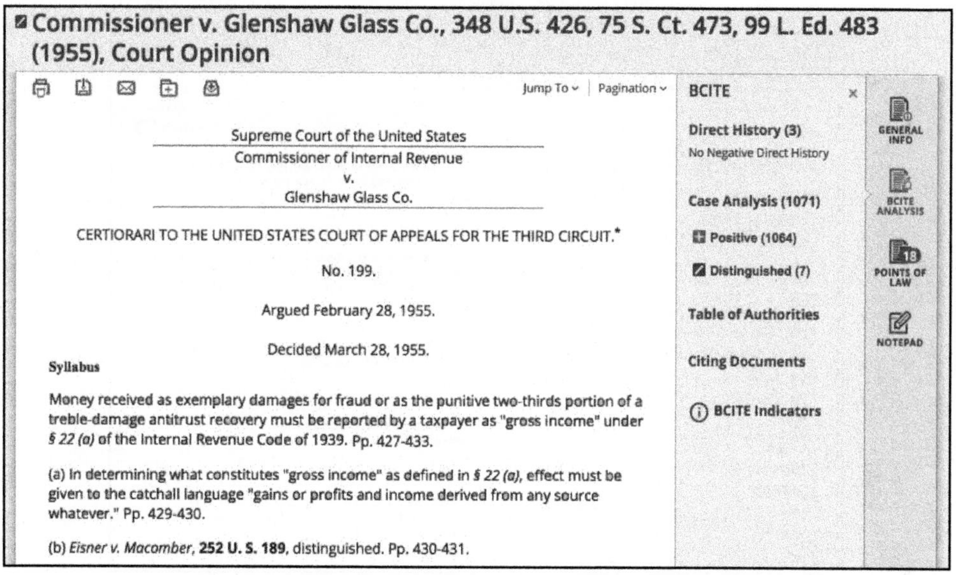

Direct History includes the history of the specific cases; it also includes cases with the same controversy and related appeals. This information can be sorted by Date, Case Status, and Court. The information can be filtered by Court, and Date.

Case Analysis is similar to its counterparts in Shepard's and KeyCite. It lists all the cases citing the cited case. You can view the excerpts from those cases that include the citation/discussion to the cited case. The material can be sorted by Date, Citation Frequency, Citing Case Analysis, or Court. You can filter the results from Case Analysis by Citing Case Analysis (how the citing case treated the current case—positive/negative), Citing Case Status (how other cases treated the case that is citing the current case), Citation Frequency, Court, Judge, and Date.

The Table of Authorities lists the cases cited by the original opinion. The material can be sorted by Date, Citation Frequency, Cited Case Analysis, Court, or Case Order. The results can be filtered by Cited Case Analysis, Cited Case Status, Citation Frequency, Court, Judge, and Date.

The Citing Documents option includes both cases and other legal materials referencing the cited case. The material cannot be sorted, but it can be filtered by Date and Content Type (BNA Portfolios, Cases, Law Reports and Journals, etc.).

While BCite has excerpts from the citing cases listed on the citation page, it does not list the exact page. To find the specific page referencing the cited case, click on the case and then use "Keywords" (located at the bottom of the page) to find the material.

BCite includes two types of cited items:

- Judicial decisions [Illustration 11-6]
- IRS documents [Illustration 11-7]

Bloomberg Law does not have a citator for law review articles or the BNA publications. You must use a general search to locate items citing those items.

Illustration 11-7. BCite Citation to Rev. Rul. 87–41, 1987–1 C.B. 296

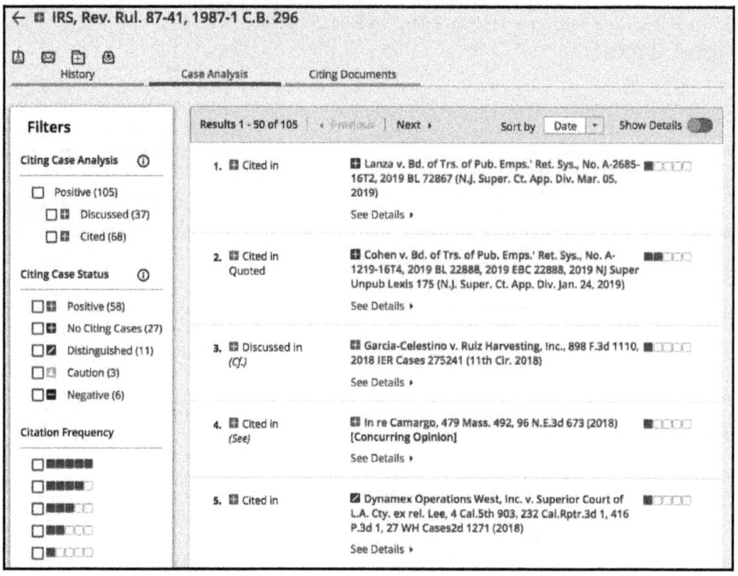

2. Smart Code

Bloomberg Law's citator for the Constitution, statutes, and regulations is called Smart Code. The information is linked directly to the source and cannot be accessed any other way. According to Bloomberg Law, Smart Code uses algorithms ("machine learning") to find the material in court opinions and then ranks the strength of discussion as Strong, Moderate, or Weak.

Smart Code can be sorted by Date, Court, and Most Cited. The material can be filtered by Date, Strength of Discussion, Court, and Topic (Tax & Accounting, Civil Procedure, etc.).

In addition to the Smart Code tab, each provision also has a tab for CFR Provisions (statutes only), Secondary Sources, and Agency Materials. These items cannot be sorted, but can be filtered by Content Type (e.g., Tax Management Portfolios, statutes, regulations).

Illustration 11-8. Smart Code Results for I.R.C. § 162

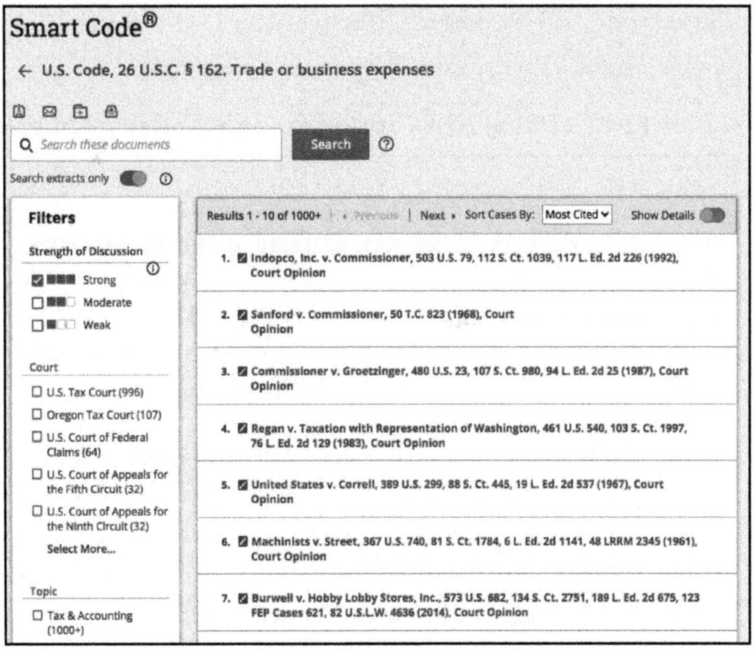

→ The materials above are sorted by Most Cited and filtered for only Strong Strength of Discussion.

G. RIA Citator

The RIA Citator began as the Prentice-Hall print citator. It is still available in print and is also carried online in Checkpoint and Westlaw Edge. The earlier volumes are available only in the print version. Checkpoint and Westlaw Edge carry only the RIA Citator 2nd series. Unless you need earlier material, the online citator will be easier to use than the print version because you will not have to use multiple volumes.[5] If you do need earlier materials, and the choice is between the RIA and CCH print citators, RIA is likely to provide more extensive results.

The online citator lets you filter your results by court. When a later case involves an issue that RIA has given a headnote, it indicates the headnote number. The online citator indicates whether the citing decision viewed the earlier item favorably (or unfavorably) or merely cited it without comment. Although RIA includes regulations as cited items, it does so by T.D. number. Unfortunately, a single T.D. may cover several regulations sections.

RIA often gives citations for both the first page and the citing page. Case citations are given to official and West services in addition to RIA services. RIA often includes U.S.T.C. citations. RIA does not use law review articles or treatises as citing items.

5 The first series covers federal tax cases from 1796 to 1954.

The RIA Citator in Checkpoint includes the following cited items:

- Regulations and IRS documents [Illustrations 11-9 through 11-11]
- Judicial decisions [Illustration 10-12, *supra* page 216]

Illustration 11-9. Using RIA Citator for IRS Notice in Checkpoint

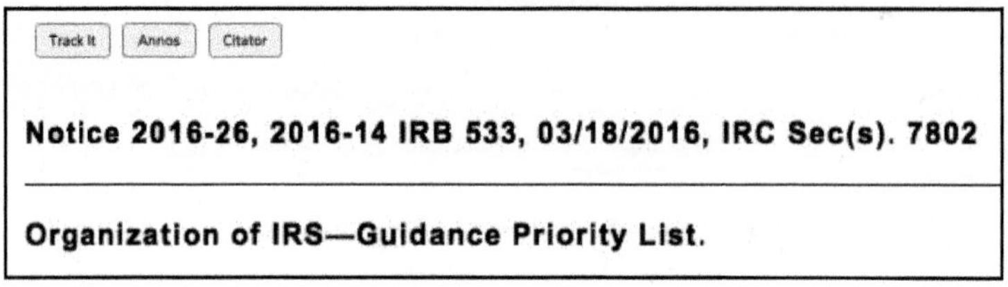

→ Click on the Citator box to evaluate Notice 2016–26.

Illustration 11-10. RIA Citator Link

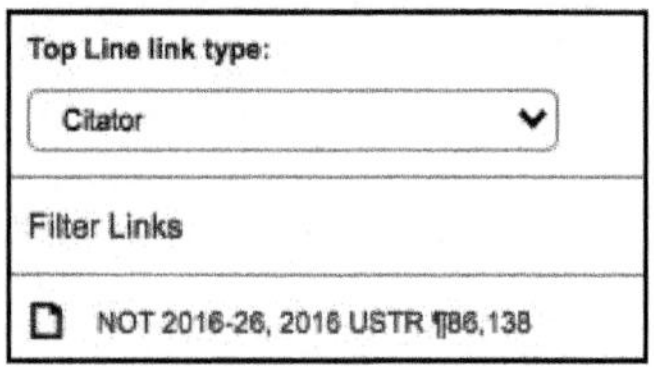

→ Click on the link to get the results.

Illustration 11-11. RIA Citator Results for Notice 2016–26

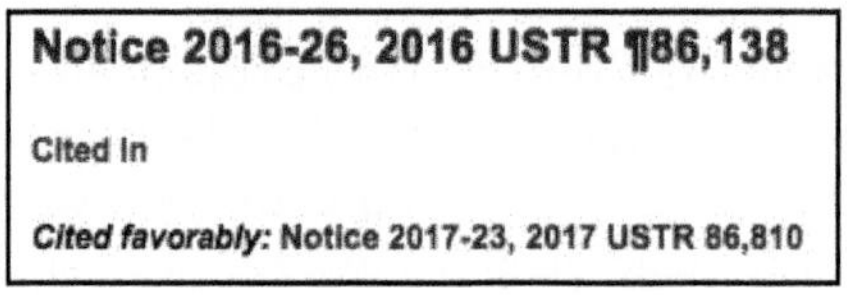

H. CCH Citator

The CCH print citator service is actually three separate services. Standard Federal Tax Reporter—Citator is a two-volume service that covers the income tax. The CCH Federal Estate and Gift Tax Reporter and Federal Excise Tax Reporter have their own citator sections, which cover those taxes.[6] The three services combined have fewer volumes than does the full RIA Citator service.[7] If you access the CCH Citator online through Cheetah, you avoid having to use separate citator services.

CCH does not assign headnote numbers to cases and so does not indicate which issue a citing case is discussing. Likewise, it does not indicate whether the citing material follows or distinguishes the cited decision. Its case citations refer to the CCH case reporters and to the official and West services. Citations to subsequent decisions in

---

[6] Although the SFTR citator volumes list non-Tax Court cases involving estate and gift taxes and excise taxes, actual citations to those cases appear only in the Citator sections of Federal Estate and Gift Tax Reporter and Federal Excise Tax Reporter.

[7] While its compactness makes it the easiest print citator to use, the CCH citator has the fewest useful features and omits, through editorial selection, many citing cases.

services other than U.S.T.C. indicate the first page of the citing case, not the page where reference is made to the cited material. Citations to U.S.T.C. are to paragraph numbers.

Citing items include CCH looseleaf services but not law reviews or treatises. Although CCH includes regulations as cited items, it does so by T.D. number. Unfortunately, a single T.D. may cover several regulations sections.

The CCH Citator in Cheetah includes the following cited items:

- Regulations and IRS documents [Illustrations 11-12 and 11-13]
- Judicial decisions [Illustration 10-13, *supra* page 216]

Illustration 11-12. Searching CCH Citator for Notice 2016–26

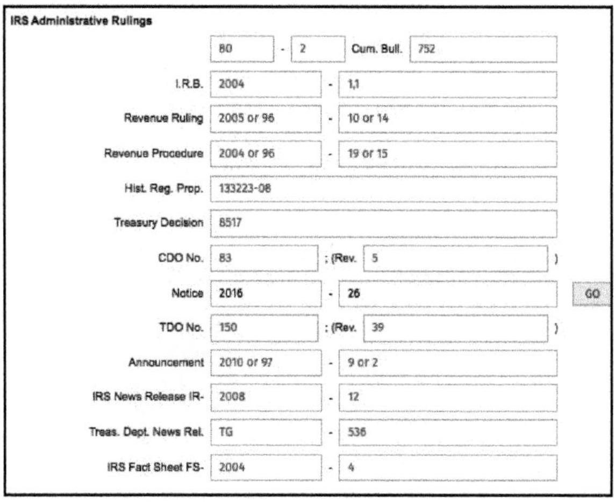

→ Because CCH does not have a citator link from the notice, you need to search directly in the citator.

Illustration 11-13. CCH Citator Results for Notice 2016–26

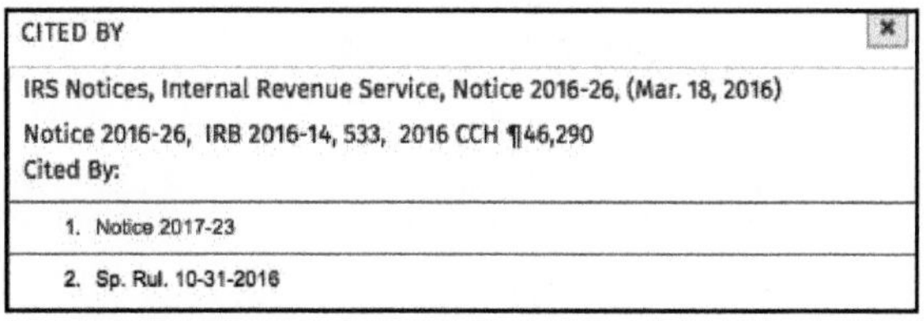

CITED BY
IRS Notices, Internal Revenue Service, Notice 2016-26, (Mar. 18, 2016)
Notice 2016-26, IRB 2016-14, 533, 2016 CCH ¶46,290
Cited By:
1. Notice 2017-23
2. Sp. Rul. 10-31-2016

→ Cheetah does not indicate how items listed ruled with respect to the cited item. It lists them simply as "Cited By."

I. Problems

1. Your instructor will assign you a primary source item to check in as many citators as are available to you. Make a list of differences in citing documents and a list of any differences in treatment. If you find differences in treatment, go to the actual citing material to determine which citators were correct.

2. Several of the problems in other chapters are easily completed with a citator. If you initially completed a problem using a particular citator, redo it using a different publisher's service and compare your results.

3. Federal Research Library, Google Scholar, and HeinOnline do not have citators, but you can often locate citing material by searching for references to a cited item. Using whichever of these services is available to you, list any items you find that cite to a judicial decision or law review article your instructor selects.

Chapter 12

LOOSELEAF SERVICES

A. Introduction

You may decide to consult explanatory materials early in the research effort, perhaps even before you read the relevant statutes.[1] If so, you are likely to use a looseleaf service. Those texts provide insight into the problem being researched. In addition, you can draw upon their liberal use of citations for a preliminary reading list of cases and administrative pronouncements. Each is updated at frequent intervals, and several have at least one related newsletter.

This chapter focuses on six looseleaf services. Four of them take a subject matter approach, but two of the best-known services are arranged in Code section order. Although this chapter describes the print versions of these services, all illustrations are to their online versions.[2] If, as is likely, you do use the online versions, remember to use the tables of contents and indexes as guides to the material you want to read.

B. Code Section Arrangement

The Commerce Clearing House[3] and Research Institute of America[4] looseleaf services take essentially the same approach. Each service's compilation volumes print the full texts of Code sections and Treasury regulations along with editorial explanations. An annotation section listing cases and rulings follows each section. Users wanting ready access to the text of the law alongside explanatory material will appreciate this format.

Because of the arrangement described above, problems involving multiple Code sections do not receive comprehensive discussion. Although the publishers supplement their looseleaf materials with newsletters and other aids, Code-based services are not as suited as are subject-based services for learning about issues involving multiple Code sections.

Although each service is arranged in Code section order, all materials are assigned paragraph numbers. A "paragraph" can be the size of a traditional paragraph, but it might be several pages long. Unless noted otherwise, each service cross-references between paragraph numbers, not between page numbers.

These services have subject matter indexes; their format makes Code section indexes unnecessary. New material arrives weekly for insertion in the compilation volumes or in a separate updating volume. These new developments are indexed

---

[1] In appropriate cases, you can use these textual materials to ascertain which statutes are involved. In addition, you should consult these materials whenever you desire additional textual information.

[2] As libraries (or publishers) cancel their print subscriptions and provide these materials only in an online format, you may hear them referred to as topical services rather than looseleaf services.

[3] Standard Federal Tax Reporter (income tax); Federal Estate and Gift Tax Reporter; Federal Excise Tax Reporter.

[4] United States Tax Reporter—Income Taxes; United States Tax Reporter—Estate & Gift Taxes; United States Tax Reporter—Excise Taxes. RIA also publishes a subject matter format service, Federal Tax Coordinator 2d.

according to the paragraph in the main compilation to which they relate, i.e., in Code section order. The online versions are also updated on a weekly basis.

Libraries often carry both services in print or online, and users eventually develop a preference for one or the other.[5] As each service's annotations are editorially selected, using both can reduce the risk that you will miss a valuable annotation. Using both may substantially increase research time, and the extra material obtained rarely justifies the additional time involved.

1. Standard Federal Tax Reporter

The discussion of this CCH looseleaf service follows the format in which it is arranged. Several volumes, such as the Citator, are discussed in greater detail in other chapters; cross-references to those discussions appear here.

SFTR is available online on Cheetah and a predecessor platform, IntelliConnect. The content on both online platforms is the same, but the interface is different. If you are using the online version, you do not need to know which volumes contain particular types of material because online links let you navigate between materials. The print and online versions are also somewhat different in their general layout. Although this chapter focuses on the Cheetah version of SFTR, we discuss Cheetah in greater detail in Chapter 17.

a. Code Volumes

These volumes print, in Code section order, all provisions involving income, gift and estate, employment, and excise taxes as well as procedural provisions. A brief explanation of amendments since 1954 (including the Public Law number and section and effective dates) follows each Code provision. These explanations include information about prior statutory language. These volumes are updated at intervals following Code amendments.

The Source Notes and Finding Lists section in Volume I covers a variety of useful legislative history information. Tables I and II provide cross-references between the 1939 and 1954 Codes.[6]

---

[5] Because budget constraints are causing many law libraries to eliminate duplicative materials, it is possible you will have neither print nor online access to a particular service.

[6] You can find these tables in Cheetah under Tax-Federal>Laws & Regulations>Internal Revenue Code. When you reach I.R.C., look at the Table of Contents on the "Contents" side panel. Cross-Reference Tables I and II are under "Finding Lists" at the bottom of the list.

Illustration 12-1. SFTR 1939 to 1954 Cross-Reference Table I

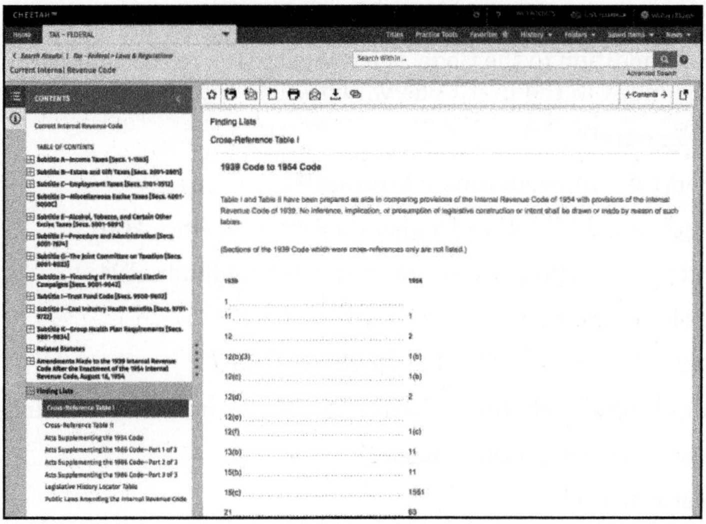

A Legislative History Locator Table lists committee reports and dates for acts that affected the Code since 1954.[7] This Table includes the act name and number, bill number, report numbers, and any Cumulative Bulletin citation. Another set of lists, which begins with 1971 legislation, covers Acts Supplementing the 1954 and 1986 Codes. These lists provide the Public Law number, bill number, date, and Statutes at Large citation for each act; they include short titles for several acts. These lists are in Public Law number order. Each act is arranged in act section order; the list indicates every Code section affected by an act section.[8] These lists do not indicate how the particular Code sections were affected.

Volume I also includes a Public Laws Amending the Internal Revenue Code section which lists Public Law number, short title, and enactment date.[9] These materials begin in mid-1954 and are in Public Law number order.

Volume I includes both a Topical Index and a Table of Contents listing all Code sections in order.[10]

Volume II prints the text of non-Code statutory provisions affecting federal taxes in the Related Statutes section that begins in 1935. Volume II also includes subject matter and Code section lists of 1954–1966 amendments to the 1939 Code. The Code section list includes Public Law number and Congress, act section, and SFTR paragraph number.

---

[7] Cheetah includes the list of Acts Supplementing the 1954 and 1986 Codes in the same place as Tables I and II above.

[8] Some libraries may have retained a special 1971 SFTR publication covering earlier acts.

[9] Cheetah includes the Public Law lists under "Finding Lists" in the Current Internal Revenue Code Table of Contents.

[10] In Cheetah, the I.R.C. Table of Contents is a sidebar. The Topical Index is more difficult to find in Cheetah. Type in "Current Internal Revenue Code Topical Index" in the search bar located in "Titles" (top menu bar). If you type in "Topical Index," it will show a list of all topical indexes available in Cheetah (e.g., "2018 IRC Topical Index").

b. Index Volume and Initial Compilation Volume

Both volumes provide useful tables and other reference material. Because it covers the annotations in addition to the Code, the topical index in the Index volume is far more detailed than the index in the first Code volume. The Index volume also includes:

- Tax calendars[11]
- IRS Service Center mailing addresses[12]
- Exemption and Standard Deduction Amounts since 2001[13]
- Tax rates since 1909 (corporate) and 1913 (individual)[14]
- Withholding tables[15]
- Depreciation tables—class life ADR; MACRS[16]
- Annuity tables, including valuation for life estates and remainders[17]
- Savings bond redemption tables[18]
- Interest rate tables[19]

  applicable federal rates since 1985

  uniform tables and procedures for compounding interest

  interest on overpayments/underpayments

  low income housing credit rates and recapture information
- Per diem rates[20]
- Checklists[21]

  for completing tax returns

  income and deductions

  medical expenses—summary of rulings and cases

---

[11] These are located under Tax-Federal>Standard Federal Tax Reporter in Cheetah. The tax calendars are located in "Tax rates and tables and tax calendar" in the "Contents" side bar.

[12] Cheetah includes the mailing addresses under "Tax Calendar."

[13] Cheetah includes the information for personal exemptions and standard deductions within "Tax rates and tables and tax calendar" (see note 11) under "Tax tables and rates."

[14] Cheetah includes the information for rates in various compartments within "Tax rates and tables and tax calendar" (see note 11) under "Tax tables and rates."

[15] Cheetah includes the withholding tables within "Tax rates and tables and tax calendar" (see note 11) under "Tax tables and rates."

[16] Cheetah includes the depreciation tables under Tax-Federal>Standard Federal Tax Reporter>Depreciation in the "Contents" side bar.

[17] Cheetah includes the annuity tables under Tax-Federal>Standard Federal Tax Reporter>Annuities in the "Contents" side bar.

[18] Cheetah includes the tables for savings bonds and notes under Tax-Federal>Standard Federal Tax Reporter>Savings bonds and notes in the "Contents" side bar.

[19] Cheetah includes the interest tables under Tax-Federal>Standard Federal Tax Reporter>Interest rate tables in the "Contents" side bar.

[20] Cheetah includes the per diem amounts under Tax-Federal>Standard Federal Tax Reporter>Per diem rates in the "Contents" side bar.

[21] Cheetah includes the checklists under Tax-Federal>Standard Federal Tax Reporter>Checklists in the "Contents" side bar.

real property tax dates by state

tax elections

information return filing

disaster areas declared in current and preceding year

The first Compilation volume includes the following reference material:

- Tax planning by topic—e.g., impact of divorce; retirement[22]
- Who Is the Taxpayer?—discussion and annotations[23]
- Constitutional and tax protest materials, including annotations[24]

c. Compilation Volumes

These volumes contain, in Code section order, the full text of the Code, proposed, temporary, and final regulations, and digest-annotations of revenue rulings and revenue procedures, letter rulings and other publicly available IRS documents, and judicial decisions. An alphabetical index is provided if the annotations section is lengthy. CCH provides an editorial explanation, including citations to the annotations, for each Code provision. [See Illustrations 12-2 through 12-5.]

Immediately after each Code section, the editors indicate which Public Laws have amended it and print text of, or citations to, committee reports; a brief T.D. history follows regulations sections. The pre-amendment text is omitted in the historical notes for both Code and regulations sections.

Regulations follow the Code section material. If a regulation does not reflect Code amendments, SFTR indicates that fact at the top of each regulations page. Because regulations are printed in Code section order, regulations from different parts of 26 C.F.R. (or even from other titles of C.F.R.) appear together. [See Illustration 12-2.] Because regulations from other C.F.R. titles follow their own prefix system, it is critical that your citation indicate Treas. Reg. (or 26 C.F.R.) for Treasury regulations and the other C.F.R. title for other regulations. See, e.g., 40 C.F.R. § 20.1, which appears in SFTR with Code section 169. [See Illustration 12-2.] If this were a Treasury regulation, the prefix 20 would indicate an estate tax regulation and the 1 following it would indicate Code section 1 (which covers income tax rates).

---

22 Cheetah includes this material under Tax-Federal>Standard Federal Tax Reporter>Tax Planning in the "Contents" side bar.

23 Cheetah includes this material under Tax-Federal>Standard Federal Tax Reporter>Who is the taxpayer, return preparers, and constitutionality in the "Contents" side bar.

24 Cheetah includes this material under "Constitutional provisions, tax protests" within "Checklists" (see note 21, *supra* page 236).

Illustration 12-2. Partial List of SFTR Grouping of Regulations for I.R.C. § 169

Contents

Standard Federal Tax Reporter (2020). §1.169-1. Amortization of pollution control facilities
Standard Federal Tax Reporter (2020). §1.169-2. Definitions
Standard Federal Tax Reporter (2020). §1.169-3. Amortizable basis
Standard Federal Tax Reporter (2020). §1.169-4. Time and manner of making elections
Standard Federal Tax Reporter (2020). §20.1. Applicability
Standard Federal Tax Reporter (2020). §20.2. Definitions
Standard Federal Tax Reporter (2020). §20.3. General provisions
Standard Federal Tax Reporter (2020). §20.4. Notice of intent to certify
Standard Federal Tax Reporter (2020). §20.5. Applications
Standard Federal Tax Reporter (2020). §20.6. State certification
Standard Federal Tax Reporter (2020). §20.7. General policies
Standard Federal Tax Reporter (2020). §20.8. Requirements for certification
Standard Federal Tax Reporter (2020). §20.9. Cost recovery
Standard Federal Tax Reporter (2020). §20.10. Revocation

→ The list of regulations appears under Related Items, directly above each subsection.

The final Compilation volume also lists IRS and Tax Court forms (numerically and alphabetically), IRS publications (numerically), Treasury and IRS personnel, IRS procedural rules, and Circular 230.

Illustration 12-3. SFTR Compilation Volume Contents

Sec. 212. EXPENSES FOR PRODUCTION OF INCOME
⊞ Legislative History
§1.212-1. Nontrade or nonbusiness expenses
§1.212-1. Nontrade or nonbusiness expenses, LR-261-76, 8/7/80.
§1.212-1. Nontrade or nonbusiness expenses, REG-166012-02, 2/26/2004.
⊞ [¶12,523] Expenses for Production of Income - Explanations
⊞ Expenses for Production of Income - Annotations
⊞ Current Developments

→ The print looseleaf uses a separate New Matters volume for Current Developments.

→ You can find this in Cheetah under Tax-Federal>Standard Federal Tax Reporter in the "Contents" sidebar by expanding Deductions-Secs. 161–250>Itemized deductions-Secs. 161–224>Expenses for production of income-Secs. 211, 212.

Illustration 12-4. SFTR Explanation

12,523.025, Expenses for Production of Income: Expenses for production of income, legal expenses

RELATED ITEMS

The deductibility of miscellaneous itemized deductions is temporarily repealed for tax years 2018 through 2025. This generally includes expenses paid or incurred for the production or collection of income (including investment advisory fees, subscriptions to investment advisory publications, certain attorneys' fees, and safety deposit box rental), or for the determination, collection, or refund of tax (including tax counsel fees and appraisal fees) that are deductible under Code Sec. 212 (Code Sec. 67(g) as added by the Tax Cuts and Jobs Act, P.L. 115-97).

Individuals are allowed to take a deduction for ordinary and necessary expenses paid or incurred (1) for the production or collection of income; (2) for the management, conservation, or maintenance of income-producing property; or (3) in connection with the determination, collection, or refund of any tax. These deductions may be taken only as itemized deductions, i.e., deductible from adjusted gross income (Code Sec. 212), and are generally subject to the two-percent floor on miscellaneous itemized deductions, and thus are not available for tax years 2018 through 2025 (Code Sec. 67; see ¶6064.01 et seq.). However, the two-percent floor does not apply to deductions attributable to property held for the production of rents and royalties (Code Sec. 62), or in connection with the administration of a trust or estate that would not have been incurred if the property were not held in a trust or estate.

→ Online looseleaf services provide hyperlinks to primary sources and to other documents. The paragraph numbers are more important when using the print service.

Illustration 12-5. SFTR Annotations

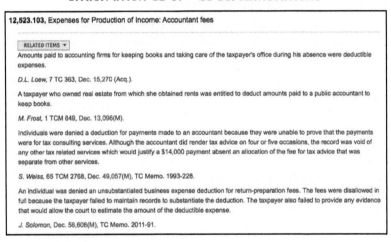

12,523.103, Expenses for Production of Income: Accountant fees

RELATED ITEMS

Amounts paid to accounting firms for keeping books and taking care of the taxpayer's office during his absence were deductible expenses.

D.L. Loew, 7 TC 363, Dec. 15,270 (Acq.).

A taxpayer who owned real estate from which she obtained rents was entitled to deduct amounts paid to a public accountant to keep books.

M. Frost, 1 TCM 849, Dec. 13,098(M).

Individuals were denied a deduction for payments made to an accountant because they were unable to prove that the payments were for tax consulting services. Although the accountant did render tax advice on four or five occasions, the record was void of any other tax related services which would justify a $14,000 payment absent an allocation of the fee for tax advice that was separate from other services.

S. Weiss, 65 TCM 2768, Dec. 49,057(M), TC Memo. 1993-228.

An individual was denied an unsubstantiated business expense deduction for return-preparation fees. The fees were disallowed in full because the taxpayer failed to maintain records to substantiate the deduction. The taxpayer also failed to provide any evidence that would allow the court to estimate the amount of the deductible expense.

J. Solomon, Dec. 58,608(M), TC Memo. 2011-91.

→ Each group of annotations has a paragraph number.

→ Note the links for each decision's text to either Tax Court or Tax Court Memo. opinions.

d. New Matters Volume

The compilation volumes' annotations receive little updating during the year involved.[25] Instead, recent material is indexed in the New Matters volume. Because the Cumulative Index (including a Latest Additions supplement) is based on the paragraph numbers used in the compilation volumes, it is easy to use the New Matters volume to find recent developments. If you use the online version, you can go directly to the Current Developments section for each Code section. [See reference in Illustration 12-3.]

[25] Cheetah has nothing comparable to the "New Matters Volume" because the online material is constantly updated.

SFTR reproduces updating material as follows:

- New Matters volume—texts of revenue rulings and procedures; digests of Tax Court Regular and Memorandum Opinions
- U.S.T.C. Advance Sheets volume—texts of decisions rendered by all other courts
- Compilation volumes—Code and regulations

The New Matters volume has a Topical Index of current-year developments, and it digests a limited number of publicly available IRS documents (e.g., letter rulings). It also includes Preambles for current year Treasury Decisions and indicates where final and temporary regulations appear in the SFTR service.[26]

A Case Table (including a supplement for Latest Additions) lists each year's decisions alphabetically. It indicates (1) which trial court is involved and where the decision appears in the U.S.T.C. Advance Sheets or SFTR New Matters volumes;[27] (2) appeals by either side and IRS acquiescence or nonacquiescence in unfavorable decisions; and (3) outcome at the appellate level.

A Supreme Court Docket, which also lists cases alphabetically, includes a brief digest of the issues involved and their disposition. This table includes cases in which the Court denies certiorari.

A Finding List of Rulings cross-references current year IRS documents to the appropriate paragraphs in the New Matters volume. If you use the print version of SFTR, consult this list in addition to the Finding Lists in the SFTR Citator when checking the status of IRS items.

e. U.S. Tax Cases (U.S.T.C.) Advance Sheets Volume

This volume contains the Preambles to proposed income tax regulations. Lists of proposed income tax regulations appear in both topical and Code section formats; the topical format is arranged chronologically rather than alphabetically.

This volume also contains the texts of income tax decisions rendered by courts other than the Tax Court.[28] You can locate these items using the Cumulative Index in the New Matters volume. Decisions appear in the order in which they are received rather than in Code section order. These decisions will later be issued in hardbound volumes as part of the U.S.T.C. reporter service discussed in Chapter 10.

f. Citator

You can use these volumes, which list decisions alphabetically, to determine if subsequent decisions have affected earlier items. The Citator also covers revenue rulings, revenue procedures, other IRS items, and Treasury Decisions. The Citator

---

[26] Cheetah includes this information in the Treasury Decisions and Notices of Proposed Rulemaking sections of its IRS Administrative Rulings & Positions subdivision.

[27] It may not indicate the state for District Court decisions and lists only decisions covered in SFTR. Bankruptcy Court cases are listed as BC-DC (Bankruptcy Court-District Court).

[28] Preambles and recent court decisions involving estate and gift taxes or excise taxes appear in the CCH services covering those topics. Court decisions involving all taxes appear in the U.S.T.C. hardbound volumes.

provides cross-references to discussions of cases and rulings in the compilation volumes. The online version of this Citator is discussed in Chapter 11.

The final item in the second volume is a list of Cumulative Bulletin citations to committee reports for sections amending the 1986 Code. These materials are in Code section order. Because Cumulative Bulletin coverage of legislation ended more than 10 years ago, these lists do not reflect recent legislation.

g. Cheetah

The CCH Cheetah service (discussed further in Chapter 17) includes the SFTR and other CCH services. Cheetah does not track the format of the print version as closely as do the online versions of some other looseleaf services described in this chapter, so you may have some initial difficulty transitioning from the print service.

Illustration 12-6. Cheetah Advanced Search for Alimony and 212

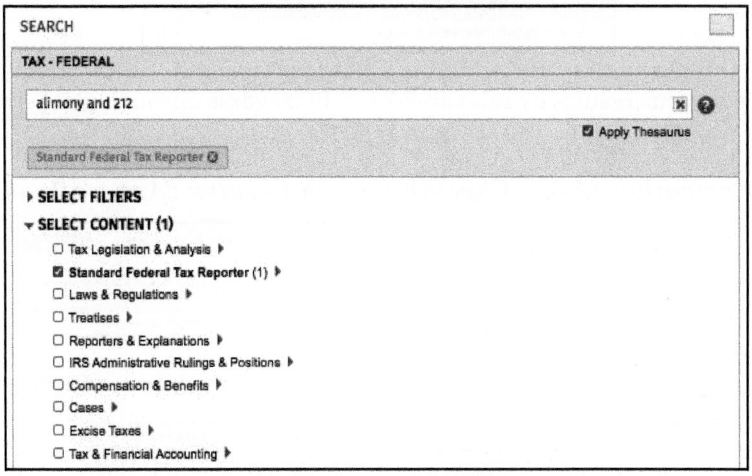

→ You can search Cheetah across different types of authority. You can also search on selected content, including SFTR.

Illustration 12-7. Cheetah Search Results

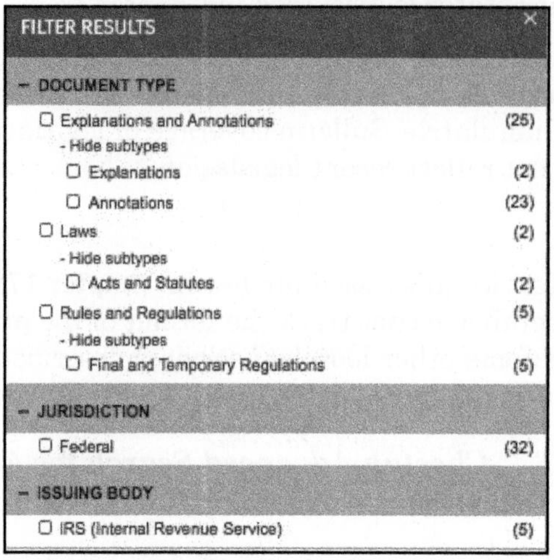
FILTER RESULTS

– DOCUMENT TYPE

☐ Explanations and Annotations (25)
- Hide subtypes
☐ Explanations (2)
☐ Annotations (23)
☐ Laws (2)
- Hide subtypes
☐ Acts and Statutes (2)
☐ Rules and Regulations (5)
- Hide subtypes
☐ Final and Temporary Regulations (5)

– JURISDICTION

☐ Federal (32)

– ISSUING BODY

☐ IRS (Internal Revenue Service) (5)

→ You can sort your results by relevance or date (reverse chronological order). You can also limit the document types you want to read.

Illustration 12-8. Cheetah Search Results: "Annotations"

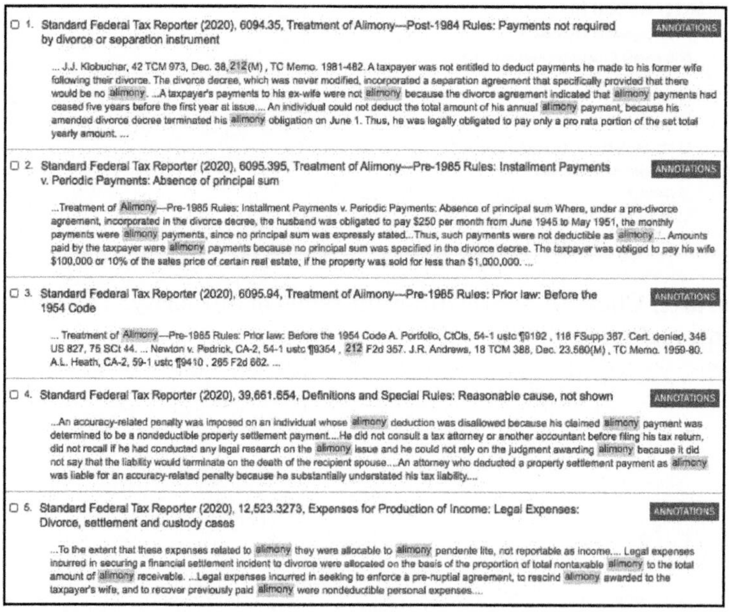
☐ 1. Standard Federal Tax Reporter (2020), 6094.35, Treatment of Alimony—Post-1984 Rules: Payments not required by divorce or separation instrument ANNOTATIONS

... J.J. Klobuchar, 42 TCM 973, Dec. 38,212(M) , TC Memo. 1981-482. A taxpayer was not entitled to deduct payments he made to his former wife following their divorce. The divorce decree, which was never modified, incorporated a separation agreement that specifically provided that there would be no alimony. ...A taxpayer's payments to his ex-wife were not alimony because the divorce agreement indicated that alimony payments had ceased five years before the first year at issue.... An individual could not deduct the total amount of his annual alimony payment, because his amended divorce decree terminated his alimony obligation on June 1. Thus, he was legally obligated to pay only a pro rata portion of the set total yearly amount. ...

☐ 2. Standard Federal Tax Reporter (2020), 6095.395, Treatment of Alimony—Pre-1985 Rules: Installment Payments v. Periodic Payments: Absence of principal sum ANNOTATIONS

...Treatment of Alimony—Pre-1985 Rules: Installment Payments v. Periodic Payments: Absence of principal sum Where, under a pre-divorce agreement, incorporated in the divorce decree, the husband was obligated to pay $250 per month from June 1945 to May 1951, the monthly payments were alimony payments, since no principal sum was expressly stated...Thus, such payments were not deductible as alimony.... Amounts paid by the taxpayer were alimony payments because no principal sum was specified in the divorce decree. The taxpayer was obliged to pay his wife $100,000 or 10% of the sales price of certain real estate, if the property was sold for less than $1,000,000. ...

☐ 3. Standard Federal Tax Reporter (2020), 6095.94, Treatment of Alimony—Pre-1985 Rules: Prior law: Before the 1954 Code ANNOTATIONS

... Treatment of Alimony—Pre-1985 Rules: Prior law: Before the 1954 Code A. Portfolio, CtCls, 54-1 ustc ¶9192 , 118 FSupp 387. Cert. denied, 348 US 827, 75 SCt 44. ... Newton v. Pedrick, CA-2, 54-1 ustc ¶9354 , 212 F2d 357. J.R. Andrews, 18 TCM 388, Dec. 23,580(M) , TC Memo. 1959-80. A.L. Heath, CA-2, 59-1 ustc ¶9410 , 265 F2d 662. ...

☐ 4. Standard Federal Tax Reporter (2020), 39,661.654, Definitions and Special Rules: Reasonable cause, not shown ANNOTATIONS

...An accuracy-related penalty was imposed on an individual whose alimony deduction was disallowed because his claimed alimony payment was determined to be a nondeductible property settlement payment....He did not consult a tax attorney or another accountant before filing his tax return, did not recall if he had conducted any legal research on the alimony issue and he could not rely on the judgment awarding alimony because it did not say that the liability would terminate on the death of the recipient spouse....An attorney who deducted a property settlement payment as alimony was liable for an accuracy-related penalty because he substantially understated his tax liability....

☐ 5. Standard Federal Tax Reporter (2020), 12,523.3273, Expenses for Production of Income: Legal Expenses: Divorce, settlement and custody cases ANNOTATIONS

...To the extent that these expenses related to alimony they were allocable to alimony pendente lite, not reportable as income.... Legal expenses incurred in securing a financial settlement incident to divorce were allocated on the basis of the proportion of total nontaxable alimony to the total amount of alimony receivable. ...Legal expenses incurred in seeking to enforce a pre-nuptial agreement, to rescind alimony awarded to the taxpayer's wife, and to recover previously paid alimony were nondeductible personal expenses....

→ The search terms (here "alimony" and "212") are highlighted. Unfortunately, the references to 212 are to case citations.

2. United States Tax Reporter—Income Taxes

The discussion of USTR follows the format in which it is arranged. Several of its volumes, and the RIA Citator, are discussed and illustrated in greater detail elsewhere in this book; this section includes appropriate cross-references to those discussions.

Illustrations of USTR are taken from the online version on Checkpoint.[29] Volume numbers aren't critical if you use the online version to find items; you can navigate using hyperlinks.

a. Code Volumes

The Code Volumes are paperback and are updated twice a year. These are in Code section order and contain all provisions involving income, gift and estate, employment, and excise taxes as well as procedural provisions. Historical information follows Code provisions that have been amended. Historical material includes the Public Law number, the Public Law section number, and the effective date of any amendments. Prior statutory language is provided for several sections.

There is a Topic Index to the Code and a listing of all Code sections.[30] An Amending Acts section includes Public Law number, date, act title or subject, and Cumulative Bulletin or Statutes at Large citation for acts since 1954. This section is not separately indexed and does not list the Code sections amended.

b. Index Volume

This begins with "How to Use United States Tax Reporter." What follows is an extensive index (main and supplementary sections), using paragraph numbers, to the material in the compilation volumes discussed below. This index uses different typefaces to denote Code section numbers and locations, location of topical discussions, and location of regulations text. It also includes a Glossary, which provides succinct definitions of terms (both words and phrases) used by tax practitioners.

c. Tables Volume

This volume contains main, supplementary, and current Tables of Cases and main and supplementary Tables of Rulings. These tables cross-reference cases and rulings to the appropriate discussions in the compilation volumes or in the online Federal Tax Update newsletter. RIA provides case citations to several different reporter services in addition to A.F.T.R. Special notations indicate paragraph numbers for decisions printed in RIA's Tax Court Memorandum Decisions service.

The case tables are not citator supplements. They merely list cases discussed in USTR and provide a citation to the discussion. This volume also includes withholding, tax rate, per diem, and interest tables.

d. Compilation Volumes

These volumes contain, in Code section order, the full text of the Code; final, temporary, and proposed regulations; and digest-annotations of revenue rulings, letter rulings, other IRS releases, and judicial decisions. Excerpted committee reports (or Cumulative Bulletin citations) are also included. Paragraph numbers assigned to these materials reflect the Code section involved.

---

[29] USTR is also available on Westlaw Edge. [See Illustration 12-14, *infra* page 246.]

[30] Checkpoint includes the USTR Topic Index under Table of Contents in the menu bar under Federal Library>Federal Editorial Materials>Federal Indexes>Code Arranged Annotations & Explanations (USTR) Topic Index.

If a regulation does not reflect a Code amendment, that information appears at the beginning of the regulation. There is an extensive editorial explanation, and citations to the annotations, for each Code provision.

Illustration 12-9. USTR Compilation Topic

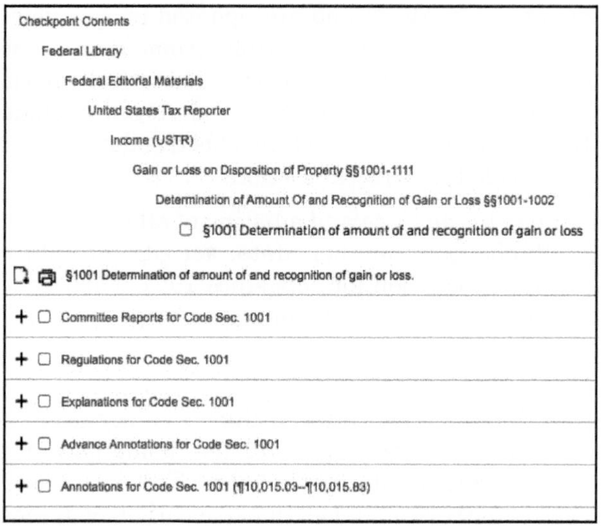

Checkpoint Contents

Federal Library

Federal Editorial Materials

United States Tax Reporter

Income (USTR)

Gain or Loss on Disposition of Property §§1001-1111

Determination of Amount Of and Recognition of Gain or Loss §§1001-1002

§1001 Determination of amount of and recognition of gain or loss

§1001 Determination of amount of and recognition of gain or loss.

+ Committee Reports for Code Sec. 1001

+ Regulations for Code Sec. 1001

+ Explanations for Code Sec. 1001

+ Advance Annotations for Code Sec. 1001

+ Annotations for Code Sec. 1001 (¶10,015.03–¶10,015.83)

→ Note how the annotation references begin with 1001.

→ In Checkpoint, the easiest way to reach the topic screen is by using the Table of Contents on the menu bar and searching in USTR Code Section.

Illustration 12-10. USTR Explanation

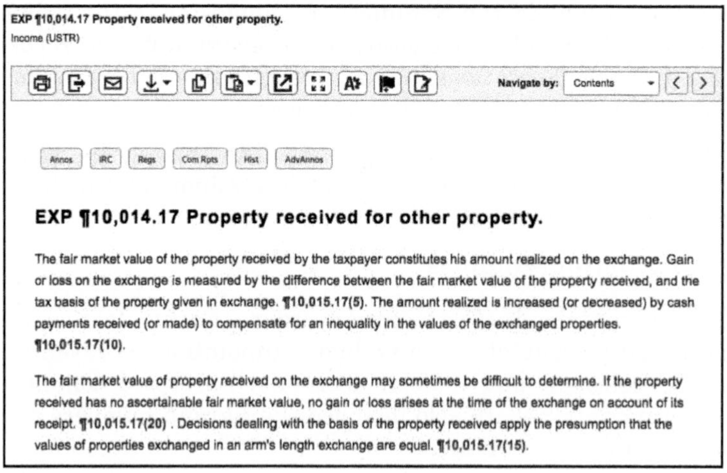

EXP ¶10,014.17 Property received for other property.

Income (USTR)

Navigate by: Contents

Annos | IRC | Regs | Com Rpts | Hist | AdvAnnos

EXP ¶10,014.17 Property received for other property.

The fair market value of the property received by the taxpayer constitutes his amount realized on the exchange. Gain or loss on the exchange is measured by the difference between the fair market value of the property received, and the tax basis of the property given in exchange. **¶10,015.17(5)**. The amount realized is increased (or decreased) by cash payments received (or made) to compensate for an inequality in the values of the exchanged properties. **¶10,015.17(10)**.

The fair market value of property received on the exchange may sometimes be difficult to determine. If the property received has no ascertainable fair market value, no gain or loss arises at the time of the exchange on account of its receipt. **¶10,015.17(20)** . Decisions dealing with the basis of the property received apply the presumption that the values of properties exchanged in an arm's length exchange are equal. **¶10,015.17(15)**.

→ Note the links to Annotations, I.R.C., etc., above the Explanation paragraph.

→ The paragraph references are hyperlinked to annotations in the electronic versions of USTR.

Illustration 12-11. USTR Annotations

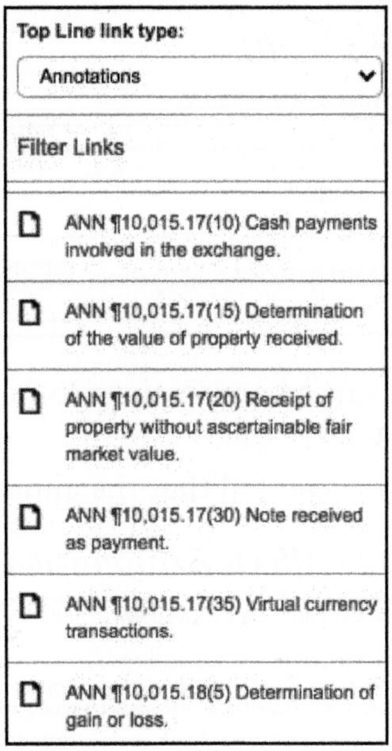

Top Line link type:

Annotations

Filter Links

ANN ¶10,015.17(10) Cash payments involved in the exchange.

ANN ¶10,015.17(15) Determination of the value of property received.

ANN ¶10,015.17(20) Receipt of property without ascertainable fair market value.

ANN ¶10,015.17(30) Note received as payment.

ANN ¶10,015.17(35) Virtual currency transactions.

ANN ¶10,015.18(5) Determination of gain or loss.

→ You can click on the hyperlink to reach the annotation or scroll through the annotations link until you reach the one you want.

Illustration 12-12. USTR Annotation ¶ 10,015.17(5)

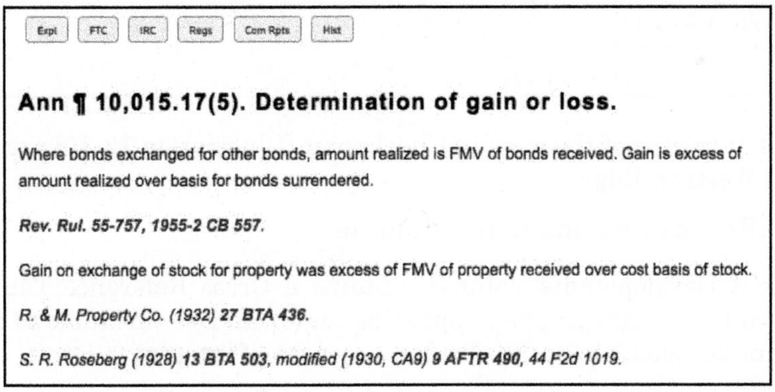

Expl FTC IRC Regs Com Rpts Hist

Ann ¶ 10,015.17(5). Determination of gain or loss.

Where bonds exchanged for other bonds, amount realized is FMV of bonds received. Gain is excess of amount realized over basis for bonds surrendered.

Rev. Rul. 55-757, 1955-2 CB 557.

Gain on exchange of stock for property was excess of FMV of property received over cost basis of stock.

R. & M. Property Co. (1932) ***27 BTA 436.***

S. R. Roseberg (1928) ***13 BTA 503****, modified (1930, CA9)* ***9 AFTR 490****, 44 F2d 1019.*

→ If there was more recent material that had not been inserted into this page, there would be an AdvAnnos box at the top of the page. [See Illustration 12-10.]

Illustration 12-13. USTR Advance Annotation Links

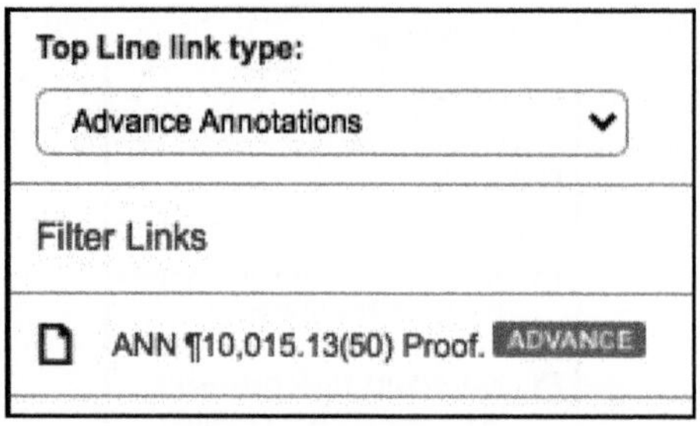

→ Make sure to check the advanced annotations to confirm that none of them relates to the topic you are researching.

→ Based on the numbering, you can tell that the annotation relates to I.R.C. § 1001.

Illustration 12-14. USTR Explanation on Westlaw Edge

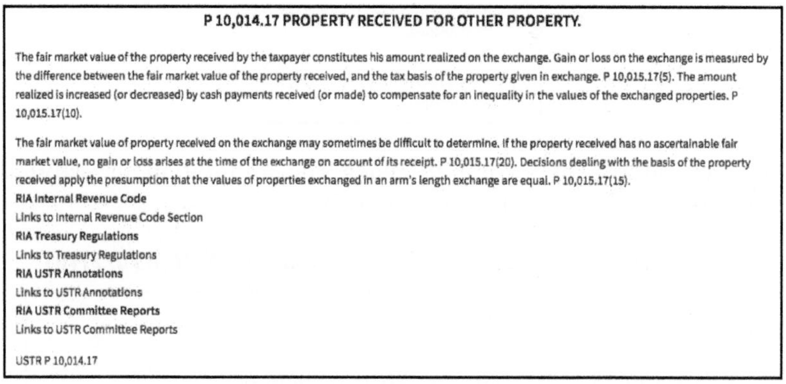

P 10,014.17 PROPERTY RECEIVED FOR OTHER PROPERTY.

The fair market value of the property received by the taxpayer constitutes his amount realized on the exchange. Gain or loss on the exchange is measured by the difference between the fair market value of the property received, and the tax basis of the property given in exchange. P 10,015.17(5). The amount realized is increased (or decreased) by cash payments received (or made) to compensate for an inequality in the values of the exchanged properties. P 10,015.17(10).

The fair market value of property received on the exchange may sometimes be difficult to determine. If the property received has no ascertainable fair market value, no gain or loss arises at the time of the exchange on account of its receipt. P 10,015.17(20). Decisions dealing with the basis of the property received apply the presumption that the values of properties exchanged in an arm's length exchange are equal. P 10,015.17(15).

RIA Internal Revenue Code

Links to Internal Revenue Code Section

RIA Treasury Regulations

Links to Treasury Regulations

RIA USTR Annotations

Links to USTR Annotations

RIA USTR Committee Reports

Links to USTR Committee Reports

USTR P 10,014.17

→ The links at the top of the page in Checkpoint [Illustration 12-10] are at the bottom of the page in Westlaw Edge.

e. Recent Developments Volume

The Recent Developments Volume contains a Cross Reference Table that cross-references from USTR paragraphs to updating material. Use this table to determine if a recent ruling or decision has been issued in any area of interest.

USTR reproduces the updating material in the Recent Developments volume (IRS rulings and procedures) or the A.F.T.R.2d Decisions Advance Sheets volumes (texts of decisions rendered by courts other than the Tax Court). The Recent Developments volume provides Public Law number, title or subject, and introduction and signing dates for recent acts. There are also tax calendars and lists of IRS publications.

f. A.F.T.R.2d Decisions Advance Sheets Volumes

These volumes contain the texts of recent income tax decisions from all courts except the Tax Court.[31] You can locate these items by Code section using the Cross Reference Table in the Recent Developments volume. Decisions appear in the order they were

[31] Recent decisions involving estate and gift taxes or excise taxes appear in the RIA services covering these topics. Decisions for all taxes appear in the A.F.T.R. hardbound volumes.

received rather than in Code section order. Decisions printed in this volume will later be issued in hardbound volumes as part of the A.F.T.R. reporter service discussed in Chapter 10.

g. Federal Tax Regulations Volume

This volume prints the Preambles to proposed regulations. Coverage is chronological. A Finding List is in Code section order. Regulations whose numbers do not correspond to a Code section appear before traditionally numbered regulations. This list indicates Federal Register publication date.

h. Citator

The RIA Citator is not part of USTR and does not cross-reference to it (except for referencing the paragraph where IRS rulings can be found). You can use this citator with any looseleaf service to determine the status of both judicial decisions and IRS items. The online version of the RIA Citator is discussed in Chapter 11.[32]

C. Subject Arrangement: Multiple Topics

This section covers four subject-based services. Many libraries lack at least one of them or carry others not discussed here. Each covers a wide range of topics using a subject matter arrangement. Each is available in print and online versions.

If you use several services, you will get quicker access to relevant items in the second (or later) service by using tables for cases and other primary sources. After you obtain these items from one service, you can use them to locate relevant discussion in the other service. If the second service lacks these tables,[33] use its topical or Code section index.

1. Federal Tax Coordinator 2d

This weekly service contains excellent discussions of all areas of taxation, with minimal coverage of employment taxes. Federal Tax Coordinator identifies most items by paragraph number. It identifies the text of Code, regulations, and treaties by page number. The online Federal Tax Update newsletter is available in both daily and weekly versions.

Material in each volume is discussed in the following paragraphs. Illustrations are from the online version in Checkpoint; Federal Tax Coordinator 2d is also available in Westlaw Edge. As is true for the Code-based services, volume placement is not important when using the online versions.

a. Topic-Index Volume

This volume contains an extensive Topic Index, which you can use to locate appropriate discussion in the text volumes.[34] There are main and current sections.

---

[32] The first series of this Citator (which was published by Prentice-Hall) covers 1863–1954. A library that holds those volumes may shelve them with the RIA Citator 2d, with other citator services, or with archived materials.

[33] For example, Tax Management Portfolios lack case and rulings tables. They have excellent Code and topical indexes.

[34] Checkpoint includes the Federal Tax Coordinator 2d Topic Index under Table of Contents in the menu bar under Federal Library>Federal Editorial Materials>Federal Indexes>Federal Tax Coordinator 2d Topic Index.

b. Finding Tables Volumes

Finding Tables indicate where items are discussed in the text volumes, but they are no longer updated in the print edition. These tables cover the Internal Revenue Code, Public Laws since 1991, other United States Code titles, temporary and final regulations, Treasury Decisions for the past six months, Labor regulations, and proposed regulations. A table of Code sections indicates the relevant volumes and chapters covering them.

A Law-Regulation Table provides a list of Code sections for which the regulations do not reflect the most recent Code amendment. This table is in Code section order and includes the relevant acts amending that Code section.

A Rulings and Releases Table gives cross-references to discussions in the text volumes or an indication that the ruling has been revoked or otherwise modified. The table arranges each type of IRS document chronologically. Letter rulings are included.

An alphabetical list of cases provides cross-references to discussions in the text volumes. This list includes citations to various case reporter services, often including both A.F.T.R. and U.S.T.C. in addition to reporters such as Federal Reporter. A Supreme Court Docket and a Court of Appeals Docket indicate where discussion of pending cases appears in the text volumes.

c. Practice Aids Volume

This volume includes sample letters to clients on a wide variety of topics.[35] [See Illustration 14-3, *infra* page 280.] It also includes planning checklists,[36] tax tables,[37] a tax calendar, interest and annuity tables,[38] and tables showing where tax return forms[39] are discussed in the text. Other reference items, such as applicable federal rates and per diem amounts, appear in the text volumes. A Current Legislation Table lists acts since 1993 by Public Law number, subject, committee reports, and relevant dates.

d. Text Volumes

The text volumes are arranged by chapters using a subject matter approach. Discussions in each chapter include liberal use of citations and analysis of unresolved matters. Each chapter has the following arrangement: a Detailed Reference Table for topics included; cross-references to topics of potential relevance discussed in other chapters; discussion of each topic, including extensive footnote references; and text of Code and regulations sections applicable to the chapters being discussed. Topics are subdivided into "paragraphs."

One of these volumes contains the texts of United States income, estate, and gift tax treaties that are currently in effect and textual material dealing with the treaties. United States and OECD model treaties are also included. This volume discusses the

---

[35] Checkpoint includes Client Letters under Table of Contents in the menu bar under Federal Library>Federal Editorial Materials>Practice Aids>Client Letters.

[36] Checkpoint includes Checklists under Table of Contents in the menu bar under Federal Library>Federal Editorial Materials>Practice Aids>Checklists.

[37] Checkpoint includes the AFR and IRS valuation tables under Tools in the menu bar under i-Tables.

[38] Checkpoint includes this information under Table of Contents in the menu bar under Federal Library>Federal Editorial Materials>Practice Aids>Tables & Rates.

[39] Checkpoint includes the Form/Line Finder under Table of Contents in the menu bar under Federal Library>Federal Editorial Materials>Practice Aids>Form/Line Finders and Return Guides. From there you will select your year, form, and line to get a list of where that information is discussed in the text.

treaties and includes a list of treaties awaiting ratification or exchange of instruments of ratification.

Illustration 12-15. Federal Tax Coordinator 2d Contents

− ☐ Federal Tax Coordinator 2d
+ ☐ Chapter A Individuals and Self-Employment Tax
+ ☐ Chapter A-7000 Alternative Minimum Tax
+ ☐ Chapter B Partnerships
+ ☐ Chapter C Income Taxation of Trusts, Estates, Beneficiaries and Decedents
+ ☐ Chapter D How Corporations Are Taxed.
+ ☐ Chapter D-2500 Accumulated Earnings Tax; Personal Holding Company Tax
+ ☐ Chapter D-3900 Exempt Organizations, Private Foundations
+ ☐ Chapter E Special Corporations and Organizations

→ When using this service online, focus on chapters, not volumes.

e. Proposed Regulations and I.R.B.

Volumes covering proposed regulations reproduce them in the order in which they were issued, along with Preambles and Federal Register citations.[40] A cross-reference table lists proposed regulations in Code section order. Proposed regulations issued as temporary regulations are reproduced only in the Text Volumes. Another volume contains reprints of the weekly I.R.B.

---

[40] Checkpoint includes the Preambles under Table of Contents in the menu bar under Federal Library>Federal Source Materials>Final, Temporary, Proposed Regulations & Preambles>Preambles to Final and Temporary Regulations (Treasury Decisions).

Illustration 12-16. Federal Tax Coordinator 2d Text

¶K-5422. "Interest" defined for purposes of business interest limitation.

Proposed regs under theCode Sec. 163(j) business interest limitation (¶ K-5420 et seq.), on which taxpayers may rely until final regs are published in the Federal Register (see ¶ K-5420.1),[30] define "interest" as that term is used in the proposed reliance regs.[31]

Under the proposed reliance regs, the term "interest" means any amount described in:

. . . Prop Reg § 1.163(j)-1(b)(20)(i) (compensation for use or forbearance of money, see ¶ K-5422.1),

. . . Prop Reg § 1.163(j)-1(b)(20)(ii) (sweps with significant nonperiodic payments, see ¶ K-5422.2),

. . . Prop Reg § 1.163(j)-1(b)(20)(iii) (amounts closely related to interest, treated as interest, see ¶ K-5422.3), or

. . . Prop Reg § 1.163(j)-1(b)(20)(iv) (anti-avoidance rule for amounts predominantly associated with the time value of money, see ¶ K-5422.4).[32]

The proposed reliance regs provide a complete definition of interest that addresses all transactions that are commonly understood to produce interest income and expense, including transactions that may have been entered into to avoid the business interest limitation (see ¶ K-5422.4).[33]

In addition to interest associated with conventional debt instruments, the proposed reliance regs apply to transactions that are indebtedness in substance although not in form.[34]

Because there's no generally applicable Code or reg provision that addresses when a financial instrument is debt or when a payment is interest, the proposed reliance regs draw on past guidance and case law, including Notice 94-47, which describes the factors that distinguish debt from equity, and *Deputy v. Dupont* (¶ K-5020A), where the Supreme Court defined interest as compensation for the use or forbearance of money (see ¶ K-5431.2).[35]

[30] Preamble to Prop Regs, 12/28/2018.

[31] Prop Reg § 1.163(j)-1(a) ["taxpayers...may apply," Prop Reg § 1.163(j)-1(c)]; Prop Reg § 1.163(j)-1(b)(20) ["taxpayers...may apply," Prop Reg § 1.163(j)-1(c)].

[32] Prop Reg § 1.163(j)-1(b)(20) ["taxpayers...may apply," Prop Reg § 1.163(j)-1(c)].

[33] Preamble to Prop Regs, 12/28/2018.

[34] Preamble to Prop Regs, 12/28/2018.

[35] Preamble to Prop Regs, 12/28/2018.

→ Federal Tax Coordinator uses paragraphs for most cross-references.

Illustration 12-17. Federal Tax Coordinator 2d Topic Search

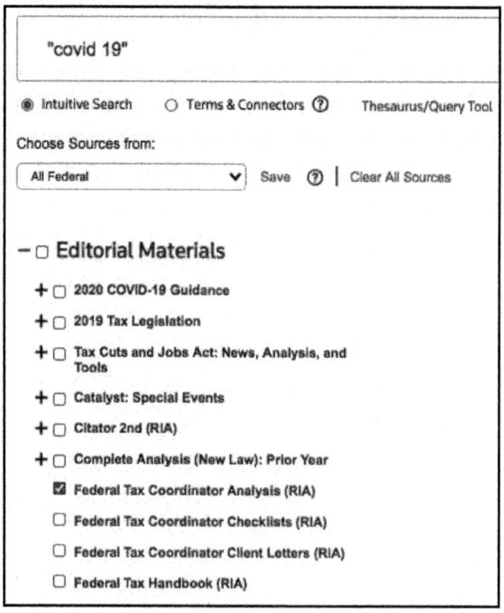

→ This Terms & Connectors topic search involved "covid 19." A list of Checkpoint terms and connectors appears in Table 17-G, *infra* page 316.

Illustration 12-18. Results of Topic Search

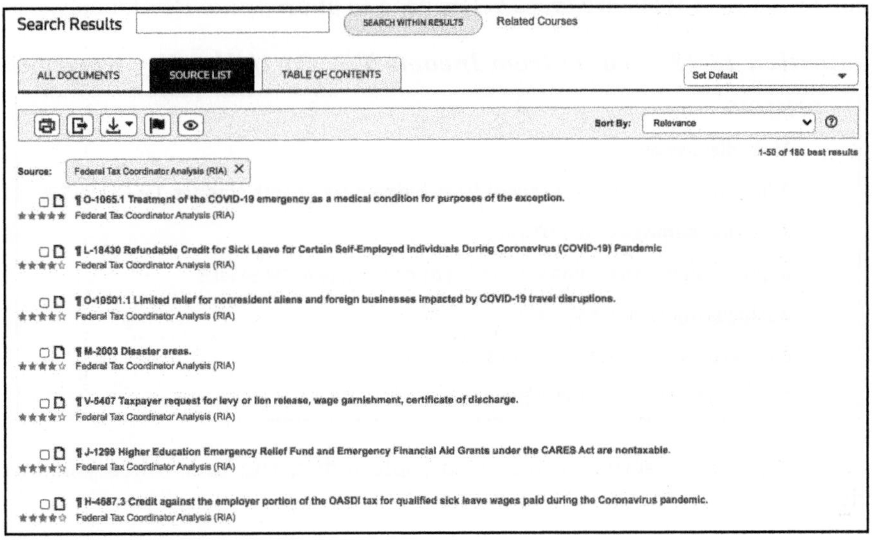

→ Checkpoint uses stars to rank items for relevance.

2. Tax Management Portfolios

The Bureau of National Affairs, Inc. (BNA) was acquired by Bloomberg in 2011, was initially called Bloomberg BNA, and is now a subgroup within the Bloomberg Industry Group (Bloomberg).[41] Bloomberg issues four main series of Tax Management Portfolios: U.S. Income; U.S. International; Accounting for Income Taxes; and Estates, Gifts and Trusts. Portfolios covering other countries are not part of the U.S. International series. You can find Country Portfolios under the International tab on the BNA: Tax home page. They are part of the Foreign Income Portfolio series. The U.S. International Portfolios are also available in this section of the website.

Bloomberg subdivides each series into several softbound booklets that cover narrow areas of tax law in great depth.[42] [See Illustrations 12-19 and 12-20.] Each Portfolio refers to other Portfolios containing information relevant to a particular problem. The print Portfolios are no longer available for purchase without an online subscription.

The print and online versions are similar in format. In addition to a Table of Contents, each Portfolio includes a Portfolio Description, a Detailed Analysis section with extensive footnoting, and a Worksheets/Working Papers section. The Worksheets can include checklists, forms that can be used as models in drafting documents, and texts of relevant congressional and IRS materials. Bloomberg supplements the Portfolios or completely revises them whenever warranted by new developments.

The print edition of the Portfolio Index includes a Portfolio Classification Guide and a detailed Master Subject Index for each series; the online version is strictly by topic in alphabetical order. A Master Code Section Index covers all series; if there is a primary

---

41 A BNA link at the bottom of the Bloomberg Law home page takes you to a page with three categories: Portfolios; Class Outlines & Notes; and Manuals. None of these is limited to tax. The home page link to Tax gives tax-focused options.

42 Subdivisions are so narrow that several Portfolios may cover one Code section.

Portfolio on point, it indicates it as "Main discussion." Numerical IRS Forms and IRS Publications Finding Tables are cross-referenced to appropriate Portfolios.

Illustration 12-19. Topic from Income Tax Portfolios Key Word Index

DAMAGES

Main discussion, TM 522

Allocation of amounts received from judgments or settlements, TM 522.VII.B.8

Antitrust damages. *See* ANTITRUST

Blight of summons damages, eminent domain law, TM 545.II.B

Business injuries, TM 501.IX.D.2

Capital assets, exclusion from status, TM 562.I.A.5

Collection of tax, unlawful IRS actions, TM 638.XVI.D

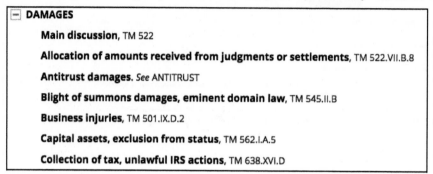

→ Although the online screen refers to a topic index, the link takes you to the Key Word Index.

Illustration 12-20. Discussion in Portfolio 522-4th

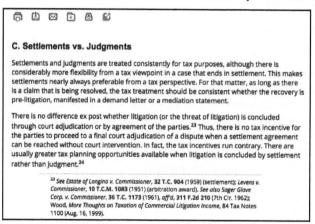

C. Settlements vs. Judgments

Settlements and judgments are treated consistently for tax purposes, although there is considerably more flexibility from a tax viewpoint in a case that ends in settlement. This makes settlements nearly always preferable from a tax perspective. For that matter, as long as there is a claim that is being resolved, the tax treatment should be consistent whether the recovery is pre-litigation, manifested in a demand letter or a mediation statement.

There is no difference ex post whether litigation (or the threat of litigation) is concluded through court adjudication or by agreement of the parties.[23] Thus, there is no tax incentive for the parties to proceed to a final court adjudication of a dispute when a settlement agreement can be reached without court intervention. In fact, the tax incentives run contrary. There are usually greater tax planning opportunities available when litigation is concluded by settlement rather than judgment.[24]

[23] *See Estate of Longino v. Commissioner*, **32 T.C. 904** (1959) (settlement); *Levens v. Commissioner*, **10 T.C.M. 1083** (1951) (arbitration award). *See also Sager Glove Corp. v. Commissioner*, **36 T.C. 1173** (1961), *aff'd*, **311 F.2d 210** (7th Cir. 1962); Wood, *More Thoughts on Taxation of Commercial Litigation Income*, 84 Tax Notes 1100 (Aug. 16, 1999).

→ The print Portfolios place the footnotes at the bottom of the page.

→ The online Portfolios place the Table of Contents as a link to the left of the Portfolio text. You can select between Full Contents and Section Contents.

Bloomberg also publishes the biweekly Tax Management Memorandum, which provides analysis of current developments, unsettled problems, and other significant items.[43]

3. Mertens, Law of Federal Income Taxation

The original Mertens service contained five sets of volumes: treatise; rulings; Code; Code commentary; and regulations. Only the treatise and rulings materials have continued in their original format. Many libraries retain the original materials, which

[43] The Tax Management Memorandum appears under News & Journals on the Bloomberg Law: Tax home page.

may still be useful for historical research. Mertens is available in print and on Westlaw Edge.

a. Treatise

The treatise volumes closely resemble general encyclopedias such as Am. Jur. 2d and C.J.S. in format.[44] Material is presented by subject matter with extensive footnoting. Treatise materials are supplemented monthly; supplements are cumulated semiannually. Supplemental material appears at the beginning of each volume rather than at the beginning of each chapter. Tables and indexes are updated quarterly.

Discussions include extensive historical background information. Because its discussions are so thorough, Mertens is often cited in judicial decisions.[45]

Illustration 12-21. Discussion in Mertens on Westlaw Edge

2 Mertens Law of Fed. Income Tax'n § 17:20

Mertens Law of Federal Income Taxation | May 2020 Update
Chapter 17. Determination of Taxpayer
Revised by Carina Bryant, J.D.

III. Receipt for the Benefit of Another

§ 17:20. Nominees

References
Nominees may be disregarded for tax purposes. [1] "A nominee is one who holds bare legal title to property for the benefit of another." [2] Nominee "connotes the delegation of authority to the nominee in a representative or nominal capacity only, and does not connote the transfer or assignment to the nominee of any property in, or ownership of, the rights of the person nominating him." [3] The same tax consequences that apply to agents and conduits apply to nominees. Indeed, the terms "agent" and "nominee" are sometimes used interchangeably. [4]

The Tables Volume (available in the print version) contains tables indicating where primary source materials are discussed in the treatise volumes. These include the Internal Revenue Code, other United States Code titles, Treasury regulations, other Code of Federal Regulations titles, and IRS materials. IRS materials covered include items printed in the Cumulative Bulletin, letter rulings, and technical advice memoranda. Two other tables provide Cumulative Bulletin citations for revenue rulings and revenue procedures. The Table of Cases Volume has similar cross-references for judicial decisions. These tables are unnecessary in the online version because you can search by citation.

The Index Volume contains a detailed topic index. The monthly Developments & Highlights newsletter in the Current Materials Volume includes lists of recent tax articles. Westlaw Edge includes Mertens Current Tax Highlights in addition to the treatise volumes.

b. Rulings

The print Rulings volumes contain the texts of revenue rulings and procedures. Notices, announcements, and other IRS items are excluded. Each volume covers a

---

44 These encyclopedias cover a wide variety of topics. Discussions of taxation appear in separate volumes within each service. A tax-oriented looseleaf service or treatise will probably provide more extensive information.

45 See, e.g., *Adolphson v. Commissioner*, 842 F.3d 478, 484 (2016); *United States v. Chaffee*, 2019 WL 8403506, at *11 (E.D. Mich. 2019); *Gerdau Macsteel, Inc. v. Commissioner*, 139 T.C. 67, 161 (2012); *Speltz v. Commissioner*, 124 T.C. 165, 178 (2005), aff'd, 454 F.3d 782 (8th Cir. 2006).

particular time period and includes rulings in numerical order, followed by procedures in numerical order. Mertens adds current items monthly.

The looseleaf current volume has Code-Rulings and Code-Procedures Tables, which provide chronological listings of every revenue ruling or procedure involving income tax Code sections or subsections.[46] There are separate tables for the current year and for prior years (beginning with 1954).

A Rulings Status Table lists the most recent revenue ruling or procedure affecting the validity of a previously published item. Mertens indicates the effect on the earlier item (e.g., modified, revoked). A separate section of this volume includes Cumulative Bulletin citations for revenue rulings and procedures. The Code-Rulings and Rulings Status Tables are not always as current as the rest of the service; citators are likely to provide more accurate information.

c. Code

Each print Code volume contained all income tax provisions enacted or amended during a particular time period (one or more years). Textual notations (diamond shapes and brackets) indicate additions and deletions. A historical note indicates Act, section, and effective date and can be used to reconstruct the prior language. The subject matter index in the looseleaf current volume cross-references each topic to applicable Code sections. This material does not cover the 1986 Code.[47]

d. Code Commentary

Looseleaf volumes of Code Commentary initially provided useful short explanations of statutory provisions as well as cross-references to the discussions in the treatise materials. More recent items are limited to references to statutory changes or to recent cases or rulings for the particular Code section.

e. Regulations

Regulations materials have undergone change since the mid-1990s. In a separate service, but using the Mertens name, the publisher currently issues a softbound set of regulations in force and proposed regulations. Regulations appear in Code section order; there is also a subject matter index. New matter issued during the year is filed in a looseleaf Current Developments and Status Table binder. The service also includes looseleaf volumes containing the Preambles issued since 1995 for proposed, temporary, and final regulations.

The volumes in the discontinued regulations service included the texts of all income tax regulations issued or amended during a particular time period (two or more years). Publication was in Code section order.

The discontinued volumes have several useful features. Textual notations (diamond shapes and brackets) indicate deletions, additions, and other changes in amended regulations. A historical note, from which you can determine the regulation's prior wording, follows. This facilitates research into early administrative interpretations.

---

[46] Although Mertens is an income tax service, these tables do cover estate and gift tax rulings. However, that coverage does not extend back to 1954.

[47] Mertens currently publishes softbound Code volumes, but they are not cross-referenced to the Law of Federal Income Taxation service.

Each volume also contains a section reproducing the Preamble to the Treasury Decision or Notice of Proposed Rulemaking announcing each proposed and final regulation.

4. Rabkin & Johnson, Federal Income, Gift and Estate Taxation

Rabkin & Johnson originally had three segments: treatise; Code and Congressional Reports; and Regulations. Only the treatise materials are currently being updated. Supplementation is frequent (but not more than monthly), with New Matter pages appearing near the beginning of each volume rather than at the beginning of each chapter. This service is also available on Lexis+ and is updated quarterly.[48]

a. Treatise

The treatise materials consist of explanatory materials and two volumes of reference material designed to facilitate research in the remainder of the set. It is arranged in chapters; each chapter is divided into sections that use chapter numbers in their prefixes. Cross-referencing is done by section number.

The initial volumes contain tables and other user aids. The following indexes and tables cross-reference to discussions in the treatise volumes: topical Index; Table of Statutory References (Internal Revenue Code and other parts of United States Code); Table of Cases; and Table of Regulations, Rulings and Releases (publicly available IRS materials in addition to revenue rulings). The Table of Cases indicates discussion in both text and footnotes. The Lexis+ version includes the topical Index.

There is a detailed User's Guide to using Rabkin & Johnson. This volume also contains checklists of deductions (arranged by the tax form involved). In addition to rates, the Tax Rates section includes imputed interest rates, annuity valuation tables, depreciation tables, and similar helpful tables. Tax Court and IRS Practice Rules also appear in this volume. This material is available in print and on Lexis+.

The remaining volumes contain textual discussion of the law. While discussions are thorough, they do not purport to cover all types of authority. Letter rulings are rarely discussed or cited as authority "[b]ecause they lack precedential value."[49]

---

[48] Lexis+ includes this looseleaf as "Federal Income, Gift and Estate Taxation." You can find it by typing the title into the search bar; the link will appear underneath. If you search for "Rabkin & Johnson," you will not find this material. You will instead find form books with the authors' names in the title.

[49] 1A RABKIN & JOHNSON, FEDERAL INCOME, GIFT AND ESTATE TAXATION § G 1.03[6].

Illustration 12-22. Discussion in Rabkin & Johnson on Lexis+

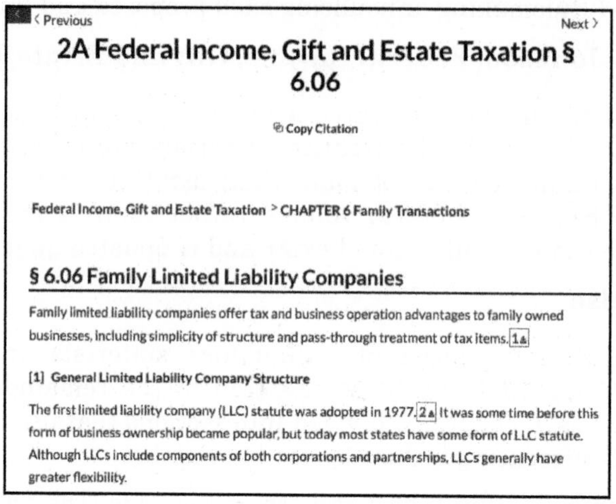

< Previous Next >

2A Federal Income, Gift and Estate Taxation § 6.06

Copy Citation

Federal Income, Gift and Estate Taxation > CHAPTER 6 Family Transactions

§ 6.06 Family Limited Liability Companies

Family limited liability companies offer tax and business operation advantages to family owned businesses, including simplicity of structure and pass-through treatment of tax items. 1

[1] **General Limited Liability Company Structure**

The first limited liability company (LLC) statute was adopted in 1977. 2 It was some time before this form of business ownership became popular, but today most states have some form of LLC statute. Although LLCs include components of both corporations and partnerships, LLCs generally have greater flexibility.

→ There are hyperlinks to primary source items in the online version. Click on the footnote number to gain access to the hyperlink.

→ Footnotes to other sources (e.g., articles) include citations but not hyperlinks.

b. Code and Congressional Reports

These volumes contain the text of the Code in Code section order.[50] You can use the Legislative History notes following each Code subsection to determine how amendments changed prior statutory language. These notes indicate the act, section, and date for amendments, but they do not provide a citation to Statutes at Large.

The legislative history notes refer to congressional committee reports explaining each provision. Relevant excerpts from these reports, including full citations, appear at the end of each Code section. These materials cover only the 1954 Code.

There is a topical index to the Code materials. There are also tables cross-referencing 1939 and 1954 Code sections. Because these tables were printed in 1963, they miss section number changes that occurred after 1963.

c. Regulations

The final volumes print 1954 Code regulations. Regulations appear in numerical order and are preceded by T.D. numbers and dates for the original version and amendments.[51] There is no list of regulations in T.D. number order. Regulations sections are cross-referenced to subject matter discussions in the treatise volumes.

Selected proposed regulations appear in numerical order. A Table of Contents contains a numerical list of included provisions. Both the Table of Contents and the

---

[50] This service omits miscellaneous excise taxes other than those involving registration-required obligations, public charities, private foundations, qualified pension plans, real estate investment trusts, and the crude oil windfall profit tax.

[51] Federal Register dates are instead given for IRS procedural rules. These materials do not include the text of a regulation's prior versions.

heading for each proposed regulation indicate the Federal Register date and a cross-reference to treatise discussion. The volumes do not include Preambles.

Table 12-A. Cross-Referencing Method

Service	*Method*
SFTR	¶
USTR	¶
Federal Tax Coordinator 2d	¶
Tax Management Portfolios	Outline
Mertens	§
Rabkin & Johnson	§

D. Subject Arrangement: Limited Scope

Various publishers issue textual materials discussing a limited number of Code sections, such as those covering S corporations.[52] These texts are extremely useful for research involving complex areas of tax law. In recent years, the number of texts covering a particular topic, and the number of topics covered, have both grown explosively. You can locate at least one text on almost any topic, from tax problems of the elderly to estate planning for farmers. While these materials are periodically supplemented, their updating is rarely as frequent as that for the services in sections B and C.

The following materials are a representative sample.

- Bittker & Eustice, Federal Income Taxation of Corporations and Shareholders
- Blanchard, Federal Income Taxation of Corporations Filing Consolidated Returns
- Blankenship, Tax Planning for Retirees
- Dubroff et al., Federal Income Taxation of Corporations Filing Consolidated Returns
- Ginsburg et al., Mergers, Acquisitions, and Buyouts
- Hardesty, Electronic Commerce: Taxation and Planning
- Hennessey et al., The Consolidated Tax Return: Principles, Practices, Planning
- Kuntz & Peroni, U.S. International Taxation
- McKee et al., Federal Taxation of Partnerships and Partners
- Schneider, Federal Income Taxation of Inventories
- Stephens et al., Federal Estate and Gift Taxation

52 Form books (Chapter 14) may also include extensive textual material.

Other potential sources include law school casebooks or textbooks, which may include copious notes. CLE providers such as Practising Law Institute regularly publish softbound volumes of course materials. Finally, the multivolume Bittker & Lokken, Federal Taxation of Income, Estates, and Gifts, provides thorough treatment of difficult issues.

E. Problems

1. Locate the paragraph reference in Standard Federal Tax Reporter or United States Tax Reporter assigned by your instructor. Then use the service's updating materials to find all updating references to the original item. Cite to each new item's location in that service and its "official" location (e.g., I.R.B. for a revenue ruling).

2. Determine if the following items are income or if their cost is deductible. (Hint: Use "checklists" in Standard Federal Tax Reporter.)

   a. Combat zone pay received for military service

   b. Reclining chair for cardiac patient

3. What was the short-term applicable federal rate for June 2005 (assuming annual compounding)? How did you find this?

4. On August 9, 2020, one of your best clients, Mr. Ginger, walked into your office to ask a question. He said his granddaughter just started college and he paid her first-semester tuition of $20,000. He read on the Internet about something called the American Opportunity Tax Credit and wants to know if he can claim the credit on his income tax return. You learned later his granddaughter is claimed as a dependent on her parent's income tax return. What did you tell him, and where did you find your authority? (Hint: The American Opportunity Tax Credit was formerly known as the "Hope Scholarship Credit.")

5. Indicate all Tax Management Portfolios discussing the I.R.C. section listed below. Your instructor will tell you whether to indicate the Portfolio titles, numbers, or authors.

   a. 74

   b. 534

   c. 1237

   d. 1253

6. Indicate who authored or revised the item below and its Portfolio or chapter number.

   a. Tax Management Portfolio: Planning for Authors, Musicians, Artists, and Collectors

   b. Tax Management Portfolio: Dynasty Trusts

   c. Mertens chapter: Constructive Receipt

   d. Mertens chapter: Preferred Stock Bailouts

7. Indicate whether there is a Tax Management Portfolio for the country listed. If there is, provide the Portfolio number from the Foreign Income Portfolios: Country Portfolios listing.

   a. Chile

   b. Ecuador

   c. Singapore

   d. Slovakia

Chapter 13

LEGAL PERIODICALS AND NONGOVERNMENTAL REPORTS

A. Introduction

This chapter provides information about periodical literature. It covers methods for locating both citations to articles and the articles themselves. It also discusses determining if a judicial opinion has cited an article or if an article has cited a judicial opinion or other authority.

Although periodical literature is a secondary source, and articles cannot be used as authority for avoiding the substantial understatement penalty, they are still important research tools. Because articles written for practitioner-oriented journals (or posted online before their actual publication in peer-reviewed or student-edited law reviews) may appear more quickly than do treatise supplements, they are valuable tools for learning about new or amended Code sections, regulations, and judicial decisions. In addition, articles may provide citations to primary source materials that you can use as authority.

This chapter also briefly covers reports issued by nongovernmental organizations. These include professional groups and think tanks. Reports issued by these groups (or testimony by their representatives at congressional or Treasury Department hearings) may impact legislation or regulations.

B. Categorizing Periodicals

Commentary on particular tax problems appears in various legal periodicals. These include general focus, student-edited law reviews, publications that focus on a broad variety of tax-related topics, and publications that specialize in a particular area of taxation.

Although general focus, student-edited law reviews occasionally include tax articles, other sources generally carry a larger number of relevant items.[1] These other sources include law-school-based law reviews (student-edited or peer-reviewed[2]) that focus on taxation, tax-oriented periodicals published by professional groups or commercial entities, and tax-oriented newsletters. Although not technically periodicals, tax institute proceedings contain useful information and are covered by several periodicals indexes.

[1] See Joseph Bankman & Paul L. Caron, *California Dreamin': Tax Scholarship in a Time of Fiscal Crises*, 48 U.C. DAVIS L. REV. 405, 410 (2014); William J. Turnier, *Tax (and Lots of Other) Scholars Need Not Apply: The Changing Venue for Scholarship*, 50 J. LEGAL EDUC. 189 (2000).

[2] Peer-reviewed publications may have student editors, who edit work that was accepted after review by faculty members or practitioners.

Table 13-A. Representative Periodicals Titles

Category	*Title*
Student-edited	Business, Entrepreneurship & Tax Law Review
Student-edited	Columbia Journal of Tax Law
Student-edited	Houston Business and Tax Law Journal
Student-edited	Virginia Tax Review
Peer-reviewed	Florida Tax Review
Peer-reviewed	Pittsburgh Tax Review
Peer-reviewed	Tax Law Review
Peer-reviewed	The Tax Lawyer
General tax focus	Journal of Taxation
General tax focus	TAXES—The Tax Magazine
General tax focus	The Practical Tax Lawyer
Specialized focus	Real Estate Taxation
Newsletter	Tax Notes Federal
Institute	Heckerling Institute on Estate Planning
Institute	NYU Institute on Federal Taxation

C. Citations to Periodicals

Your search for relevant publications may begin in a variety of sources. Citators may provide citations to articles. Other publications digest articles. Digests may cover a particular topic or a general range of topics; they generally cover fewer articles than do the other tools.

Although citators and digests are useful, periodicals indexes are the most comprehensive sources for compiling lists of articles. This section divides indexes into three categories—general legal indexes, specialized indexes, and other indexes.

General legal periodicals indexes such as Current Law Index, Index to Legal Periodicals, and LegalTrac cover all areas of law. Index to Federal Tax Articles covers only tax-related materials; its coverage begins in 1913. The third category of indexes covers areas related to law (such as political science, economics, and history) and nontax specialized legal topics (such as indexes to articles published in other countries).

The general and tax-oriented indexes differ in their indexing methods, publication frequency, and lists of publications covered. All are available in print versions; the general indexes are also available in electronic formats. Law-related indexes are available in a variety of formats.

Section F illustrates searching for articles in several sources discussed in this chapter. Those illustrations cover electronic searches (conducted in late July 2020) for articles written by Professor Gregg Polsky. These searches involved the following services and webpages: Legal Resource Index on Westlaw Edge; general law review databases on Lexis+ and Westlaw Edge; HeinOnline; SSRN; Google Scholar; the author's own webpage and his listing on his law school's Digital Commons page. The different results obtained illustrate the risks involved in compiling a bibliography from a single source.

We found only one Gregg Polsky in these databases. Our search would have been more difficult if the author had a more common name (e.g., John Smith) or had used different names at various points in time (e.g., reflecting a marriage, divorce, or other status change). An author's webpage may thus be a good starting point.

Publications discussed below are categorized by type, beginning with periodicals indexes.

1. General Legal Periodicals Indexes

a. Current Law Index; Legal Resource Index

The Current Law Index (CLI) indexed articles by subject, author/title, case name, and statute. Its Table of Statutes included a heading for Internal Revenue Code. Because that section listed articles in Code section order, CLI was the most convenient print-based general index for researching articles by Code section. However, it is no longer in print.

An online version, legal resource index (LRI), is available through Westlaw Edge; it covers material indexed since 1980. Lexis+ also carries LRI; it indicates that coverage begins in January 1977.

b. Index to Legal Periodicals & Books

Index to Legal Periodicals[3] includes tax articles in its subject matter listings. It indexes articles by subject/author, case name, and act name. Because it indexes by statute, you cannot search the print version by Code section.

ILP indexes fewer tax-related publications than do the other indexes, and it imposes page minimums for indexed material.[4] Because ILP began publication in 1908, it is more useful than CLI for historical research.[5]

ILP was initially published by Wilson and is now published by EBSCO Information Services. Its electronic offerings cover material indexed since mid-1981. The Index to Legal Periodicals Retrospective: 1908–1981 supplements the coverage available in ILP. Although this service begins in 1908, initial coverage dates vary by periodical. For example, coverage of Tax Law Review begins in 1945 (volume 1); coverage of The Tax Lawyer begins in 1967 (volume 21).

c. LegalTrac

LegalTrac by Gale (a part of Cengage), an expanded web-based version of CLI, indexes more than 1,200 law sources (law reviews, legal newspapers, specialty publications, bar association journals, etc.) and has more than 200 titles in full text in

---

[3] ILP began covering books in 1994.

[4] ILP has steadily reduced its page minimums. The minimum was five pages in volume 38, two pages in volume 39, and one-half page in volume 42.

[5] Renumbering of ILP volumes occurred in 1926. A related series was published between 1888 and 1908.

PDF format. The database also covers United States federal and state cases, laws and regulations, legal practice and taxation, as well as British Commonwealth, European Union, and international law.

There are many tax-related publications in its database. Users can search by subject, by publication, or for a word/phrase in the entire document. These searches can be restricted by date or publication.

2. Other Periodicals Indexes

Representative titles in this category include Business Periodicals Index Retrospective (1913–1982) and Business Source Elite, Index to Periodical Articles Related to Law (1958–2007), and Social Sciences Index Retrospective (1907–1983) and Social Sciences Full Text. If your problem involves another country, indexes such as Index to Foreign Legal Periodicals and Australian Legal Journals Index may be useful. As Table 13-B illustrates, many nonlaw publications print articles relevant to taxation.

Table 13-B. Examples of Tax-Related Articles in Nonlaw Journals

Ajay Agrawal et al., *Tax Credits and Small Firm R&D Spending*, 12 AM. ECON. J.: ECON. POL'Y 1 (2020)
Donald B. Marron & Eric J. Toder, *Tax Policy Issues in Designing a Carbon Tax*, 104 AM. ECON. REV. 563 (2014)
Andrew D. Cuccia & Gregory A. Carnes, *A Closer Look at the Relation Between Tax Complexity and Tax Equity Perceptions*, 22 J. ECON. PSYCHOL. 113 (2001)
Thomas W. Hanchett, *U.S. Tax Policy and the Shopping Center Boom of the 1950s and 1960s*, 101 AM. HIST. REV. 1082 (1996)
John T. Scholz & Neil Pinney, *Duty, Fear, and Tax Compliance: The Heuristic Basis of Citizenship Behavior*, 39 AM. J. POL. SCI. 490 (1995)
Leo Lawrence Murray, *Bureaucracy and Bi-Partisanship in Taxation: The Mellon Plan Revisited*, 52 BUS. HIST. REV. 201 (1978)
James A. Mirrlees, *An Exploration in the Theory of Optimum Income Taxation*, 38 REV. ECON. STUD. 175 (1971)

3. HeinOnline, SSRN, Digital Commons, and Google Scholar

You can use these services to compile lists of publications and gain direct access to their texts. HeinOnline has the largest database of publications. This service is publication-based; its database includes many law reviews in full text back to their inception. HeinOnline is discussed further in Section D (*infra* page 266), covering full text.

The Legal Scholarship Network (LSN) is a subdivision of Social Science Research Network (SSRN), an organization acquired by Elsevier (a division of RELX) in 2016. Unless an author (or the journal itself) posts an article or work in progress to SSRN, the work will not be in its database. As its name implies, SSRN is not limited to law. Thus, you can also use it to locate recent law-related literature relevant to tax. In many cases, you can download items posted to SSRN or read them online.

The bepress-hosted Digital Commons is a scholarship-hosting site. Participating institutions, including several law schools, use Digital Commons to compile, publish, and share faculty scholarship. Bepress was acquired by RELX in 2017.

Google Scholar lists articles and indicates if they are available online in other sources (e.g., HeinOnline or JSTOR).

4. Citators

You can use Shepard's, KeyCite, and BCite to compile lists of articles discussing primary authorities.[6] All three citators let you select the type of citing items to display.

Illustration 13-1. Shepard's Search for Articles Citing a Case

→ You can directly Shepardize *National Federation of Independent Business v. Sebelius*, 567 U.S. 519 (2012), if you have its citation. Alternatively, you can find the case and then Shepardize it.

Illustration 13-2. Excerpt from Shepard's List of Articles Retrieved

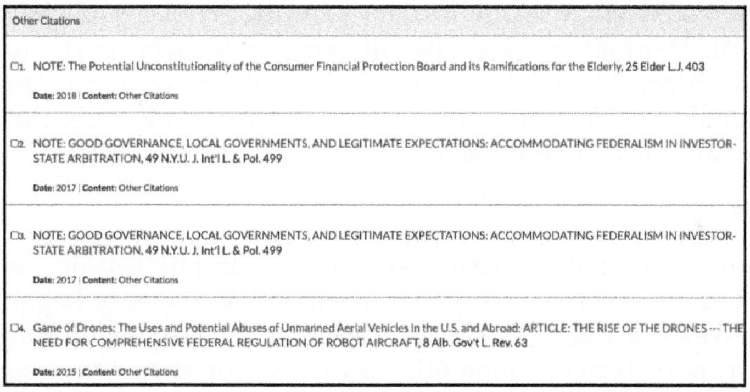
Other Citations

1. NOTE: The Potential Unconstitutionality of the Consumer Financial Protection Board and its Ramifications for the Elderly, 25 Elder L.J. 403

   Date: 2018 | **Content:** Other Citations

2. NOTE: GOOD GOVERNANCE, LOCAL GOVERNMENTS, AND LEGITIMATE EXPECTATIONS: ACCOMMODATING FEDERALISM IN INVESTOR-STATE ARBITRATION, 49 N.Y.U. J. Int'l L. & Pol. 499

   Date: 2017 | **Content:** Other Citations

3. NOTE: GOOD GOVERNANCE, LOCAL GOVERNMENTS, AND LEGITIMATE EXPECTATIONS: ACCOMMODATING FEDERALISM IN INVESTOR-STATE ARBITRATION, 49 N.Y.U. J. Int'l L. & Pol. 499

   Date: 2017 | **Content:** Other Citations

4. Game of Drones: The Uses and Potential Abuses of Unmanned Aerial Vehicles in the U.S. and Abroad: ARTICLE: THE RISE OF THE DRONES --- THE NEED FOR COMPREHENSIVE FEDERAL REGULATION OF ROBOT AIRCRAFT, 8 Alb. Gov't L. Rev. 63

   Date: 2015 | **Content:** Other Citations

→ Narrowing the results to Other Citing Sources results in displaying only law reviews and periodicals. Many of them focused on nontax aspects of this decision.

5. Miscellaneous Sources

a. Institutes

Several universities and professional organizations hold annual institutes covering taxation. Some of them make their proceedings available online; others, only in print. Institutes include the New York University Institute on Federal Taxation, the University of Miami Heckerling Institute on Estate Planning, the Southern Federal Tax Institute, and the Texas Federal Tax Institute.

---

[6] The CCH and RIA citators discussed in Chapter 11 do not include citations to articles. BCite limits its coverage to Bloomberg publications.

b. Bibliographies

Bibliographies compiled by a librarian or by another researcher may be available in the library's reference section or in law review symposium issues covering a particular area of law.

c. Current Index to Legal Periodicals

CILP indexes law review articles on a weekly basis, but it is not cumulated. It is worth consulting because it may cover an article sooner than one or more of the indexes discussed above. Articles are listed both by topic and by law review in each issue. CILP is available on Westlaw Edge. HeinOnline acquired CILP in February 2020.

d. Author and Institutional Webpages

When you search for articles by a particular author, don't ignore the Internet. Authors often list publications in a resume or publications section posted on their own or their employer's website.

D. Texts of Periodicals

1. Print

If your library subscribes to publications printing articles you wish to read, you can easily locate them. Many libraries shelve all periodicals together in alphabetical order; a library with an alcove devoted to a particular subject area may shelve specialized periodicals in the alcove. No matter which shelving method it uses, the library is likely to keep a periodical's most current issues on reserve.

2. Online

If your library does not subscribe to a particular publication, or it is in use by another researcher, try locating it online in HeinOnline, Index to Legal Periodicals Full Text, Lexis+, or Westlaw Edge. These services carry numerous publications in full text. In addition, many periodicals include full-text articles on their own websites.

If you search in Lexis+ or Westlaw Edge, you can find articles on particular topics (e.g., Code sections or cases) by using those topics as search terms. Publications in these services include hyperlinks to other materials in their online services.

You can search HeinOnline by author, title, or words in text and can use Boolean search terms. It allows direct access by citation, and it includes an electronic table of contents for each volume. Each page is reproduced as originally published. As of May 2020, it includes Akron Tax Journal (1983–2014), Boston University Journal of Tax Law (1983–1991), Business, Entrepreneurship & Tax Law Review (2017–2019), Columbia Journal of Tax Law (2010–2019), Florida Tax Review (1992–2019), Houston Business and Tax Law Journal (2001–2019), Pittsburgh Tax Review (2003–2019), Tax Law Review (1945–2018), The Tax Lawyer (1947–2020), TAXES (1923–2020), and Virginia Tax Review (1981–2019) in its extensive list of journals. There may be a time lag before this service includes the most recent volume of each publication.

Index to Legal Periodicals & Books Full Text currently provides full-text articles in numerous publications. Retrospective coverage dates vary by periodical. The collection can be searched by topic, case name, or statute name.

Illustration 13-3. Excerpt from HeinOnline

When Subchapter S Meets Subchapter C

MARTIN J. MCMAHON, JR.* & DANIEL L. SIMMONS**

ABSTRACT

It is often said that "an S corporation is a corporation that is taxed like a partnership." This statement is incorrect. An S corporation resembles a partnership only in that it generally does not pay income taxes and its income and losses pass through to the shareholders and retain their character as they pass through. Also, like a partnership, basis adjustments to an S corporation shareholder's stock reflect allocations of income, expense, loss, and distributions. However, no other rules of subchapter K governing partnership taxation apply to S corporations. Most of the rules governing the relationship between an S corporation and its shareholders differ significantly from the rules governing the relationship between a partnership and its partners. In fact, an S corporation and its shareholders are subject to the rules of subchapter C, just like a corporation that has not made an S election, with very few exceptions. This Article highlights some of the major differences between taxation of S corporations and taxation of partnerships and explores in greater detail the intersection of subchapter C with subchapter S with respect to transactional

→ HeinOnline reproduces actual pages. This page is excerpted from 67 Tax Law. 231 (2013–2014).

Bloomberg Law: Tax, Checkpoint, and Cheetah carry a more limited set of journals, namely practitioner-oriented journals published by their "family" of publishers.

3. Microform

Before starting HeinOnline, William S. Hein & Co., Inc., published many periodicals in microform. Libraries may purchase microform versions if space is limited or the print version is no longer available.

E. Citators for Articles

As noted in Section C, you can use citators to find citations to articles discussing various primary source materials. You can also use citators to determine if any court has cited a particular article. To find this information, insert the article's citation in the citator's search box. For results of a citator search in both Lexis+ and KeyCite, see Illustrations 11-3 and 11-5, *supra* pages 224 and 225.

F. Illustrations

This section illustrates checking an author's citation results in late July 2020 over several databases using Professor Gregg Polsky of the University of Georgia School of Law as an example. This exercise had two components: looking for a list of publications on his faculty page and on the law school's Digital Commons page,[7] and then consulting the databases listed below.

- Westlaw Edge: Legal Resource Index (LRI); Law Reviews & Journals
- Lexis+: Law Reviews and Journals
- HeinOnline
- SSRN
- Google Scholar

Differences in results reflect a variety of factors. These include whether the database includes the particular journal, how often the database is updated, and, in the case of SSRN, whether the author posted his article to the database. Because database inputting errors are also possible, it may be worthwhile to check more than one database. If you need the correct spelling and punctuation of an article title, try to find the text in a print or PDF version. Don't rely on the spelling and punctuation you find in an articles index.

Illustration 13-4. Author's Faculty Webpage

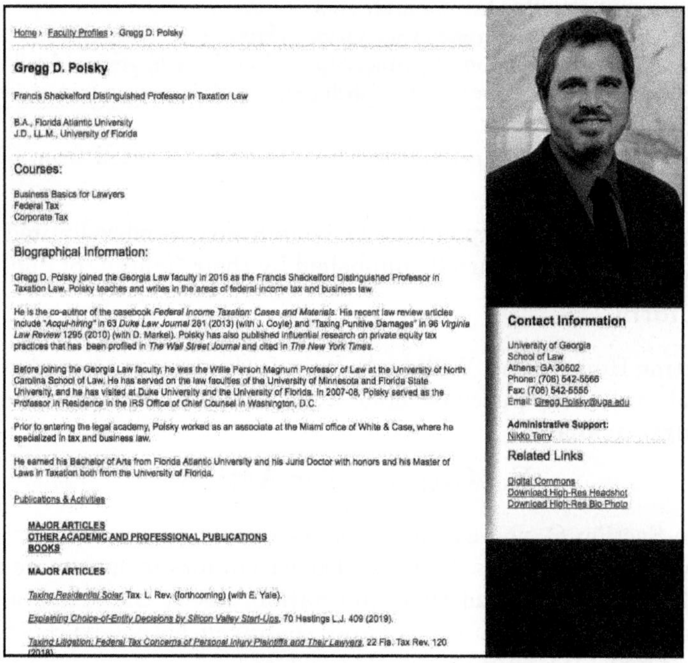

Home › Faculty Profiles › Gregg D. Polsky

Gregg D. Polsky

Francis Shackelford Distinguished Professor in Taxation Law

B.A., Florida Atlantic University
J.D., LL.M., University of Florida

Courses:

Business Basics for Lawyers
Federal Tax
Corporate Tax

Biographical Information:

Gregg D. Polsky joined the Georgia Law faculty in 2016 as the Francis Shackelford Distinguished Professor in Taxation Law. Polsky teaches and writes in the areas of federal income tax and business law.

He is the co-author of the casebook *Federal Income Taxation: Cases and Materials*. His recent law review articles include "*Acqui-hiring*" in 63 *Duke Law Journal* 281 (2013) (with J. Coyle) and "Taxing Punitive Damages" in 96 *Virginia Law Review* 1295 (2010) (with D. Markel). Polsky has also published influential research on private equity tax practices that has been profiled in *The Wall Street Journal* and cited in *The New York Times*.

Before joining the Georgia Law faculty, he was the Willie Person Magnum Professor of Law at the University of North Carolina School of Law. He has served on the law faculties of the University of Minnesota and Florida State University, and he has visited at Duke University and the University of Florida. In 2007-08, Polsky served as the Professor in Residence in the IRS Office of Chief Counsel in Washington, D.C.

Prior to entering the legal academy, Polsky worked as an associate at the Miami office of White & Case, where he specialized in tax and business law.

He earned his Bachelor of Arts from Florida Atlantic University and his Juris Doctor with honors and his Master of Laws in Taxation both from the University of Florida.

Publications & Activities

MAJOR ARTICLES
OTHER ACADEMIC AND PROFESSIONAL PUBLICATIONS
BOOKS

MAJOR ARTICLES

Taxing Residential Solar, Tax. L. Rev. (forthcoming) (with E. Yale).

Explaining Choice-of-Entity Decisions by Silicon Valley Start-Ups, 70 Hastings L.J. 409 (2019).

Taxing Litigation: Federal Tax Concerns of Personal Injury Plaintiffs and Their Lawyers, 22 Fla. Tax Rev. 120 (2018).

Contact Information

University of Georgia
School of Law
Athens, GA 30602
Phone: (706) 542-5566
Fax: (706) 542-5555
Email: Gregg.Polsky@uga.edu

Administrative Support:
Nikko Terry

Related Links

Digital Commons
Download High-Res Headshot
Download High-Res Bio Photo

→ Professor Polsky's faculty webpage lists articles. It does not include a link to a CV. Some authors provide only partial lists on their webpages and full lists on a CV.

[7] See http://www.law.uga.edu/profile/gregg-d-polsky; http://digitalcommons.law.uga.edu/ (both last visited July 18, 2020).

Illustration 13-5. Articles Listed on Law School's Digital Commons Page

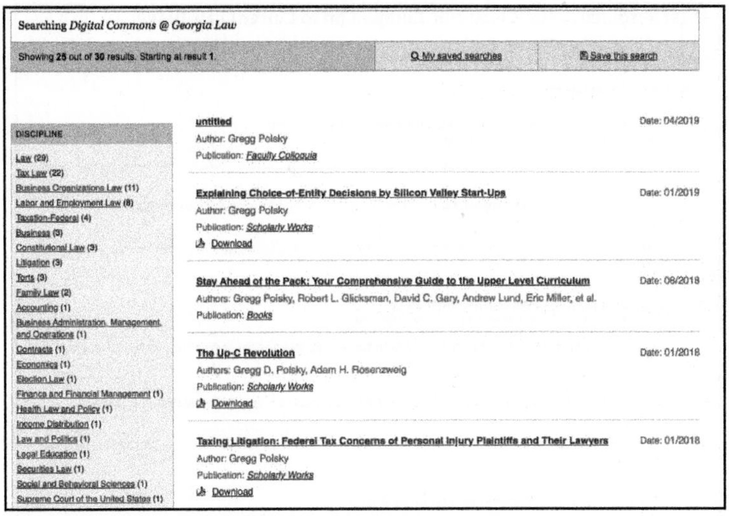

→ The Digital Commons page listed 30 results.

→ The Digital Commons page includes published articles, forthcoming articles, and faculty colloquia. It can be filtered by Discipline and Keyword and sorted by Relevance and Publication Date.

Illustration 13-6. Search in LRI on Westlaw Edge

Illustration 13-7. Results from LRI on Westlaw Edge

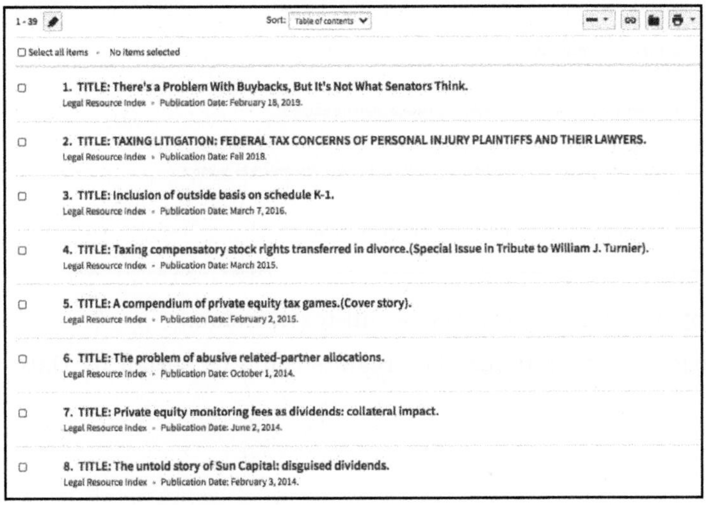

→ Legal Resource Index listed 39 items.

Illustration 13-8. Results from LRI on Westlaw Edge

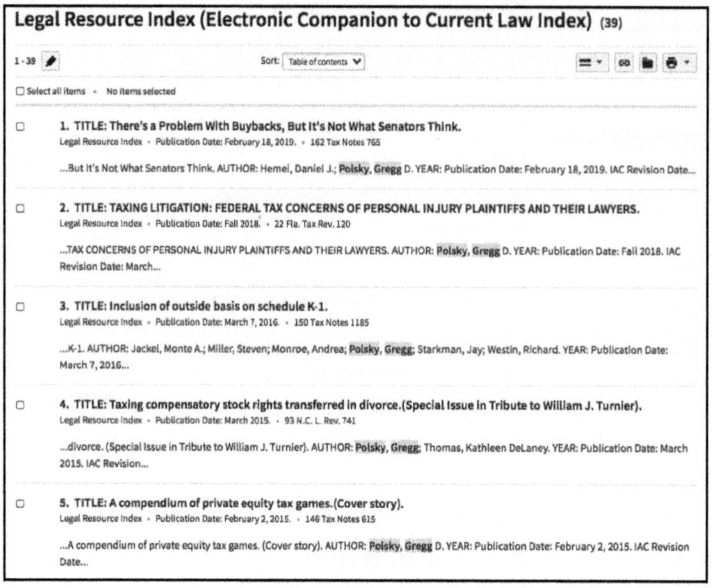

Legal Resource Index (Electronic Companion to Current Law Index) (39)

1-39 Sort: Table of contents

Select all items • No items selected

1. TITLE: There's a Problem With Buybacks, But It's Not What Senators Think.
Legal Resource Index • Publication Date: February 18, 2019. • 162 Tax Notes 765
...But It's Not What Senators Think. AUTHOR: Hemel, Daniel J.; Polsky, Gregg D. YEAR: Publication Date: February 18, 2019. IAC Revision Date...

2. TITLE: TAXING LITIGATION: FEDERAL TAX CONCERNS OF PERSONAL INJURY PLAINTIFFS AND THEIR LAWYERS.
Legal Resource Index • Publication Date: Fall 2018. • 22 Fla. Tax Rev. 120
...TAX CONCERNS OF PERSONAL INJURY PLAINTIFFS AND THEIR LAWYERS. AUTHOR: Polsky, Gregg D. YEAR: Publication Date: Fall 2018. IAC Revision Date: March...

3. TITLE: Inclusion of outside basis on schedule K-1.
Legal Resource Index • Publication Date: March 7, 2016. • 150 Tax Notes 1185
...K-1. AUTHOR: Jackel, Monte A.; Miller, Steven; Monroe, Andrea; Polsky, Gregg; Starkman, Jay; Westin, Richard. YEAR: Publication Date: March 7, 2016...

4. TITLE: Taxing compensatory stock rights transferred in divorce.(Special Issue in Tribute to William J. Turnier).
Legal Resource Index • Publication Date: March 2015. • 93 N.C. L. Rev. 741
...divorce. (Special Issue in Tribute to William J. Turnier). AUTHOR: Polsky, Gregg; Thomas, Kathleen DeLaney. YEAR: Publication Date: March 2015. IAC Revision...

5. TITLE: A compendium of private equity tax games.(Cover story).
Legal Resource Index • Publication Date: February 2, 2015. • 146 Tax Notes 615
...A compendium of private equity tax games. (Cover story). AUTHOR: Polsky, Gregg D. YEAR: Publication Date: February 2, 2015. IAC Revision Date...

→ In the "More Detail" view, the screen also shows the citation.

Illustration 13-9. Results from Law Reviews & Journals on Westlaw Edge

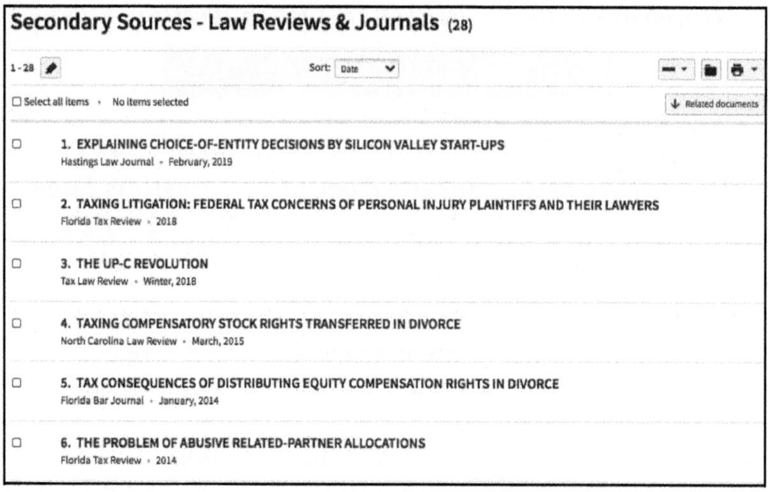

Secondary Sources - Law Reviews & Journals (28)

1-28 Sort: Date

Select all items • No items selected Related documents

1. EXPLAINING CHOICE-OF-ENTITY DECISIONS BY SILICON VALLEY START-UPS
Hastings Law Journal • February, 2019

2. TAXING LITIGATION: FEDERAL TAX CONCERNS OF PERSONAL INJURY PLAINTIFFS AND THEIR LAWYERS
Florida Tax Review • 2018

3. THE UP-C REVOLUTION
Tax Law Review • Winter, 2018

4. TAXING COMPENSATORY STOCK RIGHTS TRANSFERRED IN DIVORCE
North Carolina Law Review • March, 2015

5. TAX CONSEQUENCES OF DISTRIBUTING EQUITY COMPENSATION RIGHTS IN DIVORCE
Florida Bar Journal • January, 2014

6. THE PROBLEM OF ABUSIVE RELATED-PARTNER ALLOCATIONS
Florida Tax Review • 2014

→ Click on any of the articles to read a full-text version.

→ This database listed 28 items. The results could be sorted by Date, Relevance, or Most Cited.

Illustration 13-10. Results from Lexis+ Law Reviews and Journals

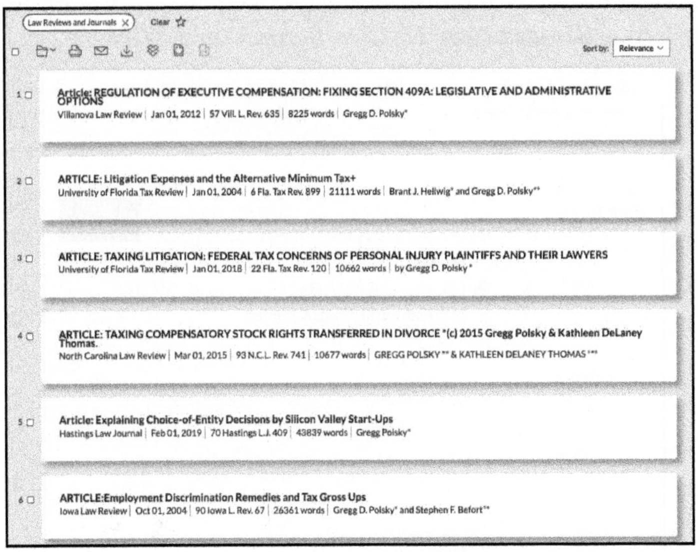

→ Click on any of the articles to read a full-text version.

→ Lexis+ listed 27 articles.

Illustration 13-11. Search in HeinOnline

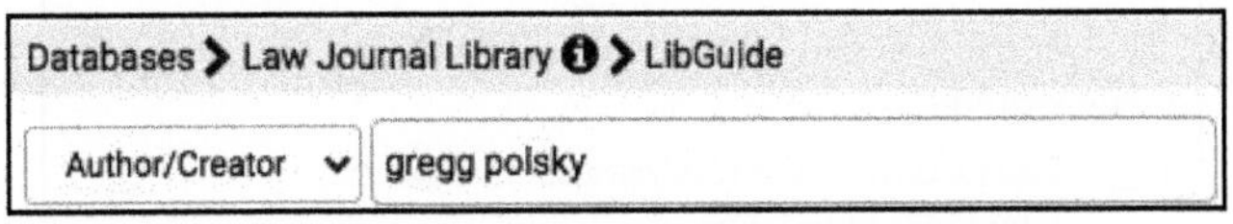

Illustration 13-12. Results from HeinOnline

→ Click on any of the articles to read a full-text PDF version.

→ HeinOnline listed 28 articles.

→ You can also search Hein using its Author Profile feature.

Illustration 13-13. Search in SSRN

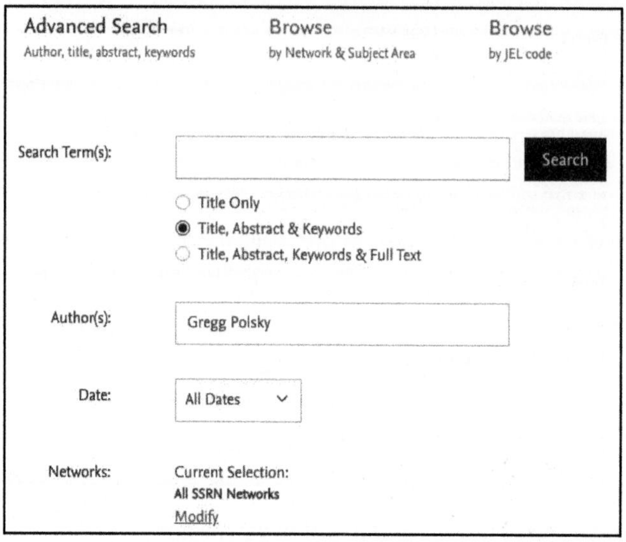

Illustration 13-14. Results from SSRN

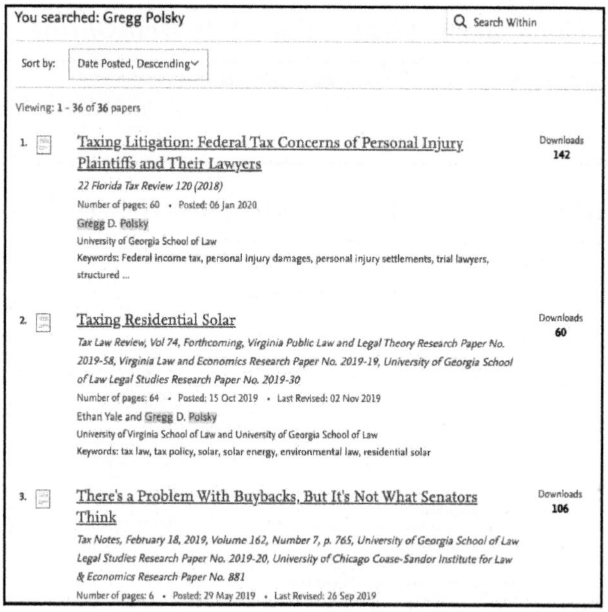

→ SSRN shows the number of downloads and when the item was posted or revised.

→ SSRN listed 36 articles.

Illustration 13-15. Search in Google Scholar

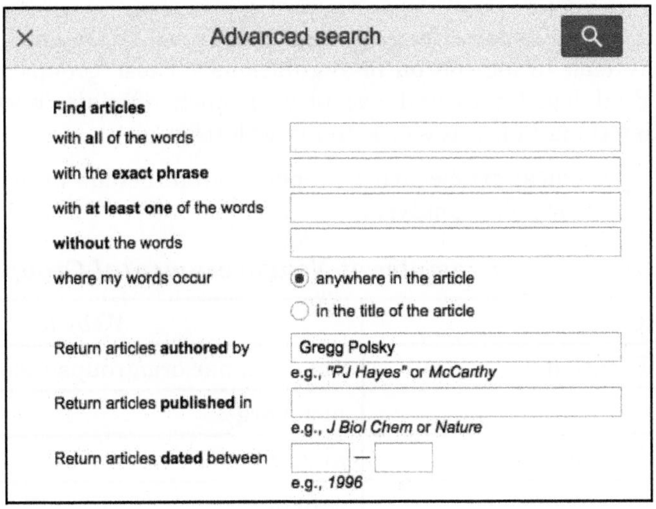
Advanced search
Find articles
with all of the words
with the exact phrase
with at least one of the words
without the words
where my words occur
anywhere in the article
in the title of the article
Return articles authored by
Gregg Polsky
e.g., "PJ Hayes" or McCarthy
Return articles published in
e.g., J Biol Chem or Nature
Return articles dated between
e.g., 1996

Illustration 13-16. Results from Google Scholar

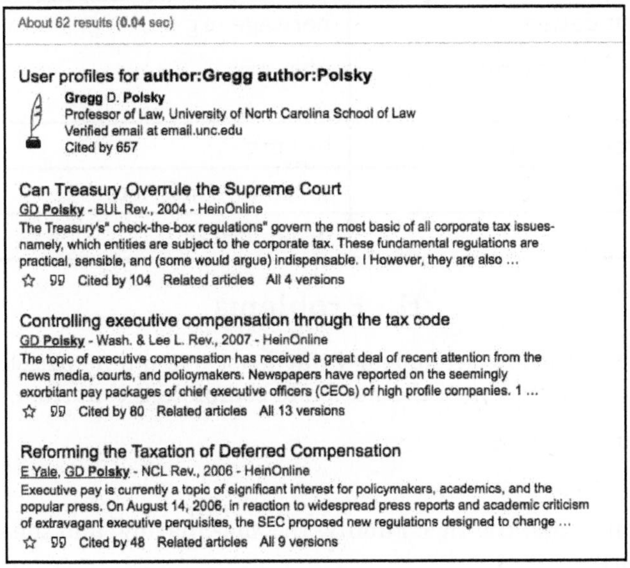
About 62 results (0.04 sec)
User profiles for author:Gregg author:Polsky
Gregg D. Polsky
Professor of Law, University of North Carolina School of Law
Verified email at email.unc.edu
Cited by 657
Can Treasury Overrule the Supreme Court
GD Polsky - BUL Rev., 2004 - HeinOnline
The Treasury's" check-the-box regulations" govern the most basic of all corporate tax issues-namely, which entities are subject to the corporate tax. These fundamental regulations are practical, sensible, and (some would argue) indispensable. I However, they are also ...
Cited by 104 Related articles All 4 versions
Controlling executive compensation through the tax code
GD Polsky - Wash. & Lee L. Rev., 2007 - HeinOnline
The topic of executive compensation has received a great deal of recent attention from the news media, courts, and policymakers. Newspapers have reported on the seemingly exorbitant pay packages of chief executive officers (CEOs) of high profile companies. 1 ...
Cited by 80 Related articles All 13 versions
Reforming the Taxation of Deferred Compensation
E Yale, GD Polsky - NCL Rev., 2006 - HeinOnline
Executive pay is currently a topic of significant interest for policymakers, academics, and the popular press. On August 14, 2006, in reaction to widespread press reports and academic criticism of extravagant executive perquisites, the SEC proposed new regulations designed to change ...
Cited by 48 Related articles All 9 versions

→ Google Scholar retrieved 62 results. The search parameters excluded articles that merely cited to Professor Polsky's work. One of the results listed by Google Scholar was actually written by a Daniel Polsky.

→ Google Scholar included PDF links for several of the articles.

→ Note that the biographical information is incorrect. Professor Polsky joined the University of Georgia School of Law faculty in 2016.

G. Nongovernmental Reports

Many groups appear before Congress and the Treasury Department to testify at hearings that may lead to legislation or regulations.[8] These groups may also submit reports to individual legislators and executive branch officials, post them on their websites, or publish them in law reviews and newsletters.

As is true for periodical articles, these reports often include numerous citations to authority to support their policy analysis.

Table 13-C. Examples of Nongovernmental Groups

Group	*Website*
ABA Section of Taxation	americanbar.org/groups/taxation.html
AICPA	aicpa.org
American Law Institute	ali.org
Cato Institute	cato.org
Citizens for Tax Justice	ctj.org
The Heritage Foundation	heritage.org
National Bureau of Economic Research	nber.org
National Taxpayers Union	ntu.org
Tax Policy Center	taxpolicycenter.org
Urban Institute	urban.org

H. Problems

1. The articles listed below all appear in at least one online articles index. Add the author name and the law review information to complete the citation.

   a. "Death Tax" Politics

   b. Trust Term Extension

   c. Love, Money, and the IRS: Family, Income-Sharing, and the Joint Income Tax Return

   d. Taxation Without Realization: A "Revolutionary" Approach to Ownership

   e. Not the Power to Destroy: An Effects Theory of the Tax Power

   f. "We Will See That You Are Troubled Right Along": Women and the Politics of the Early Federal Income Tax

2. The professor listed below will be speaking at your institution. Using whichever of the sources your instructor assigns from those illustrated in this chapter, compile a list

[8] The Resources page of the TaxProf Blog (https://taxprof.typepad.com/taxprof_blog/resources.html) includes an extensive list of organizations. It provides hyperlinks to their sites.

of the last three articles he or she has published. Use the year of publication in determining which articles are the last three published.

a. Reuven Avi-Yonah

b. Roberta Mann

c. David Weisbach

d. Shu-Yi Oei

3. The articles below were published between 1940 and 1979. Add the author name and the law review name, volume, page, and year to complete the citation.

a. Income Tax Blue Law: Imputation of Interest Under Section 483

b. An Enigma in the Federal Income Tax: The Meaning of the Word Gift

c. Some Contributions of the Income Tax Law to the Growth and Prevalence of Slums.

d. Learned Hand's Contribution to the Law of Tax Avoidance

4. The articles below were published before 1940. Add the law review name, volume, page, and year to complete the citation.

a. Frederick A. Ballard, Retroactive Federal Taxation

b. Robert B. Eichholz, Should the Federal Income Tax be Simplified?

c. Charles L. B. Lowndes, A Day in the Supreme Court with the Federal Estate Tax

d. Oscar W. Underwood, Jr., Form and Substance in Tax Cases

5. Provide a full citation to an article that includes the Code section listed below in its title. Unless your instructor tells you otherwise, find the most recent article you can.

a. 213

b. 409A

c. 6694

6. Provide a full citation to an article involving federal taxation that includes the term listed below in its title. Unless your instructor tells you otherwise, find the most recent article you can.

a. Economic substance

b. Innocent spouse

c. Cryptocurrency

Chapter 14

FORM BOOKS, CHECKLISTS, AND IRS MODEL LANGUAGE

A. Introduction

The drafter's choice of language may determine the tax consequences of a contract, lawsuit settlement, or other legal matter. To avoid adverse consequences, you might consider adapting a form book's model language to your client's situation. The author's comments explain why particular language avoids tax problems. You can also use checklists to guide you in drafting your own form. The IRS occasionally provides model language in revenue procedures and other documents and even in tax return forms. The IRS language may not be mandatory, but it does provide a safe harbor. Illustrations in this chapter cover both commercially available and IRS materials.

B. Finding Forms and Other Documents

You can find drafting language relatively easily using a form book. Relevant forms or checklists will be listed by topic or Code section or will appear along with the topical discussion. You can also use the publication's table of contents or relevant tables of authority to locate forms. The method of publication, print or electronic, should not matter.

If you are interested in IRS model language, you can locate the relevant document through an electronic search. Use such search terms as "model language," "prototype language," or "sample language." Using only "form" as a search term is risky; it may produce a significant number of references to tax return forms.

1. Form Books Available

The following list illustrates the range of available materials. Forms are most useful if the author includes citations to authority.

- Becker et al., Legal Checklists
- Bittker et al., Federal Income Taxation of Corporations & Shareholders: Forms
- Cavitch & Cavitch, Tax Planning for Corporations and Shareholders: Forms
- Foster & Long, Tax-Free Exchanges Under § 1031
- Garcia et al., Structuring and Drafting Partnership Agreements: Including LLC Agreements
- McGaffey, Legal Forms with Tax Analysis
- Murphy's Will Clauses: Annotations and Forms with Tax Effects
- Rabkin & Johnson, Current Legal Forms with Tax Analysis
- Saltzman & Saltzman: IRS Procedural Forms and Analysis

- Tilton, U.S. International Tax Forms Manual: Compliance and Reporting

2. Other Sources for Forms

In addition to using form books, you can find model language in looseleaf services, practitioner-oriented articles, and tax institute proceedings. For example, several Tax Management Portfolios include sample language in their Worksheets section,[1] Checkpoint includes client letters with cross-references to explanatory material in Federal Tax Coordinator 2d,[2] and Bloomberg Law: Tax has sample letters to clients and the IRS.[3]

Internal Revenue Service documents that include model language appear in the Internal Revenue Bulletin, which is available online through the IRS website and on commercial services. You do not need the actual citation to find these documents electronically.

In addition to model language that appears in the I.R.B., the IRS website also includes a section for tax forms and publications.[4] Although many tax return forms simply provide information related to tax liability, others include the sort of language you might find in a form book. If you are researching a topic in a treatise or looseleaf service, you will probably encounter references to relevant IRS forms.

3. Publication Format

Although form books are available in print, materials published in electronic formats have an added advantage. Users can download forms and customize them for their clients' needs. In some instances, a flash drive may accompany a print form book. Many form books are available in multiple formats.

Subscription services such as Lexis+ and Westlaw Edge include form books in their databases. The Tax Management Portfolios are on Bloomberg Law, and Federal Tax Coordinator 2d is available on Checkpoint and Westlaw Edge. As noted above, you can locate IRS forms and model language on the IRS website.

---

[1] The Portfolios are described in Chapter 12, Section C.2, *supra* page 251.

[2] In Checkpoint, you can find these by using the Table of Contents menu bar under Federal Library>Federal Editorial Materials>Practice Aids>Client Letters.

[3] In Bloomberg Law: Tax, the material is located under Sample Documents and Illustrations/Client Letters & IRS Response Letters.

[4] See generally Chapter 9, covering Internal Revenue Service documents.

Illustration 14-1. Contents Section from Rabkin & Johnson, Current Legal Forms with Tax Analysis

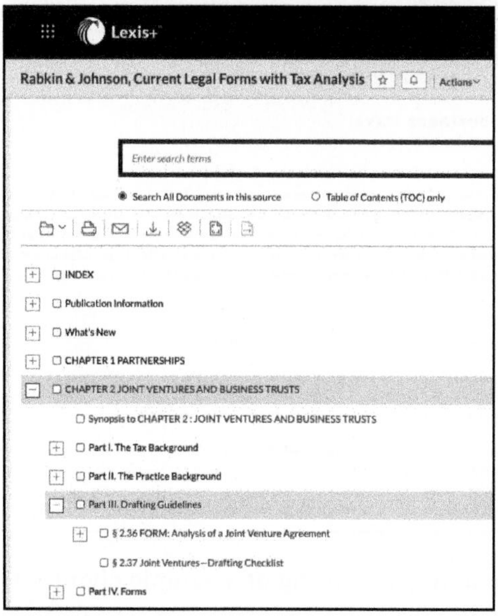

→ The table of contents shown is from Lexis+.

Illustration 14-2. Sample Form from Tax Management Portfolio 522-4th

Worksheet 4 Sample Partial Assignment of Claim Agreement

PARTIAL ASSIGNMENT OF CLAIM AGREEMENT

This Partial Assignment of Claim Agreement (the "Agreement") is made and entered into this ______ day of _________, ____ between the Assignor and the Assignees.

RECITALS

WHEREAS, the Assignor is a plaintiff in the lawsuit ______________________________ (the "XYZ Suit");

WHEREAS, the Assignor has retained __________, and _______________ of _____________, to represent him in the XYZ Suit;

WHEREAS, the Assignor wishes to recognize and reward the efforts and loyalty of the Assignees.

NOW, THEREFORE, in consideration of the foregoing recitals and the mutual covenants and promises contained herein, the adequacy and sufficiency of which are hereby acknowledged, the parties hereto agree as follows:

ARTICLE I

THE ASSIGNMENT

1.1. *Irrevocable and Unqualified Assignment.* The Assignor hereby irrevocably and unqualifiedly assigns ___% of his portion of the "net proceeds" from the XYZ Suit to the

→ Portfolio 522-4th covers Tax Aspects of Settlements and Judgments.

→ Article II of the Assignment form includes provisions dealing with taxes.

Illustration 14-3. Excerpt from RIA Client Letters on Checkpoint

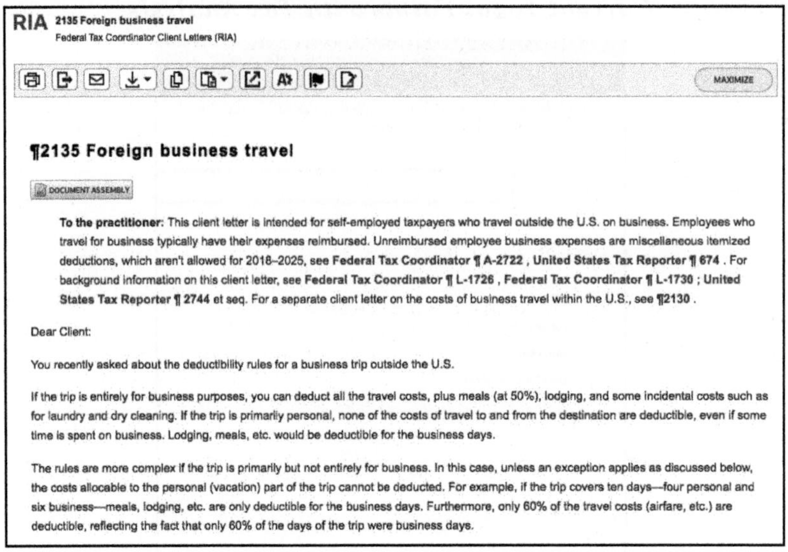

RIA **2135 Foreign business travel**
Federal Tax Coordinator Client Letters (RIA)

MAXIMIZE

¶2135 Foreign business travel

DOCUMENT ASSEMBLY

To the practitioner: This client letter is intended for self-employed taxpayers who travel outside the U.S. on business. Employees who travel for business typically have their expenses reimbursed. Unreimbursed employee business expenses are miscellaneous itemized deductions, which aren't allowed for 2018–2025, see **Federal Tax Coordinator ¶ A-2722** , **United States Tax Reporter ¶ 674** . For background information on this client letter, see **Federal Tax Coordinator ¶ L-1726** , **Federal Tax Coordinator ¶ L-1730** ; **United States Tax Reporter ¶ 2744** et seq. For a separate client letter on the costs of business travel within the U.S., see **¶2130** .

Dear Client:

You recently asked about the deductibility rules for a business trip outside the U.S.

If the trip is entirely for business purposes, you can deduct all the travel costs, plus meals (at 50%), lodging, and some incidental costs such as for laundry and dry cleaning. If the trip is primarily personal, none of the costs of travel to and from the destination are deductible, even if some time is spent on business. Lodging, meals, etc. would be deductible for the business days.

The rules are more complex if the trip is primarily but not entirely for business. In this case, unless an exception applies as discussed below, the costs allocable to the personal (vacation) part of the trip cannot be deducted. For example, if the trip covers ten days—four personal and six business—meals, lodging, etc. are only deductible for the business days. Furthermore, only 60% of the travel costs (airfare, etc.) are deductible, reflecting the fact that only 60% of the days of the trip were business days.

→ The language above is the beginning of a sample client letter.

→ Cross-references to topical discussions appear before the letter. The discussion materials include cross-references to the sample letters.

→ After clicking on Document Assembly, users can add the client's name and address.

Illustration 14-4. Search for Sample Language on IRS Website

→ The search above is for "sample language," but without the quote marks. The search could miss relevant documents (e.g., those using "model" instead of "sample").

→ This search produced 92 "hits." A search for "sample language" produced only six "hits."

Illustration 14-5. Search Results on IRS Website

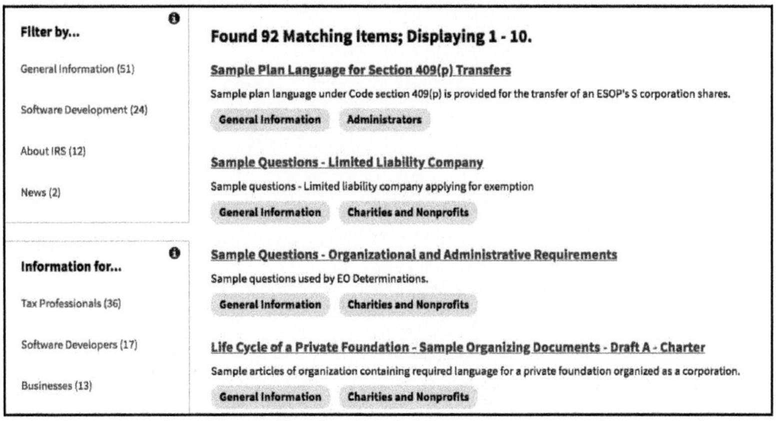

→ The results can be sorted by date or relevance. There are also filters to use in further refining results.

C. Problems

1. Locate a non-IRS produced form or checklist for
   a. Making a present interest gift in a trust
   b. Funding a charitable unitrust
   c. A golden parachute non-compete provision

2. Locate the IRS model language described below. After you find the document, check to see if the IRS has issued later guidance that affects the item you found.
   a. Model plan language a public school can use to adopt a plan that satisfies I.R.C. § 403(b) (2007 revenue procedure)
   b. Amendments for group trusts (2011 revenue ruling)
   c. Obtaining consent of the Commissioner of Internal Revenue to change a method of accounting for federal income tax purposes for I.R.C. § 446(e) (2015 revenue procedure). Are there any additional revenue procedures that you must consider before making a request to change accounting methods?

3. What is the purpose of the IRS form listed?
   a. 4029
   b. 4506
   c. 8950

Chapter 15

NEWSLETTERS

A. Introduction

Researchers in any legal specialty must update their findings or risk citing obsolete sources. When the research involves taxation, the odds of change are extremely high and the number of sources to consult may appear endless. Although keeping current requires a significant time commitment, it pays off in the long run. Regular self-education ultimately reduces your research time.

Newsletters are convenient tools for keeping up with changes in the law. While they are no substitute for updating with a citator or the new matter section of a looseleaf service, they provide a means for reviewing material issued during a predetermined time period.

Several newsletters print texts or digests of primary source material. The publisher often maintains these materials in an electronic database. If your library has sufficient shelf space for print copies, or you have electronic access, you can also use newsletters to locate and read primary source materials. Electronic versions are generally better for this purpose. They are more likely—using hyperlinks—to provide access to full text. In addition, because print versions often lack cumulative indexes, electronic searches are more efficient.

B. Categorizing Newsletters

Methods for categorizing newsletters include frequency of publication, subject matter, relationship to looseleaf services, and publication format.

1. Frequency of Publication

Newsletters may appear daily, weekly, or even monthly. Daily and weekly newsletters either offer longer excerpts from cases and rulings than do their monthly counterparts or cover a wider range of topics. To avoid extraordinary length, monthly newsletters limit their breadth or depth of coverage. The IRS's practice of issuing advance revenue rulings and revenue procedures, notices, and announcements makes daily newsletters particularly attractive. They may cover these items weeks before they appear in the Internal Revenue Bulletin.

Online publication represents the ultimate in frequency. Because electronic databases can update their newsletter files daily, subscribers enjoy instant access while avoiding the library shelving problems associated with daily newsletters. Many newsletters are available online in addition to being published in print versions.

In addition to their newsletters, many publishers email regular (in some cases, as often as daily) updates to their subscribers.

2. Subject Matter

Newsletters may be general in scope, covering all (or at least most) areas of tax. Unless a general-purpose newsletter is relatively lengthy or published very frequently, it gives limited attention to various areas or to particular types of authority. Other newsletters may limit coverage to a particular specialty, such as estate planning or oil and gas taxation.

3. Relationship to Looseleaf Services

Publishers of looseleaf services provide subscribers with pamphlet-type newsletters summarizing major events of the week or other relevant time period. Although their summaries may be short, many of these newsletters include cross-references to discussion in the relevant looseleaf. CCH and RIA publish newsletters associated with their looseleaf services.

In other instances, a looseleaf service subscription may not include a newsletter. Tax Management Weekly Report and Daily Tax Report fall into this category; neither is part of a subscription to the Tax Management Portfolios. Even if it is not included in a subscription, a newsletter may include cross-references to a looseleaf service.

Many newsletters have no relation to a looseleaf service. Some of these, including Tax Notes Federal, provide cross-references or links to sources printing full texts of items digested in the newsletter. Others simply provide citations to the primary source material.

4. Publication Format

Newsletters are available in a variety of formats, but print and online are the most common. In the past they were available on disc or microform, but publishers have moved away from both formats.

C. Descriptions of Newsletters

It is impossible to provide a detailed description of every available newsletter in an overview book of this nature. Although this section covers only a handful of newsletters and publishers, you should not overlook other resources available in print or online. This is particularly important for relatively specialized areas.

A newsletter may be available only on its publisher's website, or it may also be included in other subscription services. Several professional law or accounting organizations, and individual law or accounting firms, publish newsletters for group members, clients, or even the general public; these are likely to be available online.

1. Bloomberg Industry Group

Bloomberg Industry Group publishes the Daily Tax Report and Tax Management Weekly Report. Each print issue of the Daily Tax Report is separately paginated by date and by sections within each issue. Daily Tax Report covers congressional activity, judicial decisions, IRS materials, and regulations. Online subscribers can access many full-text documents by clicking on links to reach documents discussed in Daily Tax Report. Daily Tax Report also provides citations to other sources (e.g., government websites) for additional documents.

Illustration 15-1. Excerpt from Daily Tax Report, May 28, 2020

Tax Management Weekly Report focuses on news and analysis of current issues in addition to providing information about judicial decisions and IRS rulings.

Illustration 15-2. Tax Management Weekly Report Full Issue View

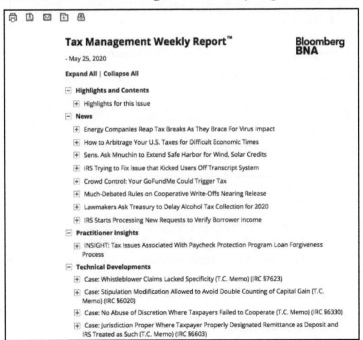

Tax Management Weekly Report™ Bloomberg BNA

- May 25, 2020

Expand All | **Collapse All**

⊟ **Highlights and Contents**

⊞ Highlights for this Issue

⊟ **News**

⊞ Energy Companies Reap Tax Breaks As They Brace For Virus Impact

⊞ How to Arbitrage Your U.S. Taxes for Difficult Economic Times

⊞ Sens. Ask Mnuchin to Extend Safe Harbor for Wind, Solar Credits

⊞ IRS Trying to Fix Issue that Kicked Users Off Transcript System

⊞ Crowd Control: Your GoFundMe Could Trigger Tax

⊞ Much-Debated Rules on Cooperative Write-Offs Nearing Release

⊞ Lawmakers Ask Treasury to Delay Alcohol Tax Collection for 2020

⊞ IRS Starts Processing New Requests to Verify Borrower Income

⊟ **Practitioner Insights**

⊞ INSIGHT: Tax Issues Associated With Paycheck Protection Program Loan Forgiveness Process

⊟ **Technical Developments**

⊞ Case: Whistleblower Claims Lacked Specificity (T.C. Memo) (IRC §7623)

⊞ Case: Stipulation Modification Allowed to Avoid Double Counting of Capital Gain (T.C. Memo) (IRC §6020)

⊞ Case: No Abuse of Discretion Where Taxpayers Failed to Cooperate (T.C. Memo) (IRC §6330)

⊞ Case: Jurisdiction Proper Where Taxpayer Properly Designated Remittance as Deposit and IRS Treated as Such (T.C. Memo) (IRC §6603)

2. Tax Analysts (Taxnotes.com)

The weekly Tax Notes Federal newsletter covers pending legislation, IRS and Treasury material, and court opinions. It also covers comments made by government representatives at tax conferences, comments by taxpayer representatives at public hearings on regulations, and comments the government receives on proposed regulations. Each issue of Tax Notes Federal includes articles by practitioners or academics.

Full text of documents (or links to full texts) are available in Tax Notes Today Federal. You can access it and other Tax Notes publications on the publisher's subscription platform.

Tax Notes publishes several specialized newsletters; these include Exempt Organizations (monthly), Tax Notes International (weekly), and Tax Notes Today Global (daily). Highlights & Documents provides daily access to relevant material.

Illustration 15-3. TOC from Tax Notes Today Federal

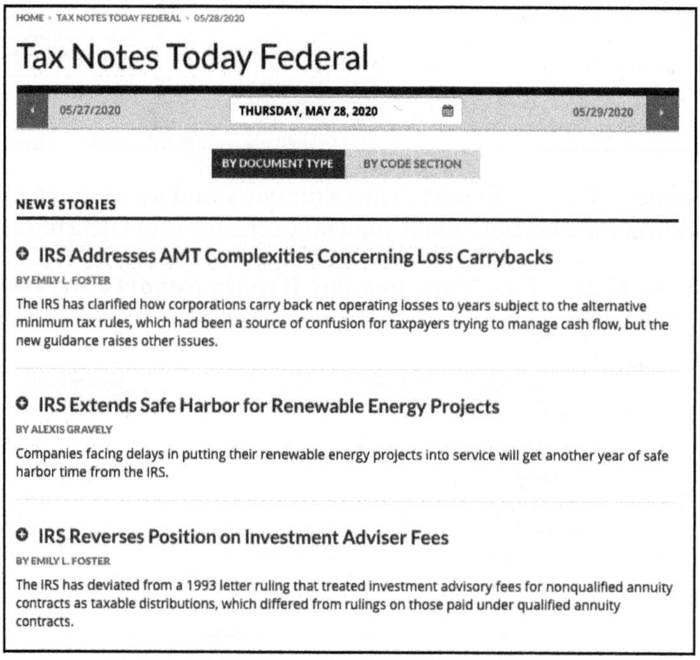
HOME › TAX NOTES TODAY FEDERAL › 05/28/2020

Tax Notes Today Federal

05/27/2020 THURSDAY, MAY 28, 2020 05/29/2020

BY DOCUMENT TYPE BY CODE SECTION

NEWS STORIES

IRS Addresses AMT Complexities Concerning Loss Carrybacks

BY EMILY L. FOSTER

The IRS has clarified how corporations carry back net operating losses to years subject to the alternative minimum tax rules, which had been a source of confusion for taxpayers trying to manage cash flow, but the new guidance raises other issues.

IRS Extends Safe Harbor for Renewable Energy Projects

BY ALEXIS GRAVELY

Companies facing delays in putting their renewable energy projects into service will get another year of safe harbor time from the IRS.

IRS Reverses Position on Investment Adviser Fees

BY EMILY L. FOSTER

The IRS has deviated from a 1993 letter ruling that treated investment advisory fees for nonqualified annuity contracts as taxable distributions, which differed from rulings on those paid under qualified annuity contracts.

3. Commerce Clearing House

Federal Tax Day and CCH Federal Tax Weekly are available online through Cheetah.[1] CCH includes links to primary source material discussed in these newsletters. There are also links to discussion in online versions of CCH looseleaf services (Chapter 12, Section B.1, *supra* page 234).

---

[1] In Cheetah, both are under Tax-Federal>Journals, Circulars & News.

Illustration 15-4. Excerpt from Federal Tax Day

Federal Tax Day - Current

WHITE HOUSE

W.1, Trump Administration Considering Further Delaying Tax Day, (May 8, 2020)

The Trump administration is reportedly considering further delaying Tax Day this year. The 2020 federal income tax filing season and 2019 tax year payment deadline was pushed back earlier this year from April 15 to July 15.

Tax Day Delay

"Things could happen like that. We have to help people," President Trump told reporters at the White House on May 7. Reportedly, the White House is considering a new tax filing and payment deadline of September 15.

Payroll, Capital Gains Tax Cuts

Additionally, the White House is calling for various tax cuts in the next economic relief package currently being negotiated between lawmakers and the White House. Along those lines, Trump again indicated in tweet this week that he wants to see payroll taxes as well as all capital gains taxes eliminated. At this time, it appears unlikely that congressional Democrats and perhaps even some Senate Republicans will support those particular tax breaks "making the cut" in the forthcoming "phase four" economic relief package.

By Jessica Jeane, J.D. – Senior News Editor

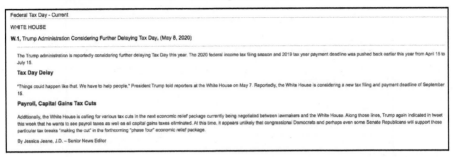

→ If primary source material is available, it is hyperlinked.

Illustration 15-5. Excerpt from Federal Tax Weekly

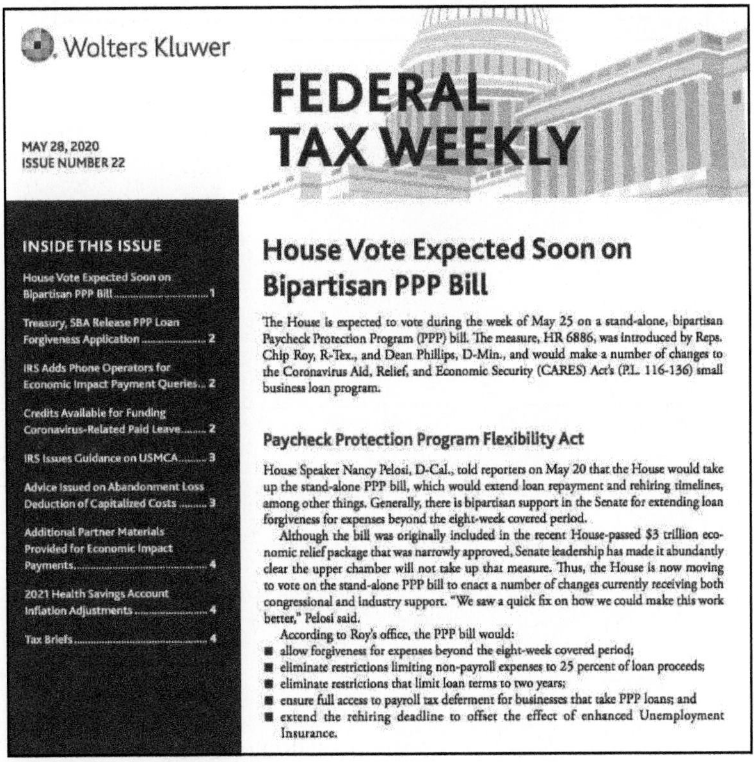

Wolters Kluwer

FEDERAL TAX WEEKLY

MAY 28, 2020
ISSUE NUMBER 22

INSIDE THIS ISSUE

House Vote Expected Soon on Bipartisan PPP Bill 1
Treasury, SBA Release PPP Loan Forgiveness Application 2
IRS Adds Phone Operators for Economic Impact Payment Queries... 2
Credits Available for Funding Coronavirus-Related Paid Leave 2
IRS Issues Guidance on USMCA 3
Advice Issued on Abandonment Loss Deduction of Capitalized Costs 3
Additional Partner Materials Provided for Economic Impact Payments 4
2021 Health Savings Account Inflation Adjustments 4
Tax Briefs 4

House Vote Expected Soon on Bipartisan PPP Bill

The House is expected to vote during the week of May 25 on a stand-alone, bipartisan Paycheck Protection Program (PPP) bill. The measure, HR 6886, was introduced by Reps. Chip Roy, R-Tex., and Dean Phillips, D-Min., and would make a number of changes to the Coronavirus Aid, Relief, and Economic Security (CARES) Act's (P.L. 116-136) small business loan program.

Paycheck Protection Program Flexibility Act

House Speaker Nancy Pelosi, D-Cal., told reporters on May 20 that the House would take up the stand-alone PPP bill, which would extend loan repayment and rehiring timelines, among other things. Generally, there is bipartisan support in the Senate for extending loan forgiveness for expenses beyond the eight-week covered period.

Although the bill was originally included in the recent House-passed $3 trillion economic relief package that was narrowly approved, Senate leadership has made it abundantly clear the upper chamber will not take up that measure. Thus, the House is now moving to vote on the stand-alone PPP bill to enact a number of changes currently receiving both congressional and industry support. "We saw a quick fix on how we could make this work better," Pelosi said.

According to Roy's office, the PPP bill would:

- allow forgiveness for expenses beyond the eight-week covered period;
- eliminate restrictions limiting non-payroll expenses to 25 percent of loan proceeds;
- eliminate restrictions that limit loan terms to two years;
- ensure full access to payroll tax deferment for businesses that take PPP loans; and
- extend the rehiring deadline to offset the effect of enhanced Unemployment Insurance.

→ Online users can access Federal Tax Weekly as a PDF file or as a text file with hyperlinks to primary source material.

4. Research Institute of America

Federal Tax Update (formerly Federal Taxes Weekly Alert) reports on major legislative, administrative, and judicial action. It includes references to coverage in Federal Tax Coordinator 2d and in United States Tax Reporter. This newsletter is only available electronically on the Checkpoint service in a text version.

Illustration 15-6 TOC Federal Tax Update, Week of May 25, 2020

Checkpoint Contents

Federal Library

Federal Editorial Materials

Federal Tax Updates

Federal Tax Update

2020

May

Week of May 25

+ Articles

− WG&L Journal Insights

- When is a rental activity considered a Section 162 trade or business? (05/27/2020)
- IRS issues new guidance on tax treatment of cryptocurrencies (05/27/2020)
- A case-based analysis of the responsibility to withhold and pay over trust-fund taxes (05/26/2020)
- Impact of the TCJA and the SECURE Act on taxpayers' financial decisions (05/28/2020)

− In Brief

- Code Sec. 61—Gross income—capital gains vs. ordinary income—partnerships—joint ventures: relinquishment of interest—sale or exchange of capital asset—settlements. (05/26/2020)
- Code Sec. 143—Qualified mortgage revenue bonds—median gross income figures. (05/27/2020)
- Code Sec. 163—Investment income—net capital gains—qualified dividend income—revocation. (05/26/2020)
- Code Sec. 168—Accelerated cost recovery system—election not to deduct additional first year depreciation—extensions—optional 10-year write-off—development and mining exploration expenses. (05/26/2020)

Chapter 16

MICROFORMS

A. Advantages and Disadvantages

Microforms have three important advantages. The first relates to space. As primary and secondary source materials proliferate, libraries can use microforms to save shelf space. A second advantage relates to availability. Your library may be able to buy non-electronic versions of some historical materials only in microform. A third advantage relates to cost. Once the library has purchased materials in microform, it has no obligation to make further outlays to ensure its access to those materials.

There are several reasons why you may prefer other formats. These relate to availability, ease of searching, mobility, space, and security. Availability may be the most critical factor. Many publishers have stopped producing microform products and have switched to electronic services. Even if a publisher no longer updates a microform service, these materials remain valuable for historical research.

Navigation and mobility are also important. Electronic sources are easier to navigate and permit word and phrase searching. Microforms are effectively used only if the compiler has indexed them well. In addition, electronic materials do not tie you to a fixed place. Microforms require a reader or reader-printer. If you have the appropriate computer configuration, you can use electronic materials anywhere.

Space and security are relevant factors for many libraries. Online systems require no library storage space; CD/DVDs require relatively little space. Although microforms require less space than their print counterparts, they do require more than the electronic versions. Finally, microforms share a problem with print looseleaf services; the individual forms can be misfiled or stolen.

B. Format and Available Materials

Microforms are available in a variety of formats (some with multiple names), including microfilm, microprint, microcard, micro-opaque, microfiche, and ultrafiche. You can use a reader-printer to produce a copy of materials you locate.

Government publications available in microform include Congressional Record, Statutes at Large, Federal Register, Code of Federal Regulations, and the Cumulative Bulletin. Other materials include Tax Court and Supreme Court case reporter services. Many libraries include briefs filed with the United States Supreme Court in their microform collections.

You are also likely to find legislative history materials available in microform. Publishers using this format include CIS (whose collections were acquired by ProQuest) and William S. Hein & Co., Inc.

The CIS Microfiche Library includes committee hearings, reports, and prints as well as Public Laws. Coverage dates for these items vary. Libraries can customize their purchases to include only certain types of documents. The print CIS Index provides abstracts of publications and a separate index. Many of the CIS publications are also available online.

Several series of Hein's Internal Revenue Acts of the United States (Chapter 6) were published in microform. These include the sets for 1909–1950, 1950–51, 1954, and 1953–72. These sets (and sets covering additional periods) are available in HeinOnline.

Some libraries may own ultrafiche copies of Tax Management Primary Sources—Series I (Chapter 6).

Law reviews and other periodicals may also be available in microform. Representative publications that Hein provided in microform include Akron Tax Journal, American Journal of Tax Policy, Tax Law Review, The Tax Lawyer, and several tax institutes. These publications are also included in HeinOnline's extensive collection of law reviews.

Because the number of materials and the microform format used varies, always consult a librarian about microform access before concluding that your library lacks a particular resource.

Chapter 17

ONLINE LEGAL RESEARCH

A. Introduction

This chapter continues the discussion of electronic research begun in Chapter 3 and continued in several other chapters. In addition to discussing advantages and disadvantages of online research, it describes three types of service: general-focus subscription services; tax-oriented subscription services; and other online services. Government websites are separately covered in chapters dealing with particular types of material and are summarized in this chapter.

B. Advantages and Disadvantages

Online legal research systems have many useful features. First, they bring research materials together in one readily accessible location. Libraries with tax alcoves require several shelf ranges to house the relevant information; libraries without alcoves may shelve these items on several floors. An online system requires only a computer, Ethernet connection or other online access tool, and a printer or other means of memorializing your research. If you have wireless access and a good battery, you can conduct online research from virtually any location.

The Internet provides a quick means for transmitting and accessing both text and graphics. More important than the time saved in gathering the material is the ability to do searches that are virtually impossible to accomplish using print materials. Because the service responds to queries based on words appearing or not appearing in its database, you could easily use an online system to locate all opinions by a particular judge or all decisions rendered in 2020, at every court level, involving the section 163 interest expense deduction.

Given these advantages, why isn't research conducted solely online? That question was raised in Chapter 3, Section E, *supra* page 12, in comparing print and electronic services. As noted there, online services may be less suited than print materials for certain research tasks, such as using looseleaf services to familiarize yourself with a topic. Some older material may not be available online, and no tax-specific articles index is available online. Publisher consolidation, discussed in Chapter 1, is also a factor. If you have access only to Westlaw Edge, for example, you currently lack access to Shepard's and Matthew Bender publications. Even if an online service offers a particular source, your subscription option may not cover it.

Cost constraints may limit the time you can spend online. If your final product requires accurate page numbers, a final check of print sources may be necessary to assure yourself that you have made no citation errors. As the discussion in Chapter 3 indicates, there is no "best source" for tax research.

C. Available Materials

Some subscription-based services include tax materials in a general database. Others focus exclusively on taxation. Nonsubscription services vary in their coverage; they may include data from a variety of sources or may focus on a single type of information. They may provide links to relevant materials rather than including text in their databases.

Materials available online may also be available in print. However, there is a general trend for publishers to encourage online subscriptions.

Keep three important rules in mind. First, you must check the time period covered for materials made available online. Don't assume a source included in an online service begins its coverage with the first print volume of that service. Coverage for many sources begins at a later date online than it does in print in both subscription and free services.

Second, remember that different systems use different search commands, rules for wildcard searches, or methods for indicating you want to use a Boolean search. You will not achieve the desired results unless you tailor your search to the rules imposed by the service you are using.[1]

Third, online systems are not static. They may add or eliminate databases or change their layout or search templates. In recent years, CCH replaced Tax Research NetWork with IntelliConnect, Cheetah, and CCH AnswerConnect), Thomson Reuters replaced Westlaw Classic and WestlawNext with Westlaw Edge, RELX replaced LexisNexis and Lexis Advance with Lexis+, and Checkpoint made changes to its search function and layout. HeinOnline and Google often add new databases. Government services are also evolving; GPO Access migrated to FDsys and then to govinfo.gov, THOMAS migrated to Congress.gov, and the IRS is constantly refining its website.

D. Subscription Services—General Focus

1. Services Covered

This section covers six subscription services: Lexis+, Westlaw Edge, Bloomberg Law, HeinOnline, ProQuest Congressional, and Law Library Microform Consortium (LLMC). The first three have extensive tax databases within their overall coverage. HeinOnline includes a significant amount of tax material, particularly material that is likely to be out of print. ProQuest Congressional is an excellent source of legislative history materials. All but LLMC are discussed in other chapters of this book.

2. Lexis+, Westlaw Edge, and Bloomberg Law: Introduction

Although they do not focus on tax, Lexis+, Westlaw Edge, and especially Bloomberg Law have extensive tax databases. You can complete many research tasks using the tax databases, but you may also need to use materials in the services' general databases.[2]

These services differ slightly in their coverage and search commands, but each offers the same type of search options. You can specify particular words that must appear or be absent in a document; if the words must be in a desired proximity, you can include that limitation. You can use these systems to locate decisions involving damages within five words of the term personal injury, or for decisions involving damages but not

---

[1] We covered a print service analogy in Chapter 12 [Table 12-A, *supra* page 257], dealing with looseleaf services. Those services vary in using outline, paragraph, and section numbers for categorizing and cross-referencing information.

[2] For example, none of these services has a tax-only articles database. Each does have a Practice Areas or Practice Centers Tax heading, where many tax-related sources are gathered. Bloomberg Law has Bloomberg BNA and Bloomberg Law: Tax, both of which include all the BNA Tax Management Portfolios. The Portfolios are discussed in Chapter 12.

personal injury. You can limit your search to particular types of authority (e.g., only Tax Court) or to particular dates.

Before formulating a search query, you should become familiar with the search term symbols used on the system you are accessing. In addition to each service's explanatory texts, other guides are available. Note that if you first used LexisNexis or Westlaw Classic, you may initially find Lexis+ and Westlaw Edge challenging to use because they include less database information on their opening screens.

3. Lexis+

a. Database Screens

From the Lexis+ home screen, you can reach the tax area by selecting the Practice Area or Industry tab and then clicking on Tax Law.

Illustration 17-1. Lexis+ Home Screen: Practice Area or Industry Option

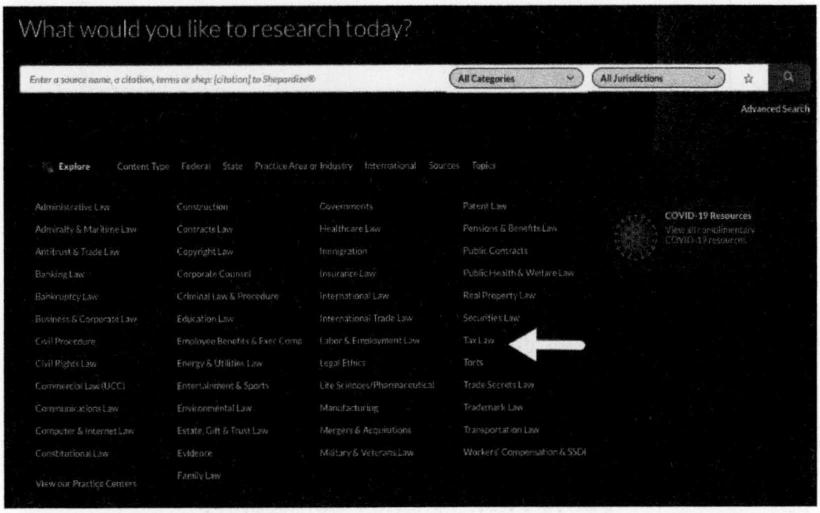

b. Database Files

You can use the Practice Area or Industry tab to locate Lexis+ databases. The practice areas are listed in alphabetical order and include Tax Law. To find a specific source in Lexis+, use the Sources tab and either type the name of your source in the search box or select View All Sources for an alphabetical list of the content within Lexis+.

Illustration 17-2. Portion of Lexis+ Tax Law Screen

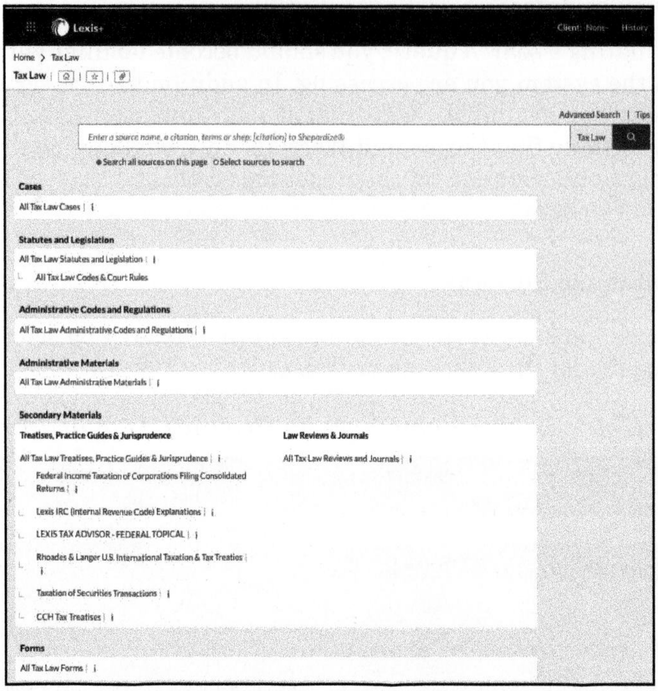

Lexis+ includes primary and secondary source materials. Secondary sources include law reviews and treatises, Shepard's Citations, and services published by Matthew Bender (e.g., Rabkin & Johnson, Federal Income, Gift and Estate Taxation).

c. Connectors and Wildcard Characters

Lexis+ lets you use Boolean and proximity connectors.

Table 17-A. Lexis+ Connectors

Term	*Meaning*
and; &	All words must appear
or	At least one of the words must appear
and not	Excludes a word or phrase
w/n; /n; near/n	Words must appear within n words of each other; either can appear first (n can be any number; less than 100 is best for avoiding usages in unrelated contexts)
w/s; w/sent	Words must appear within the same sentence (defined as within 25 words)
w/p; w/para	Words must appear within the same paragraph (defined as within 75 words)
w/seg	Words must appear in the same segment (e.g., case caption, text) (or within 100 words)

Term	*Meaning*
pre/n; +n; onear/n	First word must precede second by no more than n words
pre/s; +s	First word must precede second in the same sentence (defined as approximately 25 words)
pre/p; +p	First word must precede second in the same paragraph (defined as approximately 75 words)
not w/n	Finds the first term but there is no mention of the second term within the specified number
not w/s	Finds the first term but there is no mention of the second term within the same sentence (defined as approximately 25 words)
not w/p	Finds the first term but there is no mention of the second term within the same paragraph (defined as approximately 75 words)
not w/seg	Finds the first term but there is no mention of the second term within the same segment (defined as approximately 100 words)
" "	Exact phrase

You can use an exclamation point (!) or an asterisk (*) as a wildcard symbol at the end of the word. The exclamation point should be used only if there are at least three letters in front of it. You can also use either character within a word, in which case it will find multiple letters. You can use a question mark (?) to replace a single letter anywhere in a word except as the first letter.

Illustration 17-3. Lexis+ Tax Law Search Terms Screen

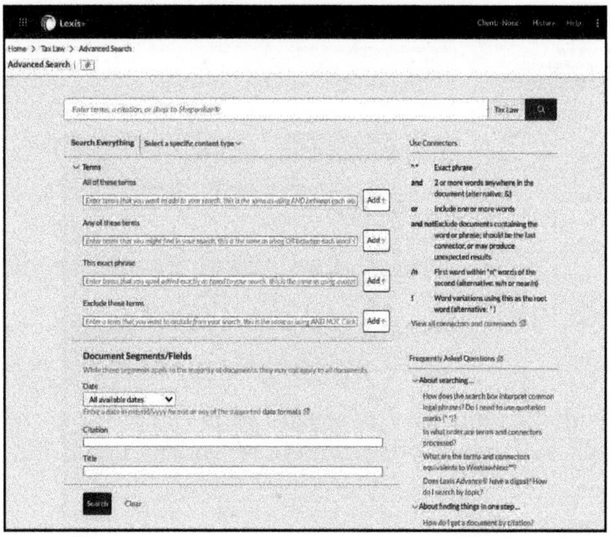

When you type search terms on the home screen, Lexis+ suggests additional search options. [See Illustration 17-4.] It does not currently do this if you are searching in the Tax screen.

Illustration 17-4. Lexis+ Suggested Legal Phrases

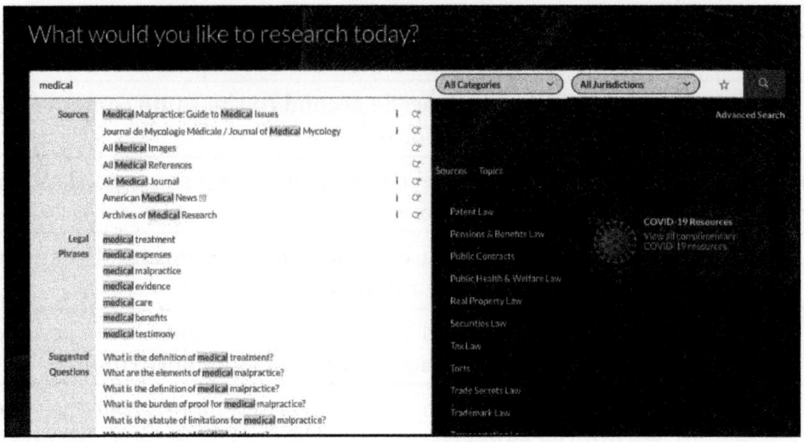

d. Search Restrictions

You can search using all sources, or you can specify a particular source (e.g., Tax Court) before you search. After you perform your initial search, Lexis+ offers filtering options for displaying your results and narrowing your search. Filters vary by the type of source you select.

Illustration 17-5. Lexis+ Display Options

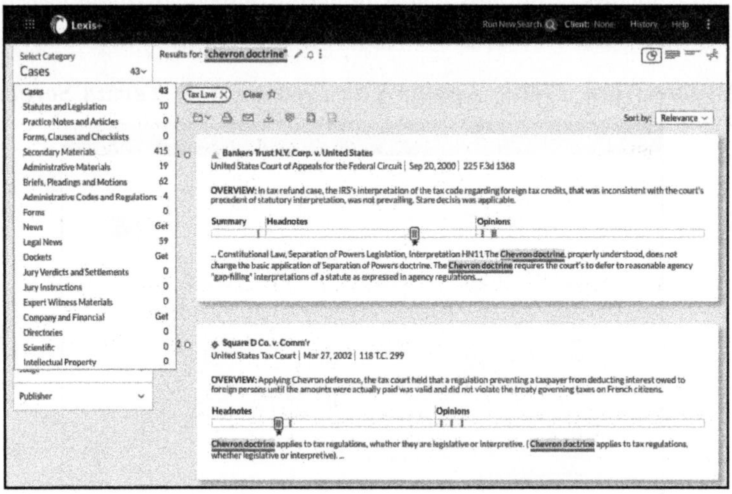

→ This is the results screen for the search term "chevron doctrine." You can then choose between cases, statutes and legislation, secondary materials, etc., for displaying results.

Illustration 17-6. Lexis+ Filters: Cases

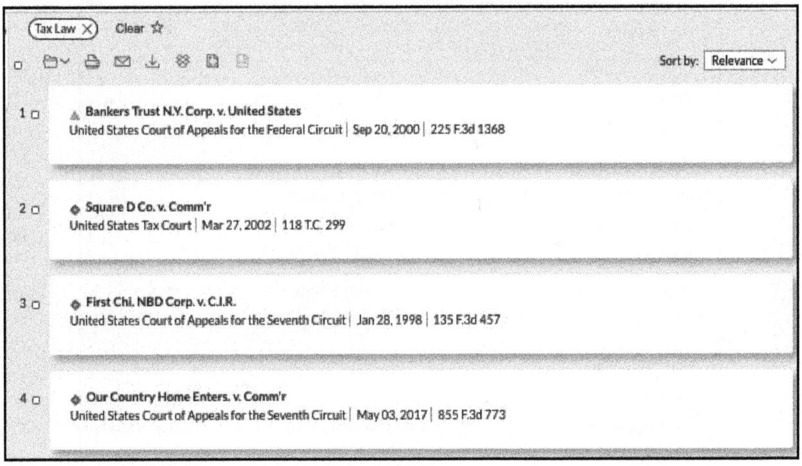

Filters for judicial decisions include court, date (timeline), publication status (reported and unreported), sources (different courts), practice area, attorney, law firm, most cited, key word, judge, and publisher.

e. Search Method Options

You can perform Lexis+ searches using the connectors and search terms described above, or you can simply enter terms into the search box and then use the filters provided by the system to narrow your search. For natural language searches, Lexis+ adds "missing" and "must include" to its search results. If the individual search results do not include one of the words in your search, it will show the missing term under the result. Directly next to that will be "must include" and the missing term. If you want that term in all your search results, click on "must include" and the search will be re-run to include that term in all your displayed results.

f. Citator

Lexis+ includes the Shepard's Citator, which is discussed in Chapter 11. Hyperlinked symbols to the left of cases or other items indicate that updating material is available. [See Illustration 10-5, *supra* page 212.] You can also enter citations directly into the citator.

4. Westlaw Edge

a. Database Screens

The Westlaw Edge All Content screen includes a variety of generic databases.[3]

[3] Thomson Reuters introduced Westlaw Edge in summer 2018. Westlaw Edge completes research tasks using artificial intelligence, including litigation analytics (determining how a judge will rule, how likely an opponent is to settle a case, etc.); new warnings for invalid or questionable law; and the ability to compare different versions of a statute using its new tool, Statutes Compare.

Illustration 17-7. Westlaw Edge Content Types Screen

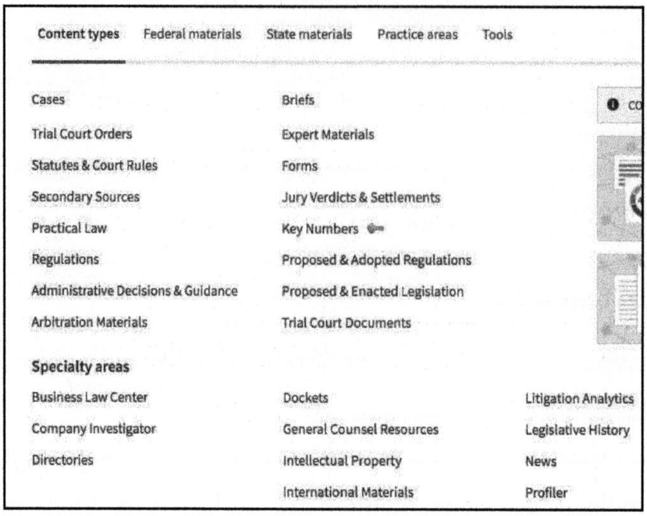

→ As with Lexis+, you can reach Westlaw Edge's tax area by selecting the Practice areas tab and then clicking on Tax.

Illustration 17-8. Portion of Westlaw Edge Tax Screen

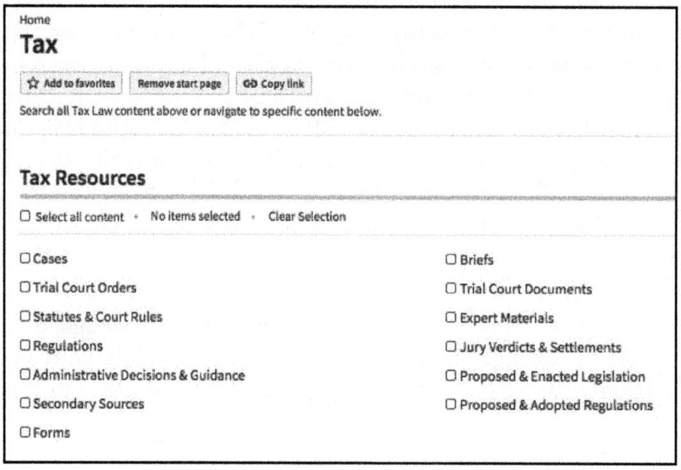

→ Selecting any of the sources gives you either tax-specific information (e.g., the most recently published tax cases in Cases) or other potentially relevant information (e.g., a list of the various tax publications in Secondary Sources).

Click on the scope icon (ⓘ) at the top of a source's page to determine what is included in each folder included in that file.

b. Database Files

The Secondary Sources files cover tax-oriented law reviews as well as treatises and looseleaf services from Research Institute of America, Warren, Gorham & Lamont, and other Thomson Reuters entities. Looseleaf services include Federal Tax Coordinator 2d, Mertens, Law of Federal Income Taxation, and United States Tax Reporter.

c. Connectors and Wildcard Characters

Westlaw Edge lets you use Boolean and proximity connectors.

Table 17-B. Westlaw Edge Connectors

Term	*Meaning*
&; AND[4]	Both terms must appear
space; OR	At least one of the terms must appear
%	Only the term before the % may appear
/n	Terms must appear within n (1–255) words of each other; either can appear first
+n	Terms must appear within n (1–255) words of each other and in the same order
/s	Terms must appear within the same sentence
/p	Terms must appear within the same paragraph
+s	First term must precede the second in the same sentence
+p	First term must precede the second in the same paragraph
" "	Exact phrase

You can use a single exclamation point (!) as a wildcard symbol (root expander) to expand words by any number of letters following the !. An asterisk (*) is a universal character and adds missing letters anywhere but at the beginning of the word. Each * represents a single missing letter. Use a # sign to turn off automatic retrieval of plural forms.

d. Search Restrictions

Like Lexis+, Westlaw Edge allows you to search all sources, or you can specify a particular source or practice area before you search. The Westlaw Edge advanced search option lets you specify whether you want all of the terms, any of the terms, or an exact phrase. You can also specify how many times each term must appear. You can also exclude terms or add a citation or a name or title.

You can restrict your search by date. Options include unrestricted and last 30, 60, and 90 days, last six months, last 12 months, or last three years. Alternatively, you can enter All Dates Before, All Dates After, a Specific Date, or a Date Range.

---

[4] You must affirmatively change your settings within the Search tab to use the words AND and OR as Boolean search terms.

e. Search Method Options

Although Westlaw Edge lets you use terms and connectors, you can also search simply by entering words into a search box. You can refine your search based on the initial results, using a variety of filters.

Illustration 17-9. Westlaw Edge Search Results

→ This illustration shows the search results for "bad debt" in the Tax Practice area.

→ You can use the results links to narrow the search results in that area. For example, Cases can filter the 5,320 cases by jurisdiction, date, reported status, practice area, judge/attorney/law firm, key number, party, or docket number.

f. Citator

Westlaw Edge includes KeyCite and RIA Federal Tax Citator 2nd; both are discussed in Chapter 11. It shows KeyCite, but not RIA Citator 2nd, on results screens.

5. Bloomberg Law

a. Database Screens

You can reach Bloomberg Law's tax area in either of two ways. You can select Browse from the home screen and under Practice Centers select Tax. This brings up a new tab in your browser for Bloomberg Law: Tax. Alternatively, you can select Tax from the Other Products list on the bottom of the home screen.

Illustration 17-10. Bloomberg Law Home Screen

b. Database Files

Bloomberg Law's tax area places a large number of tax resources at your disposal. The Tax Management Portfolios, statutes, regulations, IRS documents, case law, practice-oriented materials (forms, client letters, etc.), and news and journals are all listed on the page.

Illustration 17-11. Bloomberg Law: Tax Screen

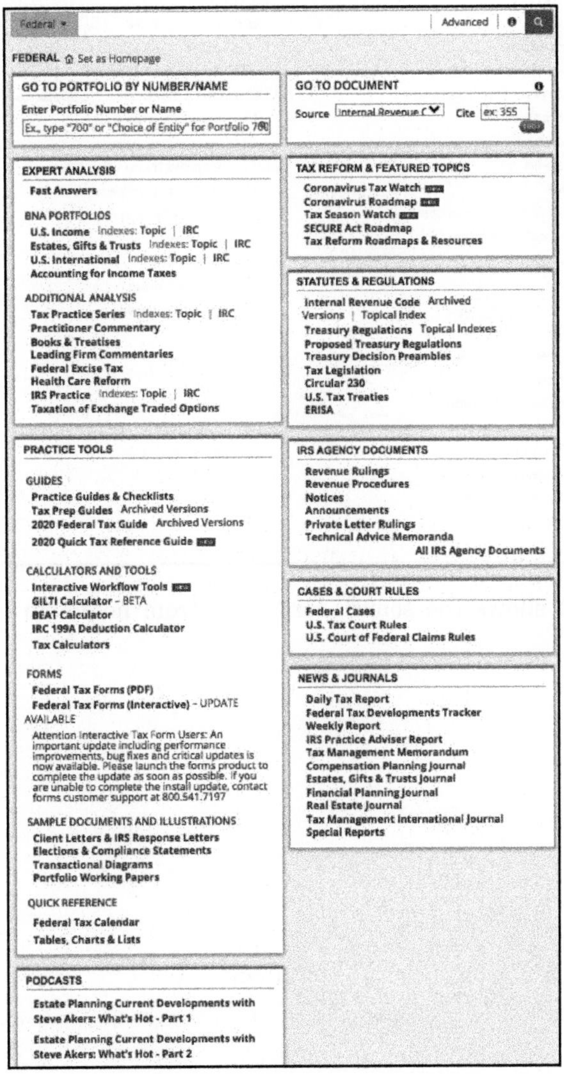

You can restrict your search by selecting one of the items listed on the page. Alternatively, if you click on Advanced at the top of the page, you can select the sources you want to search.

Illustration 17-12. Bloomberg Law: Tax Advanced Search

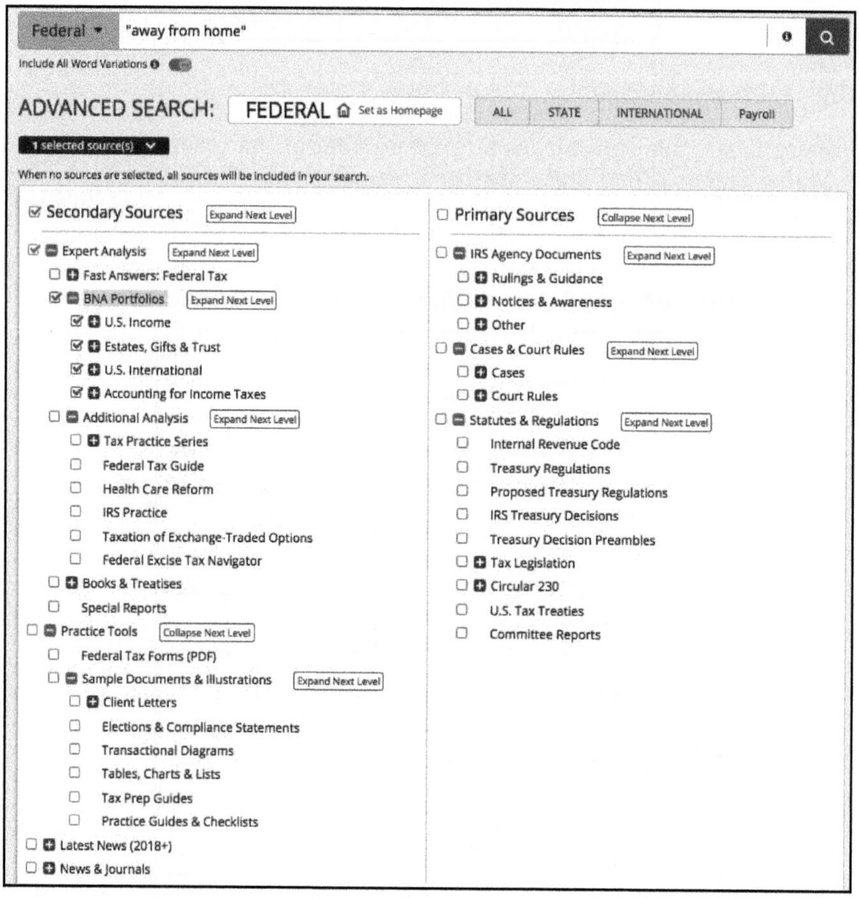

→ This illustration shows the search for "away from home" in any of the BNA Tax Portfolios.

Illustration 17-13. Bloomberg Law: Tax Search Results

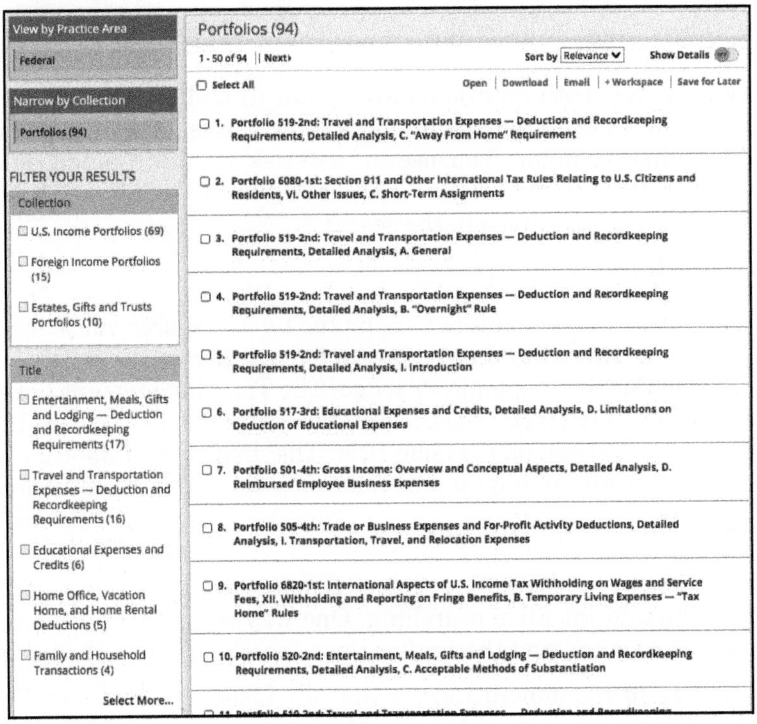

c. Connectors and Wildcard Characters

Bloomberg Law lets you use Boolean and proximity connectors.

Table 17-C. Bloomberg Law Tax Connectors

Term	*Meaning*
AND; space	Both terms must appear; AND must be in all caps
OR	At least one of the terms must appear; OR must be in all caps
NOT; AND NOT; BUT NOT	Exclude the search term; NOT must be in all caps
( )	Use parentheses to combine and order other modifiers
" "	Exact phrase or meaning
^" "	Exact phrase and case sensitive
N/x	Terms must appear within x words of each other; either can appear first
NP/x	Second term must be within x words of the first
S/	Terms must appear within the same sentence
P/	Terms must appear within the same paragraph
ATLx( )	There must be at least x mentions of the term(s) in the parentheses

Term	*Meaning*
ATMx( )	There must be at most x mentions of the term(s) in the parentheses

Bloomberg Law uses both an exclamation point (!) and an asterisk (*) as wildcard symbols. You use an exclamation point to expand words by any number of letters following the exclamation point. You use an asterisk to add a single missing letter. Bloomberg also allows you to turn on an "Include All Word Variations" option. If you do so, Bloomberg adds word variations to the search.

d. Search Restrictions

In Bloomberg Law: Tax, the filters vary by the type of source you select. The search results for cases can be filtered by date, relevant federal circuit, state, level of court (Tax Court, U.S. Supreme Court, etc.), topic, or judge. The Tax Management Portfolios can be filtered by type of Portfolio (U.S. Income; Estates, Gifts & Trusts; U.S. International; Accounting for Income Taxes), or Portfolio title. The display results are sorted only by relevance. Search terms are highlighted in yellow on the search results screen.

e. Search Method Options

Just as with Lexis+ and Westlaw Edge, Bloomberg Law allows both terms and connectors searching and intuitive searching. One way to complete your research is to use a general search to start, and then refine your search based on the initial results.

A useful feature of Bloomberg Law is that all Code sections have links (Related Content) to related subject matter in the Tax Management Portfolios, BNA Tax Practice Series, other relevant statutes, and regulations. Another useful feature is access to the Daily Tax Report newsletter.

Illustration 17-14. Bloomberg Law: I.R.C. § 213

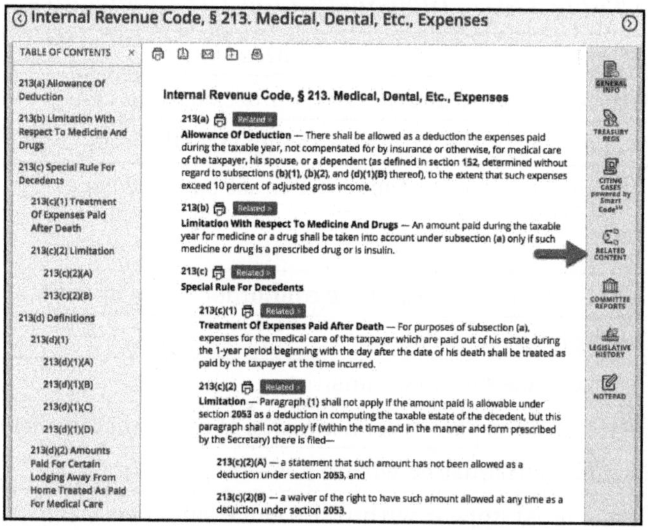

→ Note the various associated materials on the right-hand edge, including the Related Content link.

→ The Bloomberg Law: Tax Code includes the complete citation for each subsection/ paragraph/subparagraph/clause/subclause. This feature makes reading a complex statute much easier.

Illustration 17-15. Bloomberg Law: Portion of I.R.C. § 213 Related Content

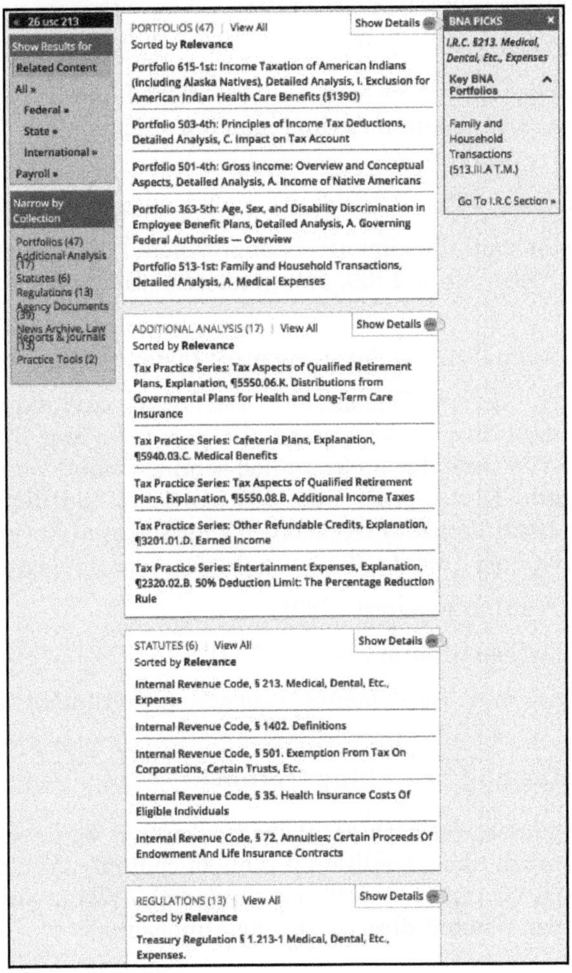

f. Citator

Bloomberg Law uses BCite for cases and IRS documents (revenue rulings, notices, etc.) and Smart Code for statutes and regulations. Both citators are discussed in detail in Chapter 11.

6. HeinOnline

HeinOnline was initially known as a site for finding old law review issues. It has since evolved into a significant source for finding full text of articles, legislative history materials, and other services. Items in this service were scanned from original documents. This feature gives you easy access to correct pagination.

a. Databases

HeinOnline databases relevant to tax research include:

- Code of Federal Regulations (since 1938)
- Federal Register Library (since 1936)
- Law Journal Library
- Taxation & Economic Reform in America Parts I and II (legislative history compilations and Seidman's and Barton's legislative history tracing materials)
- U.S. Code (since 1925)
- U.S. Congressional Documents (Congressional Record since 1873 and predecessor titles since 1789; Congressional Hearings since 1927; CRS Reports)
- U.S. Congressional Serial Set (legislative history documents since 1978)
- U.S. Federal Agency Documents, Decisions, and Appeals (Internal Revenue Cumulative Bulletins from 1919 to 2008 and Internal Revenue Weekly Bulletin Cumulation (compiled semiannually) since 2009; Reports of the Board of Tax Appeals from 1924 to 1942 and Reports of the Tax Court since 1942; Treasury Decisions Under Internal Revenue Laws of the United States from 1899 to 1942 and predecessor publications)
- U.S. Statutes at Large (since 1789)
- U.S. Supreme Court Library (since 1754)
- U.S. Treaties and Agreements Library (government and secondary sources)

b. Browsing and Searching Options

HeinOnline lets you browse each database or search it for desired information. The browse option works much like a traditional table of contents. You can browse multiple titles within a database or limit yourself to a single title. When you locate an item that looks promising, you can reach it directly through hyperlinks.

Illustration 17-16. HeinOnline Advanced Search Option in U.S. Federal Agency Documents, Decisions, and Appeals Database

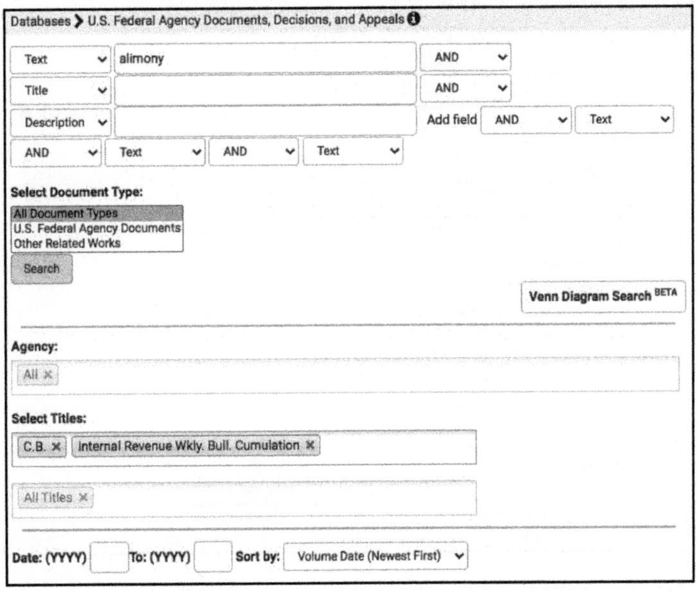

→ Because the C.B. ended publication after 2008, your search is not complete until you check the Internal Revenue Weekly Bulletin title. The Select Titles option lists the Cumulative Bulletins as "C.B." It lists the post-2008 weekly I.R.B. as "Internal Revenue Wkly. Bull. Cumulation" and "Internal Revenue Weekly Bulletin Cumulation."

→ Because HeinOnline publishes the weekly items only on a cumulated semiannual basis, use a different source for the most recent I.R.B. material.

Search options vary by database. In addition to doing a general word or phrase search, you can search many databases by field, date, and title.

Several databases have a Citation Navigator option. This is similar to the "get a document by citation" option offered in other online services.

Illustration 17-17. HeinOnline Results from Search in C.B. and I.R.B.

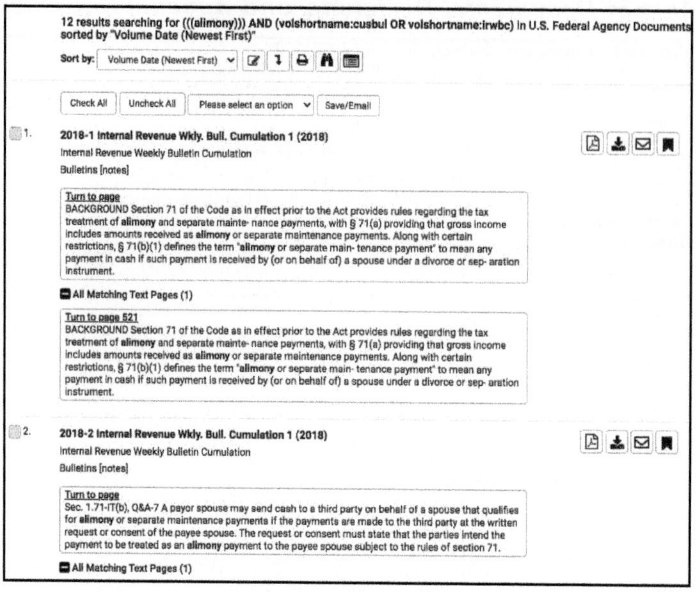

→ You can toggle the All Matching Text Pages option (the binoculars icon near the top of the illustration) to see your search term in each "hit."

→ You can sort your search results by relevance, date, or document title.

Illustration 17-18. HeinOnline Citation Navigator for C.B.

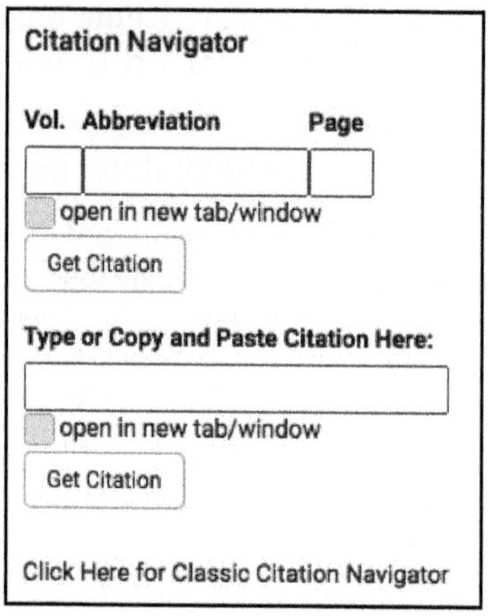

→ A faster way to locate material is using the Citation Navigator that is available in many databases in HeinOnline. To access it, click the "Citation" tab above the search bar. If available, "Citation Navigator" will appear below the search bar.

c. Connectors and Wildcard Characters

HeinOnline lets you use Boolean and proximity connectors.

Table 17-D. HeinOnline Connectors

Term	*Meaning*
AND	Both search terms must appear; AND must be in all caps
OR	At least one search term must appear; OR must be in all caps
NOT; !	The search term following NOT must not appear; NOT must be in all caps
+	The term immediately after the plus sign must appear in the document
–	The term immediately after the minus sign must not appear in the document
" "	Exact phrase
( )	Use parentheses to search grouped clauses to form sub-queries
~n	Use to search for words within n words of each other; enclose the words in quotation marks
w/#; /#	Terms must appear within # words of each other
w/s; /s	Terms must appear in the same sentence (defined as 25 words)
w/p; /p	Terms must appear in the same paragraph (defined as 75 words)
w/seg; /seg	Terms must appear in the same segment (defined as 100 words)

A question mark (?) is a universal character that searches for variations of the word you want to include in your search. For example, "ne?t" will find nest and next. The question mark can be used to replace one letter. An asterisk (*) searches for words with different possible endings or to replace more than one letter within a word.

d. Citator

HeinOnline does not have an associated citator, but it does let you find and read articles that cite to the article you are reading. [See Illustration 13-12, *supra* page 271.]

7. ProQuest Congressional

ProQuest Congressional offers PDF access to an extensive collection of legislative history materials. Its database includes bills, testimony at hearings, Congressional Record, and CRS reports.

ProQuest Congressional lets you use Boolean and proximity connectors. The Boolean operators may be in upper or lower case.

Table 17-E. ProQuest Congressional Connectors

Term	*Meaning*
AND; space	Both search terms must appear
OR	At least one search term must appear
NOT	The search term following NOT must not appear
" "	Exact phrase

Term	*Meaning*
( )	Use parentheses to search grouped clauses to form sub-queries
NEAR/n	Searches for words within n words of each other; defaults to 100 words if no value is specified
ALLCAPS( )	Searches for capital letters (e.g., IRS) corresponding to the search term within the parentheses. The search term need not be capitalized

A question mark (?) within or at the end of a word is a wildcard that replaces one letter within or at the end of the word. An asterisk (*) at the end of a word finds words that end with one or more additional letters.

ProQuest Congressional does not have a citator.

8. LLMC Digital

LLMC Digital (formerly the Law Library Microform Consortium (LLMC)) is a non-profit cooperative of libraries that works to digitize older books. Its focus is on legal literature and government documents, and it currently has the world's largest collections of those topics in digital format and in microform. If you need to find older books, LLMC should be one of the first places to look.[5]

E. Subscription Services—Tax Focus

Discussion in this section focuses on Cheetah (CCH), Checkpoint (Thomson Reuters), and two Tax Notes databases.

1. Cheetah

a. Database Screens and Contents

The content from Wolters Kluwer's CCH is currently available on two platforms, Cheetah and IntelliConnect. Both have access to the same content, but Cheetah is newer and looks more modern. Because most academic accounts were switched to Cheetah in mid-2020, Cheetah is used for all the illustrations. The contents and search parameters are the same on both platforms.

The Cheetah home screen is shown in Illustration 17-19. From there you can select from different tax practice areas or search all the content in Cheetah.

[5] Other sources for digitized older books are HeinOnline; The Making of Modern Law: Legal Treatises, 1800–1926; and HathiTrust Digital Library.

Illustration 17-19. Cheetah Home Screen

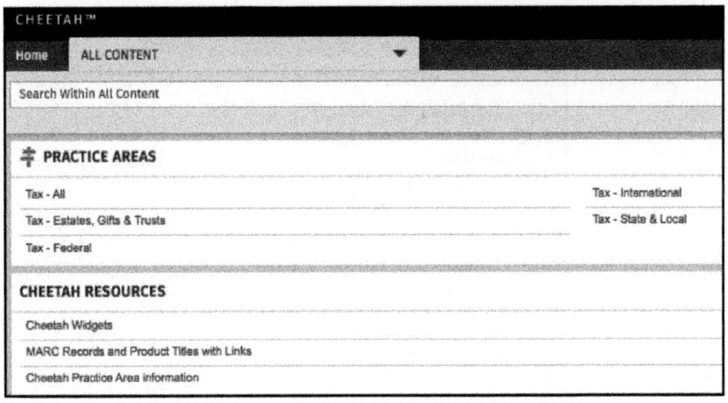

→ Click on one of the practice areas to receive more choices.

Illustration 17-20. Cheetah Federal Tax Home Screen

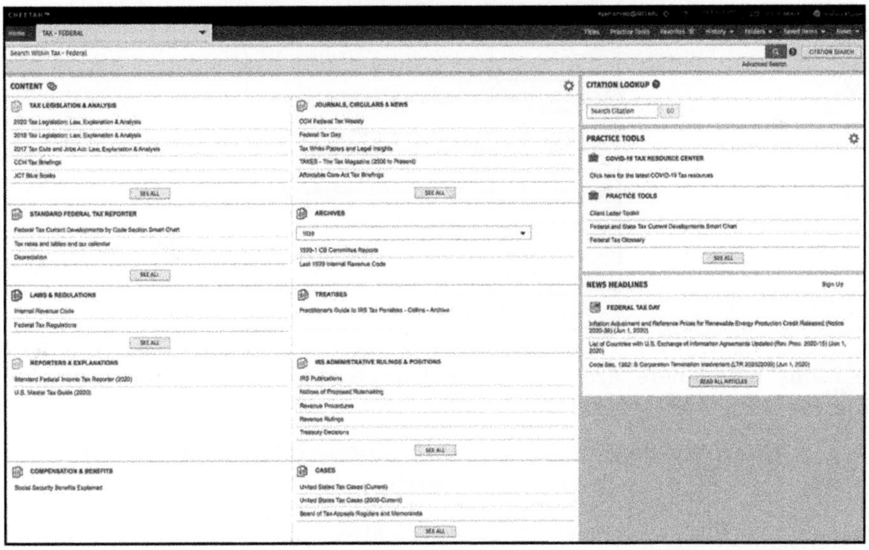

→ Tax-Federal includes Standard Federal Tax Reporter and U.S. Master Tax Guide (listed under Reporters & Explanations).

→ Tax-Federal Laws & Regulations includes the Code and regulations.

→ Tax-Federal IRS Administrative Rulings & Positions includes IRS material (e.g., letter rulings, notices, revenue rulings and procedures, and Treasury decisions).

→ Tax-Federal Cases includes judicial decisions.

→ Tax-Federal Tax Legislation & Analysis includes bills and acts, committee reports, and JCT and CRS reports.

Illustration 17-21. Cheetah Contents Screen for SFTR

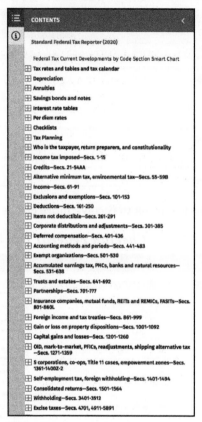

CONTENTS

Standard Federal Tax Reporter (2020)

Federal Tax Current Developments by Code Section Smart Chart

- Tax rates and tables and tax calendar
- Depreciation
- Annuities
- Savings bonds and notes
- Interest rate tables
- Per diem rates
- Checklists
- Tax Planning
- Who is the taxpayer, return preparers, and constitutionality
- Income tax imposed—Secs. 1-15
- Credits—Secs. 21-54AA
- Alternative minimum tax, environmental tax—Secs. 55-59B
- Income—Secs. 61-91
- Exclusions and exemptions—Secs. 101-153
- Deductions—Secs. 161-250
- Items not deductible—Secs. 261-291
- Corporate distributions and adjustments—Secs. 301-385
- Deferred compensation—Secs. 401-436
- Accounting methods and periods—Secs. 441-483
- Exempt organizations—Secs. 501-530
- Accumulated earnings tax, PHCs, banks and natural resources—Secs. 531-638
- Trusts and estates—Secs. 641-692
- Partnerships—Secs. 701-777
- Insurance companies, mutual funds, REITs and REMICs, FASITs—Secs. 801-860L
- Foreign income and tax treaties—Secs. 861-999
- Gain or loss on property dispositions—Secs. 1001-1092
- Capital gains and losses—Secs. 1201-1260
- OID, mark-to-market, PFICs, readjustments, shipping alternative tax —Secs. 1271-1359
- S corporations, co-ops, Title 11 cases, empowerment zones—Secs. 1361-1400Z-2
- Self-employment tax, foreign withholding—Secs. 1401-1494
- Consolidated returns—Secs. 1501-1564
- Withholding—Secs. 3401-3512
- Excise taxes—Secs. 4701, 4911-5891

→ The items listed here are covered in Chapter 12, Section B.1, *supra* page 234, discussing the Standard Federal Tax Reporter.

Illustration 17-22. Cheetah Federal Tax Contents of Journals, Circulars & News

JOURNALS, CIRCULARS & NEWS

- Affordable Care Act Tax Briefings
- CCH Federal Tax Weekly
- CCH Federal Tax Weekly - Archives
- CCH Legislation Newswire
- CCH Tax Briefings
- Federal Tax Day
- PWC's Insights
- State Tax Review - Archives
- Tax White Papers and Legal Insights
- TAXES - The Tax Magazine (1986 to 2005)
- TAXES - The Tax Magazine (2006 to Present)
- Today's Federal and State Tax News Highlights

Cheetah includes the Code, committee reports, regulations, treaties, IRS materials, and judicial decisions. The service includes Standard Federal Tax Reporter, CCH newsletters and journals, a citator, and various practice aids.

b. Connectors, Wildcard Characters, and Synonyms

Cheetah lets you use Boolean and proximity connectors.

Table 17-F. Cheetah Connectors

Term	*Meaning*
AND; space	Both terms must appear
OR	Either term must appear
NOT	Only the first term may appear
-	Search will not include words after a hyphen
w/n	The first term must appear within n words of the second (n cannot exceed 127)
w/sen	The first term must appear within 20 words of the second
w/par	The first term must appear within 80 words of the second
f/n	The first term must follow within n words of the second
p/n	The first term must precede the second within n words
" "	Exact phrase

You can use one or more question marks (?) as a wildcard symbol to insert the requisite number of characters. You can use an asterisk (*) to add missing letters; the system will replace a single * with more than one character.

Cheetah lets you find synonyms for your search term. You can also use its Thesaurus function in your searches.

c. Date Restrictions

You can restrict your search by date. Options include any day, on, before, after, and from/to.

d. Search Method Options

You can use the Search bar at the top of the Cheetah home page or you can click on Advanced Search to add additional search features. Both methods let you select searching in the entire Cheetah database ("all content") or in selected files or content. The Advanced Search tool lets you add limitations based on document type, court, jurisdiction, and date. It also lets you control the Thesaurus option.

Illustration 17-23. Cheetah Advanced Search Screen

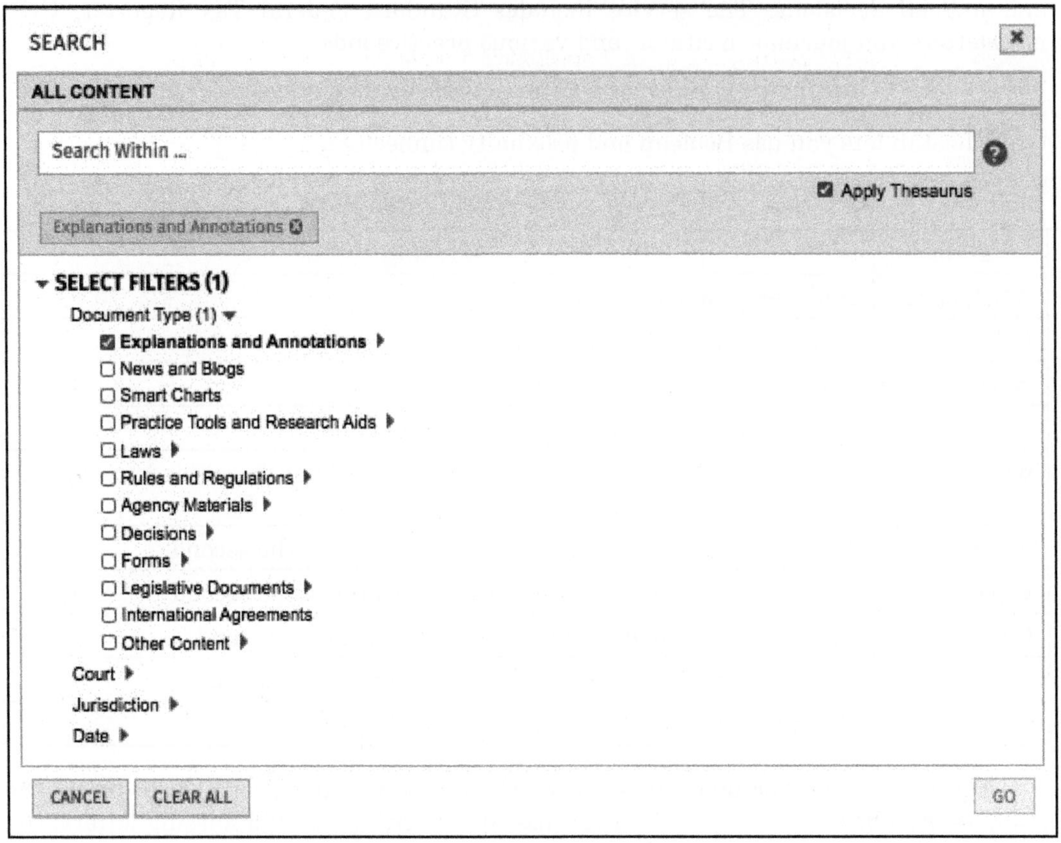

e. Citator

Cheetah includes the CCH Citator, which is discussed in Chapter 11. The looseleaf version of this citator is divided into three services, one for each of CCH's Code-based looseleaf services. Because the online version is not divided in this manner, you can find both income and gift tax cases that cite to a particular tax case with a single search. The online citator does not have an alphabetical (judicial decisions) or numerical (IRS material) browse function. You can use the online citator only if you have a citation or are using the citator after finding a document some other way.

2. Checkpoint

This service was originally named RIA Checkpoint and many users still refer to it by that name; its home screen now carries the Thomson Reuters imprint. Its content includes several RIA looseleaf services in addition to other material. Checkpoint allows you to search intuitively or using terms and connectors.

a. Database Screens and Contents

Several sections of the Checkpoint Table of Contents Screen are relevant. One is the list of available databases, which is excerpted in Illustrations 17-24 and 17-25.

Discussion and illustrations below cover various search options and browse options, including the Table of Contents feature.

Illustration 17-24. Checkpoint Table of Contents Screen

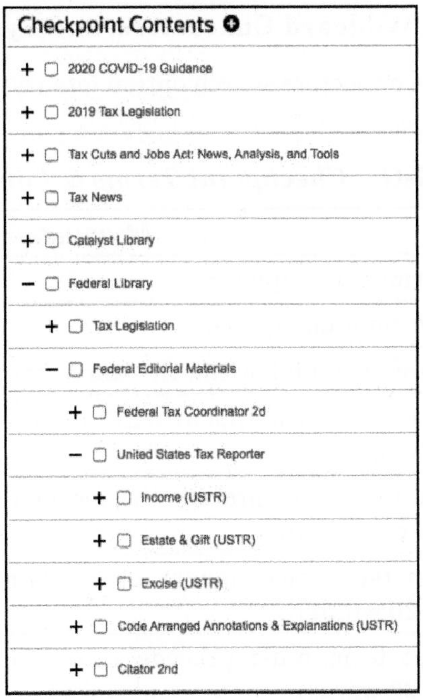

→ You can expand the Contents on this screen, or you can select a Library and go to the Search Screen.

Illustration 17-25. Checkpoint Search Screen: Federal Library

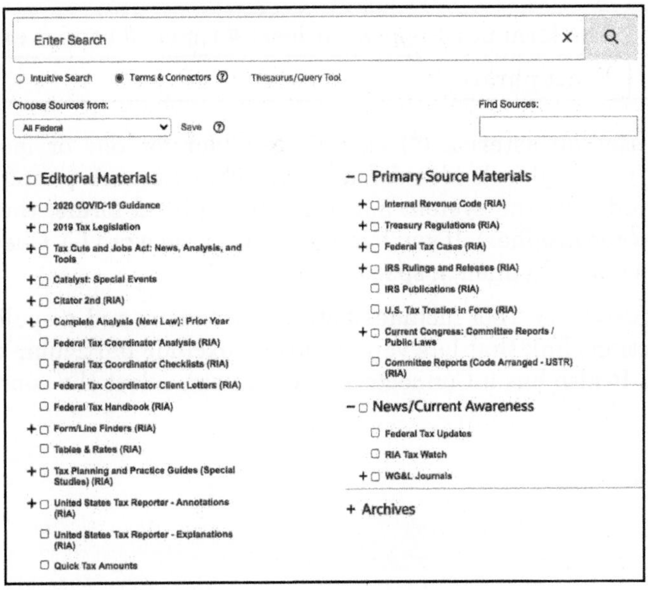

Checkpoint includes the Code, committee reports, regulations, treaties, IRS materials, and judicial decisions. The service includes United States Tax Reporter, Federal Tax Coordinator 2d, newsletters and journals, the RIA citator, and various practice aids.

b. Connectors, Wildcard Characters, and Synonyms

Checkpoint's Terms & Connectors search option lets you use Boolean and proximity connectors.

Table 17-G. Checkpoint Terms & Connectors

Term	*Meaning*
&; AND; space	Both terms must appear
|; OR	Either term must appear
^; NOT	The search term following the connector must not appear
/#	The first term must appear within # words of the second (# cannot exceed 255)
pre/#	The first term must precede the second by no more than # words (# cannot exceed 255)
/s	The first term must appear in the same sentence as the second (within 20 words)
pre/s	The first term must precede the second in the same sentence (within 20 words)
/p	The first term must appear in the same paragraph as the second (within 50 words)
pre/p	The first term must precede the second in the same paragraph (within 50 words)
atleast#	The term must appear at least # times (# cannot exceed 255)
" "	Exact phrase

Checkpoint uses an asterisk (*) as a placeholder for one or more characters; a question mark (?) is a placeholder for a single character. A pound sign (#) at the beginning of a word tells the system not to retrieve plural forms; the # sign does not affect possessives (apostrophes). If you hyphenate a search word (-), Checkpoint retrieves variations that include a hyphen, a space, or neither.[6]

The Thesaurus/Query Tool includes both a Thesaurus and a spell-checker. It also includes a Restrictions link that lets you require or exclude particular words or phrases from your search. It also has a Connectors box; you can select the connectors you want to use in your search.

6 Checkpoint indicates "e-mail" will also retrieve "e mail" and "email."

c. Date Restrictions

Checkpoint's date range search has from and to date options for searching in cases and rulings. You can add key words to these searches. The Thesaurus/Query Tool is available for these searches.

d. Search Method Options

Checkpoint's Intuitive Search "interprets your query to return the most relevant results for the terms you entered" and works no matter how you structure your search. Unless you are searching for a particular case or ruling, you use the search box at the top of the search page; it can be modified by using the Thesaurus/Query Tool.

Before beginning a search, you can specify a practice area from the Search link. You can also choose between Keyword (the default option), Date Range, and Legislation Searches. You can use this option to search in cases or rulings databases. The Legislation Search option is subdivided by year, beginning in 1996, and includes committee reports. You are limited to a Keyword search only if you select All Practice Areas.

Illustration 17-26. Checkpoint Practice Area Options for Limiting Search

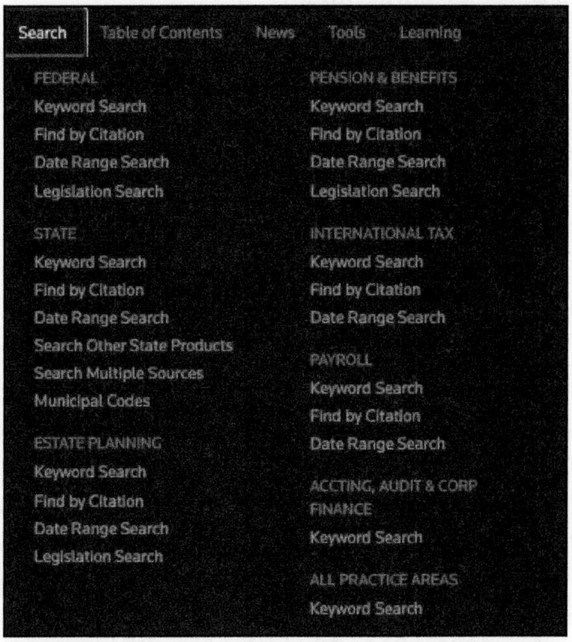

If you already have a citation, you can retrieve the document using the Find by Citation option. "More" offers a list of additional document types for which you can use the Find by Citation option.

Illustration 17-27. Checkpoint Keyword Search in Federal Tax Coordinator 2d

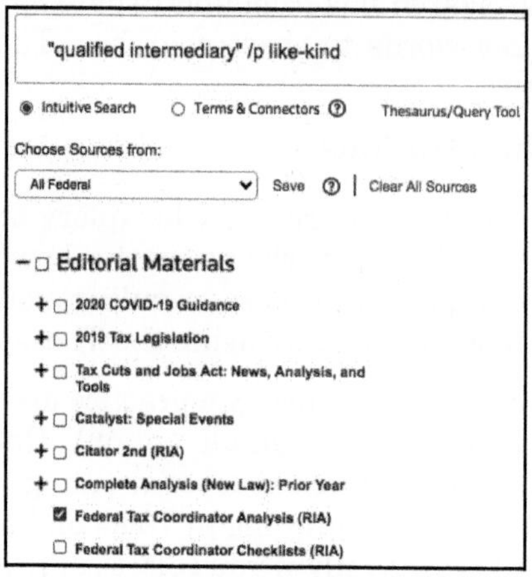

→ The search above is limited to one source and to terms within 50 words of each other but not necessarily in the same paragraph.

Illustration 17-28. Checkpoint Thesaurus Option

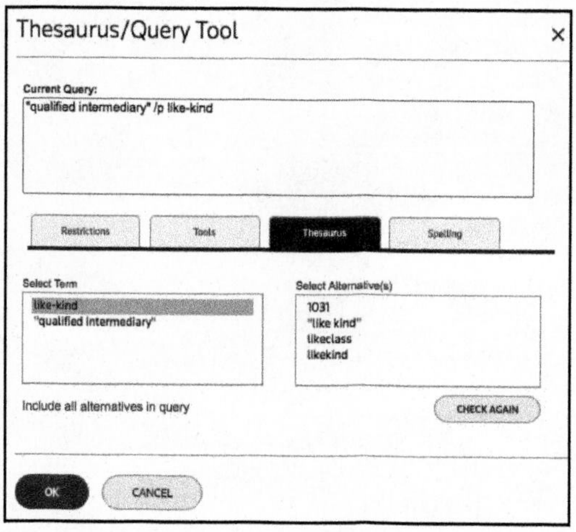

→ The Thesaurus option shows the search could be broadened by adding "1031." Then the Current Query would be: "qualified intermediary" /p (1031 | like-kind). The results would include like-kind or 1031 within 50 words of qualified intermediary.

Illustration 17-29. Checkpoint Search Results

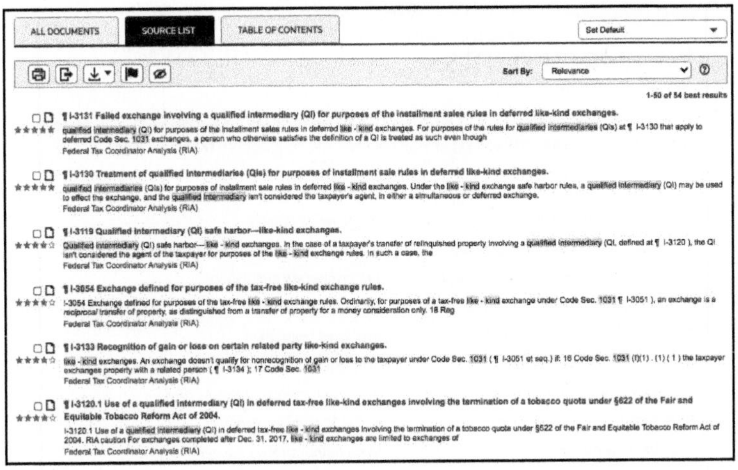

→ Checkpoint rates the found documents.

Instead of searching for documents by term, you can also browse a source's table of contents. Click on the Table of Contents link at the top of the screen and then select the particular databases you want to browse. [See Illustration 17-24, *supra* page 315.]

e. Citator

Checkpoint includes the RIA Citator 2nd. It does not include the earlier RIA (and Prentice-Hall) citator service. The Table of Contents option lets you browse the citator by taxpayer name or IRS document number. The RIA citator is discussed in Chapter 11.

3. Tax Notes Databases

Tax Notes provides primary source documents in its Federal Research Library and its Worldwide Tax Treaties service. The TaxNotes.com site also offers access to newsletters, including Tax Notes Federal. The site does not include a looseleaf service, treatises, or citator.

a. Database Screens and Contents

When you access the Tax Notes home screen, you can access material from the Key Documents tab or the Research Tools option (accessed through the Subscriptions tab).

Illustration 17-30. Tax Notes Home Screen

Illustration 17-31. Tax Notes Key Documents Page

HOME › KEY DOCUMENTS

Key Documents

Tax Notes provides daily news on all tax-related topics, including key resources and tax documents online. Sign up for a free trial and get all your tax news and insights from Tax Notes today!

Administrative Assistance	IRS Revenue Procedures
Attorney General Opinions	IRS Revenue Rulings
Congressional Joint Committee Prints	IRS Technical Advice Memorandums
Congressional Research Service Reports	IRS Temporary Regulations
Consultation Documents and Responses	News Releases
Court Opinions	Proposed Legislation
Court Petitions and Complaints	Proposed State Administrative Regulations
Federal Tax Regulations	Public Comments on Regulations
Final State Administrative Regulations	Social Security Agreements
Final State Legislation	State Administrative Rulings
Internal Revenue Bulletin	State Announcements and News Releases
Internal Revenue Code	State Court Opinions
IRS Final Regulations	Supreme Court Briefs
IRS Letter Rulings	Temporary State Administrative Regulations
IRS Proposed Regulations	Treasury Reports

→ Click on any source on this page to search within that source.

The Research Tools option lets you select between the Federal Research Library, Worldwide Tax Treaties, a Tax Directory, and the Exempt Org. Master List. These offerings are available as separate subscriptions.

The Federal Research Library has both Quick Search and Browse options. Each option covers a discrete primary source, such as the Code or Court Opinions. The Quick Search is useful if you have a citation (or taxpayer name) for the document you seek or if you know the underlying Code section. The Browse option lets you limit your search by word or phrase and includes a limited number of filters.

Illustration 17-32. Tax Notes Federal Research Library Page

FRL SEARCH

QUICK SEARCH

Code Sections

Final & Temporary Regs

Proposed Regulations

Treasury Decisions

IRS Guidance

IRS Private Rulings

Court Opinions

→ In addition to a Quick Search option, this page includes an area entitled "Most Significant Recent Documents," access to the Code, regulations, and other documents, and a Browse function for doing more-extensive searches.

Illustration 17-33. Tax Notes Code Section Resources

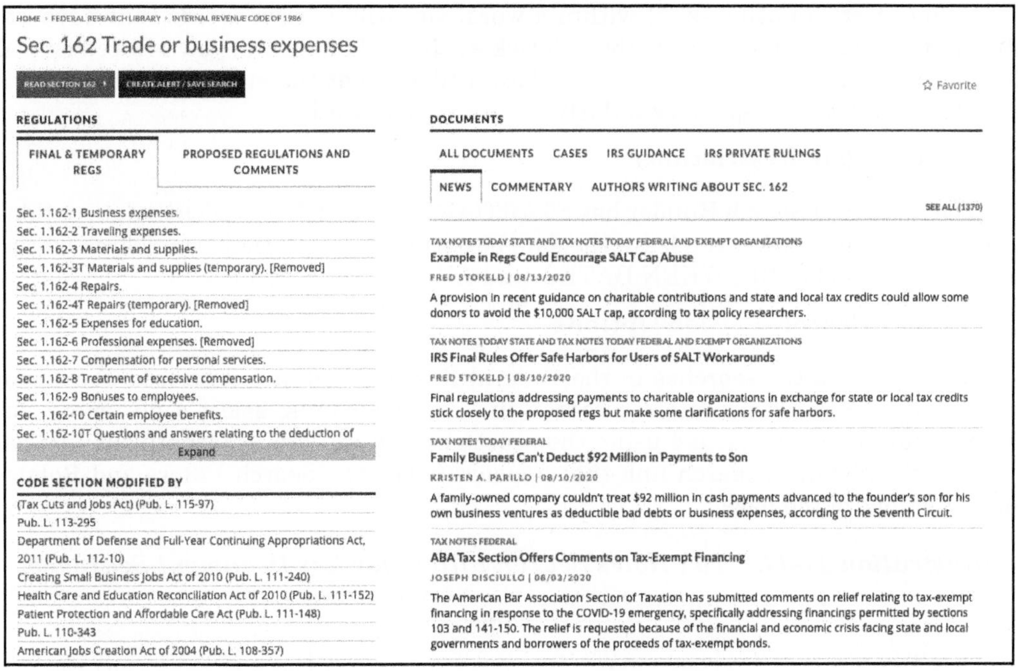

→ Although Tax Notes does not have a citator, its Resources option for Code sections provides links to both primary and secondary sources.

b. Connectors and Wildcard Characters

The Advanced Search feature lets you search the entire Tax Notes platform using key words or terms and connectors for primary source documents, commentary and analysis articles, and news stories.

Table 17-H. Federal Research Library Terms and Connectors

Term	*Meaning*
AND; space	All terms must appear; AND must be in all caps
OR	At least one term must appear; OR must be in all caps
NOT; -	The second term must not appear; NOT must be in all caps
/n	Search for a word within n words of another word or a phrase
/s	Search for a word within the same sentence as another word or a phrase
/p	Search for a word within the same paragraph as another word or a phrase

Term	*Meaning*
“ ”	Exact phrase
( )	Terms can be grouped in the search

If you insert an asterisk (*) within a word, you will retrieve words that have any letter in that space. If you insert the asterisk at the end of a word, you will retrieve all alternate endings for that word. If you place a tilde (~) at the end of a word, you will retrieve words that are spelled similarly to the original word.

c. Date Restrictions

The Advanced Search Builder has START/AFTER and END/BEFORE date options. It searches for all items if you leave the date boxes blank. The Free Form Search feature has BEFORE DATE, BETWEEN DATES, and AFTER DATE options.

d. Search Method Options

In addition to the searches in the Federal Research Library described above, you can search in Key Documents. To search in Key Documents, select a document and narrow your search as needed using the search screen's filters. Alternatively, you can click on the Advanced Search link that appears below the Search Filters and Related Topics sections of the page.

Illustration 17-34. Tax Notes Search Filters for Key Document Searches

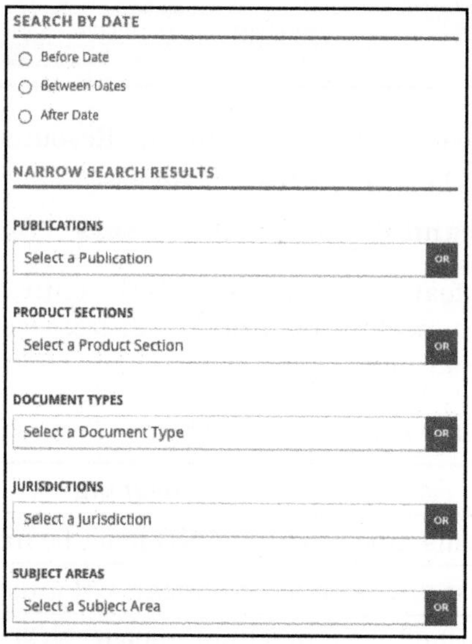

→ This screen appears after you click on a primary source in the Key Documents section of the website. Filters have drop-down menus.

→ You can also filter your search by Code section, author, judge, court, and date.

Illustration 17-35. Tax Notes Menu for the Key Documents Publications Filter

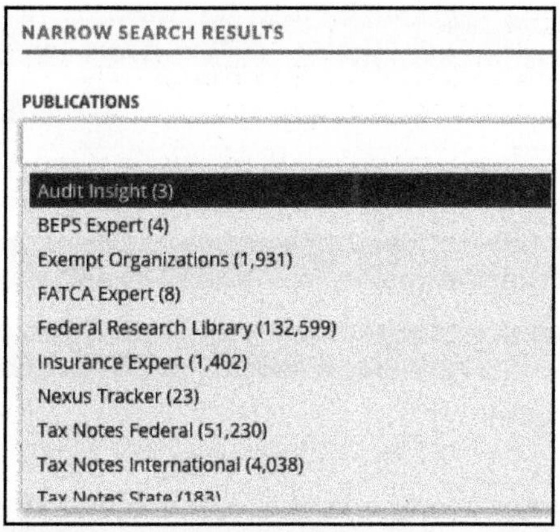

Illustration 17-36. Tax Notes Key Documents Advanced Search Screen

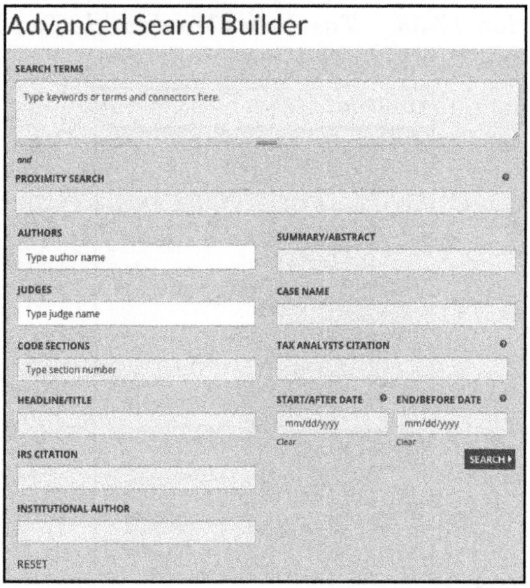

The Worldwide Tax Treaties database covers treaties to which the United States is a party, treaties between other countries, and model treaties. It allows you to browse treaties and to compare treaties. The Advanced Search function is particularly robust.

Illustration 17-37. Tax Notes Worldwide Tax Treaties Home Page

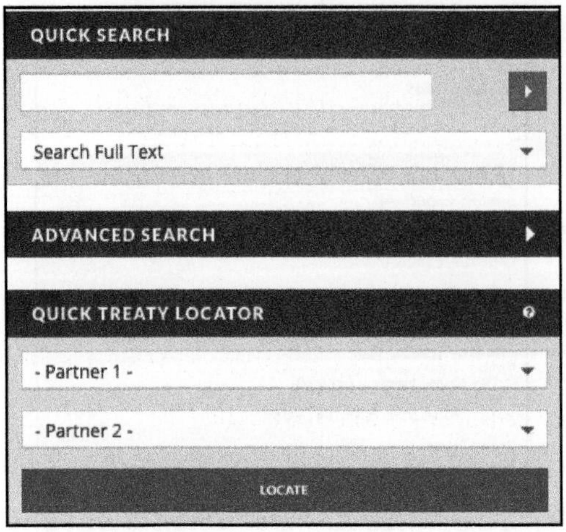

Illustration 17-38. Tax Notes Worldwide Tax Treaties Advanced Search Screen

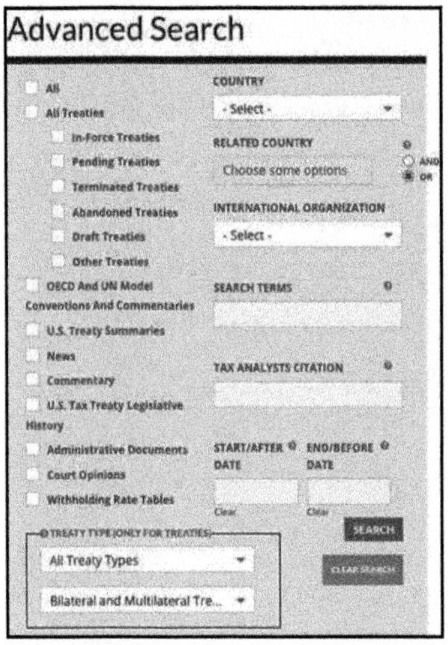

F. Government and Other Nonsubscription Sites

There are a variety of useful websites available. Some provide primary source material directly; some provide hypertext links to other websites; some perform both functions. Unfortunately, websites often change address or cease to exist altogether. You are likely to find that many of your searches lead you to at least a few nonexistent sites.

1. Government Sites[7]

This section lists a selected sample of government sites that you might use in conducting tax research. Table 17-I (*infra* page 326) lists government website illustrations appearing throughout this book.

[7] Online access to government documents is attributable to the Government Printing Office Electronic Information Access Enhancement Act of 1993, Pub. L. No. 103–40, 107 Stat. 112, codified in 44 U.S.C.

a. Govinfo.gov (Government Publishing Office)

Govinfo.gov provides text of, or links to, documents generated by all branches of the federal government. It offers PDF format for many documents, thus allowing you to cite original pagination. Govinfo.gov is particularly useful for statutes and legislative history. The website allows searching by terms; you do not need an exact citation to find many of the covered documents.

b. Congress.gov (Library of Congress)

Users can find texts of bills, note the progress of bills in Congress, and gain access to the Congressional Record and committee reports. You can use Congress.gov to find various versions of a bill, trace its history, and read it as a Public Law.

c. Congressional Support Entities

Entities that provide reports and other analysis include Congressional Budget Office, Congressional Research Service, Government Accountability Office, and Joint Committee on Taxation.

d. Treasury Department

This site includes pages for the Office of Tax Policy. Its Resource Center includes text for recently signed tax treaties that have not yet gone into effect and Treasury testimony at congressional hearings. The Resource Center also includes various reports to Congress and papers prepared by the Office of Tax Analysis.

e. Internal Revenue Service

The IRS site (discussed in Chapter 9) includes text of tax forms and publications, Internal Revenue Bulletins, the Internal Revenue Manual, IRS releases that are not included in the I.R.B., and income tax treaties that are in force. There also links to other primary source materials.

f. White House

This site provides text of presidential speeches, including bill-signing messages. It also provides links to such support functions as the Office of Management and Budget.

g. Regulations.gov and Reginfo.gov

Reginfo.gov is an excellent site for searching agencies' regulatory agendas. Regulations.gov lets you submit comments on pending regulations and read comments submitted by others.

h. United States Courts and Supreme Court[8]

The United States Courts site provides links to individual courts. The Opinions page of the Supreme Court site (https://www.supremecourt.gov) includes a Case Citation Finder. This service provides the preferred citation, as determined by the Reporter of Decisions, for all Supreme Court decisions scheduled for publication in a bound volume

[8] The United States Courts home page (https://www.uscourts.gov) "Federal Court Finder" feature includes webpage links for the Supreme Court, Courts of Appeals, District Courts, Bankruptcy Courts, Probation and Pretrial Offices, and Federal Defender Organizations.

since 1790. This site also includes PDF versions of the bound volumes of the Court's opinions.

i. United States Tax Court

This site provides text of Regular, Memorandum, and Summary Opinions. You can search the site by judge, date, taxpayer name, opinion type, and words in the opinion's text. It currently includes Regular and Memorandum Opinions since September 25, 1995, and Summary Opinions since January 10, 2001. The site also includes Tax Court rules and forms.

j. State Department

The State Department site, discussed briefly in Chapter 7, includes links to the TIAS treaty series.

Table 17-I. Illustrations of Government Websites

Source	*Illustrations*
Congressional Budget Office	6-13
Congress.gov	5-20; 5-21; 6-1; 6-4; 6-5; 6-8; 6-15
Government Accountability Office	6-14
Govinfo.gov	5-19; 6-6; 6-7; 8-15; 8-16
IRS	9-1; 9-2; 9-3; 9-11; 9-14; 14-4; 14-5
Joint Committee on Taxation	6-12
Office of Law Revision Counsel	5-22
Reginfo.gov	8-10; 8-11; 8-12; 8-13
Regulations.gov	8-20; 8-21; 8-22
Tax Court	3-5; 3-6

→ Table 7-B (*supra* page 112) lists government websites that include treaty materials.

2. Tax-Oriented Blogs

Several publishers, accountants, attorneys, and academics maintain blogs focusing on taxation. In addition to commentary on current statutes, judicial decisions, or other matters, the blogs include a variety of links to primary sources, to professional and research organizations, and to other blogs. The sites below are a small sample of those available.

- Procedurally Taxing (https://procedurallytaxing.com/)
- TaxBuzz (https://www.taxbuzz.com/blog)
- Taxgirl (https://www.taxgirl.com)
- TaxProf (https://taxprof.typepad.com/)
- 21st Century Taxation (21stcenturytaxation.blogspot.com/)

3. Other Sites

Chapter 13 includes a partial list of nongovernment entities that prepare reports on tax and economic issues. In addition, several law school sites offer text of tax-oriented material, links to sources providing that information, or research guides for finding tax materials in their libraries.

Finally, in addition to using Google as a search engine, you can use it to find full-text versions of judicial decisions (Chapter 10) and as an articles index (Chapter 13). Both functions are discussed elsewhere in this book.

G. Search Engines

Online sites have Uniform Resource Locator (URL) addresses, most of which begin with http://www (or with http:// without www); often they will start with https://. This book provides URL locations for many websites relevant to tax research. Those sites represent only a small portion of what is available online.

Navigating online can be a daunting task if you lack a site's URL or if you don't know if a site exists. Fortunately, you can use search engines and related services to locate information based on key words.

Search engines are unlikely to lead you to as much primary source material as you can locate using the subscription services discussed in Sections D and E. But search engines may find articles and other analysis that aren't in a commercial service's database.

Search engines let you customize your searches to retrieve documents by date, language, type (e.g., PDF or HTML), or website or domain. Be sure you take advantage of your search engine's capabilities to maximize the chances you will find relevant information.[9]

No matter how you locate your material, remember to determine the last time it was updated. Materials posted to websites may be current, but there is no requirement that they be. Indeed, unlike government or subscription services, there is no guarantee that items posted to a particular website were ever accurate.

Although Google has become an everyday word, it is not the only search engine option. In addition to Google, you may decide to use Bing, Yahoo, or another search engine. You will get a better idea of what each can do if you conduct the same search in several search engines.

H. Problems

You can solve many of the problems in earlier chapters using online services. For some of them, online searches are your only viable option. Those problems lack sufficient identifying information to allow searches using print materials. To practice your online research skills, try the following tasks.

1. Find recently introduced legislation on a topic your instructor selects. Follow its history through Congress.

[9] See Thomas R. Keefe, *The Invisible Web: What You Can't See Might Hurt You*, RES. ADVISOR, May 2002, at 1.

2. Track the progress of a regulations project your instructor selects.

3. Find all IRS documents released this year that mention a Code section your instructor selects.

4. Download the presidential signing statement for the Tax Cuts and Jobs Act or another act that your instructor selects.

5. Find articles posted on the web on a topic your instructor selects. Concentrate on websites for law and accounting firms.

6. Using a search engine, search for a phrase of your instructor's choice. First, conduct your search without treating the words as a phrase. Then redo the search using the search engine's advanced search options. What refinements did you need to produce more relevant results?

Appendix A

COMMONLY USED ABBREVIATIONS

NOTE: Abbreviations may appear with or without periods, depending on the service you use. The list below presents some items in both formats. Note also that abbreviations used for IRS entities may include a slash (/) between letters but will not always do so.

A	Acquiescence
ACI	Appeals Coordinated Issue
Acq.	Acquiescence
AF; AF2d	American Federal Tax Reports
A.F.T.R.; A.F.T.R.2d	American Federal Tax Reports
ALI	American Law Institute
AM	Legal Advice Issued by Associate Chief Counsel
Am. Jur.	American Jurisprudence
Ann.	Announcement
ANPRM	Advance Notice of Proposed Rulemaking
AOD	Action on Decision
APA	Advance Pricing Agreement; Administrative Procedure Act
App.	Appeals
A.R.M.	Committee on Appeals and Review Memorandum
A.R.R.	Committee on Appeals and Review Recommendation
Art.	Article
ASG	Appeals Settlement Guideline
A.T.	Alcohol Tax Unit; Alcohol and Tobacco Tax Division
ATG	Audit Techniques Guide
Bankr.	Bankruptcy
BAP	Bankruptcy Appellate Panel
BATF	Bureau of Alcohol, Tobacco, and Firearms; Bureau of Alcohol, Tobacco, Firearms, and Explosives
BCite	Bloomberg Law Citator
BL	Bloomberg Law
BNA	Bureau of National Affairs
B.R.	Bankruptcy Reporter

BTA	Board of Tax Appeals
BTC	Treasury Office of Benefits Tax Counsel
Bull.	Bulletin
CA	Court of Appeals
CB; C.B.	Cumulative Bulletin
CBO	Congressional Budget Office
CBS	Collection, Bankruptcy and Summons Bulletin
CC	IRS Chief Counsel
CC: CORP	IRS Associate Chief Counsel (Corporate)
CC: CT	IRS Division Counsel/Associate Chief Counsel (Criminal Tax)
CC: FIP	IRS Associate Chief Counsel (Financial Institutions & Products)
CC: FM	IRS Associate Chief Counsel (Finance & Management)
CC: GLS	IRS Associate Chief Counsel (General Legal Services)
CC: INTL	IRS Associate Chief Counsel (International)
CC: ITA	IRS Associate Chief Counsel (Income Tax Accounting)
CC: LB&I	IRS Division Counsel (Large Business and International)
CC: PA	IRS Associate Chief Counsel (Procedure & Administration)
CC: PSI	IRS Associate Chief Counsel (Passthroughs & Special Industries)
CC: SBSE	IRS Division Counsel (Small Business/Self Employed)
CC: TEGE	IRS Division Counsel/Associate Chief Counsel (Tax Exempt & Government Entities)
CC: WI	IRS Division Counsel (Wage & Investment)
CCA	Chief Counsel Advice or Advisory
CCDM	Chief Counsel Directives Manual
CCH	Commerce Clearing House
CCM	Chief Counsel Memorandum
CCN	Chief Counsel Notice
CDP	Collection Due Process
CEA	Council of Economic Advisers
C.F.R.	Code of Federal Regulations
Ch.	Chapter
CILP	Current Index to Legal Periodicals
CIR	Commissioner of Internal Revenue

Cir.	Circuit; Circular
CIS	Congressional Information Service
CIT	Court of International Trade
C.J.S.	Corpus Juris Secundum
Cl.	Clause
Cl. Ct.	Claims Court Reporter
CLI	Current Law Index
C.L.T.	Child-Labor Tax Division
CNTA	IRS Chief Counsel Office Special Counsel to the National Taxpayer Advocate
Comm.	Commissioner; Commission; Committee
Comm'r	Commissioner
Comp.	Compilation; Compliance
Con.	Concurrent
Conf.	Conference
Cong.	Congress
Cong. Rec.	Congressional Record
Const.	Constitution
CPE	Continuing Professional Education
CRS	Congressional Research Service
C.S.T.	Capital-Stock Tax Division
C.T.	Carriers Taxing Act of 1937; Taxes on Employment by Carriers
Ct.	Court
CTB	Criminal Tax Bulletin
Ct. Cl.	Court of Claims
Ct. D.	Court Decision
Cum. Bull.	Cumulative Bulletin
D.	Decision; District
D.C.	Treasury Department Circular
Dec.	Decision
Del. Order	Delegation Order
Deleg. Order	Delegation Order
Dept. Cir.	Treasury Department Circular
Dist.	District
Dkt.	Docket

DLB	Disclosure Litigation Bulletin
D.O.	Delegation Order
Doc.	Document
E.A.S.	Executive Agreement Series
EE	IRS Employee Plans and Exempt Organization Division
Em. T.	Employment Taxes
E.O.	Executive Orders
EO	Exempt Organizations
E.P.C.	Excess Profits Tax Council Ruling or Memorandum
E.T.	Estate and Gift Tax Division or Ruling
Ex.	Executive
Exec. Order	Executive Order
F.; F.2d; F.3d	Federal Reporter
FAA	Legal Advice Issued by Field Attorneys
FAQ	IRS Frequently Asked Questions
Fed.	Federal; Federal Reporter
Fed. Appx.	Federal Appendix
Fed. Cl.	Court of Federal Claims
Fed. Reg.	Federal Register
Fed. Supp.; Fed. Supp. 2d; Fed. Supp. 3d	Federal Supplement
FI	IRS Financial Institutions and Products Division
FOIA	Freedom of Information Act
FR	Federal Register
FS	IRS Fact Sheet
FSA	Field Service Advice; Field Service Advisory
F. Supp.; F. Supp. 2d; F. Supp. 3d	Federal Supplement
FTC; FTC2d	Federal Tax Coordinator
GAO	General Accounting Office; Government Accountability Office
GATT	General Agreement on Tariffs and Trade
GCM	General Counsel Memorandum

G.C.M.	Chief Counsel's Memorandum; General Counsel's Memorandum; Assistant General Counsel's Memorandum
Gen. Couns. Mem.	General Counsel Memorandum
GL	IRS General Litigation Division
GLAM	Generic Legal Advice Memorandum
GPO	Government Printing Office; Government Publishing Office
GSA	General Services Administration
H	House of Representatives
HCC	IRS Chief Counsel Health Care Counsel
H.R.	House of Representatives
HRG	Hearing
IA	IRS Income Tax and Accounting Division
ICM	IRS Compliance Officer Memorandum
IDR	Information Document Request
IGA	Intergovernmental Government Agreement
IIL	IRS Information Letter
IL	IRS International Division
ILM	IRS Legal Memoranda
ILP	Index to Legal Periodicals
INTL	IRS International Division
Int'l	International
IR	Information Release
IRB	Internal Revenue Bulletin
IRC	Internal Revenue Code
IRM	Internal Revenue Manual
IR-Mim.	Published Internal Revenue Mimeograph
IRS	Internal Revenue Service
ISP	Industry Specialization Program
I.T.	Income Tax Unit or Division
ITA	IRS Technical Assistance
ITC	Treasury Office of International Tax Counsel
JCT	Joint Committee on Taxation
JEC	Joint Economic Committee
Jt.	Joint
KC	KeyCite

L.	Law; Legal; Letter
LB&I	IRS Large Business & International Division
L. Ed.	United States Supreme Court Reports, Lawyers' Edition
LGM	Litigation Guideline Memorandum
LLMC	Law Library Microform Consortium
L.M.	Legal Memorandum
LMSB	IRS Large & Mid-Size Business Division
L.O.	Solicitor's Law Opinion
LR; L & R	IRS Legislation and Regulations Division
LRI	Legal Resource Index
LSA	C.F.R. List of Sections Affected
LTR	Private Letter Ruling
Ltr. Rul.	Private Letter Ruling
M.A.	Miscellaneous Announcements
Mem.	Memorandum
Memo.	Memorandum
Mim.	Mimeographed Letter; Mimeograph
MOU	Memorandum of Understanding
MS.	Miscellaneous Unit or Division or Branch
MSSP	Market Segment Specialization Paper
M.S.U.	Market Segment Understanding
M.T.	Miscellaneous Division or Branch
NA	Nonacquiescence
NARA	National Archives and Records Administration
NEC	National Economic Council
Nonacq.	Nonacquiescence
NPRM	Notice of Proposed Rulemaking
NSAR	Non Docketed Service Advice Review
NTA	IRS National Taxpayer Advocate
O.	Solicitor's Law Opinion
O.D.	Office Decision
OECD	Organisation for Economic Co-operation and Development
Off. Mem.	Office Memorandum
OIC	Offer in Compromise

OIRA	Office of Management and Budget Office of Information and Regulatory Affairs
OLRC	Office of Law Revision Counsel
OMB	Office of Management and Budget
Op.	Opinion
Op. A.G.	Opinion of Attorney General
OPR	IRS Office of Professional Responsibility
OTA	Treasury Office of Tax Analysis
OTP	Treasury Office of Tax Policy
Para.	Paragraph
PERAB	President's Economic Recovery Advisory Board
PH; P-H	Prentice-Hall
PLR	Private Letter Ruling
PMTA	Program Manager Technical Assistance
Priv. Ltr. Rul.	Private Letter Ruling
Prop.	Proposed
PS	IRS Passthroughs and Special Industries Division
P.T.	Processing Tax Decision or Division
Pt.	Part
P.T.E.	Prohibited Transaction Exemption
Pub.	Public; Published
Rec.	Record
REG	Regulations Project
Reg.	Register; Registration; Regular; Regulation
Rep.	Report; Reports; Representatives; Reporter
Res.	Resolution
Rev. Proc.	Revenue Procedure
Rev. Rul.	Revenue Ruling
RIA	Research Institute of America
RIN	Regulation Identifier Number
RISC	Regulatory Information Service Center
RP	Revenue Procedure
RR	Revenue Ruling
S.	Senate; Solicitor's Memorandum
SAM	Strategic Advice Memorandum

SB/SE	IRS Small Business/Self-Employed Division
SCA	Service Center Advice
S. Ct.	Supreme Court
Sec.	Section
Sess.	Session
SFTR	Standard Federal Tax Reporter
Sil.	Silver Tax Division
SLA	Taxpayer Advocate Service Level Agreement
S.M.	Solicitor's Memorandum
SOI	IRS Statistics of Income Bulletin
Sol. Op.	Solicitor's Opinion
S.P.R.	Statement of Procedural Rules
S.R.	Solicitor's Recommendation
S.S.T.	Social Security Tax and Carriers' Tax; Social Security Tax; Taxes on Employment by Other than Carriers
S.T.	Sales Tax Unit or Division or Branch
Stat.	United States Statutes at Large
T.	Temporary; Tobacco Division; Treaty
TA	Tax Analysts
TAM	Technical Advice Memorandum
TAS	IRS Taxpayer Advocate Service
T.B.M.	Advisory Tax Board Memorandum
T.B.R.	Advisory Tax Board Recommendation
T.C.	Tax Court Reports
TCM	Tax Court Memorandum Opinion
TC Memo	Tax Court Memorandum Opinion
T. Ct.	Tax Court
T.D.	Treasury Decision
TEAM	Technical Expedited Advice Memorandum
TECH	Assistant Commissioner, Technical
Tech. Adv. Mem.	Technical Advice Memorandum
Tech. Info. Rel.	Technical Information Release
Tech. Mem.	Technical Memorandum
TE/GE	IRS Tax Exempt & Government Entities Division
Temp.	Temporary

T.I.A.S.	Treaties and International Acts Series
TIF	Treaties in Force
TIGTA	Treasury Inspector General for Tax Administration
T.I.R.	Technical Information Release
TLB	Tax Litigation Bulletin
TLC	Treasury Office of Tax Legislative Counsel
TM	Technical Memorandum
Tob.	Tobacco Branch
Treas.	Treasury Department
Treas. Dep't Order	Treasury Department Order
Treas. Reg.	Treasury Regulation
T.S.	Treaty Series
UIL	Uniform Issue List
UILC	Uniform Issue List Code
UN	United Nations
UNTS	United Nations Treaty Series
U.S.	United States Reports
U.S.C.	United States Code
U.S.C.A.	United States Code Annotated
USCCAN	United States Code Congressional & Administrative News
U.S.C.S.	United States Code Service
U.S.T.	United States Treaties and Other International Agreements
U.S. Tax Cas.	U.S. Tax Cases
U.S.T.C.	U.S. Tax Cases
USTR	United States Tax Reporter; United States Trade Representative
UTC	U.S. Tax Cases
WG & L	Warren Gorham & Lamont
W&I	IRS Wage and Investment Division
WL	Westlaw; Westlaw Edge
WTO	World Trade Organization

Appendix B

ALTERNATE CITATION FORMS

This appendix does not cover all possible citation forms. It includes formats in the sources listed below. You are likely to find articles, particularly in practitioner-oriented publications, that use different formats. Chapters 9 and 10 provide several abbreviation formats for IRS items and judicial decisions.

Primary Sources Used

ALWD Guide to Legal Citation (6th ed. 2017)

The Bluebook: A Uniform System of Citation (21st ed. 2020)

Internal Revenue Manual 4.10.7.2 (Jan. 1, 2006)

1. Citations for Internal Revenue Code section 61

   I.R.C. § 61 (year of U.S.C.)

   I.R.C. § 61

   26 U.S.C. § 61

2. Citations for Treasury Regulation section 1.61–1

   Treas. Reg. § 1.61–1 (promulgation/amendment year)

   Treas. Reg. § 1.61–1

   Reg. § 1.61–1

   26 C.F.R. § 1.61–1

3. Citations for Temporary Treasury Regulation section 1.1041–1T

   Temp. Treas. Reg. § 1.1041–1T (promulgation/amendment year)

   Temp. Treas. Reg. § 1.1041–1 (promulgation/amendment year)

   Temp. Treas. Reg. § 1.1041–1T

   Temp. Reg. § 1.1041–1T

   26 C.F.R. § 1.1041–1T

4. Citations for Proposed Treasury Regulation section 54.9801–2

   Prop. Treas. Reg. § 54.9801–2 (month/day/year proposed)

   Prop. Treas. Reg. § 54.9801–2 (Federal Register citation/date)

   Prop. Reg. § 54.9801–2

5. Citations for Private Letter Ruling 199929039

   I.R.S. Priv. Ltr. Rul. 99–29–039 (Apr. 12, 1999)

   I.R.S. P.L.R. 9929039 (Apr. 12, 1999)

P.L.R. 99–29–039 (Apr. 12, 1999)

P.L.R. 9929039

PLR 199929039

Appendix C

POTENTIAL RESEARCH ERRORS

Statements in Appendix C reflect comments made elsewhere in this book.

- Don't assume that a library lacks a source because it is not available in its general print collection or online. Check the microform and government documents collections.
- Don't be afraid to ask your law school's reference librarian or the reference attorney at your firm about the various electronic services (Bloomberg, Lexis+, Westlaw Edge, etc.) and for help in finding sources or materials.
- Check a service's coverage dates before you begin your research. An electronic service may omit a source's initial years. A print service may not have been updated recently enough to catch a very recent item.
- Before using a service (including a government website), determine how it treats revoked items. Some services delete these items; others include them but indicate they have been revoked.
- If you check research results in a second publication, try to select a source from a different publishing group. Although corporate parents offer several imprints (Appendix D), there is no guarantee they will always use separate editors.
- If you find a Code section on point, don't forget to check effective dates and special rules that may not be codified.
- Never assume a definition in one section of the Code or regulations applies to all other sections.
- Don't ignore potentially related Code provisions merely because they don't refer to each other.
- Don't confuse an act section number with a Code section number.
- Don't assume every relevant provision is actually codified.
- Don't assume section numbers in a bill remain unchanged through the enactment process.
- Don't confuse the enactment date, effective date, and expiration date for statutes (or the comparable date limitations for treaties and regulations).
- If you use cross-reference tables to trace a statute's history, remember that these tables may not reflect changes in a section's numbering.
- Don't forget to compare the issue date of regulations and the decision date for cases against the revision date for relevant statutory amendments. Otherwise you risk citing sources whose authority has been weakened or overruled altogether. Online citators may indicate this information.

- If you want to challenge a regulation, don't limit yourself to whether its language contradicts the statute it interprets. Check the Preamble to be sure it complies with APA and other regulatory requirements.
- Remember to use the designation required by the source you are searching. For example, don't insert hyphens or dashes in IRS documents when searching online unless the service allows hyphens or dashes; remember that a service may use names other than Chief Counsel Advice for CCA documents.
- Don't forget to check for pending items (legislation, regulations, appeals from judicial decisions) that may be relevant to your project.
- Don't overestimate the degree of deference a court will accord legislative history and Treasury or IRS documents.
- Don't assume the government conceded an issue merely because it didn't appeal after losing a case. Check to see if there is an AOD or other announcement regarding the case.
- If you find a notice of acquiescence or nonacquiescence, check to make sure the IRS didn't reverse itself in a later AOD or Internal Revenue Bulletin item.
- When searching for cases using the taxpayer's name, remember that early cases are not captioned Taxpayer v. Commissioner or Taxpayer v. United States. Eisner and Helvering are government officials, not taxpayers. Likewise, remember that different services may use different caption formats for bankruptcy cases.
- Remember that U.S.T.C. is an abbreviation for U.S. Tax Cases; that case reporter service does not include United States Tax Court cases.
- Don't confuse page and paragraph numbers. Make sure you know if a service cross-references by page, by paragraph, by section number, or by outline heading. Make sure you know whether new material is located in the same volume or a different volume (and where in the relevant volume it appears). Although online services avoid this problem, you must still use the appropriate format in any memorandum or brief you prepare.
- Don't rely on a service's editor for a holding. Read the document yourself.
- Remember that early volumes of Index to Legal Periodicals omit short articles.
- Don't overlook free government websites, particularly if you need access to a document and already have a citation.
- When using electronic materials, make sure you understand the particular service's Boolean search rules and rules for limiting searches to a particular range of dates. From date 1 to date 2 is not the same as after date 1 and before date 2.
- Make sure that "s" means sentence (and "p" means paragraph) in an electronic service. Some services define sentence and paragraph by a maximum number of words rather than by grammatical rules.

- When using an electronic service, use wildcards for words with variant spellings (e.g., includible and includable).
- If a URL no longer yields the desired website, assume the site changed its URL but still exists. Use your service provider's search function (or a search engine) to search for the new URL. It is also possible, particularly for government sites, that the agency involved has been renamed or merged with another agency.
- When searching by dates, make sure to use the proper format. The date format "08/01/1999" is not the same as "8/1/1999" in many government agency search engines. Form trumps substance.

Appendix D

COMMONLY OWNED PUBLISHERS

Aspen	Wolters Kluwer
Bepress	RELX Group
Bloomberg Law	Bloomberg Industry Group
Bureau of National Affairs	Bloomberg Industry Group
Clark Boardman Callahan	Thomson Reuters
Commerce Clearing House	Wolters Kluwer
FindLaw	Thomson Reuters
Gale Group	Cengage Learning
Hein	William S. Hein & Co., Inc.
Lexis Advance	RELX Group
LexisNexis	RELX Group
Lexis+	RELX Group
Matthew Bender	RELX Group
Michie	RELX Group
Prentice-Hall[1]	
Research Institute of America	Thomson Reuters
Rothman	William S. Hein & Co., Inc.
Shepard's	RELX Group
SSRN	RELX Group
Tax Management	Bloomberg Industry Group
Tax Notes	Tax Analysts
Thomson Reuters Westlaw	Thomson Reuters
Warren Gorham & Lamont	Thomson Reuters
Westlaw	Thomson Reuters
Westlaw Edge	Thomson Reuters
WestlawNext	Thomson Reuters

→ The information above reflects ownership groups in July 2020.

[1] Still exists, but relevant titles were acquired by Research Institute of America and Warren Gorham & Lamont.

Index

References are to Pages

Bolded page numbers indicate the primary discussion of that term.